Corrections

1 - **Introduction:**
   Page 3, line 7:   Faysal called for Islamic solidarity

2 - **Introduction:**
   Page 8, line 31:   the coup plot of 1969

3 - **Prince Faysal:**
   Page 27, line 25:   Faysal's mother passed away when the young boy
                          was five months old

4 - **Prince Faysal:**
   Page 28, line 5:   at the age of sixteen

5 - **Prince Faysal:**
   Page 32, line 4:   Jiddah fell to 'Abdul'Aziz

6 - **Prince Faysal:**
   Page 35, line 1:   as well as Turkey, Afghanistan

7 - **Prince Faysal:**
   Page 37, line 26:   However, his final wish was to pray once more

8 - **PrinceFaysal:**
   Page 47, line 23:   Faysal returned to the United Nations

9 - **Prince Faysal:**
   Page 49, line 11:   Hashemite Kingdom in Jordan

10 - **Heir apparent Faysal:**
   Page 66, line 33:   When neither Abdullah Bin Abdul Rahman
   line 35:   Abdullah Bin Abdul Rahman

11 - **Heir apparent Faysal:**
   Page 68, line 35:   Washington voiced support for an
                          Iraqi-Jordanian federation

12 - **Heir apparent Faysal:**
   Page 73, line 36:   In October,1962

13 - **Heir apparent Faysal:**

Page 79, line 12:   Several of his advisors

14 - **Heir apparent Faysal:**

Page 84, line 35 :   Saudi targets in late February 1963-just a few days

15 - **Heir apparent Faysal:**

Page 85, line 7:   Conseq uently, he accepted broad

16 - **Pictures:**

Page 96, top picture: Faysal with his uncle prince Abdullah Bin
Abdul Rahman

17 - **King Faysal:**

Page 117, line 13:   Naturally, education was free. Queen
'Iffat Al Thunayyan

18 - **Divergences from the United States :**

Page 147, line 36:   a few weeks later, Hafez Al-Asad overthrew the
government in Damascus

19 - **A Modernizing Vision for an Emergent Kingdom:**

Page 191, line 25:   of the Organization of the Islamic Conference

20 - **The Faysal Legacy:**

Page 195, line 35:   Faysal's body never lay in state

21 - **The Faysal Legacy:**

Page 198, line 14:   There was never a deppegging of oil
prices to the dollar

Faysal

UNIVERSITY PRESS OF FLORIDA

Florida A&M University, Tallahassee
Florida Atlantic University, Boca Raton
Florida Gulf Coast University, Ft. Myers
Florida International University, Miami
Florida State University, Tallahassee
New College of Florida, Sarasota
University of Central Florida, Orlando
University of Florida, Gainesville
University of North Florida, Jacksonville
University of South Florida, Tampa
University of West Florida, Pensacola

FAYSAL

Saudi Arabia's King for All Seasons

Joseph A. Kéchichian

University Press of Florida

Gainesville Tallahassee Tampa Boca Raton

Pensacola Orlando Miami Jacksonville Ft. Myers Sarasota

Printed in the United States of America. This book is printed on Glatfelter Natures
Book, a paper certified under the standards of the Forestry Stewardship Council (FSC).
It is a recycled stock that contains 30 percent post-consumer waste and is acid-free.

13 12 11 10 09 08   6 5 4 3 2 1

Library of Congress Cataloging-in-Publication Data
Kechichian, Joseph A.
Faysal: Saudi Arabia's King for all seasons/Joseph A. Kéchichian.
p. cm.
Includes bibliographical references and index.
ISBN 978-0-8130-3242-9 (alk. paper)
1. Faisal, King of Saudi Arabia, 1906–1975. 2. Saudi Arabia—History—1932– I. Title.
DS244.6.K43 2008
953.805'30929–dc22   [B] 2008013690

The University Press of Florida is the scholarly publishing agency for the State
University System of Florida, comprising Florida A&M University, Florida Atlantic
University, Florida Gulf Coast University, Florida International University, Florida
State University, New College of Florida, University of Central Florida, University
of Florida, University of North Florida, University of South Florida, and University
of West Florida.

University Press of Florida
15 Northwest 15th Street
Gainesville, FL 32611-2079
http://www.upf.com

In memory of ʿIffat Al Thunayan,
a queen whose life and reign were beyond value

Contents

Preface

God, give us men!
A time like this demands
Strong minds, great hearts, true faith and ready hands;
Men whom the lust of office does not kill;
Men whom the spoils of office can not buy;
Men who possess opinions and a will;
Men who have honor; men who will not lie;
Men who can stand before a demagogue
And damn his treacherous flatteries without winking!
Tall men, sun-crowned, who live above the fog
In public duty, and in private thinking;
For while the rabble, with their thumb-worn creeds,
Their large professions and their little deeds,
Mingle in selfish strife, lo! Freedom weeps,
Wrong rules the land and waiting Justice sleeps.
God give us men;
Men who serve not for selfish booty;
But real men, courageous, who flinch not at duty.
Men of dependable character;
Men of sterling worth;
Then wrongs will be redressed, and right will rule the earth.
God Give us Men!

Josiah Gilbert Holland, "Child of the Appalachian Coalfields"

When Josiah Gilbert Holland wrote this poignant poem, he could not have had
Faysal bin ʿAbdul ʿAziz Al Saʿud in mind because the Massachusetts physi-

cian probably did not know about Arabian tribes. Still, men like Faysal not only met his criteria, but also proved to be ideal candidates for the archetype. One hundred years after his birth and, sadly, thirty years since his assassination, King Faysal continues to fascinate and bewilder as few Arab men have. The late ruler of Saudi Arabia (1964–75) captivated and astonished his countrymen, as well as most individuals he encountered, through statesmanship and poise. His determination to look after the interests of his country drew admirers and detractors alike although neither group impressed him. Simply stated, Faysal was destined for greatness because he was a dreamer with a vision, one that drew succor from faith and wisdom, not adulation. Over a relatively short period of time, the third Saudi ruler in the twentieth century adopted specific policies that became the norm for each of his successors, who, in turn, built on his many accomplishments. In fact, Faysal's overall accomplishments were so ample and varied that few absorbed their full meanings during his lifetime. What was defined, argued, defended, and implemented in a largely tribal environment with pragmatic traditions in place was nothing short of phenomenal. Few of his contemporaries believed that he could reform the Kingdom of Saudi Arabia and embark a relatively isolated society on the bandwagon of change. Many were truly surprised that he succeeded even if critics rejected his overtures. In the end, Faysal achieved most of his objectives because he believed in himself and, equally important, in ordinary Saudis.

This scholarly analysis of his accomplishments, and how he influenced the course of history, is meant to be a comprehensive work that provides careful assessment of domestic and foreign policies that shaped the monarch's political outlook. Toward that end, this analysis makes an effort to rely on the monarch's pronouncements on contemporary Saudi, regional, and international affairs. It also harvested the collective memory of a few non-Saudis who were intimately involved with the late king.

The study follows a historical approach because clear linkages between personalities and events pepper Arab memory. Given that monarchs reveal little of their inner thoughts—perhaps due to their exalted positions, especially when acolytes who aim to please surround most—the focus on how Faysal shaped, or reacted to, actual developments clarified obscure points. Although few rulers escaped the predicament of eager advisors, Faysal was one of those who made the necessary adjustments to free himself from fabricated realities. Doing so added to the burden of rule for he devoted an enormous amount of time to detail, but it also allowed him to seek counsel from men and women he trusted deeply. Little is known of many of these individuals beyond his uncles, brothers,

sons, and nephews. Yet, the one person who stood out was Queen ʿIffat Al Thunayan, whose views he regularly solicited and whose ideas he deemed valuable.
The queen was the great woman who stood behind this remarkable king and
who freely advised her husband on matters of genuine importance. This book
is dedicated to her memory precisely to recognize the contribution she made to
his rulership.

Acknowledgments

When I was a little boy growing up in Lebanon, my father once took me to the Beirut International Airport to welcome King Faysal of Saudi Arabia. It was either 1964 or 1965 and the old facility boasted an open-air balcony over the tarmac that allowed for unobstructed views. There were too many people around, but I could vaguely make out a tall slender man attired in the traditional Arabian garb as he stepped out of his plane and was greeted by a slew of dignitaries. Though the encounter was very brief and nothing else registered at the time, I often thought about my father's wish to go on the "excursion" because, he would always remind me, "Faysal is a great man and we need to express our support." One simply did not grow up in the Arab world throughout the 1960s without being impressed by Faysal. He was a towering figure who reached out to many, both inside his country and elsewhere, in the true custom of a *badu*. *Badu* is the Arabic version of *Bedouin*, a nomad or tribesman, whose roots are linked to his extended family and tribal members. This and similarly impressionistic encounters piqued my interest in the Arabian Peninsula. It was not surprising, therefore, that I have devoted much of my academic life to the Arab Gulf monarchies and, over the years, traveled extensively throughout the area, where I met decision makers, intellectuals, and many people who welcomed me into their homes. Inevitably, I often recalled my excursion to see Faysal, who earned both respect and admiration.

The idea for this book, my second on the Kingdom of Saudi Arabia, came about through two happy coincidences. In 1995, Professor John L. Esposito invited me to write the King Faysal entry for his *Oxford Encyclopedia of the Modern Islamic World*, which truly piqued my interest in the Saudi ruler. That short article took several days to compose and necessitated a careful re-reading of Jacques Benoist-Méchin's, *Fayçal, Roi d'Arabie: L'Homme, le Souverain, sa Place dans le Monde (1906–1975)*, which was published in Paris in 1975, the year the monarch was assassinated. Jacques Benoist-Méchin was fortunate because he met his subject for in-depth discussions that, in turn, provided rare analytical insights. Four decades later, the challenge to write a fresh judicious assessment of Saudi Arabia under Faysal proved to be more difficult because the subject had been transformed into a legend. Still, long after his demise, Faysal generated raw emotions given his epoch-making decisions that transformed the kingdom and affected much of the Muslim world.

The second coincidence was Faysal's centennial birthday, which was slated for commemoration through various activities, including academic works that provided new assessments of his legacy. I thought of my late father's insight of Faysal and decided to approach one of his sons for access. In his capacity as chairman of the King Faisal Center for Research and Islamic Studies (KFCRIS) in Riyadh, His Royal Highness Prince Turki al-Faysal, then ambassador to the United Kingdom, approved my proposal to write this volume. I thank Prince Turki for extending this kind invitation, for reading my manuscript, and for offering various comments that clarified obscure points. His assistant in London and Washington, Dr. Sa'ud al-Sati, was equally forthcoming in following up on my numerous requests, including access to a complete set of the *Records of Saudi Arabia*, for which I sincerely extend my heartfelt appreciation. After Prince Turki returned to Riyadh in early 2007, 'Abdallah Ashuwaish, his office director, continued the essential liaison work, including access to the rare photographs from the center's archives that are included in this book. While I readily acknowledge this unprecedented level of support and took Prince Turki's comments under advisement as I emended a few details to clarify obscure points he graciously identified, I alone am responsible for the contents of the book.

In the course of writing this book, I visited the kingdom twice, primarily to research the vast holdings of the King Faisal Center for Research and Islamic Studies. Several individuals at the center deserve special accolades for facilitating my work in the kingdom. Dr. Yahya Mahmoud Ibn Junaid, the center's affable secretary-general, quickly took an interest in the project for which I am grateful. His interventions with several depository library officials allowed for timely and productive visits. Ibrahim 'Abdul Rahman Al-Hadlaq, the director-general for administrative affairs, ensured that my stays were fruitful as well as comfortable. Dr. Awadh al-Badi, the head of the Department of Research and Studies, offered valuable comments on my text.

Several Saudi researchers, including Dr. Mazin Salah Motabbagani, a professor at the Imam Muhammad bin Sa'ud Islamic University, and Turki Al-Hamad at King Sa'ud University, exchanged valuable insights. Dr. 'Abdul Kareem bin

'Abdul Rahman al-Zaid, the deputy supervisor general at the King 'Abdul 'Aziz Public Library, Dr. Fahd bin 'Abdallah al-Semmari, the director-general of the King 'Abdul 'Aziz Research Center, and 'Abdallah bin Muhammad al-Nasir, at the King Fahd National Library, graciously extended authorization to roam through their holdings.

I owe a special debt of gratitude to His Excellency Dr. 'Abdallah Ibrahim El-Kuwaiz, now the ambassador of Saudi Arabia to Bahrain, who recommended me to Prince Turki and the KFCRIS. My friendship with Dr. El-Kuwaiz is long-standing, ever since his tenure as assistant secretary-general for economic affairs at the Gulf Cooperation Council. He has always welcomed me—in Riyadh as well as in Manama—and answered my numerous questions.

I also wish to extend my sincere appreciation to two remarkable American dip-lomats who clarified several key points: Secretary Richard W. Murphy, the former assistant secretary of state, who shared a very long breakfast in New York; and Ambassador Herman Eilts, who welcomed me in his Wellesley, Massachusetts home for a memorable interview that lasted over three hours. Both men knew Faysal firsthand and had dealt with him in an official capacity; both knew his true worth. My regret is that Ambassador Eilts did not live to see this contribution, although he never missed an opportunity to encourage my work on Saudi Arabia. It is equally important to note that repeated attempts to interview Secretary of State Henry Kissinger came to naught. Naturally, none of the individuals named above are responsible for my analysis, although each added value to this book.

My research assistant on this project, Jean-Pierre Der Mendjian, devoted a good deal of time assembling various sources and preparing several early drafts of the comprehensive chronology as well as identifying bibliographical data. Even if his efforts are not visible in the final product, his insights and attention to detail improved the overall work, avoiding embarrassing errors. J.-P. proved to be reli-able and I thank him for his diligence.

Genuine accolades go to my friend Dr. Odeh Aburdene for his unflinching loyalty and for standing by me in good times as well unfavorable ones. Odeh is that rare man with quality. He kindly brought to my attention the poem by Josiah Gilbert Holland, which was quoted in the memoirs of Senator Robert C. Byrd (D-WV), *Child of the Appalachian Coalfields*, and always prompted me to remain trustworthy with our Arab Gulf friends.

Angelica, my shining light, understands about King Faysal more than most American thirteen-year-olds. I tell her he was a great man.

Juliette, whose knowledge of the Arab world is vast and who is an ideal coun-selor, knows how much she means. Her innate intelligence and her capacity to manage difficult moments in the life of, and with, a partner who happens to be a professional writer is truly a blessing.

Finally, I wish to extend my sincere appreciation for the publications team in Gainesville, Florida, starting with Amy Gorelick, acquisitions editor at the University Press of Florida, who shepherded the first draft of the book through customary academic hurdles. Allyson Gasso, marketing assistant, ensured that the book received the attention it deserves, and Jacqueline Kinghorn Brown, the project editor, looked after every imaginable detail. Last, but truly not least, I thank Christine Sweeney, who read my text very carefully and offered useful suggestions. Copyediting is an often thankless task, but Christine's skills helped avoid embarrassing errors for which I am genuinely indebted.

A Note on Transliteration

A modified version of the Library of Congress transliteration system has been adopted throughout this book. In rendering Arabic words and names, however, I relied upon the style used by the *International Journal of Middle East Studies*. Thus, for example, Mohammed becomes Muhammad, and Mecca becomes Makkah. Whenever known, I used the common English spellings for proper nouns. Thus I refer to Saudi Arabia rather than Al- Mamlakat al-'Arabiyyah al-Sa'udiyyah and Casablanca rather than Dar al-Bayda'. Although special care was devoted to standardizing the spellings of as many transliterated words as possible, there are—inevitably—a few inconsistencies that, I trust, readers will understand. For practical purposes, all diacritical marks for long vowels and velarized consonants have been eliminated, except for the *hamza* (') and the *ayn* ('). Arabic speakers will know the correct reference for transliterated words throughout the text.

An effort was made to clarify family names as well. When referring to the proper appellation of ruling families, the Arabic word Al, which means "family," precedes the name of the eponymous founder. In Saudi Arabia, the founder lent his name to the family, thus the Al Sa'ud. A lower case al- often refers to a sub-branch of the ruling family. In this instance, Sa'ud al-Faysal is the son of the late King Faysal bin 'Abdul 'Aziz Al Sa'ud. Although the transliteration of "'Abd" (servant or slave in Arabic) is rendered as 'Abdul, I am aware that the "ul" (al) is really the article of the succeeding word and that together they mean "servant of God." In that regard the family of Muhammad 'Abdul-Wahhab is not simply Al Shaykh, but Al al-Shaykh, or "House of the Shaykh," as his descendents are called. Yet, I use 'Abdul throughout this text for two reasons: first, because that is the preferred transliteration in official Saudi correspondence; and second, because it comes as close as possible to the protocols of the Library of Congress and the *International Journal of Middle East Studies*. Arabic readers know how difficult transliteration can be and I urge patience, understanding, and forgiveness if I digressed.

Introduction

The founder of modern Saudi Arabia, 'Abdul 'Aziz bin 'Abdul Rahman Al Sa'ud (d. 1953, r. 1932–53), correctly assessed that his third son, Faysal, was particularly gifted for politics. Accordingly, he groomed his youngster for a leadership role, gradually entrusting Faysal with challenging responsibilities. Among his early accomplishments were distinguished visits to Britain and France at the end of World War I, when British authorities conferred on him the Medal of St. George and St. Michael. Faysal also led the kingdom's delegation to the 1939 London Conference on the Palestine Question, then known as the Round Table Conference, and, as head delegate, he represented Saudi Arabia at the signing of the United Nations Charter in San Francisco on June 26, 1945, making Saudi Arabia a founding member of the world body. At home, Faysal led Saudi forces in 1922 to subdue uprisings in 'Asir, and he participated in the Yemeni-Saudi War of 1934. Renowned for his poise, the young prince served his father as viceroy of the Hijaz starting in 1926, as chairman of the al-Shurah Council in 1927, and as the first foreign minister of the kingdom after 1930.

The contrast between Faysal and his immediate predecessor on the throne, King Sa'ud bin 'Abdul 'Aziz (r. 1953–64), was glaring. Under the guidance of his renowned father, Faysal (r. 1964–75) literally shaped his country's broad domestic and foreign policies, matching the prowess of the first king for good governance. If 'Abdul 'Aziz invented a monarchy, Faysal defined it and, not a negligible point, gave it an existential meaning. Immersed in a sacred environment that equipped Saudis with ideas and principles, Faysal drew succor from Islam and designed those doctrines that sealed Al Sa'ud legitimacy. As foreign minister, Faysal acted as the chief observer of the world to both his father and elder brother. Thus, what the first two kings of Saudi Arabia knew of the world was what Faysal saw first-hand and perceived in the depth of his being. Yet, as monarch, he quickly realized that his immense talents were not sufficient to rule effectively. While he still needed to watch, listen, and meditate before deciding what was better for Saudis, he concluded that the kingdom required social, economic, and political institutions to guide it. His rule was therefore dedicated to that fundamental goal, to empower Saudi Arabia with the wherewithal to succeed while remaining true to its core values.

Because of his innate awareness of local affairs, and although Faysal was steeped in foreign affairs, he nevertheless devoted a great deal of attention to various internal matters, paying particular care to economic, financial, industrial, and agricultural spheres. In fact, his interests in economic affairs were so extensive that he regularly read translations of major articles published in the London *Financial Times*. Under his careful supervision, major schemes, including the Irrigation and Drainage and the Sands projects in and near the city of Al-Ahsah, received necessary funding to encourage agriculture. Equally critical projects, ranging from the Haradh Agricultural design to the Abhah Dam outline, were addressed in toto. Various tasks equipped the country with the tools to emancipate functioning economic activities that slowly empowered Saudis in the workplace.

Naturally, while Faysal believed that it was urgent for the kingdom to propel an economic engine for the country, he realized that its required fuel, which would ensure smooth operations, was education. Toward that end, he authorized a full expansion of both general and higher education, including that for girls and women even if the latter task was truly gargantuan in a traditional tribal society. Under his rule, the actual number of university students increased significantly, with the more gifted dispatched overseas on full scholarships. Colleges established in the 1950s were rapidly expanded as several institutes were added to the growing roster. Early on Faysal realized that Saudi Arabia would remain dependent on foreign labor and, in the aftermath of the oil boom, Riyadh faced huge development challenges. With solid planning, however, oil revenues were gradually channeled toward investments designed to stimulate growth. A normal budgetary system was introduced to better manage spending. Still, all of these steps were made possible because the ruler concluded that the development of human capital, through compulsory and free education, should be the law of the land. It may be worth noting that these initiatives were controversial, as many traditional families refused to allow their children to attend school for fear that their morals would be corrupted. To alleviate such concerns and accomplish his objectives, the ruler devoted substantial time to cajoling his conservative society to adopt modernizing methods, which was a rare accomplishment indeed.

A Nascent Vision

Faysal devised a multi-pronged policy to safeguard the kingdom and the Al Sa'ud and to empower Saudi citizens. Remarkably, he accomplished these objectives by basing his beliefs on the Shari'ah (Islamic law) and on Arab as well as Muslim solidarity. Toward that end, he encouraged the establishment of the Muslim World League and conducted preferential foreign policy initiatives with several countries. Troubled by the spread of republicanism in the Arab world, which challenged the legitimacy of the Al Sa'ud, Faysal called an Islamic summit conference in 1965 to reaffirm established principles against the rising tide of modern ideologies. He dedicated himself to Muslim ideals, which he had learned in the house of his maternal grandfather and, encouraged by family members, developed values that were consonant with tribal leadership. Over the years, his religious values improved necessary secular policies because he perceived all political performances as religious acts that demanded thoughtfulness, dignity, and integrity.

The monarch proceeded cautiously when he introduced Western technology into the kingdom. In fact, he was compelled to deal with the insistent demands of Westernized associates to move faster and the equally vociferous urgings of the 'ulamah to end all innovations. 'Ulamah is the plural form of 'Alim, a learned man of Islam, who is versed in theoretical and practical sciences. Theologians, religious judges, and university professors who specialize in Islamic studies may also be known as 'ulamah. Not surprisingly, the adroit ruler opted for a middle ground, both to compromise with and assuage equally powerful forces that defined Saudi society. Moreover, Faysal earnestly believed that correct religious orientations, which he supported wholeheartedly, would almost always mitigate adverse effects of modernization if there were any. For example, when in 1965 the introduction of television broadcasts offended some and produced violent demonstrations against his policy, Faysal refused to withdraw his support for the project.

Equally important, Faysal believed that internal reforms protected and promoted Saudi interests. Yet, early on he understood that Riyadh was destined to play a leading role in Arab history and, toward that end, he redefined his country's ties with its neighbors. He firmly placed the kingdom in the Arab cocoon, sponsoring and supporting the League of Arab States (LAS) in 1945, and championed the core Arab question—the fate that befell Palestine—throughout his life. Simultaneously, Faysal pursued pro-Western and both anti-Communist as well as anti-Zionist policies, which earned him the wrath of most Western diplomats, analysts, and journalists. These "rave reviews" notwithstanding, the Saudi monarch remained consistent and true to his beliefs and almost always placed the interests of his brethren ahead of everything else.

A Farsighted Foreign Policy

Even before Faysal assumed his country's foreign policy mantle, he perceived regional affairs through the prism of the Arabian Peninsula, where boundary disputes abounded. Shortly after acceding to the throne, the monarch reached a final border agreement with Jordan in August 1965 before signing a similar delineation with Qatar. The Continental Shelf Agreement with Iran in October 1968 established the separate rights of Iran and Saudi Arabia in the Persian Gulf, and an understanding was reached to discourage foreign intervention, although both Riyadh and Teheran then concentrated on the Soviet Union. Even the formation of the United Arab Emirates in 1971, which was deliberately left in diplomatic abeyance by Riyadh because of the long-standing dispute over the Buraymi Oasis, was addressed in 1974 as Saudi Arabia extended political recognition. To be sure, the two countries signed a treaty in 1974, but at the time Riyadh and Abu Dhabi failed to delineate a proper border accord.

As discussed in the body of this book, while remarkable progress was recorded under Faysal's rule, at his death Saudi Arabia was still burdened with several unsettled frontiers. Although a partial agreement was signed in 1934, no dispute proved to be more ominous than the putative settlement of the border with Yemen, a perennial dilemma for all Saudi and Yemeni leaders. In August 1965, King Faysal and President Gamal 'Abdul Nasir—whose troops were deployed in Yemen—agreed to an immediate cease-fire, the termination of Saudi aid to the royalists, and the withdrawal of Egyptian forces from Yemeni territories. Unfortunately, Yemeni representatives from opposing sides botched the resolution of their differences, which inevitably led to renewed hostilities. Royalist forces, which were supported by Riyadh, claimed extensive victories. Republican units, buttressed by Cairo, retrenched before the Egyptian air force bombed royalist installations and towns in southern Saudi Arabia. Tensions escalated as Faysal's domestic foes sought to influence his policies; King Sa'ud, then a resident of Egypt, extended financial assistance to the Yemen Arab Republic. He even broadcast lackluster intentions to return from exile "to save the people and land of Saudi Arabia." No settlement of the border was thus possible.

After Cairo was humiliated by defeat in the 1967 Arab-Israeli war, Nasir accepted the reconciliation offer made by Faysal at the Khartoum conference in August. That gathering, wherein the Saudi emphasized the necessity to rely on one's faith, sealed the elevated status of the king within Arab circles as his influence amplified throughout the Arab world. With Jerusalem under occupation, the Saudi position gathered added support, which further strengthened the ruler's prestige. Riyadh led on moral grounds and proved to be particularly generous with front-line states, which were desperate for financial assistance. As a corollary, Saudi Arabia secured a firm Egyptian commitment to untangle from the Yemeni quagmire, as Nasir and Faysal compromised.

By this time, Saudi Arabia spoke with rare authority in Arab circles, and when a significant incident in Jerusalem—a suspicious fire at the Al-Aqsah Mosque on August 21, 1969—mobilized public opinion, Faysal was ideally poised to call for a conference. The Islamic Summit Conference in September 1969 in Rabat, Morocco intensified various efforts to deal with the repercussions of the fire, including "mobilized public opinion," with the Israeli occupation of Jerusalem, and although Israeli military forces continued their occupation, the tone of peace negotiations changed. A significant shift was under way as oil-producing countries flexed their growing economic muscles. In July 1973, Saudi Arabia and its oil-producing allies threatened to reduce deliveries if the United States, the key Western power broker in the region, refused to balance its policies toward the Arabs and Israel. As discussed in some detail below, the threat was finally actualized during the October 1973 War, when the Organization of Arab Petroleum Exporting Countries (OAPEC) imposed an oil embargo on the United States and the Netherlands for supporting Israel unilaterally. The oil embargo was a political protest aimed at obtaining Israeli withdrawal from occupied Arab territory and recognition of the rights of the Palestinian people, and while that goal was not achieved, it nevertheless elevated Saudi Arabia to the highest levels in international discourse.

One of the fundamental consequences of the 1973–74 oil crisis was the recognition of the Palestine Liberation Organization (PLO) as the legitimate representative of the Palestinian people. In November 1973, the Algiers Summit of the League of Arab States (LAS) adopted this plank, which was driven by Faysal and Saudi Arabia, even if Jordan, and King Hussein bin Talal in particular, rejected it. The Jordanian monarch was eventually persuaded by Faysal to attend the follow-up conference in Rabat in October 1974 that made the decision unanimous. The PLO would thus speak for the Palestinians and, in return, Saudi Arabia pledged to the Kingdom of Jordan U.S.$300 million a year for the next four years. This was generous but Faysal believed that increased revenues should be devoted where they were needed most. His commitment to Arab and Muslim causes continued unabated until the day he was assassinated—March 25, 1975—a day that ended his cherished dream to pray once again in Jerusalem.

A King for All Seasons

For all his mercurial policies, Faysal strengthened the hold of the ruling Al Sa'ud family, equipped the country with a sense of fiscal responsibility, and protected his brethren from internal uprisings. Immediately after acceding to rulership in 1964, the monarch quickly set out to modernize the country, starting with a sorely needed cleansing of the kingdom's finances. His first two official acts were protective in nature, directed toward safeguarding the Al Sa'ud from potential internal as well as external threats. Faysal appointed his brother Khalid as heir apparent and his brother Fahd as second deputy prime minister to prevent a succession struggle—which nearly destroyed the ruling family between 1958 and 1964. He also appointed his brother 'Abdallah as head of the National Guard to train and add discipline to *badu* levies, entrusting them with internal security as well as protection of the ruling family. Moreover, he entrusted Sultan, another brother serving as minister of defense and aviation, with the task of modernizing the military. It was under his rule that the kingdom was equipped with a rudimentary air defense system to protect growing petroleum reserves.

Faysal aligned Saudi Arabia with Egypt when Anwar Sadat launched his October 1973 surprise attack on Israel and helped to impose a selective oil embargo on the United States and the Netherlands (for providing military transfers to the Jewish state) without, nevertheless, reneging on his fundamental objectives. For Faysal, an avowed anti-Communist, the problems of the Middle East were a byproduct of the East-West conflict. There was never any doubt about which side he and Saudi Arabia were on.

Before he was twenty, Faysal had visited key Western capitals, World War I battlefields, including Verdun, and major museums such as the Louvre in Paris and L'Hermitage in St. Petersburg. He had also attended various operas in London, Paris, and Moscow and visited countless factories and industrial sites. Even by the standards of the twenty-first century, few leaders were ever exposed to such a variety of cultures that, by definition, fostered greatness.

Yet, this education and foresight earned him scorn because Faysal never compromised as he staunchly protected and promoted his country's interests. Recent references to his alleged anti-Semitism further illustrated the passion that his independent mindset created.[1] Faysal was the quintessential Semite who defined his own passion and articulated his own vision.

The ways in which Faysal's background, history, and heritage molded his personality and, undoubtedly, his worldviews were of paramount importance. At the risk of oversimplification, and to simply highlight a thematic impression, it may be safe to posit that Saudi Arabia evolved under Faysal within three principal themes.

The first was a legacy of strong political leadership provided by the ruling Al Sa'ud family, as amply illustrated throughout this volume. He is credited with rescuing the kingdom's squandered finances and for implementing strict rules for all ruling family members who benefited from the treasury. It was under Faysal that the Al Sa'ud instituted strict expenditure rules that rewarded participation in the affairs of the State.

The second was the legacy of strong puritan Islamic values maintained by descendents of Unitarian (Wahhabi) reformers within the Al al-Shaykh. In fact, Faysal was a product of both of these legacies because his father was the founder of the modern Saudi state and his mother was an Al al-Shaykh. Moreover, he was tutored in Islam by his maternal grandfather and could go toe to toe with any religious leader who challenged his domestic policies of "modernization without secularization" or his foreign policies that reflected the bipolarity of classical Islamic theory of international relations. Various attempts are made to illustrate how these two legacies affected Faysal, including a sampling of his published speeches and his attention to Islamic foreign policy, which give eloquent testimony to how bipolar Islamic theory and the Cold War itself helped mold the monarch's foreign policy during the Cold War.

The third legacy was his desert culture. It is widely believed in the West that Saudi women are downtrodden and that cannot be further from the truth. There was and still is an ancient custom of division of labor, in which women run the home and their extended families and men are protectors and providers outside. But within that structure, women have always had vast influence. Just as the founder's blood sister Nurah was one of his most influential advisors, so Faysal's wife, Queen 'Iffat, was one of his most influential advisors, particularly on women's issues. The story of how Faysal stopped by Istanbul to see if she would be a suitable political wife for his father and then married her himself was but a small vignette that made their very private relationship come alive.

Methodological Approach

Saudi policies were influenced by realpolitik and the Cold War for much of the period under investigation in this study. Between 1932 and 1975, Riyadh perceived that many, if not most, of its interests were protected and advanced by a close association with Western powers, especially the United States, Britain, and France. The end of the Cold War in 1990, and the dramatic changes in the region since then, called for variations in this eclectic approach, but the trends of Saudi responses were clearly set in the early 1970s. If his successors managed to pursue more independent foreign policies and promoted closer ties with the West as well as with both Iran and Iraq, it was largely because the third monarch had set the stage that allowed for such advances. Riyadh emphasized that its long-term needs required cooperation with many different countries, to avoid thorny confrontations, and this too was a legacy of Faysal.

To better address these contentions, this study relies on extensive narratives, interviews, and primary documents, first examining Saudi Arabia and the Al Saʿud before Faysal, discussing the ruling family and its institutional legacy. Chapter 1 deciphers contenders to authority to better determine what the Saudi *raison d'état* was and how the kingdom's doctrine and Alternative strategies were designed before Faysal came to power.

Chapter 2 discusses Prince Faysal between 1906 and 1953, concentrating on his innate diplomatic skills and added political responsibilities that introduced him to major political actors throughout the world. A detailed analysis of his numerous visits is provided to set the stage for his assumption of the ministry of foreign affairs. His trips to the United States are also scrutinized in some detail to determine how he faced various diplomatic challenges. The chapter closes with the accession of Prince Saʿud bin ʿAbdul ʿAziz to rulership, which divided the family for several years hence.

Chapter 3 assesses Faysal as heir apparent to King Saʿud between 1953 and 1964. In particular, an effort is made to evaluate how King Saʿud perceived the United States, especially his understanding of, and responses to, the Eisenhower Doctrine. Faysal's regency is also scrutinized to better ascertain how regional confrontations, ranging from the 1958 Iraqi Revolution to the end of the Yemeni monarchy to various internal challenges, influenced his decisions. The chapter closes with the deposition of King Saʿud and the actual transfer of power.

Chapter 4 provides a detailed assessment of Faysal's actual rule from 1964 to 1975. It ascertains that the monarch remade the ruling family before tackling his gargantuan re-creation of the kingdom itself. In particular, an attempt is made to identify the consequences of his overhaul of the armed forces, especially after the uprisings of the 1950s, the Royal Saudi Air Force defections in 1962, and the coup plots between 1969 and 1977. It argues that Faysal literally empowered military officers because he understood that no nation could be successfully reconstructed without loyal armies. The chapter then turns to the critical oil arena, which formed the nexus of decisions that allowed OPEC and OAPEC to become effective political instruments. The purpose of this discussion is to identify the roles of oil security both on the internal as well as external levels. It then delves into the use of oil as a weapon and discusses its role in the October 1973 War, as well as providing an appraisal of its consequences.

Because so much of Saudi foreign policy is directly tied to the United States, Chapter 5 looks at the divergences with Washington, starting under the Johnson administration. A special effort is then made to evaluate the relationship between Henry Kissinger, the U.S. secretary of state, and King Faysal especially during the 1973–74 period.

Chapter 6 provides a detailed review of the modernizing vision of King Faysal for the emergent monarchy. It considers pan-Islamism and the establishment of the Organization of Islamic Conference (OIC); the monarch's quest for Arab leadership; the many clashes over the Palestine question; the search for stability in the Gulf region, including nascent ties with the smaller Gulf states; the Iranian seizure of the Abu Musa and Tunb islands; the establishment of diplomatic ties with the United Arab Emirates; and the tense relationship with the shah of Iran. The chapter closes with a review of the ideological conflict with Communism.

Finally, the book culminates with a considered opinion of the Faysal legacy, including the impact of his tragic death, the investigation that followed, and the post-Faysal evolution of the Kingdom of Saudi Arabia.

To better assist the reader with sources, several vital speeches and key documents are reproduced in the appendices, along with a detailed chronology of the many stations Faysal crossed throughout his life. The comprehensive bibliography should allow for additional investigations.

Post–9/11 Saudi Arabia

Although this volume concentrates on a specific time frame, it is now amply clear that everything written on the Kingdom of Saudi Arabia in the post-9/11 framework will be assessed against the tragic developments of that day. For many detractors, a clear linkage exists between the fundamentalists who devised those attacks and the policies of the kingdom devised under King Faysal through OIC initiatives. Yet, in its assessment of the 2001 attacks on the United States, *The 9/11 Commission Report* provides both an exoneration—that the government of Saudi Arabia "funded" anti-American organizations—and an allowance—that Al Qa'ida "raised money from a variety of donors and other fund-raisers, primarily in the Gulf countries" and in the kingdom.[2] While the report is critical in other aspects, it proposes to determine whether the two societies can build a closer political relationship, which could strengthen long-standing and time-tested economic as well as military ties. By recommending such an approach, the *Report* recognizes the existence of a critical relationship between the two countries and the likelihood that it would remain so for the foreseeable future.

Still, generalizations and half-truths have dominated heated public debates, often with bigoted agendas and confusing rhetoric. Newspaper articles, films, and countless books have been published to demonize Saudi Arabia, lock, stock, and barrel. No one and nothing was spared. From the ruling family to government institutions—especially the country's educational and financial organizations—everything came under microscopic scrutiny. More ominous were sharp criticisms of Islam and the creed practiced in the kingdom. Recent such "analyses" claim to identify the root cause of all the ills that befall Saudi Arabia and, by association, the United States.[3]

In summary, these lofty pronouncements have concluded that Saudi *disorders* originated in Wahhabi Islam, and any efforts to tolerate it on grounds of piety were inimical to supporting the "enemy." Bombarded with sustained and carefully tailored negativism, many Americans have concluded that Saudi Arabia is a foe, certainly not a trusted ally. For many, Riyadh is under the control of an autocratic regime that oppresses minorities—and women—and is dominated by a "fanatical" religious establishment determined to conquer the Muslim world by spreading narrowly defined views. Wahhabi Islam is, allegedly, extremist and thus incompatible with either East or West. Faysal may have been many things, but he was not an anti-Semite and he certainly did not hate Christians. On the contrary, he admired all believers even as he demanded reciprocity. He justified and protected the rule of the Al Saʿud ruling family, developed concrete views of the kingdom, and worked tirelessly to introduce genuine development plans that would transform sleepy hamlets into modern cities. He worked tirelessly to empower the *badu*, catapulting him into the modern world, while retaining his values. More important, Faysal imagined a vision for his country, both as an Arab and as a Muslim monarchy, that would allow it to join the nations of the world.

1

Saudi Arabia and the Al Saʿud before Faysal

Modern Saudi Arabia is largely the creation of the ruling Al Saʿud family.[1] The family's sheer size and complexity, in terms of both its internal structure and composition as well as its connections to Saudi society, make the Saudi political system markedly different from other past and present monarchies.[2] Indeed, family politics developed in the context of vast wealth and profound transformations that have, in turn, altered the face of Saudi Arabia. Thus, it is on this basis that family politics is analyzed with an emphasis on determining the interplay between politics and policy on the one hand, and the balance between cohesive and disintegrative forces within the family on the other. These implications for Saudi behavior have had a direct bearing on Saudi power and succession before Faysal bin ʿAbdul ʿAziz acceded to rulership. In turn, these assumptions help elucidate some of the rationale that secured the succession of Faysal bin ʿAbdul ʿAziz to rulership.

To assess the legacy of King Faysal bin ʿAbdul ʿAziz—certainly one of the leading Al Saʿud figures in the twentieth century—it is necessary to examine the role that the country's founder played, and how ʿAbdul ʿAziz bin ʿAbdul Rahman branded the country into his image. A brief assessment of the ruling family will clarify the many changes that occurred within it when Faysal inherited the mantle of power. To be sure, ʿAbdul ʿAziz's progeny institutionalized the kingdom's political features, ranging from governance to succession, and did so with distinction. Remarkably, and despite serious challenges, they managed to preserve the dynasty's authority. In less than a century, the founder and his successors further legitimized their own power bases, adding value to both crown and country. Even if ʿAbdul ʿAziz's two immediate successors—Saʿud and Faysal—were relatively ensured of their positions, both had to distinguish themselves and come to terms with the many limitations that the complex Al Saʿud entity represented.

The Al Sa'ud Ruling Family until 1902

Long before 'Abdul 'Aziz bin 'Abdul Rahman reconquered Riyadh and unified central Arabia, the pattern of succession and intra-family politics determined, to a large extent, his preferences and behavior. The problems inherent in the Saudi pattern of succession and maintenance were very evident to the future monarch as he contemplated the history of the first (1744–1818) and second (1822–91) Saudi Kingdoms.[3] 'Abdul 'Aziz realized that different branches of the family struggled to fill vacuums in the line of succession when foreign powers interfered and disrupted the relative tranquility that permeated throughout the peninsula.[4] Even without external influences, the balance of power among rivals for the throne frequently broke into open warfare because self-preservation required family leaders to protect and provide for their members. Out of a total of fourteen successions between 1744 and 1891 only three were uncontested. The eleven contested successions included assassination, civil war, and, in a few cases, bloodless revolution.

The first great Saudi leader was Muhammad bin Sa'ud (1742–65). Having joined forces with Muhammad bin 'Abdul Wahhab (the founder of the Unitarian movement pejoratively known as Wahhabism) in 1744, Muhammad bin Sa'ud expanded the family's power base to control most of central Arabia within two decades.[5] The Al Sa'ud secured the land, and the Al Shaykh, as the family of Muhammad bin 'Abdul Wahhab came to be known, provided religious legitimacy. Not only was the combination an effective tool to retain power but, equally important, it guaranteed political stability for several generations.

It was in Dir'iyyah, the first Saudi capital, that a bond of friendship and mutual respect formed between Shaykh Muhammad bin 'Abdul Wahhab and Muhammad bin Sa'ud. The two men entered into a political alliance and, upon the latter's death, ties between the two branches were resealed in 1765 with the ruler's successor, 'Abdul 'Aziz bin Muhammad bin Sa'ud.[6] At this critical period, when the physical dominion of the Al Sa'ud was limited to portions of Najd province, the "Shaykh" exercised great power, for he was the supreme judge dealing with religious affairs. Religion literally ruled the land and 'Abdul Wahhab became an intimate advisor to 'Abdul 'Aziz. The relationship, however, was not limited to legal interpretations but included counseling on questions ranging from domestic affairs to war with enemy tribes. In fact, the jurist accommodated theory and practice because he shared a mutual goal with 'Abdul 'Aziz. Both men aimed to the establishment of a kingdom under Shari'ah (Islamic law). Within this vision, the state would thus form an integral part of the religious establishment, itself affixed to politics.[7]

After Muhammad bin Saʿud, the first two successions went unchallenged, as power passed from ruler to eldest son. In addition, these two successors, ʿAbdul ʿAziz bin Muhammad (1765–1803) and Saʿud bin ʿAbdul ʿAziz (1803–14), confirmed their tenure by further expanding Saudi landholdings. Potential claimants from either the lineal or lateral lines were either too young or too undistinguished in battle to challenge the two leaders, although several established family branches that would appear in later dynastic politics. Saʿud bin ʿAbdul ʿAziz was a fierce warrior who won several key battles in Najd, which naturally enhanced his credibility as chief. In 1788, his father appointed him heir apparent—with Shaykh Muhammad bin ʿAbdul Wahhab's full consent—and, most important, without known objections from any member of the extended family. To be sure, Saʿud's prowess in battle, especially in absorbing the difficult provinces of Hasah in 1793, Karbalah in 1802, and Makkah in 1803, endeared him to all. Thus, when a revenge-minded Shiʿah from Karbalah assassinated ʿAbdul ʿAziz bin Muhammad, Saʿud was proclaimed leader without opposition.[8]

A victim of his own successes, Saʿud bin ʿAbdul ʿAziz (1803–14) was quickly challenged by the Ottoman Empire, which directed its viceroy in Egypt, Muhammad ʿAli, to invade the Hijaz and defeat the Unitarian movement. Like his father and grandfather, Saʿud bin ʿAbdul ʿAziz groomed his eldest son, ʿAbdallah, for the throne. At first, ʿAbdallah proved successful in defeating the invading Egyptians, although he lost the Hijaz in 1812. When Saʿud died of fever in May 1814, ʿAbdallah became ruler but faced internal challenges in part because of his poor performance on the battlefield. The emerging family rivalry was resolved by the Egyptian invasion when Dirʿiyyah fell (1818). Several senior Al Saʿud members were captured and carted off to Cairo, where many simply disappeared. ʿAbdallah, who was also arrested and taken to Egypt, was beheaded in 1819 in Constantinople. Without a doubt, Ottoman officials were after the Al Saʿud—as well as the Al Shaykh—and aimed at the total elimination of the Unitarian movement on the Arabian Peninsula. In the event, Turki bin ʿAbdallah successfully escaped the Ottoman Empire's net, hiding in the harsh environment of the Najd, where few Ottoman or Egyptian levies survived.[9] Within a few years, occupying Egyptian forces lost interest and, by 1822, most had withdrawn from central Arabia. The Al Saʿud entered a period of intense internal rivalry in the absence of a single recognized leader or dominant branch of the family. With the collapse of family order, several rivals sought the support of Egypt against their brothers, clearly abandoning the fundamental consensus principle that had seen them through difficult times. This too was not lost on ʿAbdul ʿAziz bin ʿAbdul Rahman Al Saʿud.

Al Sa'ud power was restored in August 1824, when Turki bin 'Abdallah (a grandson of Muhammad bin Sa'ud and an uncle of the beheaded 'Abdallah bin Sa'ud bin 'Abdul 'Aziz) returned to Riyadh, captured it, and claimed it as a new capital. He appointed Mish'ari bin Nasir (from the collateral Mish'ari branch) as governor of Riyadh. Importantly, Turki was the first leader of the 'Abdallah bin Muhammad line to assume leadership, thereby introducing an alternative to the 'Abdul 'Aziz line.[10] In time, several captured Al Sa'ud leaders managed to escape from Egypt and returned to Arabia. Among these was Faysal bin Turki, who quickly rose to prominence and became his father's designated successor. Still, the Al Sa'ud were boxed in central Arabia because, by this time, the British Empire had appeared over the horizon. In the absence of additional landholdings, the instinct to survive aggravated dynastic rivalries, as the Al Sa'ud, once again, fell prey to internecine conflict. Turki bin 'Abdallah survived a challenge from his cousin Mish'ari bin 'Abdul Rahman in 1831 but was finally assassinated by Mish'ari's agents in 1834.[11] This was the foremost political murder recorded since the alliance of 1744, which established the first Saudi state. As fate would have it, Mish'ari's tenure on the throne was very short, since he too was killed, by Turki's son Faysal, who captured Riyadh in 1834 and proclaimed himself ruler.[12]

Faysal's rule was cut short in 1838 by the return of agitated Egyptian forces who were concerned with the rising influence of the British in and around the peninsula. The Egyptians expelled and replaced Faysal bin Turki with a puppet ruler, Khalid bin Sa'ud, who, at least theoretically, restored the original dominant branch of the family to power. As alluded to above, the British soon pressured their Egyptian suzerain Muhammad 'Ali—who was earlier instructed to send troops to Arabia—to withdraw his forces in 1840. Soon after, Khalid was overthrown by a distant cousin, 'Abdallah bin Thunayan bin Ibrahim.[13] For the first time in contemporary Saudi affairs, a member of the Al Thunayan branch of the family assumed power, even if the tenure would be short. 'Abdallah bin Thunayan was deposed in 1843 by Faysal bin Turki, who had successfully escaped Egyptian captivity. The popular Faysal bin Turki assumed rulership for the second time as he ushered in, by far, the most stable period in the history of the peninsula up to that time. What Faysal bin Turki did—circumstances that were carefully studied by 'Abdul 'Aziz bin 'Abdul Rahman Al Sa'ud several decades later—was legendary.[14]

First, he gently persuaded the 'ulamah—who tended to recognize whichever prince won the secular struggle for power during these byzantine and bloody periods—to preach faith and conciliation. Second, Faysal bin Turki succeeded in establishing a more cohesive though smaller Saudi realm, satisfied with the Najd,

Hasah, and Jabal al-Shammar. He accepted Ottoman control over the Hijaz—at least temporarily—because he simply could not rule it with meager resources. Third, and perhaps as important as any measure ever taken by a Saudi official, Faysal bin Turki restored order within the family. Loyalties were fostered through appointments, marriages were blessed among various young and promising princes, and financial concessions were encouraged for burgeoning trade efforts. These, as well as other steps, enhanced internal stability.[15]

With Faysal's death in 1865, however, the ruling family was again plunged into a long period of struggle and civil war. Unlike the previous period of family strife, which had stemmed from the vacuum created by foreign invasion, the struggles after Faysal's death were the result of a failure to share power among various heirs. Following the pattern of other strong rulers, Faysal had designated his eldest son, ʿAbdallah, as heir apparent, but the latter was challenged by his younger half brother Saʿud. The consequence was more than a decade of civil war that included attempts by rival princes to make alliances with external powers, this time with the Ottoman Empire, against each other. By 1871, Saʿud bin Faysal had succeeded in deposing ʿAbdallah bin Faysal. At Saʿud's death in 1875, his younger full brother ʿAbdul Rahman ascended the throne, only to be deposed that same year by ʿAbdallah bin Faysal, who returned to power with Ottoman support. With ʿAbdallah bin Faysal's death in 1889, his younger half brother ʿAbdul Rahman again ascended the throne. By this time, however, the Al Saʿud dynasty was so weakened by internal fighting that Riyadh was captured by a rival family from Haʾil in northern Arabia, the Al Rashid.[16] After leading an unsuccessful revolt against the Al Rashid in 1890, ʿAbdul Rahman, the last surviving son of Faysal bin Turki, was forced to seek exile in Kuwait along with his immediate family. It was one of ʿAbdul Rahman's sons, ʿAbdul ʿAziz bin ʿAbdul Rahman Al Saʿud, who recaptured the family seat and founded the third Saudi state.

ʿAbdul ʿAziz bin ʿAbdul Rahman Al Saʿud

Beginning from exile in Kuwait in 1902, ʿAbdul ʿAziz captured Riyadh and expelled the Al Rashid. Over the next three decades, ʿAbdul ʿAziz defeated a host of enemies—including Ottoman Turks, rival Arabian families, rebellious tribes, and even rival princes from the Al Saʿud family—to establish the present Kingdom of Saudi Arabia in 1932. What ʿAbdul ʿAziz bin ʿAbdul Rahman concluded was that constant challenges to the dominant branch within the family substantially weakened the ruler, and that rivalries from collateral branches, although limited, were equally harmful. Simply stated, there were too many claimants whose quests for power could not be sustained. Moreover, the founder of the third state realized that lineal challenges were detrimental to the survival of the family, and partly to address this problem he reintroduced an additional mechanism to support his own heir apparent, namely the *bay'ah* (oath of loyalty or compact of rule). Faithful to the 1744 alliance between the Al Sa'ud and Al Shaykh, the *bay'ah* was bestowed to his designated heir by the Ahl al-'Aqd wal-Hall (literally, those who bind and loosen; a group composed of senior family members, religious, tribal, and town notables), who ensured a modicum of stability. Much like the first Saudi state, which had been achieved through a combination of religious fervor and tribal ethos, Arabia would be reconquered by 'Abdul 'Aziz bin 'Abdul Rahman using similar methods. Among key features, the alliance with the *'ulamah*, neglected when expediency gave way to principles, was restored in full. Likewise, unheeded consultations with key tribal leaders were also reinstated, as was the diligent application of a strict legal system. Only by adhering to such values, reasoned 'Abdul 'Aziz, could the Al Sa'ud transcend intertribal feuding. Although personal authority and demonstrated prowess were helpful, internal unity was absolutely necessary to successfully challenge outside foes. Finally, 'Abdul 'Aziz also noted that both states that had preceded his own failed to create basic institutions that would assume the burden of governance and, in a real sense, establish a buffer between the population and the leadership on one level, and among leaders on the other. He set out to address these concerns systematically even before 1932 to ensure that his own successors did not engage in fraternal struggles.

Contenders to Authority after 1932

In Najd, a different type of conflict loomed on the horizon for the Al Sa'ud, as the Al Rashid challenged tribal authority. In fact, the Al Rashid bid led 'Abdul 'Aziz to devise an ambitious plan centered on the establishment of two hundred new settlements that combined military, agricultural, and missionary functions. Inhabitants in these settlements were the Ikhwan (the Muslim Brethren) whose devotion to strict Hanbali rites helped 'Abdul 'Aziz rebuild Saudi Arabia between 1910 and 1930.[17] For approximately twenty years, 'Abdul 'Aziz held the religious title of imam, as he earned unparalleled legitimacy. In 1921, he supplemented his religious title with the secular designation of sultan and, after his conquest of the Hijaz, the title of king. By acquiring a monarchical title, 'Abdul 'Aziz sealed the traditional jurists' interpretation that the "caliphate had become a dynastic monarchy."[18] This was further reinforced by the well-established relationship between the king and the *'ulamah*. The arrangement was so satisfactory that senior religious figures often sided with 'Abdul 'Aziz against the extremist Ikhwan, whose random raids across the peninsula produced embarrassment as well as diplomatic friction between the king and his neighbors. The Ikhwan were eventually defeated as the monarch moved to set up a regular army to retain superior capabilities over renegade tribes. His nascent army, which was formed in 1929 and primarily staffed by loyal tribal levies, eventually became the National Guard.

In 1912, 'Abdul 'Aziz occupied Hasah province in the east and gradually received the allegiance of tribes living in the area. In turn, this development brought him to the attention of the British, who, following the signing of the 1915 'Uqayr Treaty, recognized him as the "governor" of Najd, Hasah, Qatif, and Jubayl.[19] This international treaty was the first signed by 'Abdul 'Aziz that strengthened his status and allowed him to counterbalance Ottoman plans on the Arabian Peninsula. Still, relations with London deteriorated sharply because Britain supported the Hashemite Sharif Hussein in the Hijaz. Ironically, successive Al Sa'ud victories in the Hijaz brought the "sultan" Soviet recognition, even if London demurred. 'Abdul 'Aziz's second son, Faysal, visited Moscow in 1932, where he met senior officials, including Vyacheslav Molotov. Soviet leaders received the Saudi delegation warmly as Moscow opened a diplomatic mission in Jiddah.[20] As discussed below, the mission was closed in 1938, after the Soviet Union became disillusioned with Riyadh.

The 'Uqayr Treaty, which brought London and Riyadh closer than Moscow anticipated, was further compounded by American oil companies' attention to 'Abdul 'Aziz. A decade before Washington opened its first legation in Saudi Arabia, the Standard Oil Company of California (SOCAL) received an oil concession from the ruler. That agreement of July 1933 led to the historic meeting between 'Abdul 'Aziz and the U.S. president, Franklin D. Roosevelt, aboard the USS *Quincy* on the Great Bitter Lake in Egypt on February 14, 1945. The two men discussed three specific issues: (1) the establishment of American bases in Saudi Arabia; (2) the Palestine question, about which Roosevelt promised to consult with both Jewish and Arab leaders before making any decisions concerning the status of the disputed area; and (3) oil concessions.[21] As a result of the meeting, the United States built military bases in Dhahran, al-Khobar, and al-Aghissiyyah, as Saudi Arabia entered into the Western defense orbit. The Palestine issue, however, introduced a chill in Saudi-American relations when war broke out in 1948 and President Harry Truman refused to respect his predecessor's solemn pledge.[22] Despite this lapse, 'Abdul 'Aziz did not forego cooperation with oil companies because he desperately needed their expertise as well as political support. When the British tried to curb American tanker traffic through the Suez Canal, or when they attempted to thwart the construction of Tapline (the pipeline connecting Dhahran with Zahrani, Lebanon), 'Abdul 'Aziz asked for and received assistance from Washington. These initiatives illustrated the monarch's diplomatic skills as he balanced ties with both Britain and the United States. At times, the ruler would not hesitate to use one against the other; at other times, he would be the victim of the London-Washington axis. Still, Saudi Arabia did not enjoy full British support because the Buraymi Oasis conflict pitted Riyadh against London.

Sa'ud bin 'Abdul 'Aziz Al Sa'ud

Ruling family politics under King Sa'ud (1953–64) were marked by a sharp division of power between the monarch and the heir apparent that escalated into a bitter feud.[23] As discussed in some detail in chapters 2 and 3, disagreements between the two men spilled over into sharp political confrontations as well as military ones.

When Sa'ud began appointing his inexperienced young sons to major governmental positions, senior members of the ruling family became concerned about the monarch's tendency to make hasty decisions, which bypassed older and more seasoned uncles and nephews. Many feared that such appointments signaled that Sa'ud was planning to transfer succession to his offspring. Such concerns, coupled with observations of Sa'ud's spending habits, increased overall dissatisfaction to the point that senior family members urged Sa'ud to relinquish power to Faysal. On March 24, 1958, and under much duress, Sa'ud issued a royal decree transferring executive powers to Faysal.

Armed with emergency powers, Faysal fortified his position by implementing a number of foreign and domestic policies (including a ten-point reform program) to meet various crises.[24] By 1964, and literally at the end of his patience, Faysal mounted a palace coup by inviting the leading religious figures and princes to convene in Riyadh and consider a formal settlement of the persistent feud.[25] Sa'ud was muzzled but the damage was done. The 'ulamah stripped Sa'ud of his powers though they retained him as monarch and, while the decree they issued was specific, additional conditions were quickly imposed which further complicated relations between the two leaders.

It must be emphasized that relations between the two brothers worsened over the Yemen conflict that pitted Sa'ud, favoring a military intervention on behalf of Imam Badr, the Yemeni leader, and Faysal, who considered the Saudi army too weak to confront the Egyptian military. Within his own camp, Faysal was chastised for not showing firmness toward Washington, which had adopted an ambiguous attitude toward Nasir's Yemeni policies while extending lukewarm support to Riyadh. Deteriorating relations between Sa'ud and Faysal led the latter to call on the Council of Ministers and the 'ulamah to hear his grievances. On

March 30, 1964, the struggle for power ended, with the clerics introducing an unusual solution. They declared that Saʿud was "unable to carry out the affairs of the state" because of his "state of health" and "current circumstances," but he would remain king and still have "the right to respect and reverence." The ʿulamah further stated that Faysal would "carry out all the internal and external affairs of the King, without referring back to the King in this regard."[26] On April 1, 1964, Khalid bin ʿAbdul ʿAziz, the deputy prime minister, notified senior ministers of the decision and asked them to approve it by signing the decree (*fatwah*). Saʿud would reign but would no longer govern.

Such a situation could not go on without creating unnecessary disputes within the royal family especially since several members disapproved of Faysal's brilliant internal diplomatic maneuvers. Others concluded that the heir apparent was not empowered to exercise full authority as long as the monarch reigned. Not surprisingly, what transpired throughout the following months was managed chaos, as the country's—as well as the family's—interests were severely affected by top-level disagreements. By early November 1964, Faysal was ready to end the discord that ensued, as the Council of Ministers and the ʿulamah were summoned to make a final decision. A decision was brokered to depose Saʿud and to proclaim Faysal king.[27] A religious decree confirming the latter was issued on the same day and made public—along with the Council of Ministers' decision as well as King Faysal's first royal edict—on November 3, 1964. Faysal immediately became king, and Saʿud, along with several of his sons, went into exile. Although the highest-ranking family members settled into a new arrangement, the country faced the consequences of its earlier sociopolitical dilemmas, which certainly deserved careful assessments. The ways in which Saudi leaders devised various institutions, and how they developed the kingdom's doctrinal and strategic imperatives are worthy of attention.

Continuum in Saudi Arabia

Having successfully extended his rule throughout most of Arabia, ʿAbdul ʿAziz bin ʿAbdul Rahman Al Saʿud took the title of king of the Hijaz and announced, on August 31, 1926, the adoption of a constitution. The latter stipulated that the kingdom was a monarchical constitutional Islamic state whose capital would be Makkah.[28] This document placed no limits on the monarch's authority, except to confine his rule to be compatible with Shariʿah. In addition, the constitution of 1926 introduced the concept of succession in calling for the appointment of an heir apparent who would assist the ruler and who would seek the cooperation of as many administrators as necessary to direct the affairs of the kingdom. Finally, this first modern constitution called for the establishment of a consultative council, which would meet once a week and debate pertinent questions on the agenda prepared by the heir.[29] This was the first attempt to institutionalize consultation, even though the practice was widespread among Arabia's tribal communities. In the event, this constitution was never fully implemented, but it served as a basis for future permutations.

On September 18, 1932, the name of the country was changed to The Kingdom of Saudi Arabia, and while a new heir apparent was named as successor, the kingdom was essentially ruled by decree until 1953. Between 1932 and 1953, the Council of Ministers executed the ruler's domestic and foreign policies. Originally, there were two ministries: Finance and Foreign Affairs, and in 1944 a Ministry of Defense was duly established. With additional revenues generated through the sale of petroleum, Saudi Arabia earned $160 million in 1953, leading 'Abdul 'Aziz to expand various government functions.[30]

The Council of Ministers

Approximately one month prior to his death, 'Abdul 'Aziz promulgated a decree establishing a new Council of Ministers, as heir apparent Sa'ud was named prime minister. The council convened its first session on March 7, 1954 in Riyadh, after the founder had passed away. One of the new ruler's first decrees, issued on March 26, 1954, defined the statutes of the council, which was expected to supervise the implementation of domestic and foreign policy, approve budgets, authorize the foreign minister to sign treaties and international agreements, and grant oil concessions as necessary. Significantly, the monarch, who was also his own prime minister, presided over council meetings even if he could not vote. This was a technical matter with little importance since all council decisions were subject to the ruler's approval.[31] The decree of March 26 further provided for the establishment of a secretariat-general, an audit office, a grievances post, and a group of technical experts, who were attached to the council.[32] These new positions formed the Cabinet of the Council of Ministers and were part of Prince Faysal's doing as he sought to delegate administrative powers to qualified individuals. Parenthetically, King Sa'ud, in his capacity as prime minister, presided over the first council meeting only. Faysal chaired all succeeding meetings after he became prime minister.

With respect to internal reforms, and largely at the insistence of senior family members, Sa'ud issued another critical decree on March 23, 1958, which gave Faysal full authority over foreign affairs, internal policy, and finance. When this authorization was deemed insufficient to resolve the political crisis that mired the ruling family, Saʿud promulgated a new edict (May 11, 1958) that expanded the prerogatives of the Council of Ministers. That initiative transformed the council "from a purely advisory [institution] into a formal policy-making body with both executive and legislative powers under Faysal."[33] Although the king retained a veto power, the council was in effect given legislative and executive privileges, which established the framework for future constitutional changes. While the decree of May 11, 1958 was not a formal constitution, its fifty paragraphs could, indeed, be classified as constitutional articles.[34]

According to the decree, each cabinet officer would be responsible for his department's affairs to the prime minister, who would, in turn, be responsible to the king (Article 8). The Council of Ministers would "draw up the policy of the State [in] internal and external, financial and economic, educational and defense, and in all public affairs" and "supervise its execution" (Article 18). In addition, all government commitments regarding public spending would have to conform to the provisions of the budget authorized by the cabinet (Article 34), and no extra spending would be permitted without the council's authorization (Article 36). All government requests would be submitted for approval to the ruler, who would decide within thirty days whether to endorse or reject them. Only after following this procedure could the prime minister act independently and inform the cabinet of his decisions (Article 23).

Although many differences separated Saʿud and Faysal, raw political interests—the appropriation of authority within the Council of Ministers—enlarged the gap that existed between the two brothers. The point is worth repeating that poor management of the kingdom's limited resources threatened the country with bankruptcy, which, in turn, compelled senior princes to trust the administration of the state to the more capable Faysal. The heir instituted strict spending limits and introduced severe austerity measures that were unpopular among Saʿud's supporters. The latter pressured the monarch to force his brother's resignation on December 19, 1960. When Saʿud formed his own cabinet on December 21, 1960, he included six "liberal" princes, including Talal bin ʿAbdul ʿAziz and ʿAbdallah Tariqi, who was then director-general of the Department of Petroleum and Mineral Resources.[35] The new team began working on a constitutional project, which pretended to create a national assembly for Saudi Arabia. In fact, the zeal of several liberal princes was not new and may have started in 1958, when executive powers were transferred to Faysal. At the time, Tariqi claimed "exultantly: we in Saudi Arabia have just taken a step forward to a constitution. Eventually this country will become a constitutional monarchy."[36] The young technocrat, who had proved himself a staunch supporter of the kingdom during negotiations with oil companies and other founding members of the Organization of Petroleum Exporting Countries (OPEC), may have ignited the flame of political participation. Yet, it was Talal bin ʿAbdul ʿAziz who provided detailed constitutional proposals that led Saʿud to break his ties with "progressive" ministers and entrust, once again, the premiership and foreign ministry to Faysal on March 15, 1962.[37]

Following harrowing events from March to November 1964, the statutes of the Council of Ministers were duly revised on November 18, 1964, allowing the monarch to resume direct control of the Council's presidency—a provision that has remained applicable ever since. In fact, the council was the only effective political institution in Saudi Arabia, although a draft constitution first drawn up in 1960—and which called for the establishment of an independent national assembly—lingered.

The Saudi *Raison d'État*

If the Council of Ministers was the construct through which various institutions were created, the kingdom's *raison d'état* came about as a "will to power" emerged under Faysal. Although the founder articulated his "Saudi" identity, the will to power was first tested under Faysal, who confronted an ideological challenge from Egypt. To be sure, King Saʿud was also aware that the survival of the regime was directly linked to order and the triumph of Al Saʿud ideology, but it was his heir apparent who enlarged the parameters through which ideology was understood. Faysal envisaged a logically constructed view of social and political life containing elements of myth and symbolism that were used to communicate his message in simplified form. For him, ideology was a lens through which the world was viewed as normative and positive judgments, used to form subjective assessments. The kingdom's ideology thus identified and criticized what it considered to be deleterious behavior. It also identified values and outcomes worth striving for. Ideology, in its normative role and as applied by King Faysal, was the source of views on the proper allocation of resources in society, the desirable qualities of rulership and authority, and, by implication, the source of the regime's legitimacy.

Because there was no palpable distinction between Saudi Arabia and the ruling Al Saʿud ruling family, it was amply clear that the 1744 alliance between the Al Saʿud and the Al Shaykh families formed the focal point of all pressure points. It was that alliance, which formed the principal pillar of the Saudi *raison d'état*, that was first challenged by radical Arab forces who called on the religious leaders to distance themselves from allegedly incompetent and unworthy political leaders.

Faysal buttressed his ideological principles and defended his rule by relying on Hanbali Islam.[38]

The Kingdom's Doctrine and Alternative Strategies

As Saudi values and norms arose from a particular ideological view of the world, they were transformed into more rigid principles specifying concrete political goals. This was the kingdom's doctrine, which, arguably, was inherently less flexible than its ideology. To be sure, the two served different purposes: ideology to attract supporters and provide legitimacy and doctrine to accomplish clear political and organizational goals. Faysal was ideological but not doctrinaire. As a concrete embodiment of ideology, political doctrine involved elements of strategy, policy, and constitutional structure, all of which Riyadh espoused with vigor starting in 1964. Indeed, Faysal relied on Hanbali writings to sanction the emergence of the monarchy in exchange for the monarch's vow to uphold the tenets of Hanbali Islam.[39] In addition to forming an institutional embodiment of ideology, Saudi doctrine permitted ideology to be reaffirmed by spelling out concrete political goals. Throughout the 1960s, Faysal developed and articulated a clear doctrinal imperative that redefined the parameters of the Saudi monarchy. Henceforth, Riyadh would defend Islam, even if this imperative remained subordinate to the more important need to use doctrine as a means by which to stay in power, remove external ideological or doctrinal threats, and maintain internal legitimacy. In other words, Saudi Arabia championed this core value, although anyone who questioned the constitutional status quo became—by definition—a doctrinal liability. When an individual, or a group, was equipped with the influence or capabilities to overturn the reigning constitutional order, he or they became a national security risk, and sometimes a military hazard. It was for these fundamental reasons that Faysal never authorized financial support to extremist religious groups inside the kingdom or elsewhere in the Arab and Muslim worlds.

To implement their doctrinal imperatives, the Al Saʿud did not shy away from tough measures, as demonstrations with strong political rhetoric were dealt swift blows in the past. In the 1920s, Riyadh did not hesitate to put down religious uprisings, with the full support of senior *ulamah*. Furthermore, and largely to placate any doctrinal opposition to Riyadh, Faysal accelerated the introduction of various socioeconomic reforms even if the Majlis al-Shurah, first envisioned in 1927, was never fully empowered under his rule.[40] On November 6, 1962, the heir apparent proposed the establishment of a Basic Law

for the Government of the country, drawn from the Koran and the Traditions of His Prophet and the acts of the Orthodox Caliphs, that will set forth explicitly the fundamental principles of government and the relationship between the governor and the governed, organize the various powers of the state, and the relationship among these powers, and provide for the basic rights of the citizen, including the right to freely express opinion within the limits of Islamic belief and public policy.[41]

Yet, by appointing a whole slew of well-qualified individuals to advise him, the monarch aimed to neutralize doctrinal opposition. His actions surely presaged eventual political revisions. Although fundamental constitutional reforms were not on Riyadh's agenda in the 1960s and 1970s, Faysal was nevertheless capable of using powerful tools at his disposal to make changes as needed.

King Faysal foresaw "strategem" for Saudi Arabia in very specific ways. He envisaged several strategies to defend the monarchy against internal or external ideological or doctrinal challenges. To remove external threats, for example, Riyadh systematically engaged in a "game of nations" tactic, playing one set of nations off against another. In a scheme of riyalpolitik, Riyadh would buy off potential regional troublemakers with financial aid, and in a strategy of media domination, it would control dozens of Arab news organizations. Moreover, to maintain the regime's internal legitimacy, several approaches were also designed to co-opt counterelites and wayward ruling family members as well as build domestic credibility (and foreign influence) by means of awqaf (religious endowments) and da'wah (propagation of the faith) donations. Still, and because specific military, political, and economic capabilities and influences were required to turn a strategy into concrete and effective action, Saudi Arabia relied on its intrinsic capabilities: oil production and purchasing power. In fact, it was this latter strategy that Faysal adopted starting in the early 1970s, when he eagerly restored—through a series of bold and relatively radical economic moves (including privatization, foreign investment, and oil production cuts)—the country's moribund economic health.

The elements of this analytical construct do not describe either a mutually exclusive or a mutually exhaustive paradigm. Rather, they capture a substantial part of what policy formulation was all about, which, under Faysal's custodianship, was exercised with zeal. Of course, interactions between various elements of the construct seemed obvious, but this was not always the case. For example, the legitimacy of the kingdom's ideology, which enhanced its influence, was questioned throughout the 1960s. It may also be useful to note that authority improved the types of doctrinal goals, which Riyadh was readily capable of setting for itself and achieving, as Faysal gained self-confidence after he became a ruler. Indeed, Saudi Arabia's influence throughout the vast and growing Muslim world was in its infancy when Faysal became the monarch. It was only augmented when the visionary ruler placed his impressive economic, political, and religious instruments to the service of the worldwide Muslim community. Finally, the various threats the kingdom faced affected its doctrinal goals, and strategies further required Faysal to maximize whatever capabilities were available. To succeed in this realm, therefore, Faysal relied on a firm internal base of support. That base was the ruling Al Saʿud family. Faysal engaged in a systematic winnowing, promoting loyal members of the family and isolating those who expressed doubt, to ensure internal stability as well as ward off external threats. His rule was epoch-making for it restored Al Saʿud responsibilities while fulfilling the original vision espoused by the founder. In 1964, Saudi Arabia was secured, but by 1975, it was safely placed on the path of stability.

2

Prince Faysal (1906–1953)

Few political figures started their apprenticeship in international affairs at the tender age of thirteen. Even fewer assumed the burden of responsibility for over fifty years. Faysal bin ʿAbdul ʿAziz Al Saʿud was such a leader. Born in a desert tribe, Prince Faysal ascended to the rulership of one of the most enigmatic countries in the world following a unique apprenticeship. It would indeed be an understatement to emphasize that little did he know at the time that he would be called upon to carry a sword in one hand and the Holy Qurʾan in the other, to administer justice as his name's moniker required. For in Arabic "Faysal" also means a mediator or a judge.[1]

When Faysal was born in Riyadh on April 9, 1906, his father was barely twenty-six, but he was already impressive both by stature and popularity. A handsome and tall leader, ʿAbdul ʿAziz bin ʿAbdul Rahman was a tenacious man, yet savvy to fundamental tribal nuances. His management of Najdi communities served him and his descendants well as he galvanized former enemies into putative allies. Few resisted his charm and fewer stood in the way of several audacious conquests. ʿAbdul ʿAziz bin ʿAbdul Rahman was a man in a hurry, eager to reunite the various Arabian Peninsula tribes under his control, and reestablish the third Saudi monarchy. Whether he sought revenge was not improbable given his recollections of his own father's defeat and expulsion from Najd in 1890. At an impressionable age, ʿAbdul ʿAziz was determined to resurrect a phoenix from the desolate landscape that was then Arabia. His daring conquest of Riyadh in 1902 was more than legend, which, without a doubt, buttressed his leadership claims.

Faysal was ʿAbdul ʿAziz bin ʿAbdul Rahman's third son but the first one to be born in Riyadh. Although the name Riyadh—"Garden" in Arabic—left the impression that this was a bustling oasis, in reality the place was austere and did not count more than a few thousand *badu*. What Riyadh offered, above all else, was water in the Wadi Hanifah region. Because of this vital resource, a few nomads' farms, date palms, and fig trees, lined the area. The city was laid in open desert, surrounded by ridges and some vegetation, but it lacked the natural protection of Dir'iyyah. In the heart of Najd, the small village was exposed to the elements, stifling heat during the day and bitter cold at night. Such conditions literally shaped the Najdi character, rugged in temperament, intuitive in outlook, and careful in trusting outsiders. Najdi men and women were consequently introverted, drawing succor from their religious beliefs and a methodical application of age-old rituals that served their ancestors well.

Faysal's mother, Tarfah bint Al Shaykh, bore no other son to 'Abdul 'Aziz. Yet she resealed the 1744 bond that united the Al Sa'ud with the Al Shaykh. As a descendant of Muhammad bin 'Abdul Wahhab, she was the critical link that legitimized the military-religious alliance, a linkage that has retained all of its value ever since. Like all *badu* children, Faysal played bare-footed in the desert, climbed trees, and, perhaps when he was five or six years old, mounted on a mare to learn to ride, a most critical activity. Although Faysal was less athletic than several of his contemporaries, he displayed prowess and excelled in riding. His courage was displayed in other areas as well. To show their bravery, young Najdi boys would hold their nose and jump "thirty foot or so into a deep well, swimming round by a dog stroke, until a rope was let down with a basket in which they could be drawn up."[2] Reportedly, Faysal was fearless when his initiation came about, a feat that earned him much respect among young Najdis. News of his young son's progress reached 'Abdul 'Aziz bin 'Abdul Rahman, who roamed around the Arabian Peninsula to subdue warring tribes.

Faysal's mother passed away in 1912, when the young boy was five years old. Consequently, his maternal grandmother reared him, but even before he reached the age of seven, his upbringing was entrusted to his maternal grandfather, 'Abdallah bin 'Abdul Latif Al Shaykh. Few men influenced Faysal as much as this pious gentleman, who instilled values of piety in the young man's character. The elder Al Shaykh taught Faysal the scriptures and instilled a deep love and respect for Arabic poetry. In addition to piety, Shaykh 'Abdallah insisted that his young charge absorb modern skills, including reading and writing at an advanced level, which were not then widely practiced. These skills would prove vital to Faysal, who conducted massive and simultaneous correspondence sessions with dozens of Arab leaders over the years.[3] His mentor guided him in a critical area during his youth, as the elder tutor foresaw the young man's potential.

Like his elder brothers, Turki and Sa'ud, Faysal would also delve into the military arts. At the time, these consisted of expert riding and the manipulation of the sword, preferably while on horseback. Over several years, his father entrusted Faysal with key expeditions, to instill responsibilities and to lead men into battle. As 'Abdul 'Aziz organized his tribal levies into the Ikhwan, Faysal joined in pivotal battles in 'Asir Province and attended settlement negotiations when the founder successfully subdued rebellions.[4] At the age of fourteen, Faysal commanded his father's forces in 'Asir and, in 1921, led troops in the region around Jabal Shammar, whose main stronghold of Ha'il fell before long. A year later, he conquered Abhah at the head of an expedition of four thousand men before consolidating his control over northern 'Asir. Throughout this period, Faysal learned both war and politics from his master, developing patience and discretion as necessary. In fact, one of the early lessons Faysal learned from his father was the art of political readiness, whereby a leader is taught patience.[5] Given that Najdi leaders were well acquainted with tribal politics, 'Abdul 'Aziz instructed his sons to show magnanimity, recruiting local tribesmen to the ultimate cause of joining forces with the Al Sa'ud. After battles were settled, the Al Sa'ud introduced effective mechanisms to further induce survivors into the growing political fold that the founder created.[6] Faysal learned to persuade by introducing benevolent taxation and the Unitarian creed. According to his contemporaries, the young prince was often seen in a pensive stage, turned reflexively inward as he analyzed tribal negotiations.

'Abdul 'Aziz bin 'Abdul Rahman faced unmistakable internal foes, but it was Britain that delayed his conquests. When he set out to conquer the Lower Gulf shaykhdoms, London protested and, in the case of the Buraymi Oasis on the border of Oman, Abu Dhabi, and Saudi Arabia, warned 'Abdul 'Aziz before opposing him. Doubtless, the British veto disappointed him, even if the decision taught Faysal a critical lesson. He would henceforth cooperate with others but only rely on himself. As Faysal witnessed how British and, to a lesser extent, Ottoman leaders behaved with his father, he may have drawn a lifelong instruction from this experience. When Britain sided with the Hashemites in World War I, 'Abdul 'Aziz turned his attention inward. He waited for the conflict to end, as the repercussions of the secret Sykes-Picot agreement of 1916—whereby Britain and France carved the Middle East to serve their particular interests—surfaced. As British machinations against the Hashemites drew severe criticisms, particularly during the Versailles conference then meeting near Paris in the aftermath of World War I, London extended a separate invitation to 'Abdul 'Aziz to discuss the best mechanisms to defuse tensions. He accepted the invitation but opted to delegate his thirteen-year-old son Faysal to represent him. Faysal was seconded by Ahmad bin Thunayan, who emerged after 1919 as the founder's principal advisor, chief clerk, and foreign affairs executive.

In the absence of any relevant records, we cannot know what instructions ʿAbdul ʿAziz may have issued to his son. Nevertheless, we do know that in Bahrain Faysal embarked on the HMS *Lawrence* for Europe. The young man was probably instructed to be careful, but he was already fully mistrustful of the British, who had betrayed and disappointed the Al Saʿud by preventing a full conquest of Arabia. British officers on the dedicated warship quickly noted Faysal's demeanor, especially when contrasted with that of the Kuwaiti delegation also making the trip, as the young man stood his ground.[7] After a brief stop in Bombay, Faysal and his small retinue—which included several Ikhwan warriors acting as bodyguards—embarked on a German vessel, the *Kigoma*, and set off for Plymouth, England, where they arrived on October 14, 1919. Harry St. John Philby, later an advisor to ʿAbdul ʿAziz, welcomed the delegation, although the reception at Paddington Station in London was wanting. If Faysal was displeased with the reception or the mix-up in their accommodations—which were only addressed after Philby intervened with Lords Cromer and Curzon—he never shared it with anyone. The wily Curzon quickly repaired the diplomatic faux pas, designating the group as the "Central Arabian Delegation" and Prince Faysal as his "Royal Highness."

On the sidelines of multilateral negotiations, Faysal encountered classic but tactful British arms-twisting, as key officials pressured him to end the feuds between the Al Saʿud and the Hashemites. Despite the honorific bestowed on the young Saudi prince, the visit to the Foreign Office was a disaster, as Lord Curzon allegedly treated his guests "like children and so patronizingly that they left England enraged," swearing never to return.[8] More important, London was eager to secure a new agreement that would clearly delineate the Hijaz-Najd border and, not surprisingly, called for a reassessment of British financial subsidies to the Al Saʿud for their various services.

On October 30, 1919, King George V received Faysal at Buckingham Palace, before the young Saudi visited the House of Commons and other prominent British institutions. His most memorable stop was in the City, where he assessed, perhaps for the first time by an Arab official, the financial might of the British Empire. He also visited the Greenwich Observatory, where he watched stars in daylight, and, with Philby acting as a guide, Trinity College in Cambridge to acquaint himself with a modernizing educational institution. In an ironic twist of fate, Faysal then stopped in Cardiff, then one of the world's most important coal producing cities. He was repeatedly told that coal, which fueled the empire's ships, was an unparalleled source of power. Little did anyone then know that within a few years oil would dethrone coal from its pedestal and with it introduce new global powers. The "Central Arabian Delegation" ended its visit with no accords on Al Saʿud-

Hashemite differences as neither Faysal nor Ahmad bin Thunayan were empowered to concede. Faysal and his group then went to Ireland, where they visited Dublin and Belfast, before returning to Britain. In Birmingham, they stopped at the Small Arms Factory and the Wolseley Motor Works to appraise British industry before returning to London in late November. There, Faysal attended a performance of *The Mikado*, as well as several other theatrical productions.[9] Although too young to comprehend the full horror of war, Faysal and his entourage visited the fresh battlefields of France and Flanders that, without a doubt, left an undeniable mark on the prince. Amiens, Reims, and Verdun were inexplicable, but Faysal was not immune to a profound cultural catharsis that visitors to such battlefields experienced, especially so soon after armistice was declared and when so much lay in ruins.

Escorted by Major Norman Napier Evelyn Bray, who served with Lawrence of Arabia in ʿAqabah, the Saudis next stopped in Paris, where Faysal ascended the Eiffel Tower to admire the City of Lights. Bray actually continued his negotiations with Faysal and Ahmad bin Thunayan about Arabia's future and the tribal warfare then underway. In the event, the Saudis committed to a three-year cease-fire, which was meticulously honored, even if few could prevent occasional provocations. Ironically, while Faysal was in the French capital, the city also hosted Faysal bin Hussein, Sharif Hussein's son. Bray took it upon himself to arrange a meeting between the two, but Ahmad bin Thunayan was too steeped in diplomacy to subject his young prince to such an ordeal. He attended the hastily arranged meeting himself, but, not surprisingly, it floundered after Faysal bin Hussein made snide remarks about Ikhwan bodyguards. Less than five years later, Faysal bin ʿAbdul ʿAziz would become viceroy of the Hijaz, following a full-fledged military routing of all Hashemite forces from western Arabia. Still, the episode left a negative image of British interference, even if Bray's intentions were honorable and his ultimate goal was peace. Faysal communicated his sentiments to his father, signing his letter with these memorable words: "Faysal bin ʿAbdul ʿAziz bin Saʿud, son of the King [Malik] of the Diyar [territories] of Najd and Chieftain of its Tribes."[10] The impact of European diplomacy—with titles and personal references carefully tailored to meet various positions—was clearly flowing into the young prince's mind as he substantially sharpened his observation skills. A few days later, the Saudi delegation boarded the SS *Neuralia* in Marseilles, France bound for home. The visit was an immense success especially since it awakened Faysal's innermost political instincts. A lifelong diplomat who cherished worldly affairs, Faysal was marked for life by this inaugural exposure to foreign affairs. He knew what to look for even as his father and cousin, Ahmad bin Thunayan, as well as key advisors, deserved recognition for trusting a thirteen-year-old with such lofty responsibilities. Equally important, Faysal etched in Western minds the notion that a nascent entity—which would soon become a kingdom—was slowly emerging on the Arabian Peninsula, led by capable leaders who earned legitimacy from their actions. His early decisions ensured that the kingdom would gain value long before it became a petro-monarchy in the 1970s.

A Warrior-Diplomat in the 1920s

Soon after Faysal had returned home, 'Abdul 'Aziz designated him commander of the expedition to finally subdue 'Asir and establish order in the province. In 1921, the prince distinguished himself in this reconquest, as the Idrisi rulers again acquiesced to Al Sa'ud authority. He was seconded by Khalid bin Luway, a tested Ikhwan officer who was from the Sharif clan but chose to ally himself to 'Abdul 'Aziz because of the latter's overwhelming charisma and fair dealings.[11] When the Idrisis had reneged on their commitments, perhaps cajoled in this foolish opposition by the sharif of Makkah, Faysal returned to 'Asir to crush all resistance in 1924. His legendary triumph was not limited to battlefield successes. Rather, Faysal persuaded his father to establish a protectorate over 'Asir in 1926, although the territory was not properly incorporated into Al Sa'ud territories until 1930.

Concurrent to these epoch-making developments, the Hashemite dominion over Makkah entered a dark era, as Sharif Hussein recognized his weakened position. Unfulfilled British promises to the Hashemites created distinct opportunities for the unhurried Al Sa'ud. 'Abdul 'Aziz waited patiently, and in 1924, when Mustafa Kamal—later known by his moniker Ataturk—abolished the Ottoman Caliphate, none other than the sharif of Makkah unwisely took the title. This was intolerable to the Al Sa'ud, who launched a massive attack on the Hijaz, expelled those who did not flee, and subjugated the remainder. Looting and massacres were common, especially in Ta'if, even though 'Abdul 'Aziz issued specific instructions calling on his Ikhwan troops to exercise maximum restraint.[12] He and Faysal entered Makkah as pilgrims, although Ikhwan forces were less restrained. Decorations and sacrilegious ornaments were forcefully expunged or trampled ostensibly to return the holy places to their pristine conditions. Still, the destruction was undeniable and not necessarily a positive legacy with which to initiate one's rule among a relatively sophisticated population. To avoid a repeat of such mistakes, 'Abdul 'Aziz entrusted Faysal to "take" Jiddah, instructing him to respect foreign legations and property. In fact, a specific command was issued not to assault the urban setting, which, under Faysal's leadership, was largely spared. A year-long siege followed that witnessed internal decay as living standards plunged to dire conditions. 'Ali bin Hussein, who had been empowered by his fleeing father, Sharif Hussein, to defend the Hijaz, finally escaped to join his younger brother Faysal bin Hussein in Iraq. Jiddah fell to Faysal 'Abdul 'Aziz without a single shot being fired.[13]

The conquest of the Hijaz assured, 'Abdul 'Aziz informed all tribal leaders that he intended to protect the holy cities, and that he would only rule over them as an *Amir al-Mu'minin* (Commander of the Faithful).[14] Faysal, who foresaw the need for a political as well as a religious settlement, wrote the declaration in the hope that the Al Sa'ud would be accepted as legitimate rulers. The young prince's style, as much as his substantive preferences, endeared him to many local inhabitants. As his triumphs increased, the ruler appointed Faysal viceroy of the Hijaz in August 1926 to fulfill the Qanun al-Asasi (Basic Law) that was negotiated with notables of Jiddah and Makkah. As *na'ib al-malik* (viceroy), Faysal organized his own Majlis al-Shurah (Advisory Council), with five notables from Makkah, three from Madinah, another three from Jiddah, and one each from Yanbu' and Ta'if. The council was mandated to advise "the viceroy about legislative matters, the budget, concessions and licenses, and general communal interests."[15] To his credit, Faysal perceived the council's institutional value and, as viceroy, practiced consensus politics by surrounding himself with local personalities whose views he assiduously sought. In turn, these men were placed in a hierarchical order, which strengthened Al Sa'ud rule. Those who opposed the preference, including the Ikhwan, were ostracized as the ruler acquired more legitimacy.

Throughout these early years, 'Abdul 'Aziz bin 'Abdul Rahman was single-mindedly preoccupied with tribal politics that left an impregnable mark on his sons. Faysal acknowledged the tension and fought bravely whenever called upon to fulfill his father's designated tasks. When a particular mission necessitated negotiations with foreign powers, Faysal assumed the burden of familiarizing himself with the "other" and, inasmuch as his task was to follow the founder's wishes, of not straying off from specific instructions.

In August 1926, Faysal returned as a goodwill emissary to London, an assignment that further sharpened the young man's diplomatic prowess. Little did the prince realize how convoluted international accords were or could become especially when contrasted with complicated but altogether much smoother tribal compromises. In the event, the viceroy fulfilled his objective and returned home to help his father address the Ikhwan revolt, which lasted until 1930. His unwavering implementation of all of 'Abdul 'Aziz's directives seldom earned Faysal, or other members of the ruling family, support from lascivious interlocutors. In fact, according to Cecil Gervase Hope Gill, the British chargé d'affaires in Jiddah at the time, Faysal was described by local public opinion—that opposed draconian measures introduced to restore law and order—as a "bum" and a "nonentity."[16] It was during this initial unification period that Faysal first became conscious of Al Sa'ud notables' relentless reliance on the treasury. He further noted how his father's disapproval of his uncle Muhammad strained family unity. Muhammad bin 'Abdul Rahman was certainly qualified to lead, although 'Abdul 'Aziz worked tirelessly to establish a smooth succession with his designated heir Sa'ud.[17] Whether Faysal concluded that the ruling family lacked leadership at the time was impossible to determine. Yet, subsequent initiatives, especially those that addressed the country's emerging economic crisis, certainly illustrated his growing consciousness. Over the years, Faysal twice gave his brother Sa'ud a *bay 'ah* (oath of allegiance) because he concluded that family schisms were deleterious and because he deduced that loyalty was, above all else, the key ingredient for unity.

Visits to Europe

In between these critical developments, Faysal returned to Europe, where he visited several major capitals. Naturally, his first stops were in Britain, France, and the Netherlands, the three countries that first extended diplomatic recognition to 'Abdul 'Aziz in February 1926 and that maintained legations in Jiddah. Whatever was accomplished during these early visits marked the young prince in more ways than imaginable even if his presence on the European continent was significantly and often misunderstood. In fact, Faysal's European visits elicited the most ill-informed diplomatic reporting, which reflected, more than anything else, the bewilderment of otherwise competent attachés. For example, Richard M. Tobin in The Hague cabled to the secretary of state in Washington that the Dutch government had hosted a luncheon for Faysal because it "desired to ingratiate itself" with the Al Sa'ud. Tobin remarked that the Netherlands "display[ed] at all times towards the Mohamadan population of the Indies the greatest kindness and paternal solicitude" and was, therefore, eager to extend a warm welcome.[18] The astonishment was not limited to diplomats stationed in Europe. The U.S. ambassador Alexander K. Sloan in Baghdad reported that this latest whirlwind European tour had tired Faysal and that he was literally overwhelmed by heavy social obligations in the Iraqi capital, where the Saudi delegation had stopped on its way back home. Sloan described the prince as "a tall, slender, handsome young man of the true Arab hook-nosed type" and, relying on an Iraqi minister's assessment, concluded that he had "not yet shown any indication that he has energy enough or strength of character enough to govern the kingdom of the Hejaz and Nejd."[19] This was comical enough, but the envoy further revealed that his sources had informed him of how inadequately Faysal had performed during his European visits. In fact, Sloan reported that Faysal had "incurred his father's displeasure and would in all probability be imprisoned when he returned to Riyadh," presumably because both he as well as Fu'ad Hamzah—"the power behind Ibn Saud's throne"—had failed to secure sorely needed loans.[20] These interpretations were, of course, figments of Iraqi imagination, but they passed for serious diplomatic discourse when measured and better assessments were direly required. In the event, Faysal's latest visit to London sealed British recognition of the Al Sa'ud as legitimate rulers over large chunks of the Arabian Peninsula, which, not surprisingly, represented something of a dilemma for the pro-Hashemite crown. Still, over time, London acknowledged that it had little choice but to negotiate with the Al Sa'ud as 'Abdul 'Aziz secured vast chunks of territory. For his part, Faysal proved to be a consummate diplomat who was capable and at ease with grandiose trappings.

Remarkably, the young prince learned the way diplomats in various countries reciprocated his inquisitive questions, often to his benefit. He received critical political briefings on French interests in the Arab world and reciprocated by declaring that 'Abdul 'Aziz was beholden to the British. He also inquired about Paris' intentions toward the region and underscored how beneficial their cooperation would be. As France played a relatively neutral role over the Hijaz conflict by refusing to sell arms to King Hussein, Faysal assumed that French policies were noble, and never tired of stressing this point to his interlocutors. Of course, he did not then know about the secret 1916 Sykes-Picot Accords dividing the Middle East between Britain and France, which may have certainly affected his perceptions. Nevertheless, since Faysal was not privy to these covert agreements, his initial views of French diplomacy were certainly positive, echoing his father's jubilant assessments.[21] If, over time, Faysal learned of what London and Paris jointly concocted for the Middle East, he opted to keep his sentiments to himself, especially as French policies toward the Arab world changed dramatically in the early 1960s. In the event, and although American prospectors "discovered" oil in Saudi Arabia, Faysal recognized various French engineering firsts, including the successful detection of large underground aquifers starting in 1956.[22] Oil revenues naturally allowed the foraging but, in the desert, water sustained life itself. How it was harvested, and with whose assistance, never escaped Faysal.

On his third overseas journey, which lasted close to six months, Faysal stopped in Italy, Switzerland, France, Britain, Holland, Germany, Poland, and the Soviet

Union, as well as Turkey, Iran, Iraq, and Kuwait. Inasmuch as he was his father's foreign minister, Prince Faysal introduced Saudi Arabia to every head of state who welcomed him, always imparting the most positive impressions even if negotiations were often condescending and bitter. Few viewed Saudi Arabia in positive terms and many considered the Al Saʿud as no more than illiterate *badu* ruling over savage tribes. It was up to Faysal to change such misguided perceptions, earn the world's respect, and seek long-term commitments to invest in initial oil-prospecting projects.

The convoluted Iraqi-inspired evaluation of his 1932 trip notwithstanding, the warrior-diplomat left a remarkable impression in every European capital he visited. His most memorable encounters were in the Soviet Union because the Al Saʿud shared so little with Communism. It was worth noting that the Union of Soviet Socialist Republics (U.S.S.R.) extended official recognition to ʿAbdul ʿAziz Al Saʿud on February 16, 1926 and reconfirmed its diplomatic exchange on April 15, 1927. Still, and given British diligence over affairs in the Arabian Peninsula, what was truly surprising was the move by Al Saʿud to expeditiously acclimatize themselves with Moscow. Yet, it would be an error to conclude that the Al Saʿud were eager to pursue closer ties with the Soviet Union. Rather, what motivated them primarily was an opposition to "British" imperialism, with Moscow certainly useful as an equalizer.

As the Soviet Union was the first country to recognize the independence of the Kingdom of Najd and Annexed Territories (1927), Moscow prided itself in recognizing the Sharif Hussein of the Hijaz in 1924 and its successor on February 15, 1926. The first Soviet diplomatic envoy to ʿAbdul ʿAziz, Nazir Tyuryakulov, handed his letters of credence as minister plenipotentiary and envoy extraordinary of the Soviet Union on February 26, 1930.[23] ʿAbdul ʿAziz "was pleased that Moscow was building relations with him on an equal footing," although he primarily perceived Soviet ties as a counterbalance to Britain.[24] It must be emphasized that the Al Saʿud were aware of severe restrictions imposed by Communism, and while they privately deplored the atheist ideology, an evolving strategic awareness propelled them to seek the development of economic relations. Little is actually known of Tyuryakulov's tenure in Jiddah although several meetings were held with ʿAbdul ʿAziz, some of which were attended by Faysal.[25] When the third European trip was finalized, Faysal and his principal advisors quickly added Poland and the Soviet Union to the itinerary, being appreciative of the opportunity that the voyage presented for the prince. On May 28, 1932, he and his delegation arrived in Moscow from Warsaw, where they had spent three days visiting various personalities. Although Faysal was given a warm reception by the

Soviets, visiting the Red Army House, a horse show, the October Camp, the Military Aviation Academy, and the AMO Automobile factory—then renamed Stalin Automobile—in Moscow, he did not meet Stalin. Indeed, various foreign ministry commissars received him, as did Mikhail Kalinin, the president of the Central Executive Committee. Vyacheslav Molotov, the chairman of the Sovnarkom, as the government was then known, as well as Nikolai Alexandrovich Bulganin, then the head of the Moscow Soviet, received him too.[26] Both men were close to Stalin and Faysal probably broached the issue of obtaining a line of credit to import goods. It must be reemphasized that while Faysal received an elaborate welcome, with the Saudi flag [duly inscribed with the Qur'anic verse "There is no God except God and Muhammad is His Prophet"] flying above main train stations in Moscow and Leningrad, the Soviet government failed to extend any credits.[27] Faysal and his delegation attended two productions of the Bolshoi Theater—*Don Quixote* by Miguel de Cervantes and *Carmen* by Georges Bizet—and heard *The Barber of Seville* by Gioachino Antonio Rossini. They made a side visit to St. Petersburg—then Leningrad—on June 3–4, where they toured the renowned Hermitage Museum, before leaving for Odessa and Istanbul.[28]

His Soviet hosts favorably impressed Faysal. Nevertheless, he was disappointed that Moscow overlooked one of his concerns, namely the credit issue. In fact, given that the young prince was convinced that Soviet industry was "growing and . . . being developed," he may well have recommended that the Al Sa'ud enhance their ties. Moscow's stillness on the matter, aloof to strongly held religious beliefs or, perhaps, aware of British influences throughout the Arabian Peninsula, resonated loud and clear. In hindsight, Moscow's silence was surely a monumental Soviet strategic error, as Faysal ended his first and last visit to the Soviet Union favorably impressed by the potential of the country but dissatisfied by Soviet leaders' inclinations toward his requirements.

By 1938, 'Abdul 'Aziz concluded that the Soviet diplomatic mission in Jiddah no longer added any value to his foreign ties, and he terminated it. Whether this pause constituted a break in diplomatic ties was debatable although later contacts indicated that Riyadh preferred to keep a certain distance from Moscow (see chapter 3).

Before leaving for this tour, and almost a year prior to the formal creation of the Kingdom of Saudi Arabia, Faysal was entrusted with the leadership of a Council of Deputies (Majlis al-Wukala') to better govern the emerging political entity. At the time, Faysal was the only individual carrying the title *wazir* (minister), even if the ruler appointed 'Abdallah Sulayman and his brother Hammad Sulayman to key finance department posts to maintain a semblance of unity. According to G.

Hope Gill, 'Abdul 'Aziz "carefully planned this development" to fully empower Faysal. Barely twenty-eight but already viceroy of the Hijaz, Faysal was his father's foreign minister, internal affairs minister, and head of the Council of Deputies. Internal affairs ministry responsibilities included "health, education, execution of the *Shari'ah*, the police, the quarantine of pilgrims, and the control of the telegraph system."[29] It was fortuitous that Faysal was young and capable for the entirety of his duties was truly overwhelming. As foreign minister, he would be called upon to assume additional responsibilities that, over time, would see him in most world capitals.

Foreign Minister of Saudi Arabia

Faysal shaped Saudi foreign policy by giving it an ideological base, insisting on a strict balance with internal developments, and adopting a level of consistency unparalleled throughout the Arab and Muslim worlds. This consistency was amply visible throughout the 1960s and early 1970s when the kingdom faced a challenge from Gamal 'Abdul Nasir. At the time, Riyadh responded to the rising wave of Arab nationalism by emphasizing core Islamic values, which were the basic foundations of its foreign policy. Rejecting both secularism and socialism, for example, Faysal supported Yemeni tribes who favored the monarchy and, in the aftermath of the 1967 Arab-Israeli War, sought a rapprochement with Egypt to end the Arab Cold War (1957–67). By early 1973, however, Faysal perceived the need to link the kingdom's oil power to the unending Arab-Israeli conflict, especially as Washington took note of Saudi pleas. Following the outbreak of the 1973 Arab-Israeli War, and the American decision to create a weapons air-bridge to Israel, Faysal authorized an oil embargo against both the United States and the Netherlands. But ever the astute statesman, the king rescinded his decision when Washington reactivated its moribund peace efforts through U.S. secretary of state Henry Kissinger's famous shuttle diplomacy. However, his lifelong wish to pray at Jerusalem's Al-Aqsah Mosque never materialized.

If this summary of Faysal's foreign policy was perceptible in the mid-1970s, it was not always this clear, as the young prince assumed the gargantuan burden of developing a consistent ideology and creating the mechanisms and institutions to implement it.[30] Because of internal Al Sa'ud family rivalries as well as a dearth of qualified leaders, 'Abdul 'Aziz relied on a restricted "privy council" of fellow Arabs to help negotiate with foreign governments and oil companies eager to sign preferential concession rights. Two Syrians in particular, Fu'ad Hamzah and Yusuf Yassin, were the founder's principal advisors, but both may have overreached their mandates, although the latter fared better than the former. According to reliable British sources, 'Abdul 'Aziz had a row with Hamzah in July 1930, ostensibly because his outlook was deemed too "Europeanized." Yassin, who was a more pious Muslim, was promoted to foreign policy advisor in lieu of Hamzah. Unhappy with Hamzah, the ruler thrust the problem into Faysal's lap when he named his son foreign minister in December 1930. Hamzah was appointed undersecretary of the newly created foreign ministry.[31] Luckily for Faysal, Hamzah's tenure was cut short when the undersecretary fell ill, necessitating prolonged absences. The energetic prince would have one less battle to settle as the looming economic crisis—poorly managed by the director-general of finance, 'Abdallah Sulayman—required that Faysal align himself with other privy council members to restore spending discipline. Such personnel shifts were not easy to address especially when few qualified individuals could then replace those who had been moved or removed. Therefore, when Faysal became Saudi Arabia's first foreign minister in 1930—an office he held almost without interruption until his death in 1975—and led his country's delegation to the conference in San Francisco in April 1945 in which the United Nations was established, he was essentially running a shoestring operation. He established the Ministry of Foreign Affairs from scratch, equipping it with the basics to conduct Al Sa'ud diplomacy, even if he was personally acquainted with most of the leaders that marked the twentieth century. According to Gerald de Gaury, by the time Faysal became foreign minister or a few years after assuming that burden, he had "met, and remembered . . . a greater number and variety of his fellow men than anyone else alive, except the Duke of Edinburgh," a professional host.[32]

American Recognition of Saudi Arabia

'Abdul 'Aziz bin 'Abdul Rahman proclaimed himself king of the Hijaz, Najd, and its dependencies in 1927. By 1931, the United States had recognized him personally—through a series of written exchanges with President Franklin Delano Roosevelt—although full diplomatic relations were not established until February 4, 1940. Because neither country contributed to the other's economic welfare at the time—a condition for the establishment of diplomatic ties according to Cordell Hull, the U.S. secretary of state and the father of reciprocal trade—there was no haste in establishing legations in either capital. It was the California-Arabian Standard Oil Company (CASOC) that nudged Washington to take the initiative, not only to look after the growing number of Americans working in the oil industry, but also to deny Germany and Japan, which were keenly interested in enhancing their influence with the Saudis, from winning concessions of their own. Consequently, the American ambassador to Egypt, Alexander C. Kirk, was also accredited to Saudi Arabia.

As significant progress was achieved in the oil field, much to 'Abdul 'Aziz's delight, it was natural that high-level political contacts would ensue. Yet, these contacts were eye-openers because they highlighted fundamental ideological differences over Palestine, a central concern that predated the establishment of the State of Israel in 1948. Even if 'Abdul 'Aziz and his successors placed the Palestine question second to their own survival and national security, it was nevertheless a core concern that could not be neglected. The founder formally raised the Palestine question in his correspondence with President Roosevelt, and the latter, to better ascertain Saudi views, authorized Harold Hoskins, the son of American missionaries and an Arabic speaker, to visit Saudi Arabia for face to face conversations with the monarch. The purpose of the encounter was to ascertain whether Riyadh would consent to meet with Chaim Weizmann or other representatives of the Jewish Agency.

Hoskins heard an earful. First, the American envoy received detailed confirmation of Weizmann's attempt to bribe the Saudi—via H. St. John Philby for £20 million—to advance the Jewish cause in Palestine. Second, 'Abdul 'Aziz recounted how his worst fears were materializing as Jewish immigration to Palestine accelerated. He further expressed fears that, over time, the Palestinians would be wiped out as the majority population.[33] Above all, Hoskins reported, 'Abdul 'Aziz was astonished how Weizmann would offer Roosevelt's "guarantee" without—as far as it was known and widely assumed—having secured such an assurance from Roosevelt himself. The Saudi king pondered long and hard on the source of such audacity on the part of a civilian who was not even an American citizen. Not surprisingly, Roosevelt was irritated by Weizmann's approach toward the Saudi when he heard Hoskins, but, as far as it is known, he did not share that irritation with any Saudi official. On the contrary, he thanked the Saudi monarch for the gifts that the princes Faysal and Khalid had presented to him during their visit to Washington and expressed a desire to meet 'Abdul 'Aziz at the first opportunity. On his return trip from the Teheran conference, Roosevelt flew over the kingdom, but pressing engagements did not allow for a stop. Nevertheless, he must have realized the awesome power of the country's potential, especially as oil discoveries poured in at a regular pace.[34]

Roosevelt, certainly a giant figure in American politics with ingrained foresight and a rare knack for effective diplomacy, finally invited 'Abdul 'Aziz to meet with him in February 1945 on board the USS *Quincy* on the Great Bitter Lake in the Suez Canal. The encounter was friendly on a personal level and Roosevelt gave 'Abdul 'Aziz one of his wheelchairs as a sign of affection. Much has been written about the encounter over the years, but among several topics that were covered two stood out: the security of the kingdom (as well as that of the Al Sa'ud ruling family) and Palestine.

In his personal account of the meeting, William Eddy—an American military officer who was born in Sidon, Lebanon and who was fluent in Arabic—reported that Roosevelt underscored that "(1) He personally, as president, would never do anything which might prove hostile to the Arabs; and (2) the US Government would make no change in its basic policy in Palestine without full and prior consultation with both Jews and Arabs."[35] Importantly, Roosevelt reiterated these pledges in a letter of April 5, 1945 to 'Abdul 'Aziz, ironically dated one week before his death, when Truman betrayed the deceased president's pledges.

It is worth noting, once again relying on Eddy's memoirs, that 'Abdul 'Aziz asked Roosevelt for "friendship" before the meeting ended, highlighting his tribal inclination to embed his associations in honor as well as personal etiquette. Roosevelt's pledges certainly reflected a fine understanding of the impact they would have on men such as 'Abdul 'Aziz. They also left their marks on the likes of Colonel Eddy, who, shockingly, opted to resign his post in May 1946.[36]

Eddy, it was later reported, had been privy to Truman's decision to forego Roosevelt's pledge to the Saudi (see below) and, having concluded that his credibility with the Saudis had literally evaporated into thin air, took the high road. This noble resignation earned Eddy respect for he proved to be honorable and loyal to both his country and his Saudi host. He betrayed neither even if he knew that his resignation confirmed how Truman had diminished Roosevelt's stature with 'Abdul 'Aziz. This was doubly tragic because President Truman, in his turn, had reiterated several times to 'Abdul 'Aziz that no changes in American policy were foreseen and that Washington would take no action in Palestine without consulting both Arabs and Jews. Still, Truman changed his mind, more for political convenience than out of conviction. According to Eddy, but seconded by other foreign service officers, Truman concluded a top-level briefing by American ambassadors accredited throughout the Middle East on November 10, 1945 by stating: "I am sorry, gentlemen, but I have to answer to hundreds of thousands who are serious for the success of Zionism; I do not have hundreds of thousands of Arabs among my constituents."[37] Truman, it must be clarified, dismissed objections raised by several senior cabinet officers, including James Forrestal, the secretary of defense.[38] Remarkably, how the ruler dealt with American counterparts served as a model for his successors. Because Truman, whether nudged by the

State Department or not, expressed his full support for the territorial integrity and independence of Saudi Arabia and offered to defend the kingdom—and especially the Al Sa'ud—from putative Hashemite or British-orchestrated designs, the Saudis could not articulate and defend a richer agenda. Later on, regional hegemonies, including Yemen, Iran, and Iraq, would be added to the list of countries Saudis would need to be protected from. No Saudi leader could, understandably, voice major displeasure when the American commitment was so clear. Yet, by accepting a compromise on an issue that they themselves championed, it was the Al Sa'ud who may have erred in American eyes. The Palestine question was not an American priority and Arabs, including the Al Sa'ud, were not willing to sacrifice useful political and nascent military alliances that were forged with successive American administrations. Even "oil embargoes," which would eventually be used (unsuccessfully in 1967 and with mixed results in 1973), would not make a dent. It was amply clear that dual track patterns were laid in the 1940s. In turn, these permitted westerners to manipulate Arab leaders, including Saudis, at will. Over time, the task of redressing such errors would increase as opportunities to reap benefits from specific developments would draw scarce.

The Impact of Oil Resources

Although oil was first discovered in Saudi Arabia in 1933, it was not commercially exploited until 1936–37, when it would revolutionize the kingdom. Life was certainly austere before when 'Abdul 'Aziz made do with little save for meager revenues from pilgrims. His income was indeed limited and his expenses grew by leaps and bounds because Ikhwan forces displayed a generous appetite. Moreover, the Al Sabah in Kuwait demanded full repayment of advances made around the turn of the century, which did not surprise the founder. Internal needs, along with Al Sa'ud family necessities, added to the ruler's financial burden. To be sure, Al Sa'ud preferences centered around the discovery of water—which would, in turn, encourage the development of agriculture—even if 'Abdul 'Aziz was happy that oil flowed freely after American prospectors first discovered the large Hasah pool. Before long, the ruler was confronted with a critical decision to grant exploitation rights to a specific concession then contested by both British and American companies. In fact, the competition was not simply among rival companies but also pitted Britain against the United States, with the wily H. St. John Philby carefully informing his true masters of whatever details he could gather. Philby's recommendations—to grant the concession to British enterprises—notwithstanding, 'Abdul 'Aziz opted to sign an accord with Standard Oil of California because the latter accepted Saudi requirements. A token $450,000 payment was made to Riyadh with a promise to disburse 18¢ per barrel for all production until the contract expired in 1999.

In a magisterial move, 'Abdul 'Aziz denied the contract to London, remembering how Britain sided with Sharif Hussein in the aftermath of World War I, and the overall condescending attitudes displayed by successive British officials toward the *badu*. According to Karl S. Twitchell, who successfully negotiated the accord, 'Abdul 'Aziz favored American companies because he believed that American corporations enjoyed greater autonomy and thus could be more generous, and because the United States—at some physical distance from the Arabian Peninsula—harbored no political ambitions toward his nascent kingdom. Faysal's pro-American sentiments probably influenced this decision as well given that the Al Sa'ud slowly drifted to the American orbit under his expert guidance.[39]

Faysal's First Visit to the United States

With the oil concession secured, Faysal embarked on his first trip to the United States, where he would meet several American leaders and where he would establish solid contacts that would serve him well for several decades.

In Washington, D.C., President Franklin Delano Roosevelt and Secretary of State Cordell Hull received the young prince and, as state visitors, the Saudi delegation was housed at Blair House, across from the White House. Faysal gave Roosevelt "a fine Arab sword, its blade damascened, its hilt bejeweled and the scabbard mounted in gold."[40] This was a generous present reciprocated by the American president in a major dinner, for which the vice president, members of the Cabinet, senators, and congressmen as well as other guests living in the capital were invited. Roosevelt met Faysal a second time on November 9, 1943 for a private encounter before his party traveled to New York, where meetings with business leaders were scheduled. The visit presented an opportunity to see something of the Big Apple, including ascending to the top of the Empire State Building. They party also visited Princeton University and met Professor Philip Hitti, then the most knowledgeable specialist of the Arab world living in the United States.

Following this East Coast tour, Faysal and his delegation—which included the future King Khalid—took a cross-country train to Los Angeles and San Francisco, with stops in Texas, New Mexico, and Arizona. Texas and Standard Oil Companies, then the two ARAMCO partners, arranged various sightseeing calls, as well as several agricultural, educational, and entertainment sojourns. The party returned east via Denver and Detroit before disembarking in Washington, D.C. There, additional conversations were held with Edward Stettinius, acting for the secretary of state from whom he was taking over, as well as Assistant Secretary

Adolf A. Berle Jr. These last meetings were particularly meaningful as Faysal was told of lend-lease requirements and provisions to create a silver currency for Saudi Arabia. He was also given a memorandum supporting Washington's favorable views on building a refinery in Dhahran by the California Arabian Standard Oil Company.[41] Prince Faysal's first sojourn to the United States ended with a stop at the United States Naval Academy in Annapolis, Maryland, a brief introduction to Baltimore, and then back to New York from where the delegation boarded a British Overseas Airways clipper service (via the Bermudas) to London and, eventually, home.

Faysal returned to Saudi Arabia impressed with the American "can-do" attitude as well as its risk-taking spirit. He contrasted this experience with his earlier visit to the Soviet Union, where few leaders were willing to make the slightest commitments. Consequently, he duly informed his father, and other members of the family, of what he had witnessed and shared with them his own perceptions. More important, he concluded that Americans could be reliable allies to Saudi Arabia, as he further solidified his growing pro-American views. These, he determined, were the natural result of fundamental compatibilities of interests between the two countries.

The Airfield That Gelled the Partnership

Washington's early successes with 'Abdul 'Aziz occurred under the watchful eyes of the United Kingdom, whose undeniable presence on the Arabian Peninsula may well have irritated Saudis and Americans equally, but whose influence could be neglected by neither. Following significant setbacks in gaining oil concessions for British companies, London attempted to persuade—even threatened—the Saudi ruler to abandon the American plan for a major airbase in Dhahran, first proposed in 1944. Colonel William A. Eddy, the U.S. minister plenipotentiary to Saudi Arabia, informed Washington of this putative interference in no uncertain terms. Assistant Secretary of State Adolf A. Berle Jr. reportedly lost his composure with Michael Wright, the British deputy chief of mission in Washington, when he exclaimed: "There is no law in heaven or earth which entitles anybody to interfere with our building an airfield for legitimate purposes in Saudi Arabia."[42] As this episode was not isolated in the very active U.S.-U.K. competition for political and economic domination of what was then the so-called free world, Secretary of State Cordell Hull and Foreign Secretary Anthony Eden were called upon to sort out differences between the two allies. In May 1945, London relented and communicated its nonobjection—or approval—of the project to 'Abdul 'Aziz.

Even if the Dhahran Air Base was completed after the Japanese surrendered on

September 2, 1945, it stood against some odds as a symbol of U.S.-Saudi cooperation. Construction of the base represented, at least from the Saudi point of view,
a concession of sovereignty. What 'Abdul 'Aziz wanted to achieve by acquiesc-
ing was twofold: (1) to display his independence from London; and (2) to secure
the goodwill of an emerging superpower. Washington, for its part, intended to
lock in its presence on the Arabian Peninsula to further consolidate its growing
commercial monopolies, as well as to enlarge its footprints for power projection.
Naturally, Riyadh delighted in the facility, which included a ten thousand foot
long hard-surface runway, and Washington gained the vital means to protect its
expanding oil concessions. In other words, a strengthened military presence further enhanced American political and economic interests in Saudi Arabia.

Although certain British officials, especially Ambassador Stanley R. Jordan—
who was not particularly liked by the Saudi monarch—may have precipitated
the level of cooperation between Riyadh and Washington, it was clear that the
Al Sa'ud were far more pragmatic than generally credited. Its leaders perceived
the decline of one power and the rise of another. They opted, for purely nationalistic reasons, to align themselves with the emergent one. In fact, the 1945 re-
negotiations of the British-Saudi Cable and Wireless Accord—which was first
signed in 1926 under duress by a power losing a significant colonial monopolizing
vestige—was another example of this awareness. In the event, 'Abdul 'Aziz authorized an American company to build an external electronic communications
system, further strengthening the security relations between Saudi Arabia and the
United States. In response, London, then in serious financial difficulties, reduced
its traditional disbursements to the Saudi monarch—instituted several years earlier to keep various tribal leaders on the Arabian Peninsula in check. It also coaxed
Washington to emulate its own efforts, allegedly because the Arabian-American
Oil Company (ARAMCO) was now earning enough to cover Saudi Arabia's expenses.

Rather than follow the advice of its British ally, the United States embarked on
a diametrically opposed track because the opportunity was too good to let it slip
away. In one of the most clairvoyant and long-lasting maneuvers toward embel-
lishing its bonds with Saudi Arabia, the United States granted the kingdom direct
financial assistance under the Lend-Lease Act of 1941. The act, which established
American bilateral assistance to foreign powers, required a presidential "finding."
Edward Stettinius, then the lend-lease administrator, requested that President
Roosevelt declare the defense of Saudi Arabia as being "vital to the United States."
This was promptly done on February 18, 1943. In fact, this "finding" confirmed
that "Saudi Arabia's defense was an integral part of US defense."[43] Importantly, the

language of the finding was emended at the end of the war, thereby retaining its validity ever since. While other measures followed, Roosevelt's foresight—served by brilliant advisors who knew the region and 'Abdul 'Aziz well (Eddy spoke his language fluently and was succeeded by half a dozen top diplomats who were eager to advance U.S. benefits)—secured long-term American interests. It may be worth repeating that while the Al Sa'ud were fearful of the British, because the latter physically surrounded their kingdom, they nevertheless played one power against another rather brilliantly. Yet, it was Washington that took advantage of its purse string in what could only be described as an effective display of dollar diplomacy.

The Meeting on the USS *Quincy*

Although Saudi Arabia was left on the sidelines of World War II, and as stated above, the key meeting between President Roosevelt and 'Abdul 'Aziz bin 'Abdul Rahman Al Sa'ud on February 14, 1945 in the Red Sea sealed the course of events and further brought the kingdom into the American fold. The meeting was carefully prepared for by Prince Faysal during his earlier visit to New York and Washington, as he perceived the encounter as a prelude to closer Arab-American ties.[44]

Roosevelt, fresh from his Yalta conference at which Washington, London, and Moscow settled on new understandings, greeted 'Abdul 'Aziz with legendary panache: "Very glad to meet you. What can I do for you?" Without missing a beat, and too artful for such charm, 'Abdul 'Aziz retorted with some celebrated prose of his own: "Since you've asked to meet, I presume that it is you who came to ask for something."[45] As the American president was eager to secure Al Sa'ud commitments for additional oil resources, he emphasized political and economic advantages to a rapprochement before inquiring about the ruler's perceptions of the future Middle East.

It was then that 'Abdul 'Aziz provided a clear expose on the post–World War I implosion that toppled the Ottoman Empire and replaced it with violent colonial powers, which occupied most of the region. According to those present, the Saudi leader opined that a confederation of independent Arab states ought to be allowed to gather forces to better serve and protect the Arab world. Roosevelt was not necessarily opposed to such an outcome, especially as that would have weakened British control over a region becoming vital to U. S. national security and that would fit nicely with America's anti-colonialist "image." But when Roosevelt broached the Palestine question, opining that Arabs must accept a Jewish homeland and welcome a large immigration of Jews from Europe, 'Abdul 'Aziz rejected these conditions rather firmly. Parenthetically, it was entirely possible that Roosevelt made this point to confirm earlier rumors that he would be predisposed toward a deal with Zionist leaders, even if no evidence existed or has surfaced since then. Yet, according to the pusillanimous H. St. John Philby, at a meeting with the Zionist leader Dr. Chaim Weizmann on September 27, 1939, Philby apparently confided that 'Abdul 'Aziz bin 'Abdul Rahman Al Sa'ud "would accept the idea of a Jewish home in Palestine, provided that he were given twenty million pounds Sterling for use as compensation for displaced Arabs."[46] This farcical description may have encouraged Weizmann to seek support from Prime Minister Churchill and pledges to raise the "required" sum "with ease in America." Not only was this perfidy vintage Philby—an arriviste par excellence—but it was also contrary to the king's vision and preferred policies. Roosevelt broke the tension that emerged between the two men when he donated one of his walking chairs to 'Abdul 'Aziz. He left the Red Sea meeting satisfied that some things were accomplished but later confided to Bernard Baruch that "among all the men that I had to deal with during my lifetime, I have met no one than this Arab monarch from whom I could extricate so little: the man has an iron will."[47]

Roosevelt's jovial prose notwithstanding, he assured 'Abdul 'Aziz that "he would take no action hostile to the Arabs," which was a significant commitment.[48] Even if his successor opted to overlook the significance such a pledge entailed, tradition-bound Saudis, as principled as any other people, were stunned by Truman's theatrics. Although Truman received credit for establishing diplomatic ties with Israel in 1948, Faysal, who admired Roosevelt as well as Truman because he perceived both as honorable leaders, was nevertheless stunned when Truman reneged on Roosevelt's word. The lesson stood the test of time and marked Faysal for the rest of his life.

Faysal at the United Nations

At the end of World War II, Faysal returned to the United States, where he signed the United Nations Charter on behalf of the kingdom. Addressing the General Assembly in San Francisco, Faysal delivered a remarkable speech in which he condemned Nazism and Fascism, discussed close Arab-American relations, and underscored Al Sa'ud confidence toward Washington (see appendix 2). He emphasized that he fully trusted the champion of anti-colonialism to stand by smaller states eager to gain their independence from traditional powers. The address, a genuine illustration of firm beliefs that the United States actually honored its promises and upheld its commitments, surprised Arab commentators in Cairo and Damascus but Faysal was adamant in his confidence. Stopping in Egypt on his way back, he reiterated his views to wary Egyptian officials, who were on the threshold of serious internal upheavals.

In his brief but meaningful speech, Faysal first thanked allied powers for their sacrifice "for the security of mankind" and firmly placed Saudi Arabia within the Western camp. He singled out President Roosevelt for planting the seeds that germinated into the United Nations, championing anti-colonialism, and respecting small states. Faysal's speech was a genuine expression of trust, and, while he realized that the charter did "not represent perfection as visualized by the Small States," he was positively inclined toward the United States as a world leader. Moreover, aware of the generous powers that the five permanent members of the Security Council bestowed on themselves, Faysal believed that the United States in particular would protect developing countries. If the Saudi presentation was not well received in nationalist Arab circles, it was applauded in San Francisco, where clear lines were drawn at the dawn of the bi-polar world.[49] To reiterate, Faysal certainly foresaw problems with the veto power, and he discussed the matter at some length with American officials, including two powerful senators, Arthur H. Vandenberg (R-Michigan) and Thomas T. Connally (D-Texas), both of whom served on key foreign affairs committees, yet he still opted for the United States. The latter's credibility and prestige were intact for the young prince.

Faysal returned to the United States in 1947 to address the United Nations Conference on Palestine as London declared that it would terminate its mandate over the territory, which had been granted by the League of Nations on April 25, 1920. At the time, Western delegations favored the creation of two states: the State of Israel next to Palestine. Arab officials voiced their concerns and opposition. Faysal may well have received American assurances, most notably from Ambassador George Wadsworth, that Arab rights would be preserved. He confided to his Arab colleagues that the United States did not favor an outcome that would create permanent clashes and was confident that the proposed partition plan would not materialize as then envisaged. In fact, he confided to other Arab delegations present in New York that the Security Council would refrain from any precipitous actions. But when President Harry S Truman met with Dr. Chaim Weizmann and changed American policy, Faysal was devastated. Washington recognized the newly created State of Israel on May 14, 1948 within a few minutes after the latter declared its independence.[50]

Truman's sovereign decision profoundly disappointed Faysal, who was, perhaps, under the impression that American confidences were genuine. Worse, the declaration made the Saudi loose credibility in front of his Arab colleagues, several of whom concluded that he was a naïve individual. According to one observer, the Truman fiat had a serious impact on Faysal and made "him mistrustful of the American Administration." He reconciled with facts on the ground although "it took him a long time to recover."[51] The heretofore pro-American Saudi left New York dejected but, perhaps, awakened to major power politics. What awaited him in the region and at home proved to be equally devastating.

Unable to defend the kingdom from envious and politically more emancipated neighbors, 'Abdul 'Aziz was forced to swallow his pride and accept loss of prestige throughout the Arab world. He further conceded that his American "friends" reinterpreted pledges or poorly defined terms and acquiesced on the question of Palestine as well as the creation of Israel in 1948. Saudi Arabia was in need of technical and developmental assistance from the United States. Perhaps inevitably, because the Saudis needed a powerful ally, they discovered that they were in a subservient position. After 1947, the founder of the kingdom, like his successors, was called upon to provide the most powerful country in the world, and especially its omnipotent presidents, with the kind of political handicaps that no other country would be asked to provide. In addition to such political concessions, Saudis were expected to safeguard the kingdom's oil resources and ensure their availability at reasonable prices. These were not negligible demands, and all 'Abdul 'Aziz (as well as his successors) could secure in exchange was a commitment to support the territorial integrity and independence of the kingdom—a commitment that the United States routinely made to countless other countries. Whether Al Sa'ud leaders understood the level of this commitment is difficult to tell because Washington used a standard international legal formula—support for the territorial integrity and/or independence of a country—to "manage" its policies with a ruling family. From an American point of view, this was a pragmatic, even if cold, step. It also was correct and straightforward. America was not offering "friendship" to Saudi Arabia—as 'Abdul 'Aziz requested from Franklin Roosevelt—but pledging its clinical assistance to advance its own national interests.

To be sure, the American choice in "managing" Arab affairs was probably a consequence of the very active British role in the region, especially with London's Hashemite allies in Jordan and Iraq. Yet, it is also important not to overread into this formulation as the balance of power shifted even before the start of World War II. Oil, not necessarily tribal politics, was the determining factor, although the British stood to lose ground on both issues.[52] Washington would not interfere in minutiae, but it upped the ante by opposing any form of Arab union that professed to unite various factions even if the parties were less than friendly. In time, London relented but let local matters fester. Why support controversial and grandiose plans, such as King 'Abdallah's concept of a Greater Syria, for example, if Washington was not in favor? Britain needed American assistance elsewhere and proved to be quite accommodating on the Middle East. It even nudged the United States to adopt policies that were not too far off from those that promoted and protected its own long-term interests, pretending that these were not necessarily what it wished.

By September 1949, when London favored the establishment of a parallel Hashemite kingdom in Iraq, a full-fledged political diversion was unfolding in earnest. 'Abdul 'Aziz was livid because, along with Kuwait, the borders between Saudi Arabia and Iraq were not yet demarcated. He expressed his displeasure to American officials, who, in turn, shared these conclusions with Britain. Even though the United States was quick to restate its pledge to come to the defense of Saudi Arabia in case the latter were attacked, it was not in favor of arming the country as the founder had requested on several occasions. Saudi Arabia saw an opening in the British position on Iraq, ostensibly to defend the northern oil pipeline (known as Tapline) that would crisscross disputed territories on its way to a Mediterranean seaport, but the United States would not welcome 'Abdul 'Aziz's request for arms. Instead, it reissued the standard support statement. Reluctantly, the Saudis focused on the assistance side of the message, but they were deeply irritated, especially since they knew that Washington and London had not refrained from such practices elsewhere. In tribal tradition, however, such developments were far less important than the personal gestures that Washington offered. President Truman dispatched his personal physician, Major-General Wallace H. Graham, to care for the ailing monarch. The monarch was, naturally, grateful and, progressively, came to accept the postures of the American president on defense matters and on Palestine, especially after his health deteriorated.[53]

As recorded in his memoirs, Truman asserted that "the American view on Palestine is that we want to let as many of the Jews into Palestine as it is possible to let into that country. Then the matter will have to be worked out diplomatically with the British and the Arabs, so that if a state can be set up there they may be able to set it up on a peaceful basis. I have no desire to send 500,000 American soldiers there to make peace in Palestine."[54]

Even if Truman refrained from using more colorful language in his memoirs, he nevertheless communicated his views, often in blunt language as was his habit, to the Saudis. Of course, one of Truman's successors would send over 500,000 American soldiers to liberate Kuwait from Iraqi occupation, and, no small matter, protect Saudi Arabia as well as its vast and expanding oil resources, but that would only occur in 1991. At the time, it was not Truman's policies that were difficult to fathom—for Truman was as straightforward a politician as there was—but ʿAbdul ʿAziz's reluctance to object to such steps. In hindsight, the Saudi monarch proved to be as cunning as Truman, clarifying and adopting narrow definitions of Saudi Arabia's national security interests to better serve his country and family. From a Saudi perspective, the defense of the kingdom was "guaranteed" by the United States; its income, generated by oil exports, was growing; ephemeral calls for Arab union were checked; problematic Arabs (Hashemites and others) were restrained; the British Empire was rapidly vanishing (even if London held on—with all its might—to its "protecting power" role in Palestine and throughout the Lower Gulf region); and health needs for the monarch, as well as his entourage, were provided for by the same team that looked after the most "powerful man in the world." All of these accomplishments were amply satisfactory and the Al Saʿud were pleased. Nevertheless, all were meager triumphs compared with the achievable. In fact, what was missing then was a "will to power." Perhaps ʿAbdul ʿAziz could not do more, but his successors, along with most of the Arab world, had to live with the consequences of this flagrant omission. Washington, naturally, was glad to let time foster even greater Al Saʿud dependence on it. ʿAbdul ʿAziz was a "great man," especially since he accepted American guidance, but his grandeur was limited.[55]

First Diplomatic Challenges

When ʿAbdul ʿAziz created the Kingdom of Saudi Arabia in 1932, Egypt, the preeminent Arab power, refused to recognize it. In fact, Egypt's King Fuʾad I had rejected the de facto Al Saʿud control over Makkah and Madinah of 1924, which set the precedent for ties throughout the 1920s. Relations remained lukewarm as both sides adopted immovable views of each other. Riyadh and Cairo froze all political dialogue in 1929, but they restored contact seven years later and, in 1936, signed a treaty that recognized the independence and sovereignty of Saudi Arabia.[56] Still, while trade and commerce expanded nascent ties, periodic upheavals severely limited what could have been one of the more critical Arab alliances. The major crunch came early and with vengeance when the monarchy was overthrown by Egyptian military officers.

The 1952 Revolution

On July 23, 1952, a coup d'état led by General Muhammad Naguib ended monarchical rule in Egypt. An internal military struggle followed until Captain Gamal 'Abdul Nasir assumed power in November 1954. In Riyadh, a more peaceful
change occurred on November 9, 1953 when Sa'ud bin 'Abdul 'Aziz succeeded
his father. Although Sa'ud watched the Egyptian political struggle from a distance and Riyadh remained neutral, a few months later, Sa'ud embraced Nasir
as a model of future Arab leadership. To be sure, the Al Sa'ud acquiesced to the
collapse of a fellow Arab monarchy because they had few options, but also because
Sa'ud actually believed that he could reason with Nasir. In hindsight, he failed
to understand fully the consequences of his decision, especially as Arab socialism
did not hide its preference for opposing oligarchies. At the time, however, Sa'ud
and Nasir at least shared a zest for change.

In the mid-1950s, Sa'ud and Nasir entered into an informal strategic relationship, because both fought the Baghdad Pact, which had been orchestrated and
created by westerners. In the event, the alliance, which had been inspired by the
British and seconded by the Americans, effectively contained revolutionary Iraq
as Saudi Arabia and Egypt tightened their nascent security relationship. Nasir
sent a 200–member military training mission to Riyadh along with civil service
officers to bolster the fledgling Saudi leadership. In exchange, Sa'ud extended
financial aid to Nasir, who in turn championed anti-colonial policies throughout
the Arab world.[57]

By late 1954, Nasir was the most popular Arab leader and Sa'ud wanted to
capitalize on the Egyptian's immense popularity, at least among the masses.[58]
To conservative rulers, warm receptions and the mass appeal of Nasir outside of
Egypt presented a genuine challenge. For all of their own traditional dialogue
with their subjects, Saudi leaders could not match the genuine appeal that Nasir
exuded. Not surprisingly, the charismatic Egyptian ruffled many feathers, which,
in turn, affected relations with fellow Arab countries. When Nasir crossed the
Rubicon by calling for an entirely new Arab nationalist outlook, Al Sa'ud ruling
family members were distressed. Throughout the late 1950s, and because of this
added new dimension in the relationship, Saudi-Egyptian ties vacillated between
a close strategic alliance to displays of outright hostility.

Overthrow of the Iraqi Monarchy

Before its unification, Saudi Arabia faced British threats chiefly from the north.
The British viewed Iraq, then under the suzerainty of the Ottoman Empire, as a

strategic asset. Turkey's entry into World War I, in late 1914, prompted a British expedition to the territory that, subsequently, became modern-day Iraq. London exploited the Ottoman Empire's lack of control in non-Turkish Iraq and used its position in the Persian Gulf to undo whatever gains its main rivals, Germany and Russia, may have achieved in the area. British control of the former Ottoman provinces of Mosul, Baghdad, and Basrah enhanced claims that Iraq fell under its singular protection. Throughout this time, 'Abdul 'Aziz bin 'Abdul Rahman Al Sa'ud was earnestly consolidating his control over the Arabian Peninsula, notwithstanding territorial feuds between the Najdi and the pro-Ottoman Sharif Hussein in Makkah.

Partly to settle the Najd-Hijaz disputes, Sir Percy Cox, then a British political agent, unilaterally established boundaries for Saudi Arabia, Iraq, and Kuwait in 1922.[59] Remarkably, 'Abdul 'Aziz refused to ratify the border treaty drafted by Cox, claiming that his negotiators exceeded their authority in surrendering key tribal allegiances to King Faysal in Iraq.[60] Instead, 'Abdul 'Aziz proposed a reconsideration of the boundaries and, surprisingly, Cox agreed. In November 1922, the 'Uqayr Protocols and the Treaty of Muhammarah were signed, ushering in temporary security for the Al Sa'ud.[61] While suspicious of British machinations in Baghdad, Riyadh was satisfied with the political outcome in the north. Even if the Hashemites were empowered to rule in Iraq and Jordan, the Saudis shared—so they reasoned—identical monarchical aspirations with their adversaries. Counting on this basic belief, the Al Sa'ud established working relations with their nemeses and cooperated with both countries. A period of benign neglect followed, allowing all parties to size up each other's powers, alliances, and potential in an increasingly volatile region of the world.

The Baghdad Pact

In part to strengthen its position vis-à-vis the Soviet Union, Britain invited all Arab countries to join in the creation of the Baghdad Pact. Not coincidentally, this sponsorship commenced after the 1952 coup in Egypt that ended, for all practical purposes, British influence in Cairo. King Sa'ud did not find much merit in the pact. Nevertheless, he was concerned enough with developments on the banks of the Nile to pursue a closer security relationship with Cairo. Sa'ud perceived the Iraqi participation in the pact as a resurgence of the dormant Hashemite threat. Wary of Iraqi hegemonic aspirations, Al Sa'ud leaders feared that Iraq would seek Western assistance to dominate the Arab world. Moreover, the Al Sa'ud were deeply concerned that the Iraqi military build-up would allow Baghdad to recover the Hijaz.[62]

Given these basic assumptions, Sa'ud approached Nasir, determined that Riyadh would pursue a neutralist policy. After Iraq formally joined the alliance, Sa'ud concluded a mutual defense treaty with Nasir in October 1955.[63] In hindsight, therefore, cooperation with Nasir was necessary to isolate Iraq and prevent Syria and Jordan from joining the pact. Simultaneously, the Saudi ruler emulated Egyptian tactics, appealing to Iraqi, Syrian, and Jordanian citizens to reject Western (mainly British) neo-colonialism. Still, the Saudi rapprochement was problematical because it occurred despite a fresh arms accord between Egypt and the Soviet Union and, equally important, because of rising tensions in Yemen.[64]

Disputes with Yemen

The perception of a Yemeni threat to Saudi Arabia first emerged in 1934 over a border dispute in the 'Asir province. A series of border violations were recorded when farmers from both countries decided to till land that was improperly demarcated. To defend their brethren, Yemeni soldiers crossed into Saudi Arabia, attacked a border post, and occupied parts of the city of Najran.[65] 'Abdul 'Aziz entrusted the "liberation of Najran" to the princes Sa'ud and Faysal, which, sure enough, touched off a bloody war between the two monarchies. Faysal penetrated deep into Yemen and occupied the port city of Al-Hudaydah in one of his early military exploits.

'Abdul 'Aziz reasoned that the attacks, although not explicitly enunciated, were to secure new borders for an expanding kingdom. A defeated Yemen accepted a cease-fire and concluded the 1934 Ta'if Treaty that ended the state of war by creating a demarcation of a mutual, albeit incomplete, border. According to Saudi interpretations, 'Abdul 'Aziz refrained from imposing further demands, nor did he advance new territorial claims against Yemen as recommended by his advisors.[66] Relations between the two countries moved expeditiously until the 1962 Yemeni revolution.

Sa'ud, King of Saudi Arabia

When 'Abdul 'Aziz bin 'Abdul Rahman appointed his son Sa'ud as his heir on September 18, 1932, he breached tribal protocol by designating a successor while still alive. Islamic practices frowned on choosing an heir, preferring to allow family elders the privilege of a conclave after a ruler passed away. Moreover, while honored traditions always identified the eldest male offspring of a deceased ruler, other siblings were considered if a majority of ruling chiefs rejected a particular claimant. It was only after the immensely powerful Faysal al-Dawish (a leading Ikhwan ruler representing the 'Artawiyyah settlement) and Nayif bin Hathlan (the ruler of the influential 'Ajman tribe) were subdued that Sa'ud could be named heir apparent. The two men died in prison in 1931 and 1934, respectively, and it may be useful to note that 'Abdul 'Aziz waited seven years after he declared himself monarch before he was comfortable enough to name a successor.[67] In the end, 'Abdul 'Aziz settled on Sa'ud for a variety of reasons, including his familiarity with key tribal leaders and his proven military prowess and, especially, because his eldest brother, Muhammad bin 'Abdul Rahman bin Faysal Al Sa'ud, was a potential contender. Uppermost on the mind of the monarch was the passionate rivalry that existed between Muhammad and Sa'ud; that is, between uncle and nephew. In fact, Faysal went to Makkah in September 1932 to persuade his uncle Muhammad that his *bay'ah* to Prince Sa'ud bin 'Abdul 'Aziz was critical, which finally sealed family harmony.[68]

'Abdul 'Aziz wrote his heir Sa'ud a congratulatory telegram that also admonished his eldest son to follow three specific obligations. At first, Sa'ud followed his father's recommendations, often accompanying him to prayer services. In fact, it was during one of these visits that Sa'ud literally saved his father from death when a disgruntled individual attacked the ruler inside the Makkah Holy Mosque. Unfortunately, Sa'ud would not always follow advice, although it may be said that Faysal applied their father's counsel to the letter. In the famed 1933 telegram, 'Abdul 'Aziz cautioned his heir:

1. Keep your intentions decent, so that your life and character may enjoy the commandments of Allah over all and may help the religion of God (Islam).
2. Be diligent in looking after the affairs of those who will be under Sa'ud's control and seek their advice openly.
3. Mind the affairs of Muslims generally and the affairs of Al Sa'ud family especially.[69]

'Abdul 'Aziz further recommended that Sa'ud seek the company of righteous and learned *'ulamah*. "Sit with them and respect them," he advised his heir; "take their counsel and be strict in teaching them the doctrines of the religion and literature, for people are nowhere if God and knowledge do not help them." He also expected Faysal to stand by Sa'ud, even if Sa'ud competed with Faysal on this score, as the latter enjoyed a more focused religious upbringing.[70]

Although Faysal was not particularly close to most tribal leaders, he drew on his religious inner strength, which had been carefully nurtured by his study of religious texts. According to Zaki Yamani, his long-time minister of petroleum,

Faisal also had a special talent for dealing with all of the forces of Saudi society. He could manage it for several reasons. First, because his mother was from a famous religious family, the Al-Ashaikh [sic]. It enabled him to deal with that group. Second, because he himself was respected as a religious man. None of the religious groups would challenge him. Third, he had a sense of the country's need to move forward, so he was respected by the progressives. Believe me, he was very powerful.[71]

Beyond these attributes, Faysal stood out for his modest display of wealth. In an open and rather transparent society where the *badu* fraternized with their leaders, ostentatious displays of wealth were bound to create envy and resentment. Given Sa'ud's propinquity for such displays, it was only a matter of time before serious disputes arose of a variety that would and could topple regimes.

Dispute with Sa'ud

Sa'ud bin 'Abdul 'Aziz was not a leader equal to the challenges then facing the Kingdom of Saudi Arabia. Moreover, his well-established reputation as a spend-thrift, which preceded his accession to rulership, crippled the Al Sa'ud, who were in an intractable family bind. How could the Al Sa'ud extricate themselves from the constraining authority imposed by Sa'ud while maintaining unity and har-mony?

To his credit, Sa'ud generously maintained tribal acquiescence, as he favored the creation of a large palace guard, the so-called White Army.[72] This was in ad-dition to the nascent military, including the long-established National Guard, which competed for recruits from some of the same tribes. At the time, revenues were limited, especially when subsidies to various foreign groups and family ex-penditures were factored in. Suffice it to say that by 1958 the Saudi riyal was deval-ued nearly 80 percent despite annual oil revenues in excess of U.S.$300 million.

What triggered the actual dissatisfaction with Sa'ud by key ruling family mem-bers was difficult to pinpoint, except that conservative societies seldom tolerated wasteful expenditures, especially when harsher conditions were still fresh in many memories. It may well have been the slow development of public projects, or even the dearth of educational institutions throughout the 1950s, modest initiatives notwithstanding. It may even have been the overall low wages both for Saudis as well as the growing labor force. Except for a select few, living conditions were still primitive as Saudis witnessed the extravagance of the new king with mixed feel-ings. In a society where ordinary citizens, shaykhs and *badu* herdsmen alike called each other by their first names, few tolerated personal aggrandizement. Moreover, the contrast between Saʿud and Faysal, one steeped in conservative outlook while the other was eager to adapt to change, could not be more blatant. Naturally, it was not long before dissatisfaction gathered steam, especially among more liberal princes as well as the sons of the rising middle class educated in Lebanon, Egypt, or even in Europe. A steady awakening gathered momentum, and it was under Saʿud's rule that the first labor strikes at ARAMCO occurred in 1953 and again in 1956. The stage was set for a serious political confrontation between the ruler and his heir. For the first time in its contemporary history, Saudi Arabia faced a genuine clash of vision, which would unravel over a decade-long period.

3

Heir Apparent Faysal (1953–1964)

Over the span of several decades, a charismatic leader with political foresight care-fully unified Saudi Arabia. To his credit, ʿAbdul ʿAziz bin ʿAbdul Rahman Al Saʿud never lost sight of what mattered most, and he toiled in earnest to secure his kingdom. He fought necessary battles, imposed strict Shariʿah, and displayed immense generosity. As he reached advanced age, he sealed the ruling family's legitimacy by addressing two significant preoccupations. For ʿAbdul ʿAziz, what were essential were Saudi Arabia's worldwide role as well as a smooth Al Saʿud succession. In both instances, he was confident that his eldest sons would rise to the occasion, the heir seconded by an even more charismatic brother. To accom-plish his stated objectives, he counseled his sons often and stirred them to remain true to their beliefs as well as each other. He reminded his sons that strict adher-ence to religion was the single most powerful governance tool at their disposal and that they should always put their trust in God.

As a committed adherent, ʿAbdul ʿAziz ordered a massive reconstruction of the holy sites in Makkah and Madinah starting in the late 1940s, which, in turn, drew thousands of artisans and workers to both cities. Given the scope involved, the task to oversee needed repairs to the finish fell on his successors' shoulders. ʿAbdul ʿAziz did not live long enough to see the completion of these major alterations as the work was extensive and meticulous. Under Saʿud, additional funds were allocated, as he authorized more elaborate arrangements. In 1955, Fay-sal ordered an even more extended enlargement of the Makkah shrine to simul-taneously accommodate three hundred thousand pilgrims. Going against estab-lished traditions, the vision of Prince Faysal necessitated the forced removal of thousands of Makkahans from their dwellings, but the decision was irrevocable. Makkah was the center of both the Islamic universe as well as Faysal's emerging vision. The heir apparent to King Sa'ud never lost sense of his mission, especially as his father coached him and, after 1953, as it forged his innermost nexus.

The preoccupation of the founder with his succession posed a far greater challenge than upholding Shari'ah or the reconstruction of the holy sites. According to Gerald de Gaury, in 1945 and "with a tear in his eye," 'Abdul 'Aziz confided to an advisor that he "only wish[ed he] had three Faisals."[1] His declared preference notwithstanding, the king designated Sa'ud not only because he was the eldest, but also to fend off opposition from his own brothers. Faysal, for his part, upheld the choice made by his father because he was a stickler for family order. In fact, Prince Faysal never entertained any digressions from the established succession line and rebuffed everyone who questioned his older brother's claim to authority. 'Abdul 'Aziz made his sons swear that they would not quarrel and would accept his preferences for Sa'ud to become king and for Faysal to be Sa'ud's heir apparent. Faysal swore and gave his brother an unwavering *bay'ah*. As later events demonstrated, the *bay'ah* to Sa'ud was highly contentious, yet it was never compromised for its own sake. Although Faysal eventually withdrew his oath and refused to obey the king, he went through a formal, at times complicated, process that involved the kingdom's senior religious clerics along with high-ranking decision makers in the ruling family. Nevertheless, when King 'Abdul 'Aziz passed away in Ta'if on November 9, 1953, the tribal unifier par excellence left a considerable void that few could fill. After his impressive rule of five decades, Saudi Arabia was relatively secure and boasted extraordinary gains. Still, the remainder of the 1950s and the first few years of the 1960s presented serious internal as well as external challenges, which ushered in a devastating decade. Both Sa'ud and Faysal were severely taxed as the country fell on the brink of financial ruin as unprecedented hazards threatened the very stability of the ruling family.

Sa'ud bin 'Abdul 'Aziz on the Throne

Ruling family politics under King Sa'ud (1953–64) were marked by a sharp division of power between the king and the heir apparent that escalated into a bitter feud over policy differences.[2] In the prolonged struggle that ensued, the balance between Sa'ud and Faysal shifted back and forth several times as the ruling family was split apart in innovative alignments. The contest was finally resolved in favor of Faysal nearly at the point of bloodshed. In the event, Saudi domestic and foreign policy suffered from confusion and reversals because the ruling family was not united.

Sa'ud bin 'Abdul 'Aziz succeeded his father during a smooth transfer of power. Faysal became heir apparent, and over the following few years the founder's eldest sons shared both power and responsibility. With some exceptions, Sa'ud strengthened his power base within the family, while Faysal concentrated his efforts in the Council of Ministers. Although the nascent monarchy was fully engaged in state-building efforts, the pattern of appointments indicated internal schisms. For example, Faysal's supporters included his son 'Abdallah (minister of the interior) and his half brothers Fahd (education) and Sultan (communications), while Sa'ud installed his sons as commander of both the National and Royal Guards, chief of the Diwan, minister of defense, and as governor of Riyadh. Whatever arrangements existed began to break down under the strain of two developments. Internally, the finances of the kingdom deteriorated amid charges of corruption and extravagance.[3] Externally, the rise of Gamal 'Abdul Nasir in Egypt—on a wave of Arab socialist ideology—confronted the conservative Saudi establishment with an unprecedented foreign threat.[4] By early 1958, the impulsive fiscal policies of the monarch, coupled with his hasty foreign adventures, had resulted in a head-on family collision.[5] Faysal believed that the kingdom should draw succor from its intrinsic capacities—that, in the end, the most valuable and true revolution was the Islamic one, preferably under Saudi leadership—and that King Sa'ud should be wary of nationalist or socialist rhetoric. His cautionary remarks fell on deaf ears in Riyadh as Sa'ud entered into temporary alliances with Nasir rather than demonstrate independence as a leader who could rally Arab masses in his own right. Nowhere was this more apparent than in Saudi-American ties immediately after President Eisenhower announced a fresh "doctrine" for the region.

King Sa'ud and the United States

The opportunity to harvest the fruits of the nascent Anglo-American competition for influence dissipated even before the founder of modern Saudi Arabia died in November 1953 as the Cold War erupted in earnest. Everyone expected to be either "with Washington or with the Communists." In the Middle East, both the Truman and Eisenhower Doctrines were rapidly applied, ostensibly to sort out an increasingly messy checkerboard. A reinvigorated Soviet Union threatened Greece, Turkey, and Iran. Soon, Iraq, Jordan, and Lebanon were added to the list as Ba'athism in both Baghdad and Damascus gained a new ally in Moscow. Egypt and Yemen followed, especially after major Western miscalculations in the aftermath of the 1952 Egyptian revolution. From the American perspective, the dominant Cold War rhetoric came to fashion foreign policy, as containment became the primary objective even of the country's *raison d'être*. From the Saudi perspective, it was the rapid fall of several "monarchies" that formulated what passed for timid and rather limited policies.

Saudi Arabia and to a lesser extent Jordan were pleased that the United States changed its strict, perhaps even arbitrary, policies to sell them defensive weapons to field a modicum of fire-power against Egypt. The firebrand identification of President Nasir of Egypt and his call for Arab nationalism unsettled conservative monarchies, including Saudi Arabia. King Saʿud bin ʿAbdul ʿAziz, for his part, knew that in Arab hearts and minds Nasir was "the great man," even if his own father, just a few years earlier, had been labeled as such by no other statesman than President Truman himself. Nasir's shadow ran deeply on the Arabian Peninsula, and not just in Yemen, affecting Saʿud's increasingly close association with the United States. What mattered for Riyadh was limiting the negative perceptions that this close association generated for Arab public opinion. Pressing Arab concerns—ranging from the Palestine question to nationalism to necessary economic development—became secondary. What was at stake was the survival of the regime.

As President Dwight D. Eisenhower and his able and generally well-informed secretary of state, John Foster Dulles, relied on their Cold War vision to deal with the entire world through a single prism, the Saudis—and most Arabs for that matter—quickly sought to lay various claims to Washington's limited attention span. In May 1953, King ʿAbdul ʿAziz had raised the "friendship" bar with Secretary Dulles, requesting U.S. political assistance against Britain in the Buraymi conflict.[6] The villages of the Buraymi Oasis, like the vast majority of border questions near or on the Arabian Peninsula, were disputed territories sitting on largely unknown and uncharted oil deposits. Whether with American nudging or not, Saudi monarchs grasped the importance of "sovereignty" over this undemarcated land, which was disputed among several claimants. Other rulers throughout the Lower Gulf, including the Al Saʿid in Oman and the Al Nahyan in Abu Dhabi, were equally determined to advance their assertions. What role ARAMCO officials played in the Buraymi conflict will never be fully known, but it was amply clear that Saudis committed a cardinal error in assuming that the U.S. oil company and the U.S. government shared identical interests. The Arabian-American Oil Company sought to secure its holdings and add to them as time went by, whereas Washington aimed to influence policy, align countries to its worldwide crusades, and manage regimes that would be favorably inclined toward its policies.[7]

Where American leaders proved naïve was to assume that local leaders were always ready to acquiesce to ensure regime survival. While this was often the case, there were times when unknown circumstances arose that complicated what passed for diplomacy. Such was the case with the Buraymi conflict.

Emboldened by his putative oil holdings, on September 17, 1952, 'Abdul 'Aziz invoked a previously declared (including in writing) American commitment to "preserve the independence and territorial integrity" of Saudi Arabia. Ironically, he did not invoke this clause to protect the kingdom from Egypt or Iraq or Yemen or even the Soviet Union. Rather, the Saudi government was calling on the United States to defend it from the United Kingdom, one of Washington's closest allies. Not surprisingly, the United States stalled and delayed a response, calling for quiet diplomacy to settle whatever differences existed between the two sides. It also did not want to be dragged into a turf war between various oil companies vying for fresh concessions. In the event, and almost a month later, 'Abdul 'Aziz changed his mind and stepped away from U.S. mediation. He sought, instead, American assistance to freeze all movements on the ground and received a commitment that London would resume discussions with Riyadh. The British desired arbitration whereas the Saudis preferred a tripartite commission between themselves, the Americans, and the British.[8] London won the day. After all, America was not about to set aside its peerless "special relationship" with the United Kingdom for a land dispute that most State Department officials found incongruous and absurd. Faysal bin 'Abdul 'Aziz, the heir apparent who was then visiting Washington, was seriously disappointed—but perhaps should not have been—by the lack of support. He opted to wait and see how the incoming Eisenhower administration would react to Saudi requests. Neither Eisenhower, nor John Foster Dulles, nor for that matter Walter Bedell Smith, the new undersecretary of state, offered a different position from those held by the previous administration. On the contrary, all insisted that arbitration was the order of the day, albeit with the understanding that the United States would look at allegations of aggression on all sides. This last point was critical because it planted the idea that Washington was ready to control the Middle East, including the vital Persian Gulf, even if the opportunity to emasculate Britain would not present itself until 1956. The far more important American concession in 1953 was to find Saudi Arabia "eligible for military assistance under the 1951 Mutual Defense Assistance Act."[9]

Again, this was another key departure from previous American policies, especially as Saudi Arabia understood that the United States would not go to war against Britain to defend it. Rather, Eisenhower reiterated Washington's standard "territorial integrity and independence" formulation in his letter of June 15, 1953 to 'Abdul 'Aziz, but he also pledged to sell the kingdom additional military hardware to better defend itself. In May 1953 Dulles warned his Saudi hosts in Riyadh not to compromise American policies by bringing up local and regional disputes, although he also assured Saudi Arabia that the United States was an ally that could be counted on.[10] The usually reserved Dulles cajoled his interlocutors into accepting military aid, meager as it was, to further demonstrate the resolve and commitments of the United States. That was the best that Riyadh could "harvest" from the Buraymi opportunity. In hindsight, it was not much, even if Saudi claims to the oasis were legally unsettled.

At the time, neither Prince Sa'ud nor Prince Faysal contemplated acting on his visible anger toward the United States. To be sure, Faysal may well have said to Ambassador George E. Wadsworth that U.S. Point IV technical assistance would no longer be needed, or that Riyadh would not "bother the U.S. Government," but these were classic diplomatic maneuverings meant to express disappointment. At no time were the Saudis even thinking of linking the U.S. position on Buraymi, or Palestine, or any other political decision to either the vital oil concessions or the Dhahran Air Base Accord. Even Soviet and Chinese overtures, ostensibly to provide unlimited quantities of weapons, were not taken seriously, although given the Cold War climate, several Washington officials must have spent restless nights over such matters. What Faysal purported to achieve was to devise a formula to deal with American power. Equally important was the conclusion reached by Riyadh that the Saudi-U.S. bond would only intensify if and when security accords were solidified.[11]

If 'Abdul 'Aziz ensured that a regime emerged in Saudi Arabia, Sa'ud's task, or so it seemed, was to ensure its survival. And it was up to Faysal to create and seal the accord. Toward that end, on November 30, 1955 King Sa'ud formally requested that Washington provide guidance for a five-year military training plan without the usual strings attached to such grants.

Because the kingdom was then earning an estimated $250 million yearly from oil exports, it was legally necessary to inform the U.S. Congress that the government of Saudi Arabia had made a specific request and that a linkage existed to justify it as a payment for use of the Dhahran Air Base. In American eyes, the facility was critical for regional defense (to buttress Baghdad Pact members—Iraq, Iran, Turkey, Pakistan, and the United Kingdom, with the United States as an "observer"—even if the scheme was part of the Eisenhower administration's overall plans), but not at any price. Still, as Cold War preoccupations colored regional views held by Washington, King Sa'ud was fully cognizant of the growing influence that President Nasir enjoyed throughout the Arab world. Little of what engrossed his father—chiefly Palestine—was pressing for his successor—at least not enough to insist that American officials address Arab concerns. Once the Suez War started on October 29, 1956, Sa'ud was pressed to make epoch-making choices.

The Israeli invasion of Egypt, rapidly followed by British and French interventions, was vigorously condemned by the United States. In this context, and while Washington and London sided together at the United Nations Security Council many times, Britain vetoed a 1956 Security Council resolution sponsored by the United States that condemned the attacks on Egypt. Saʿud backed Egypt and, along with several other Arab states, broke diplomatic ties with Britain and France on November 6, 1956. Such an abrupt decision went beyond an illustration of Arab solidarity. It also was an act of frustration—over the Buraymi conflict—as well as an act of desperation. Granted, Washington had stood with the Arabs—in the eloquent words of the Indian prime minister Jawaharlal Nehru at the United Nations General Assembly, "America had, at last, located its soul"—but, in reality, this was a reflection of larger international considerations. Eisenhower could not keep a straight face as both the champion of colonialism and anti-Communism. In a polarized world, the peoples of the world were increasingly called upon to reject Communism and align themselves with the West. The latter, its champions posited, stood for freedom, pluralism, and basic rights, all packaged in a capitalist cloak. Nevertheless, to be effective, the capitalist argument could not be advanced while several of its major supporters practiced colonialism, not to mention racially discriminatory policies.

From Riyadh's perspective, the Suez War—and the subsequent visit to Washington by King Saʿud in 1957—created an opportunity to secure additional military purchases. A key agreement was reached on February 9, 1957 under whose terms the United States agreed to develop the nascent Royal Saudi Air Force, as well as furnish and maintain a batch of eight T-33 aircraft. In addition, Washington agreed to sell eight M-47 tanks and several light coastal patrol boats. The total sum for these items did not exceed $200 million but that was almost as much as Saudi annual oil revenues at the time.[12] In April 1957, the Dhahran Air Base Accord was renewed but, and this is worth repeating, the relationship between the United States and Saudi Arabia was further isolated in a security framework. The Al Saʿud, whether consciously or not, were further immersed in a one-dimensional policy.

Far from being unique, the security framework was also the favored policy that the Eisenhower administration pursued toward Egypt. In May 1953, Dulles was keen to underscore to Prime Minister Muhammad Naguib and Colonel Gamal ʿAbdul Nasir, the actual leader of the Revolutionary Command Council (RCC), that Washington was willing to build up the Egyptian military. This, it was further posited, would allow Egypt to become the natural leader of the Arab world. Remarkably, these discussions were held despite the fact that Britain still had a huge facility at Suez and was quite eager to keep it in place. In the event, the

RCC rejected the offer made by Dulles because it would not accept that Cairo become a "chosen instrument" of the United States. When the Baghdad Pact was established on February 24, 1955, Cairo perceived this as a grave development, certainly a Western challenge to its "natural leadership" role. If Nasir was miffed at Eisenhower (who did not invite him to visit the United States), or was, perhaps, perceived by Dulles as a minor regional leader, neither side managed to salvage the steady erosion of influence. Dulles set Nasir's economic needs—wheat and the Aswan High Dam—aside. These key omissions, whether to spite Nasir, or through ignorance, or both, set the stage for the Egyptian decision to nationalize the Suez Canal Company on July 23, 1956, which, in turn, set in motion the Suez crisis and, eventually, war. For King Sa'ud, who certainly sympathized with the Arab world's fundamental nationalist changes, Nasir was an alluring leader even if he represented a real affront to traditional regimes. Bluntly stated, King Sa'ud was unaware, nor was he ready to deal with the gargantuan Egyptian political phenomenon.

Sa'ud and the Eisenhower Doctrine

King Sa'ud accepted the invitation extended by President Eisenhower to visit the United States in 1957. Although the Saudi ruler's formal reception on arrival in New York was frigid, the American president welcomed him at the airport in Washington, D.C.[13]

Eisenhower was eager to win Sa'ud over and explained his doctrine in some detail. In turn, Sa'ud declared that he wished to make it acceptable, which necessitated the inclusion of positive features to better serve Arabs. In short, Sa'ud pleaded that the Eisenhower Doctrine offer more than Nasir proposed, especially if the objective was to win the hearts as well as the minds of Arab masses. Because the Suez Canal was nationalized and its revenues rechanneled to serve Egyptians, Sa'ud suggested that Washington attach a positive and financially advantageous package to its strategic venture. In other words, the American promise to protect Arabs from Communism, while valuable, was insufficient. Eisenhower pondered the request for a whole week before agreeing to authorize a significant military build-up for the kingdom, along with a $250 million loan. Partly to ingratiate himself with his host, Sa'ud promised to explain the doctrine to Arab leaders and renewed the Dhahran Air Base commitment for another five years. Eisenhower was so pleased with Sa'ud's graceful acceptance of his vision that he placed his personal aircraft at the disposal of the king to fly him and his entourage back to Europe and home.[14]

Sa'ud first stopped in Spain—where General Franco extended a lavish reception with Madrid's famed Moroccan Guards saluting an Arab monarch in a Western capital—before flying to Morocco, Tunisia, Libya, and Egypt. At every stop, the ruler expounded on the Eisenhower Doctrine as promised and, in Cairo, discussed the matter with President Shukri Quwatli of Syria, and King Hussein of Jordan, both of whom were visiting Nasir. At 'Abdine Palace, Nasir and Quwatli rejected the Eisenhower offer and warned Sa'ud that they would not accept being drawn into the American alliance.

The return stop in Cairo was not meant only to cajole Nasir but to deliver concrete initiatives. The genuine popularity of the Egyptian at home was already at its zenith, something that was clearly obvious to the monarch. Not since the Crusades almost a thousand years earlier had an Arab leader stood up against a colonial power. Nasir had seized the opportunity to oppose two colonial powers (Britain and France) simultaneously. For Sa'ud, this was food for thought, even if the United States, along with Britain, France, and Israel, cavalierly dismissed the emergence of yet another Third World leader. During their onward Cairo discussions, Nasir agreed to seek U.S. aid through Sa'ud. It was clear that Sa'ud, by offering to intercede in Washington, was on a salvage mission to add value to his own credibility in the eyes of the most popular Arab leader. But when he raised this particular issue—providing Egypt with specific financial support—with Dulles, Dulles rejected it, cautioning Sa'ud to tread carefully. Ultimately, Sa'ud could not even secure a wheat deal and, on his return stop in Cairo, garnered the sarcasm and ridicule of Nasir. Soon, anti-Sa'ud radio broadcasts filled the airwaves and, goaded by Dulles to stand firm against Nasir, Sa'ud was reluctantly dragged into Washington's larger Cold War formulation for regional security.

Faysal and the Eisenhower Doctrine

As Sa'ud delved into diplomacy, in June 1957 Faysal left for Italy and the United States, where he was operated on twice, first to remove his gall bladder and then a nonmalignant tumor. During his five-months long convalescence, Faysal met with Eisenhower to reassure him that "no Arab country in the Middle East was in danger from Syria or elsewhere."[15] The Washington establishment did not necessarily take this declaration as a final truism, but the fact that American and British troops were preparing to go into Lebanon and Jordan in 1958 probably reassured the president. Moreover, the United States had just hosted King Sa'ud and received specific assurances, as well as strong support. Faysal's divergent pronouncements were carefully recorded but, at the time, few reacted to them.

On his way back from this long sojourn in the United States, Faysal lingered throughout the entire month of January 1958 in Cairo, where he met Nasir on at least four separate occasions. It was remarkable that the future monarch remained staunchly pro-Egyptian even as Nasir initiated his notoriously anti-monarchical oratory that bordered on the hysterical. Faysal was aware of these machinations and understood Nasir's motives—to extricate additional financial assistance— but, above all else, he wished to demonstrate that Saudi Arabia was an independent Arab country capable of distinguishing between friendships and long-term interests. He further advised Nasir to weigh the consequences of union with Syria, as Cairo and Damascus were engaged in a haphazard alliance that, in hindsight, did not withstand the pressures of intra-Arab politics.

Faysal as Regent

What occurred next was epoch-making, even if waggish, as Nasir accused King Sa'ud of plotting his demise. According to *Al-Ahram*, the official government daily mouthpiece, Sa'ud and his secretary, Yusuf Yassin, were "engaged in an attempt, cost what it might, to undermine the Syrian-Egyptian union by having Nasser assassinated."[16] Egyptian and Syrian newspapers, seldom engaged in investigative journalism, provided details substantiating numerous allegations in the form of letters, checks, and bank account deposit slips, but never mentioned were Sa'ud's generous financial disbursements to both Cairo and Damascus, which nurtured Nasir and Shukri Quwatli.[17] Against this carefully orchestrated litany of rumors and half-truths, Sa'ud kept silent, leaving the impression of gullibility if not outright culpability. Naturally, the situation was untenable, as the Arab world's rumor mills churned quantities of exquisite lies. While entertaining, the copious reportage damaged the credibility of Saudi Arabia in general and that of the ruling Al Sa'ud family in particular. Consequently, King Sa'ud's inability or unwillingness to respond heightened Al Sa'ud concerns. Because Sa'ud failed to rally his brothers around the throne and explain his problematic understandings, several concluded that the king's "leadership was dangerous to the country financially and vis-à-vis Egypt politically."[18] Led by the monarch's uncle, a group of senior decision makers decided to confront the king to seek his abdication.[19] On March 24, 1958, the future king Fahd bin 'Abdul 'Aziz along with eleven other princes confronted the ruler, who was waiting with his uncle and brother for Ramadan prayers and Iftar, the evening meal for breaking the daily fast. Reportedly, the princes declared that they "had sworn to save [the king] and in doing so save [them]selves and the Kingdom." When neither Muhammad bin 'Abdul Rahman nor Faysal objected, as both were privy to the move, the king apparently rejoined: "What do you want me to do?" Muhammad bin 'Abdul Rahman then spoke for everyone present: "We decided to demand your abdication, but your brother Faisal opposed the idea and asked that you remain on the Throne. We have accepted on one condition, that you hand over all your power to Faisal."[20] Sa'ud accepted and, within an hour, a decree was issued to seal the accord of the family because the deteriorating economic situation added to the urgency of the action taken by the princes.

Financial Discipline and Its Consequences

Faysal immediately moved to introduce sorely needed order to the country's internal requirements as well as external relations. On April 18, 1958, he delivered an eloquent speech that was distinguished by its transparency. To be sure, he was not particularly hopeful that Arab nationalists would welcome his government, but neither was he ready for the onslaught that followed.

On the domestic front, Faysal wasted no time in tightening the financial belt of the country, given that he had inherited a debt of 400 million riyals (approximately $100 million) owed to banks and local merchants. What followed was unique in Saudi annals. The prime minister ordered massive program cutbacks, adopted a balanced budget, and ordered the Saudi Arabian Monetary Agency, which was established in 1952, to maintain a 15 percent liquidity for all deposits. These immediate measures were so drastic that, by the end of 1958, Riyadh realized a small surplus to retire some of its accumulated debt. To set an example, Faysal slashed the privy purse by two-thirds, albeit over a six-year period, which earned him nothing but scorn even though the drastic measure probably saved the country from default.[21]

Yet, by setting an example, Faysal was able to refocus attention on more important needs. Education and health programs were his top priorities and these received preferential spending. Simultaneously, nonessential government expenditures were either postponed or cancelled outright. Above all else, Faysal limited specific amounts allocated to members of the ruling family, many of whom had grown accustomed to free money under Sa'ud. Prime Minister Faysal continued to live in his modest home and relinquished most princely trappings, including heavy—and costly—escorts, and countless body guards that protected the ruler from his subjects. Consequently, he took the habit of driving himself to the office of the prime minister every morning, where he received dignitaries, officials, 'ulamah, and an unending stream of visitors.[22]

In June 1958, Faysal suspended official purchases of new cars and most luxury goods and placed strict controls on foreign remittances. He also withdrew the small contingent of Saudi forces deployed in Jordan to buttress the Hashemite monarch and froze the £5.5 million subsidy given to Amman. If King Hussein was unhappy with the decision, he did not publicly voice any criticism. Many Saudis, however, were far less diplomatic. Disgruntled courtiers and agents for luxury items that were supplied to various royals, along with several nobles themselves, voiced displeasure.

As if these internal pressures were not sufficient, soon Egyptian and Syrian radio broadcasts reached abusive levels, this time targeting not just Saudi Arabia but Faysal himself. Encouraging stances made earlier by Nasir—but especially between 1952 and 1958—were literally reversed as Faysal drew the Egyptian leader's wrath. Vituperative statements notwithstanding, what truly irked Nasir was the Saudi decision to freeze all financial disbursements. Gone was Sa'ud's unlimited generosity, which had helped bankrupt Saudi Arabia.

Regional Upheavals

Like other Arab leaders, the Al Sa'ud did not know how to contain Nasir, especially his fiery rhetoric. In July 1956, they supported him when Egypt nationalized the Suez Canal, but in August 1956, they altered course.[23] Earlier, and in the wake of the 1955 upheaval within the Royal Saudi Air Force, the king expelled all Egyptian military advisers, who, allegedly, had inspired their Saudi colleagues.[24] After a brief period of renewed solidarity over the 1956 Suez Crisis—which culminated in a new coalition between Saudi Arabia, Iraq, and Jordan in 1958—Cairo and Riyadh exchanged increasingly hostile charges.[25] Throughout this period, Egypt also pursued closer relations with the Soviet Union, which clearly alarmed Sa'ud. It was in this connection that Riyadh renewed the lease on the Dhahran Air Base, which facilitated additional U.S. military sales.[26]

The Impact of the 1958 Iraqi Revolution

Saudi leaders were "shocked" when they learned that a fellow monarch, King Faysal II, had been murdered in Iraq. For all of their differences, Saudi Arabia found a modus vivendi with a fellow monarchic regime in its independent years. To make matters worse, the coup orchestrated by Brigadier General 'Abdul Karim Qasim reversed the pro-Western orientation in Baghdad. Qasim enunciated his intentions to adhere to Arab nationalist tenets. He further declared that Iraq would distance itself from Western strategic objectives and, to buttress his claims, withdrew from the Baghdad Pact shortly thereafter. Turkey, Iran, and Pakistan, the other full members, renamed the pact the Central Treaty Organization and moved its headquarters to Ankara. Despite its fundamental differences with potential Iraqi hegemony in the region, Riyadh recognized some intrinsic value to the Baghdad Pact, namely that it kept the Soviet Union at bay. After the 1958 Iraqi Revolution, however, it altered its views sharply, considering Iraqi nationalist aspirations throughout the Arab world to be far more dangerous.

The Qasim nationalist vision called for the removal of all Arab monarchies and, in the case of Saudi Arabia, to carve up the kingdom into smaller entities.[27] By 1961, Iraq had declared Kuwait an integral part of its territory, which led to a British military expedition to protect the shaykhdom. A few months after the British deployment, the League of Arab States replaced the force with its own peacekeeping operation under the leadership of a Saudi commander. This crisis illustrated how Qasim intended to deal with states on the peninsula. At the time, Riyadh and Cairo cooperated in earnest to counter Iraqi expansionism.[28]

In hindsight, it was the Iraqi coup that brought Saudi Arabia closer to Egypt and away from the United States. It also allowed Faysal the opportunity to galvanize his allies within the ruling family against Sa'ud. Assessing the implications of Sa'ud's errors, Faysal adopted a policy of appeasement toward Nasir by declaring his support to the Egyptian leader as well as consenting to suspend several agreements with Washington. Thus, by mitigating pro-Egyptian and Arab nationalist sentiments within the kingdom (especially in the armed forces, where sympathy for Nasir caused several mutinies), Faysal fed fodder to anti-American proponents. In doing so, however, he positioned himself to wrestle power away from Sa'ud as soon as senior members of the family became aware that the long-term consequences of these decisions were devastating. Faysal argued that fragile Al Sa'ud interests required a steady hand, sound anti-revolutionary policies, cooperation with powerful allies, and, above all, full unity at home.[29]

Thus, and although the Al Sa'ud ruling family was severely jolted by the bloody Iraqi Revolution, Faysal, ever the realist, recognized the new government in Baghdad even if 'Abdul Karim Qasim and his generals failed to inspire confidence. Faysal flew to Cairo on August 19, 1958 to reach a fresh understanding with Nasir. Whether a new deal was brokered between the two men was pure speculation, although Egyptian attacks on Saudi Arabia ceased for a while. In all likelihood, Nasir thought it appropriate to reassess his posture on the Arab scene for fear that firebrand rhetoric threatened a loss of control in Baghdad and Damascus.

Against the paper tiger that was the United Arab Republic (the 1958 union of Egypt and Syria), Washington voiced support for an Iranian-Jordanian federation with potential Saudi membership. Even if Secretary of State John Foster Dulles perceived these "entities" as defensive rooks on the American-Soviet chessboard, any Hashemite alliance was bound to raise Saudi eyebrows. Not surprisingly, the entire scheme collapsed after the coup in Baghdad on July 14, 1958. By precipitating himself in the larger Arab political arena, Saʻud had further weakened the kingdom as it added fellow Arab countries to its list of enemies. Rather than maintain its distance from the superpower rivalry, Saudi Arabia sank even deeper in the American orbit for purely defensive purposes. In less than a decade, two major Arab monarchies had disappeared and, by the late 1950s, the threat against Kuwait imperiled the Saudi monarchy too.

Kuwait, by virtue of its 1899 agreement with Britain, was, for all practical purposes, a British protectorate. Yet, as oil income redefined it, the need to show its "Arab" credentials increased. The Al Sabah quickly settled large parts of their borders with the Al Saʻud, including a joint accord over a neutral zone. Kuwait and Britain then replaced their 1899 agreement with a sweeping treaty on June 19, 1961 that essentially granted London the right of intervention to defend the small but rich shaykhdom.[30] Less than a week later, the Iraqi strongman ʻAbdul Karim Qasim rejected the Anglo-Kuwaiti actions and declared that Kuwait was "an integral part of Iraq."[31] Saʻud was stunned. He announced that aggression against Kuwait would be tantamount to aggression against Saudi Arabia. Most Arab states, including Egypt and Syria, were also opposed to the Iraqi claim.

On reports that two Iraqi army divisions (even in those days the Iraqi military was portrayed as a super powerful entity) were moving toward Kuwait, the British, with full American support, landed a battalion of six hundred Marines in Kuwait on July 1, 1961. The Saudis sent a small paratroop battalion on the same day, which was soon augmented by token Egyptian, Jordanian, and Sudanese troops operating under a mandate by the League of Arab States. Arab opinion then, both official and public, was unanimous in its opposition to Qasim's posturing. Hussein bin Talal of Jordan, who maintained that the Iraqi claim to Kuwait was legally valid, opposed Qasim. Saʻud bin ʻAbdul ʻAziz was equally committed to the defense of Kuwait. Even if some leaders perceived the dispute as British posturing against Iraq, it was nevertheless clear that yet another security dilemma was "created" for all Arabs.

After an initial stabilization period, London withdrew its troops starting on July 11, 1961, but the League peacekeeping force—commanded by a Saudi because of Riyadh's initiative and largest contribution (almost fifteen hundred men)—remained in place.[32] The United States recognized Kuwait as an independent country and exchanged ambassadors, although the U.S. envoy was simultaneously assigned and resided in Saudi Arabia. Still, such diplomatic exchanges irritated Iraqis but Baghdad was powerless to affect any change. It must be underlined that the presence of a significant Saudi contribution in Kuwait, while welcomed as part of a League of Arab States peacekeeping deployment, was also viewed with suspicion. The Al Sabah then trusted the British—and only the British—and, in time, signed an important security agreement with Qasim's successor, Colonel 'Abdul Salaam 'Arif, on October 4, 1963. What irritated the Saudis were the rapid exchanges between Kuwait and Baghdad—official visits and the extension of generous financial "loans"—that, at least from the Saudi perspective, essentially meant a Kuwaiti acquiescence to an anti-monarchical regime. Naturally, the Saudis understood why Kuwait would want to pursue a double-edged policy toward Iraq: granting financial incentives to appease Baghdad while reinforcing their tight military alliance with London. What they could not accept was the ease with which the United States and the United Kingdom interjected themselves in regional Gulf affairs. Security alliances were mushrooming while monarchies were disappearing and the Al Sa'ud leadership, particularly Prince Faysal, took notice.

Ba'athism in 1963

The security threat to Saudi Arabia increased in February 1963 when a group of Iraqi "Free Officers" assassinated 'Abdul Karim Qasim. Unable to consolidate its power, however, the new regime was toppled in November 1963 when other military leaders took power. Calls to support Saudi Ba'athists rose, as regular broadcasts lambasting Saudi leaders further poisoned the atmosphere. Baghdad opted for a neutral policy in the East-West conflict and turned its efforts to strengthening relations with Arab states, especially Egypt. Because of the civil war in Yemen, as well as Egypt's controversial role in supporting anti-royalist forces in Aden, the Saudis were "pinched" between Iraq and Egypt. The threat to the kingdom was now multidirectional. It was this strategic development that solidified one of the principle ideological interests of Saudi Arabia: the need to emphasize Islamic solidarity. Faysal, certainly a pious Muslim, appealed to his brethren around the world to fight all ideologies that were inconsistent with Islam, specifically Ba'athism and Communism.[33] Whatever support Faysal extended to fellow Muslims after this epochal development was to defeat ideological threats to core values.

The End of Monarchy in Yemen

On September 27, 1962, Imam Muhammad Al Badr was deposed in Sana'a. This was a historical turning point for Saudi Arabia because a fellow monarchy was replaced with two non-monarchical regimes.[34] Riyadh was caught off guard by the coup because King Sa'ud had been ill and Prince Faysal was attending a meeting of the United Nations General Assembly in New York. When asked about the Yemeni coup, Faysal declared that this was a domestic Yemeni issue and that Riyadh did not concern itself with the internal affairs of other countries. Still, when President Kennedy personally sought Faysal's views on the ʿAbdallah Sallal coup d'état, the Saudi counseled not to hasten diplomatic recognition. Naturally, Riyadh was troubled about the fall of the monarchy and correctly saw Egypt playing a role to destabilize Arab monarchies even before everyone realized that the fallen imam was still alive and seeking assistance. The United States, in contrast, was eager to ingratiate itself with Egypt, perhaps hoping to play a moderating role in Arab affairs. It was also impressed with the quick diplomatic maneuverings initiated by the Soviet Union—extending full recognition to the Sallal government in Yemen on September 29, 1962, which prompted Kennedy to mimic it on December 19, 1962.[35]

Irrespective of tactful pronouncements made in public declaring noninterference, Saudi Arabia quickly welcomed members of the Yemeni monarchy to settle in the kingdom and provided them with the basic necessities.[36] In the event, Saʿud did not commit the kingdom to provide defeated monarchists with financial assistance, but Faysal was quick to propose alternative initiatives to regain the upper hand. After Imam Badr's forces rallied and organized their initial opposition, Egyptian troops opened several new fronts, including aerial bombardments of Saudi cities in Najran and Jizan. On January 3, 1962, Faysal mobilized his military forces and broke diplomatic ties with Cairo.[37]

The Al Saʿud knew that the United Arab Republic, the latest proposal to unite distant Arab lands separated by geography and background, could not survive because of major ideological differences between Nasirists and Baʿathists. Saʿud and Faysal, along with other family members, chose to buttress the tribal attributes of Syria to accelerate the collapse of the United Arab Republic. Faysal pushed for a pan-Islamic policy that protected Saudi interests while blocking Nasirist and Baʿathist gains. Against Nasirism, Faysal championed Islam, the ultimate unifying force. A forum—the Muslim World League—was created in Makkah in 1962 to organize Islamic affairs while serving intrinsic Saudi security objectives. This bold policy was not fully endorsed by Saʿud, who disagreed with Faysal. Unlike Saʿud, who favored a policy of co-option, Faysal argued for a two-pronged approach: to assume a leadership role within the Muslim world and to foster closer ties with Western powers. In fact, it may be argued that Faysal feared Nasir's antimonarchist mind-set far more than he feared Western colonial influences. His predictions proved correct when Egypt entered the Yemen civil war to help oust a conservative monarch from power.[38]

The 1962 Egyptian Bombing of 'Asir

The coup that ousted the monarchy from Sana'a led to an open military confrontation between Saudi Arabia and Egypt. A chaotic war followed in which Nasir backed republican forces and Saudi Arabia supported monarchists. In November 1962, Egypt broadened its involvement by conducting air strikes against several Saudi border towns in Najran, Jizan, and Abhah provinces.[39] Nasir sought to create a state of unrest in Saudi Arabia to lend credibility to widespread rumors that the monarchy was close to collapse.[40] The borders of the kingdom were never this exposed.

In this conflict, Saudi Arabia primarily sought to secure an Egyptian withdrawal from Yemen and only secondarily to restore the imam in Sana'a. Reaction to Egyptian attacks on Saudi Arabia, however, required a concerted response. First, the kingdom ordered a general mobilization and canceled army leaves. Second, it dispatched three air force squadrons to a base near the Yemeni border and moved antiaircraft guns to Najran. Finally, Riyadh asked for and received a small number of Jordanian troops to join Saudi forces on the southern border.[41] Simultaneously, it disbursed generous financial assistance to royalist forces in Yemen, thereby polarizing that country's body politic. In April 1963, a full six months after the bombings, the Al Sa'ud discussed their strategic decision, reiterated the assistance to royalist forces, and encouraged the spread of the conflict to Sana'a itself. Faysal explained his policy in the town of Muna, where he declared: "Friends, with what do we help our brothers in the Yemen? If we are helping some of them with food and with other things to enable them to preserve their lives, would that be considered as assistance? We did not send fleets, planes, and tanks to burn villages, houses, children and aged people. Nevertheless, we have offered to agree on the principle that all foreign forces in the Yemen be withdrawn."[42]

This was as forthcoming as Faysal would be at the time, but the message was clear: Yemen would not be abandoned. The heir apparent promoted the Saudi position throughout the Arab and Western worlds in the hope that the Egyptian adventure in the Yemen would end quickly. In September 1963, he met with an Arab League mission to discuss the crisis and informed it of his personal desire to avoid further clashes between Saudi and Yemeni troops. He expressed Saudi desires to cooperate fully in strengthening Arab solidarity and the restoration of normal relations among all Arab states.[43] Furthermore, diplomatic contacts were enhanced with Jordan, Lebanon, and Kuwait, all of which expressed concern over Egypt's role in the Yemen crisis. What resulted was a buildup of a regional consensus against Cairo. In October 1963, Faysal met with President John F. Kennedy in Washington, D.C. to discuss the Yemeni situation in some detail. Faysal articulated the Saudi position by stating that Yemen was no longer independent, that the Egyptian military was, in effect, in control of Yemen, and that a large-scale intervention into the kingdom was imminent. He concluded by stating the obvious, that any of these developments would severely affect American interests in the Red Sea region.[44]

It must be emphasized that the ʿAsir bombing taught the ruling family a valuable lesson in determining long-term Saudi strategic interests. With Faysal in ascent over Saʿud, the former carved the policy-making environment of the kingdom into his image. Within the political realm, Faysal geared his security interests on Islamic solidarity as a counterweight to socialist radicalism espoused by revolutionary Arabs. He encouraged the formation of the Organization of the Islamic Conference (OIC) to upstage and dilute Nasirism, and he improved ties with non-Arab Muslim states, including Iran and India.[45] Moreover, Faysal emphasized the development of an effective defense capability for the kingdom by focusing on increasing the firepower and strength of the Royal Saudi Air Force.[46]

The bold strategy proved effective. A confident Faysal met Nasir at the Arab Summit in Alexandria in September 1964, at which the two men agreed to "fully cooperate in mediation with the concerned parties, namely royalist and republican Yemenis, to reach a peaceful solution of all problems in Yemen, and to continue these efforts until conditions stabilized there."[47]

King Saʿud and Internal Challenges

Although few members of the Al Saʿud ruling family challenged Faysal on foreign policy matters, his rule was not free from turmoil, as a confrontation loomed over the horizon. If the 1958 arrangement stripped King Saʿud of most of his powers, senior members of the ruling family were both concerned and embarrassed at Saʿud's tendency to appoint his inexperienced young sons to major governmental positions, rather than older and more seasoned uncles and nephews. Many feared that such appointments signaled that Saʿud was planning to transfer succession to his offspring. Such concerns, coupled with their observations of Saʿud's lavish spending habits, increased overall dissatisfaction to the point that senior family members urged Saʿud to relinquish power to Faysal. As discussed above, on March 24, 1958 Saʿud issued a royal decree transferring executive powers to Faysal after senior princes insisted. The heir apparent turned the distressing financial situation around, although reductions in family expenditures infuriated Saʿud. Gradually, however, the monarch usurped the legally sanctioned political privileges instituted by Faysal, which, not surprisingly, limited the authority of Faysal in the role of prime minister. The monarch opposed his heir apparent's systematic appointments within the Council of Ministers, especially after Faysal gained personal control over the Ministries of Foreign Affairs, Interior, Commerce, and Finance.[48]

The very success of Faysal's efforts—to address the financial and foreign policy crises facing Saudi Arabia—created opportunities for Sa'ud to reclaim full power. For example, because strict financial restrictions were necessary to restore Saudi fiscal standing, Sa'ud relied on tribal and commercial circles (the two groups that paid dearly), promising fundamental changes. It was typical that most would support him against Faysal. The concentration of power by the heir apparent further created a faction of disgruntled younger princes who advocated constitutional reforms. Sa'ud endorsed the "free princes," not because he believed in their advocacy, but because they posed as natural allies against the power and authority of his brother. By late 1960, Sa'ud had engineered a complete reversal in concert with the free princes, as Faysal and his supporters were swept from the Council of Ministers. The monarch appointed himself prime minister and replaced several cabinet officials with some of his sons. Key supporters, including the princes Talal, 'Abdul Muhsin, and Fawwaz bin 'Abdul 'Aziz, were brought in as well.[49] Faysal and his Council of Ministers tendered their resignations.

Family politics then entered an extraordinarily complex period, with three sets of main competitors: King Sa'ud and his sons (the "little kings"), the free princes, and heir apparent Faysal and his supporters. Yet, because Sa'ud was conservative at heart, tensions quickly developed between him and Prince Talal, especially over the latter's calls for constitutional reforms.[50] The growing influence of Sa'ud's sons, as well as the division of power between members of the family and the Council of Ministers, amplified the overall anxiety. Sensing an opportunity to further weaken Prince Faysal, Sa'ud played Talal against him. In September 1961, he managed to remove the most troublesome of the free princes, including Talal, yet denied Faysal and his supporters any positions in government. By fragmenting the free princes and frustrating Faysal, Sa'ud was strengthening the power of his sons—especially Muhammad bin Sa'ud, the minister of defense who was being discussed as a possible successor.

At the height of his power, however, Sa'ud's health deteriorated, and in December 1961 he flew to the United States to receive medical care. This marked the beginning of Faysal's return to power.[51] About the same time, civil war broke out in Yemen, and Egyptian forces arrived to support revolutionary elements there against Saudi-supported royalists. Steeped in international politics, Faysal perceived the inherent advantages of the Egyptian intervention to secure and strengthen his authority. With Sa'ud indecisive, Faysal seized the crisis to assume full executive powers and, in a foresightful move, appointed a new Council of Ministers composed of loyal princes. These included confirmed supporters such as Prince Fahd (interior) and Prince Sultan (defense), but also a key new ally, Prince Khalid, as deputy prime minister. Given his critical ties to the Jiluwi branch of the family, the Khalid alliance with Faysal severely undercut Saʻud's traditional power base. In 1963, Faysal appointed ʻAbdallah bin ʻAbdul ʻAziz as commander of the National Guard (in place of Saʻud's son Saʻad), and Salman bin ʻAbdul ʻAziz as governor of Riyadh (in place of Saʻud's son Badr).[52]

By late October 1963, tensions between the two camps had escalated to a point of no return. Faysal, ever so conscious of his 1953 oath to his father, refused to go along with a palace coup that would have ended Saʻud's many "interferences" in the affairs of state. Simultaneously, he warned his loyal brothers that he would no longer lead the state without full authority. The ball was now in the court of the "Family Council," and Faysal counted on one of its leading members—Prince Khalid bin ʻAbdul ʻAziz—to untie the Gordian knot. In late October 1963, King Saʻud, supported by his son Muhammad—who was defense minister under his father's previous government and who was married to Sarah bint Faysal bin ʻAbdul ʻAziz—launched a last effort to regain sovereignty, but it was too little too late. Senior princes, led by the Sudayri Seven (then Interior Minister Fahd, Defense Minister Sultan, Deputy Interior Minister Nayif, Governor Salman of Riyadh, along with Turki, Ahmad, and ʻAbdul Rahman), and members of the religious establishment were all united in their decision to force an abdication.

Deposing King Saʻud

Armed with emergency powers, Faysal fortified his position by implementing several foreign and domestic policies (including a ten-point reform program) to meet the Yemen crisis.[53] Saʻud, however, made one last effort to recover his powers. In January 1964, he met with President Nasir of Egypt over the Yemen situation and arranged for the return of the free princes (who had earlier fled to Cairo) to Saudi Arabia to prepare yet another comeback. By doing so, however, he brought the ideological struggle that had boiled within family circles for almost half a decade to a head when he ordered that all his executive powers be restored. The foreign excursion of the king notwithstanding, a major mismanagement of the Saudi economy, coupled with the significant blunder with Egypt, essentially froze King Saʻud's effectiveness as ruler. Ill health added to the burden of the monarch, which, in time, allowed Faysal to step in at the right moment. In effect, Faysal assumed rulership as heir apparent after October 1962, even if the king could step in at a moment's notice. The drama between the two men was bound to reach an eventual climax and this occurred in early 1964.

To achieve his desperate aim, Sa'ud appealed to the *'ulamah* for a decision on March 13, 1964. In response, and literally at the end of his patience, Faysal mounted a palace coup by inviting the leading religious figures and princes to convene in Riyadh and consider a formal settlement of the persistent feud.[54] Faysal's decisive victory was sealed by a series of proclamations from the *'ulamah* and the Council of Ministers following the meeting at Prince Muhammad bin 'Abdul 'Aziz's palace on March 25. On March 26, a delegation composed of religious leaders—including Muhammad bin Ibrahim Al Shaykh, 'Abdul Malik bin Ibrahim Al Shaykh, 'Abdul 'Aziz bin Baz, and Muhammad bin Harakan—confronted King Sa'ud at his Nasiriyyah palace. Four specific demands were made: (1) attach the Royal Guard to the armed forces, (2) attach the personal guards of the monarch (the Khuwiyyah) to the Ministry of the Interior, (3) abolish the Royal Diwan, and (4) reduce royal expenses "to reasonable amounts and investment of saved funds in development projects."[55] Not surprisingly, Sa'ud rejected these demands and immediately mobilized the Royal Guard around the palace. What followed was a classic coup d'état because Defense Minister Sultan and National Guard Commander 'Abdallah had surrounded both the palace as well as the Royal Guard with their respective forces. Sa'ud was, perhaps, expecting support from his traditional tribal allies, but none was forthcoming. In the event, Faysal struck first and, in the melee that followed, had Sultan bin Sa'ud placed under house arrest. The Royal Guard yielded within twenty-four hours, declaring its allegiance to the heir apparent. Sa'ud still refused to abdicate. On November 2, 1964, the Council of Ministers, under Deputy Prime Minister Khalid bin 'Abdul 'Aziz, "asked the Kingdom's Ulama to examine the 28 October 1964 letter from the ruling family—deposing King Sa'ud and proclaiming Faysal monarch—from a canonical point of view, and to issue a suitable fatwa [religious decree]."[56] A *fatwah* confirming the latter was issued on the same day (November 2, 1964) and made public—along with the decision of the Council of Ministers as well as the first royal decree issued by King Faysal—the next day.

An Assessment of the Transfer of Power

Fully empowered to put order in the affairs of the kingdom, Faysal earned the reputation as a doer, and he enjoyed the support of family elders as well as religious leaders. Importantly, Faysal enjoyed the endorsement of Prince 'Abdallah bin 'Abdul 'Aziz and that of the Al Fahd, or as they were generally known the Sudayri Seven. A confrontation inevitably developed when Sa'ud expressed his displeasure with key changes. Some of these changes affected the monarch himself; others denied his sons certain emoluments, although few senior Al Sa'ud family members were spared the financial ax that Faysal introduced.

The Evolving Security Partnership with the United States

For a variety of reasons, seasoned historians of the Middle East, analysts, and observers have concluded that Saudi Arabia and the United States initiated their relationship not for "normal" diplomatic purposes but purely for convenience. This may well have been the rationale relied upon by both sides, but what emerged during the past several decades was nothing short of miraculous. In fact, few countries enjoyed such an in-depth security relationship, albeit lopsided in favor of the United States. The anchor of the first contacts was oil. It was important then and it has remained the single most important feature of all U.S.-Saudi contacts ever since. How the relationship germinated, developed, and reached its current shape was complicated and perplexing. Although both eerie and fascinating, most of it developed under Faysal when he was heir apparent.

Faysal and the United States

The heir apparent Faysal bin 'Abdul 'Aziz confided to the U.S. ambassador Parker T. Hart, "Since 1943, I have considered the interests of my country and community to be the same as those of the United States. We differ in nothing basic. ... After Allah we trust in America."[57]

Although Faysal eventually became a truly great monarch in many respects, he feared for the stability of the kingdom. In 1943, for example, he requested and received American assurances that the United States would object to any encirclement of Saudi Arabia, whether from Hashemites supported by the British, or any joint Arab efforts. Policy clarifications by the United States, that it would support all Arabs to choose their own governments, that "unions" would be subjected to popular agreements in accordance with the terms of the Atlantic Charter, reassured him. At the time, the language of Deputy Under Secretary of State Adolf A. Berle was well understood by the seasoned Faysal.

Still, Faysal encountered his first American "crisis" in 1945. When he stopped in Washington on his way back from the United Nations conference in San Francisco, he received assurances from Joseph C. Crew, who was then acting secretary of state, that, as far as he knew, there had been no changes in American policy toward Palestine. Faysal returned home believing that his enthusiastic reception was, in fact, meaningful. Within two years, that is after the 1947 UN partition plan for Palestine that was supported by the United States, Faysal (as well as his father) would don a permanent doubt of American intentions in the Middle East. Between 1945 and 1962, Faysal assumed his role with aplomb, negotiating whenever he could to further advance Saudi interests. To satisfy internal Saudi requirements, he stepped up to fulfill the role he was, perhaps, destined to shoulder all along.

In contrast, it may be worth recalling that Saʿud was prone to commit egregious errors. During his private visit to the United States for medical examinations in late 1961, for example, he met John F. Kennedy in a nonofficial encounter in West Palm Beach, Florida, and serious disagreements emerged. Saʿud agreed to have lunch with the newly elected president at the White House. That encounter did not go well either even though Saʿud was pleased with his own performance. Several of the his advisors took on far more assertive postures—on the Arab-Israeli conflict in particular—that, not surprisingly, did not sit well with a president who had been elected by the narrowest of margins and who was preoccupied with looming crises in Cuba and Vietnam. What mattered at this stage was the continued vital American military presence in the Kingdom of Saudi Arabia and how to best accomplish that in the absence of the Dhahran facility.[58] Whether Saʿud fully grasped what Kennedy focused on was difficult to know. In fact, for the Kennedy administration, security dominated the Saudi-American relationship, something that was not always clear in Riyadh. Shortly after this meeting, the U.S. Military Training Mission, ostensibly in place for over a decade, was fully reactivated with 250 officers dispatched to Riyadh. Washington perceived the mission as a serious undertaking and appointed an army general to command it, with a colonel in charge of its air force section.[59] Simultaneously, a navy communications unit was moved to Bahrain by mid-1962. Nevertheless, and despite these advances, Saʿud acted out of pride (by this time, he had ousted Talal bin ʿAbdul ʿAziz—by Al Saʿud standards the royal with the most impeccable Arab nationalist credentials—from his post at the Finance Ministry), and terminated the Dhahran Air Base Accord. Washington then opted to remove from the base literally everything that could be moved out, without allowing the hapless defense minister, Muhammad bin Saʿud, either to buy the equipment or order replacements in time. Clearly, the action illustrated how American pride had also been hurt, further complicating ties. Whatever trust existed between the two parties had significantly eroded, as Assistant Secretary of State Phillips Talbot told Muhammad bin Saʿud on February 13, 1962: "The Saudi Government was obtaining, free, a working airport worth $250 million."[60]

From the Saudi perspective, however, Riyadh was not receiving a base for free. It was regaining control over a facility, rightfully its own, that had served American interests for over a decade. Moreover, the Saudis, who measured—perhaps mistakenly—their relations in terms of human values (friendship, and so forth), were baffled by the bureaucratic approach favored in Washington, which measured the value of every "movable" piece of equipment. This grave American error—to know the price of everything save the value of a privileged relationship—would set a pattern that would be long remembered. Eventually, the Saudis would be able to operate the facility as the Dhahran International Airport with what was left of the equipment (and with purchases of the rest of what was needed) but, again from a Saudi perspective, the experience was educational. For years, Saudis had come to trust Americans, cooperating and assisting in the exploration and production of large quantities of oil at very favorable terms without the nickel-and-diming that the Dhahran Air Base transfer brought to the surface. Seldom had they adopted a legalistic approach, but after 1962 younger Saudis embraced similar matter-of-fact steps as increasingly difficult negotiations over oil contracts demonstrated.

What further complicated matters for Sa'ud was Kennedy's gradual efforts to win over Nasir. Sa'ud was concerned that Washington, so opposed to Nasir just a few years earlier, would now cajole him—at the expense of America's traditional Arab "friend." Simultaneously, the United States would opt to deal directly with Faysal, the heir apparent, concluding that King Sa'ud was, perhaps, no longer capable of handling Saudi-American affairs.[61]

Faysal and Kennedy

On October 5, 1962, President John F. Kennedy hosted Prince Faysal in their last face-to-face meeting before Kennedy was assassinated. While the two men liked each other and got along well—a meeting of minds in the tradition of 'Abdul 'Aziz and Franklin D. Roosevelt—Faysal was eager to take Kennedy's pulse on his contemplated action toward Arab concerns. What he sought, and received, from Kennedy was a reaffirmation of previous American commitments to Saudi Arabia, especially its territorial integrity and independence. More important, Kennedy "enlarged" his understanding of what would constitute a threat. "In response to a query" by Faysal, Kennedy stated that "the United States would consider its pledge of general support to apply to threats against Saudi Arabia *activated from without and from within*,"[62] This was, to say the least, a breakthrough that strengthened Faysal's resolve. Then and there, he promised Kennedy that he would abolish slavery, institute basic civil rights, and strive to eliminate corruption. Kennedy perceived Faysal as a man of honor, someone with whom Washington could chart a special relationship, even if sensitive subjects were not raised during their White

House tête-à-tête. In fact, Faysal was far more interested in seeking Kennedy's reactions to the September 27, 1962 coup in Yemen that toppled yet another Arab monarchy.[63] It must be underscored that Faysal was apprehensive over the Yemen, not only because of the immediate crisis that the revolution precipitated, but also because of its historical legacy. For decades, the two countries had fought bitterly, with the Saudis wresting both the Jizan and Najran provinces from the imamate. Even if the 1934 Ta'if Accord recognized the new border, and even if the British continued to occupy Aden—and thereby remained a thorn on the southern flank of the kingdom—the Al Sa'ud were troubled by successive internal Yemeni problems. Chronic poverty, the forced immigration of Yemeni Jews to Israel, the successful Soviet and Chinese foreign aid programs, and a slew of tribal disputes, all of which necessitated high-level intervention, preoccupied Faysal greatly. In short, Faysal wanted to find out what Kennedy intended to do about the Yemen, including the role of Nasir in its denouement.

The Saudi prince left the meeting with Kennedy with certain assurances, as Washington concluded that Faysal was its best chance to restore order to the kingdom and, not a negligible point, of clipping Nasir's wings. Nevertheless, from an American perspective, what was troubling was the categorical assertion made by Faysal that the kingdom would provide substantial financial and military assistance to Yemeni royalist opposition forces. That such assistance was considered by Washington to be harmless at first—as long as "internal" reforms were under way—but, consequently, extremely grave, spoke volumes. Naturally, Washington was surprised when Faysal broke diplomatic ties with Cairo and provided military assistance to royalist forces, but it gradually came to accept the Saudi perspective. In fact, in 1963, several messages from Kennedy to Faysal pledged to send American military forces to assist Saudi Arabia during the crisis, indicating an unmistakable acceptance of the initiatives advanced by Faysal.[64]

Kennedy, for his part, hoped that Egypt and Saudi Arabia would fall to his charisma, even if both Cairo and Riyadh held diametrically opposed views on basic ideological issues. By coupling this hope with specific views on the Arab-Israeli conflict, it was not too difficult to conclude that Washington, including Kennedy, would only support Faysal as long as he heeded American calls. No clash occurred between the two men before Kennedy was assassinated on November 22, 1963 in Dallas, Texas. Nevertheless, Faysal's "experiences" over the Yemen crisis, so well managed by American diplomats, were instructive. He perceived Kennedy and the U.S. government as practitioners of the realist school in that Washington recognized the vital importance of Saudi Arabia essentially for its oil resources. In short, Kennedy adopted pure Cold War policies, and Faysal observed them carefully to better protect and promote Saudi interests. Whether Kennedy trusted Nasir not to take Egypt into the Soviet bloc or whether he thought that the Egyptian adventure on the southern shores of the Arabian Peninsula would not expand into the kingdom were highly questionable.

By then, several critical agreements were signed between Cairo and Moscow, and Faysal, for one, was not about to entrust his security interests to Nasir. He may also have been optimistic that Yemeni royalist forces would wage a successful guerilla war and return to power. Faysal, effectively in charge of Saudi diplomacy as King Sa'ud was convalescing in Europe, believed that Washington would not impose a settlement based on the fait accompli. In this respect as well he was wrong because Kennedy insisted that Nasir withdraw his forces from Yemen in exchange for American recognition of the Yemen Arab Republic. Nevertheless, Kennedy was too quick to concede, pressuring the weaker Saudis at the expense of the stronger Egyptians. Remarkably, the Egyptian president played a successful bluffing game with the Kennedy administration, arguing that failure to recognize the Yemen Arab Republic would be tantamount to pushing the Yemenis into the Soviet orbit. Nasir, relying on back-channel diplomacy through his foreign policy guru, Muhammad Hassanein Haikal (the editor of the daily *Al-Ahram*), further asserted that Saudi Arabia was ripe for revolt anyway.[65] This was, of course, a tactical Egyptian error further illustrating how little Levantine Arabs knew about and understood their Gulf brethren. Unable to persuade Washington not to concede to Egypt so fast, Faysal acquiesced, but the episode taught the acerbic monarch another hard lesson: for major world powers, the Al Sa'ud were simply entrusted to protect the oil resources of the kingdom. The rest was subject to negotiations.

By early November 1962, Faysal was convinced that Washington was ready to recognize the Yemen Arab Republic, even if the U.S. ambassador in Jiddah was still "sounding him out."[66] Like King Hussein bin Talal of Jordan, who had dispatched a few planes to Ta'if to provide Yemeni royalists token assistance, Faysal was considered to be too "emotional." Both men may well have been emotional even if this was a highly subjective assessment and, more important, highly doubtful. Both Hussein and Faysal were seasoned rulers with intimate knowledge of their societies, the Arab world in particular, and international politics in general. Yet, both were militarily weak, but what they were not was cold blooded in their calculations.

The Yemen crisis brought Saudi Arabia closer to Jordan. To be sure, the gesture buried four decades of Hashemite resentment against the Al Sa'ud, as custodianship over the two holy Islamic cities was now firmly in Saudi hands. Yet, the Jordanian shift did not mean that the Hashemites or King Hussein was turning a page out of weakness. Rather, Amman rallied around Riyadh because of their commonly perceived Nasirite threat and, equally important, because of the anti-monarchical aspect of the Yemeni revolution.[67] This aspect was also of some concern to rulers throughout the Persian Gulf, even if all of them were under British suzerainty. What was even worse was the near incapacity of Britain, deliberate or not, from intervening on the royalist side. This was clearly noticed by all concerned, underscoring the slow decline of British influence and the designed rise of American power in the Middle East.[68] The contours of an emerging American empire were in their formative stages, which became obvious to alert officials. Naturally, these deliberations were not entirely pertinent to events in Yemen, as the revolution unfolded and a slew of countries, including most independent Arab states as well as the United States, extended diplomatic recognition to Sana'a. But Riyadh was equally determined to forge its own sense of "national security interests" and "sovereignty of decisions."

Indeed, Faysal was determined to strengthen his position further after being confronted with the Kennedy *fait accompli* of November 1962 that, surprisingly, spelled out a detailed (and Egyptian preapproved) plan of action. Riyadh would end its support to royalist forces, Cairo would phase out its troops from Yemen, and Washington would recognize Sana'a. To make matters worse, Faysal was made to understand that he should concern himself with Jordan more than the Yemen, as Washington viewed with suspicion—in reality, it did not approve of—the Hussein-Sa'ud alliance, even if Kennedy had written King Hussein that Washington "acted with Jordanian and Saudi interests in mind."[69] Presumably, Sa'ud was goaded by a wily Hussein to infiltrate Saudi forces with spies in order to verify their loyalty to the Al Sa'ud. At least, this was the American version; besides its comical aspect, the inference was that King Sa'ud was a buffoon who reached such a momentous decision—letting non-Saudi Arabs in the armed forces of the kingdom—without the acquiescence of Faysal, the heir apparent. What was clearly at stake, from an American perspective, was the development of intra-Arab alliances. Truth be told, these were not favored because the preference was for—and remained centered on—bilateral ties. Washington cherished its bilateral relationships with key countries and insisted on continuing on the same wavelengths.

Events on the ground in Yemen compelled the United States to take a more direct interest in its settlement formula. As Egyptian bombardments of Saudi border villages accelerated, and as Saudi military assistance to royalist Yemenis increased, Washington called on Cairo to stop its repeated violations of Saudi borders. Simultaneously, it called on Riyadh to end its provocations and, toward that end, to suspend its aid to royalist forces. When Saudi air force pilots—along with their American instructors—spotted parachuted weapons on the coast in mid-February 1963, Faysal was furious.[70] He insisted that foreign diplomats in the kingdom examine the collected evidence and judge for themselves. Machine-guns and ammunition for an estimated one thousand soldiers had been dispatched by Nasir in this one instance. Allegedly, Nasir's aim was to assist rebellious units within Saudi Arabia to organize a coup, but the attempt was averted in extremis because ringleaders had second thoughts. At the time, a very large Al Sa'ud gathering was under way in nearby Jiddah and it was likely that Nasir thought the time opportune to decapitate its leadership. Kennedy did not take up the recommendation of his own ambassador to send a few fighters and deny Egyptian incursions from Yemen. Although a token force was eventually deployed, no matter how understanding Faysal may have been, he was not pleased with the hesitancy. In fact, while Kennedy was still committed to the security of the kingdom, he was not willing to support any "royalist" interests. On the contrary, Kennedy prodded Faysal to push ahead with his internal reforms and, simultaneously, let Nasir know that the Al Sa'ud were off-limits to his own vision of Arab leadership monopoly or false grandeur. Kennedy even persuaded U Thant, the UN secretary-general, to abandon his plans for a Rome tripartite summit—grouping Faysal, Nasir, and 'Abdallah Al Sallal, the president of the Yemen Arab Republic—after his advisors realized what a paltry meeting that would be.[71] In any case, none of the heads of states were on speaking terms at the time, and the proposal was dropped. But even in this instance what was apparent was the haphazard nature of the concept and how disjointed it was from the realities of the Middle East. Personalities mattered just as much as ideas, and policies could not be imposed by fiat. In time, Kennedy realized that the Saudi-Egyptian row over Yemen could not be settled through the usual diplomacy, but required the attention of a seasoned negotiator. Ellsworth Bunker, who had experience in both the business community and the foreign service and was a successful mediator between Indonesia and the Netherlands over the West New Guinea/West Irian dispute, was chosen for the task.[72]

Accompanied by Talcott Seelye, a career foreign service officer with Middle East experience, Bunker arrived in Saudi Arabia to meet with Faysal on March 6, 1963. He reiterated how Kennedy envisioned a settlement of the conflict, which shocked the heir apparent. Ironically, the disappointment was aggravated because Washington looked the other way when Egyptian air force fighters attacked several Saudi targets in late February 1963—ironically just a few days before the meeting between Faysal and Bunker.

American conditions, whether interpreted in a strict or loose sense, were crystal clear. Faysal conceded. Although several of his aides discussed various issues with U.S. officials in the kingdom, Faysal remained optimistic that a favorable settlement would be reached, even if he was far better attuned to reading subtleties and nuances in diplomatic language. He concluded that it was no longer useful for Saudi Arabia to prolong what many perceived as Faysal's own obstinacy, even if his efforts were solely geared to promoting the long-term interests of the kingdom. Consequently, he had accepted broad conditions imposed by Kennedy, but, surprisingly, the American delegation returned with the same set of conditions in mid-March 1963. As a caveat, Bunker told Faysal that Washington was privy to insights that a "revolutionary spirit" was brewing inside the kingdom.[73] This was amateurish at best on the American side, and Faysal, ever the vigilant and astute listener, reminded his guest that he had already accepted the earlier proposal offered by Kennedy. What was new to him was Washington's observation that the Saudi government faced revolutionary elements within the kingdom. Faysal, ever the practical man, steered the conversation back to the issue at hand, namely Egyptian military attacks on Saudi Arabia, including land incursions in the south. What were, he queried, the levels of American military commitments to assist him in case of need? Could he rely on Kennedy?[74]

Bunker responded with the usual opening (almost bordering on a religious *fatihah* or preamble), namely, that the United States was committed to the territorial integrity and independence of Saudi Arabia and that Washington had strongly protested to Cairo following its most recent incursions from the Yemen. Of course, Faysal knew that he was militarily weak and that he desperately needed U.S. assistance, but it must have occurred to him that the United States was placing the burden of proof on the weak, as it insisted Riyadh end its support of royalist elements. This was really the only chip on Faysal's board and Kennedy wanted it. In other words, Faysal was faced with a truly astonishing request, namely that the most powerful leader in the world was asking for a handicap from an undermined partner.

Bunker then engaged in shuttle diplomacy between Egypt and Saudi Arabia, trying to identify vulnerable points on each side, cajole wary leaders into accepting the magic potion brewed by Washington, and settle this festering dispute on his just terms. All of this was ostensibly to deny the Soviet Union a victory where none was likely to occur. Or, conceivably, it was to see to it that the ephemeral "Arab unity" vision articulated by Nasir stayed at that chimerical level. Faysal, responding to a well-orchestrated Egyptian public relations coup—effectively undermining the Bunker-brokered peace initiative—spoke at a rare Saudi rally, which was attended by an estimated one hundred thousand people. At the public gathering, he emphasized that the main concern of the kingdom was and remained the Egyptian interference in the internal affairs of neighboring Arab countries. He called on the United Nations to implement the Bunker accord expeditiously.[75]

It is critical to note that the entire Saudi-Egyptian crisis over the Yemen was negotiated and settled with Faysal, not King Sa'ud. To be sure the latter was ill, recuperating overseas, or generally disinterested. Moreover, and as heir apparent, Faysal was essentially fully in command. Yet, it was still odd that Washington was not at ease with Faysal, despite Kennedy's positive views.

As a corollary to the Bunker mission, and perhaps to stiffen Faysal's resolve, U.S. military activity in Saudi Arabia accelerated. Port visits by U.S. naval units became more frequent and Green Beret commandos were deployed in the Dhahran area to begin counterinsurgency instruction to Saudi officers. Even Operation Hardsurface—deployments carried "titles" even in those days— the actual line up of an air squadron (eight F-100Ds with a single command-support aircraft and six KB-50 tankers), was born out of this need.[76] An estimated 850 tactical and support vehicles were required for this long-delayed mission. Needless to say, the United States wanted the squadron to be based at Dhahran, allegedly because facilities there were much better (they were) and because it would not be perceived as an intrusion at Jiddah at the height of the Hajj season (even if the deployments were modest, compared to recent figures). Faysal, ever attentive and foresightful, insisted that the squadron be deployed in western Saudi Arabia to deter Egypt.[77] This was, after all, the primary reason why the squadron was in the kingdom to begin with. If Washington meant to test long-range deployment and initiate training programs with the nascent Saudi air force, both of which Faysal supported in principle, he was vigilant nevertheless to derive political capital out of the deal. In the event, Dhahran was chosen as the primary base, with a secondary facility at Jiddah and frequent "crossings" from east to west.

Deployment was delayed from early May to early July 1963 after several hiccups threatened to sabotage the entire effort. First, there was the rabid Egyptian press, which further tightened the "progressive" noose around pro-American Saudis. Second, there were various requirements to change Saudi entry restrictions to U.S. personnel who happened to be Jewish. Finally, there was the American political step to conclude the deal.[78] Both Saudis and Americans handled negative publicity, which passed for journalism in Cairo, rather well. On-the-job training over a period of years had stiffened their backs and, truth be told, both Saudis and Americans could and did dish out as much propaganda of their own as they took in.

The issue of Jewish-American soldiers proved to be more difficult to address, but Faysal was allowed to save face by declaring that American soldiers on a mission were not subjected to normal visa regulations. As people of the book, both Jews and Christians could therefore be allowed in the kingdom, and they would come under Muslim protection. What Faysal objected to was the political aspect, namely American support of Israel and Zionism and the influence of American Jews on Middle East affairs in the United States. On this score, Faysal was humbled and had to acquiesce to U.S. demands. When Egyptian air force units attacked Abhah on June 23–24, Faysal was finally persuaded that the deployment was urgent. Washington, of course, had scored a rounding success because it had quelled Saudi support for royalist opposition forces, preserved and even enhanced its military presence in the kingdom, and demonstrated—to Faysal and others—that its political capabilities were considerable.

In the meantime, with the UN Yemen Observer Mission (UNYOM) team in place, tensions did not abate, as Egypt was determined to score its elusive political victory. It even resorted to the use of poison gas, although verification of such allegations was difficult.[79] Comically, and while serious problems existed within Washington's larger Cold War strategy, American military officials contemplated pulling the token aircraft deployed in the kingdom within two months. Meanwhile, a few thousand Egyptian troops had pulled out of the Yemen, even though Saudi non-assistance to royalist forces was mostly enforced. There were a few instances when aid continued to cross the border, but this was largely through private smuggling and quantities were rather small.[80] Even Egyptian payments for UNYOM expenditures—equally divided between Cairo and Riyadh—were either suspended or frozen. At a loss as to what to do next, the United States asked Faysal how détente could be achieved. Prince Faysal was formal: détente would be achieved when Nasir got out of the Yemen.[81] Kennedy called on Faysal's sense of honor not to jeopardize American prestige—how could Washington break relations with the Yemen Arab Republic after establishing them a few months earlier? Once again, it was up to the emasculated party to provide a handicap to the powerful one. For several months, American promises to "persuade" Nasir to pull the bulk of his forces from Yemen produced little. Faysal, a patient man by habit, was losing what patience he had left even though he was fully aware that he and Saudi Arabia had no alternative options. Turning to the British or the French—both of which supported the UNYOM action and recommended a settlement brokered by the UN—was not possible as neither was still fully awakened to its potential in the kingdom. Likewise, Kennedy may have also placed a good deal of pressure on Nasir (although Kennedy's tragic death altered the tone of U.S.-Egyptian discussions), but Washington was fully aware of the substantial drain that the Yemen adventure was causing Cairo. Such preoccupations certainly prevented, or severely limited, putative Egyptian preparations on the Arab-Israeli arena.[82]

Once in office, President Lyndon B. Johnson reaffirmed American support for Faysal and for Saudi Arabia in the usual strong terms that the Al Saʿud were "privileged" to hear. By January 1964, the token F-100Ds of the U.S. Air Force had been withdrawn, although the now regularly funded UNYOM continued to monitor deployments, rotations, and other belligerent activities, mostly Egyptian and some Saudi. Nasir finally broke the ice and invited all Arab heads of states to attend a League of Arab States meeting in January 1964, at which he reached a political understanding with King Saʿud and Prince Faysal. The latter still thought that the United States should deny Nasir economic assistance, assuming he wanted to get Egypt moving on the pace of stability, so that Egypt would be forced to leave Yemen. Washington, naturally driven by specific Cold War strategies, did not contemplate such drastic measures. Once again, Faysal was made to cave in, which further disappointed him. Having exhausted his energies, and being exhausted by endless American diplomatic vagaries, and this is worth repeating, he confided to Ambassador Parker T. Hart in September 1963: "Since 1943, I have considered the interests of my country and community to be the same as those of the United States. We differ in nothing basic. . . . After Allah we trust in America."[83]

President Lyndon B. Johnson of the United States welcomed the accession of Prince Faysal to rulership on November 2, 1964 in a congratulatory telegram that was broadcast on Makkah Radio. Faysal enjoyed American support and considered it vital that all Saudis—as well as all Arabs—knew it. Even if his accession to rulership was an internal Saudi affair, Washington was pleased with the result because Faysal enjoyed its full support. The new monarch needed the United States and he knew it well. What he failed to appreciate fully, however, was that the United States needed him just as much. Washington was confident that Faysal truly grasped full control over the kingdom and protected its vast oil resources. Moreover, it supported the kingdom to "bleed" Nasir's Egypt in Yemen for as long as possible and, more important, to weaken him further on the larger Arab scene.

Figure 1. Prince Faysal in full *badu* garb in the United Kingdom during his 1919 visit, when he was twelve years old.

Figure 2. Faysal at fourteen years of age, in 1921.

Figure 3. Faysal *(center)* at the Moscow train station during his 1932 visit to the Soviet Union.

Figure 4. Faysal at the Moscow train station in 1932 with Nikolai Krestinsky, the first deputy foreign minister of the Soviet Union.

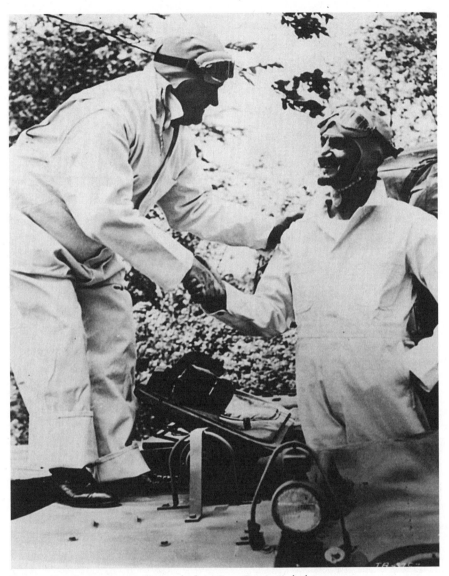

Figure 5. Faysal inspecting a military vehicle in Great Britain in the late 1930s.

Figure 6. Faysal following his father, King ʿAbdul ʿAziz (*front, center*), and ARAMCO officials at the Raʾs al-Tanurah oil facility in 1938.

Figure 7. King ʿAbdul ʿAziz *(center, seated)* at the inauguration of the Raʾs al-Tanurah oil facility in 1938. Faysal is standing behind the ruler, leafing through a brochure.

Figure 8. Faysal *(seated)*, as head of the Saudi delegation to the San Francisco inaugural conference, signing the charter establishing the United Nations in 1945.

Figure 9. Faysal as the heir apparent (ca. 1953).

Figure 10. Faysal *(right)* and his brother King Saʿud (ca. 1960).

Figure 11. Faysal *(front, right)* with his uncle Prince Musaʿid bin ʿAbdul Rahman *(holding glasses)* during Hajj ceremonies. Princes Fahd and ʿAbdallah are immediately behind them (ca. 1960).

Figure 12. King Faysal *(center)* participating in a traditional Saudi festival. Princes Khalid and Fahd are behind him (ca. 1964).

Figure 13. King Faysal *(front)* and his brothers Fahd, Khalid, and ʿAbdallah *(left to right)*, all future kings of Saudi Arabia (ca. 1965).

Figure 14. King Faysal *(center)* praying at the Al-Aqsah Mosque in Jerusalem in 1966. King Hussein bin Talal of Jordan is on the far right.

Figure 15. Muhammad Reza Pahlavi, shah of Iran, and King Faysal in 1965.

Figure 16. *Seated, left to right:* King Faysal and President Gamal 'Abdul Nasir of Egypt, accepting presents from children in Cairo, and Prince Sultan bin 'Abdul 'Aziz (ca. 1968).

Figure 17. *Left to right:* King Faysal, President Hafez al-Asad of Syria, and Prince Fahd bin 'Abdul 'Aziz in Damascus (ca. 1968).

Figure 18. King Faysal and President Habib Bourguiba of Tunisia during Faysal's 1969 visit to North Africa.

Figure 19. King Faysal with President Léopold Sédar Senghor of Senegal during Faysal's visit to Dakar in 1969.

Figure 20. King Faysal with U Thant, United Nations secretary general, in New York in 1966.

Figure 21. King Faysal with President Lyndon B. Johnson in Washington, D.C., in 1966.

Figure 22. King Faysal and President Charles de Gaulle in Paris during Faysal's 1967 state visit to France.

Figure 23. King Faysal with Queen Elizabeth II during Faysal's 1967 state visit to the United Kingdom.

Figure 24. King Faysal with Emperor Hirohito of Japan *(far right)* during Faysal's official visit to the Chrysanthemum Throne in 1971.

Figure 25. King Faysal with President Richard M. Nixon at the White House in Washington, D.C., in 1971.

Figure 26. King Faysal listening to President Richard M. Nixon in Jiddah during Nixon's visit to the kingdom in 1974. Standing behind them are Secretary of State Henry Kissinger and Prince Fahd bin ʿAbdul ʿAziz.

Figure 27. Secretary of State Henry Kissinger and King Faysal in Saudi Arabia in the aftermath of the 1974 oil embargo.

4

King Faysal (1964–1975)

If the Yemen crisis precipitated fundamental changes in intra-Arab affairs, it probably further accelerated King Saʿud's abdication and hastened the accession of Prince Faysal to rulership. Almost three years after the start of hostilities—which Nasir did not foresee lasting more than a few weeks—a League of Arab States summit meeting in January 1964 generated unusually positive comments on Saʿud, enveloping the latter in a deceptive sense of grandeur. Indeed, ʿAbdallah Sallal, the revolutionary president of Yemen, showered Saʿud bin ʿAbdul ʿAziz with false praise. Emboldened by this newly found reputation as a genuine reformer, Saʿud attempted a quick return to full power, even if he had little or no intention to introduce sorely needed changes to his country.

Throughout the first few months of 1964, however, senior Al Saʿud princes objected to the monarch's stratagems. Most perceived Saʿud as an obstacle to reforms, "which had become imperative if they were to survive" as a ruling elite.[1] Naturally, Prince Faysal was aware of these objections, but on several occasions he rejected family pleas to depose the king. As late as October 29, 1964, in other words, only a few days before Saʿud actually abdicated, Faysal asked the ʿulamah to first settle their differences with the ruling sovereign before proclaiming the heir as their new monarch. When pressed to acquiesce to demands that he accede to the throne, Faysal rejoined: "In the house of ʿAbdul ʿAziz we do not depose the King except after all attempts at persuasion have failed. Have you exhausted all means of persuasion?" Moved by his interrogation, "members of the delegation replied: 'Truly, you are King.'"[2] Al Saʿud emissaries, composed of senior princes and leading ʿulamah, then dedicated several days to finally convince Saʿud to concede, but it was Faysal who, on October 31, 1964, confronted his sovereign in a final political encounter that determined the fate of the kingdom.[3] Little of what transpired between the two men ever surfaced, although Faysal assured Saʿud of his good will toward him, as illustrated by how well Saʿud was cared for after he left the country. Faysal insisted that a violent coup d'état was out of the question and that he would not orchestrate such action. Nevertheless, he called on his brother to respect, as he promised to do likewise, decisions reached by the Council of Princes. Speaking to the Lebanese journalist Salim Labaki a few days after his accession, Faysal acknowledged that he "sought to bring [Saʿud's abdication] about" ... although his "efforts were in vain."[4] In the event, senior Al Saʿud princes withdrew their *bay ʿah* from Saʿud on November 2, 1964, and pledged themselves to Faysal. On the same day, the *ʿulamah* issued a religious decree proclaiming Faysal monarch, as well as a letter signed by leading Al Saʿud family members vowing themselves to Faysal. Over the next two days, tribal delegations poured into Riyadh to affix their legitimizing vows, a procedure that buttressed the new king. The deed was completed when National Guard commanders committed their oaths on November 4, 1964.

Faysal was fifty-eight years old when he became monarch. Although he saw light in an established ruling family, and was the son of a major political figure who earned fame and title, Faysal was not born a king. He became one because he trusted in God, applied sheer determination to all his tasks, exercised immense patience, lived fully content, and adopted a genuine self-denial style.[5] His apprenticeship lasted forty-five years, and while his reign would only stretch over ten years, his legacy would be felt for decades.

When he became king, Faysal was probably the most experienced living Arab leader, having interacted with world leaders on matters great and small. He was a head of state, yet his views of monarchy were reminiscent of just princes who ruled Arabian lands in earlier times. Responding to a question concerning the evolution of monarchical regimes, Faysal emphasized that "the important thing about a regime is not what it is called but how it acts." He did see an impediment to tackling gargantuan problems because he was an absolute ruler, but he believed that "there are corrupt republican regimes and sound monarchies and vice versa." He declared that "the only true criterion of a regime—whether it be monarchical or republican—is the degree of reciprocity between ruler and ruled and the extent to which it subsidizes prosperity, progress and healthy initiative."[6] This was the mind-set of a leader who tackled numerous internal, regional, and international tasks with aplomb and poise. Not surprisingly, his first obligation was to restore order to the ruling Al Saʿud family, which was seriously weakened after prolonged internecine confrontations.

Remaking the Ruling Family

Under King Faysal bin ʿAbdul ʿAziz, Al Saʿud family politics developed in a fundamentally different way, though the transformation was gradual and not without setbacks. Altogether, Faysal's rule was marked by increased centralization of power, greater internal stability, and clearer policy direction, all of which were in sharp contrast to the 1953–64 period. These developments had a direct bearing on the distribution of power within the family as well as on key foreign policy planks that altered the image of the kingdom more or less permanently.

As discussed earlier, the division of power between the ruling family and the Council of Ministers under King Saʿud proved to be a source of dispute, with the position of prime minister shifting back and forth between the king and his heir apparent, and with the powers of the deputy prime minister remaining undefined until 1962. By contrast, King Faysal combined the powers of his throne with formal control over the Council of Ministers for the entire period of his reign.[7] Although this fusion of power enhanced his intrinsic capabilities, it also stalled the strengthening of the cabinet to balance the immense prerogatives of the king. This was particularly the case since the deputy prime minister, Prince Khalid, was not active in daily affairs, serving instead as Faysal's representative during his absences.

Resolution of the succession issue, like the division of power between the Al Saʿud and the Council of Ministers, also remained unresolved during Saʿud kingship. Indeed, Saʿud's numerous attempts to promote his own sons to succeed him were a significant political issue in the struggle between the two eldest sons of the founder. Still, under Faysal, the basis for a smooth succession—from brother to brother—was gradually established. Whether the discerning Faysal had any aspirations for his own progeny was difficult to verify. At the same time, the formation of an alliance with the princes Muhammad, Khalid, Fahd, and ʿAbdallah—officials with close ties to influential tribal groups—indicated that Faysal preferred family consensus over expediency. Given that his calculated maneuvers ended the reign of his predecessor, a different succession formula would have, at the very least, appeared in the eyes of all Al Saʿud princes as being disingenuous. To cement his alliance, Khalid was appointed deputy prime minister in 1962, a position that implied priority in the line of succession. Even if Khalid was not officially decreed heir apparent until 1965, the delay probably reflected a desire to consolidate various positions and to avoid provoking family rivalries at a time when Saudi Arabia was beset by internal and external threats stemming from the civil war in neighboring Yemen.[8]

In addition to Khalid, Faysal relied on several other supporters, including Prince Fahd, who sided with Faysal from the very beginning of the family dispute.[9] In October 1967, Fahd was appointed second deputy prime minister in addition to holding the interior ministry portfolio, which he had held since 1962. Much like the earlier designation of Khalid in the same post, the new position of Prince Fahd implied priority in the line of succession after the designated heir apparent. Therefore, Faysal, like his father, attempted to establish a line of succession for the next two kings, and in this respect he accomplished his objectives.

In addition to temporarily resolving the succession issue, Faysal carefully distributed several key positions to his closest allies and, in the process, ensured a modicum of internal stability within the family. The Council of Ministers that was first appointed in 1962, which had included Prince Fahd (interior) and Prince Sultan (defense), and Ahmad Zaki Yamani (a trusted commoner who would run the petroleum ministry for over two decades), remained virtually unchanged. Other important positions, such as commander of the National Guard (Prince 'Abdallah) and governor of Riyadh (Prince Salman), were also mobilized.

Ironically, the long tenure of these princes in such visible posts would become a critical factor in the pattern of family politics after Faysal's death, as each developed his own office into a personal power base. Sophisticated patron-client networks were created and inevitable nepotism ensued.[10] For example, Prince Sultan's younger full brother, Prince Turki, was appointed deputy defense minister in July 1969, and another full brother, Prince Nayif, was made deputy interior minister in June 1970. To be sure, the political supporters of King Faysal were not the only ones benefiting from such appointments and, in truth, the kingdom desperately needed qualified senior Al Sa'ud family members in positions of authority. Even some of the "free princes" were incorporated into the new family equation. These included Badr (deputy commander of the National Guard, 1965), 'Abdul Muhsin (governor of Madinah, 1965), Nawwaf (adviser to the king, 1968), and Fawwaz (governor of Makkah, 1971). To some extent, these appointments served to conciliate political discontents, but they also balanced other princely factions, especially since the majority were deeply indebted to King Faysal.[11]

Still, neither Talal bin 'Abdul 'Aziz nor any of King Sa'ud's sons were rehabilitated by Faysal. Indeed, several of Sa'ud's sons, including Khalid, Mansur, Badr, and Sultan, joined their father in exile and supported his efforts to regain the throne.[12] The deposed monarch was most active from 1964 to 1967, when President Gamal 'Abdul Nasir gave him refuge in Egypt and even allowed him propaganda time on Radio Cairo.[13] After the June 1967 Arab-Israeli War, however, King Sa'ud lost Egyptian support, finally settling in Greece, where he died in 1969.[14]

A final significant political development during Faysal's reign was the introduction of several previously uninitiated princes into politics. These included some of the founding ruler's younger sons, such as Sattam (deputy governor of Riyadh, 1968) and Ahmad (deputy governor of Makkah, 1971). In addition, a number of the founder's grandsons were entrusted with their first assignments, including sons of Faysal, Fahd, 'Abdallah, and Sultan.

Because of his political preeminence and the overall success of many of his policies, Faysal faced little or no serious opposition from within the family, especially after the initial purges distanced many of his foes.[15] Still, Faysal's rule was distinguished by several trends on this critical matter.

First, the monarch established a secure line of lateral succession, as a strong presence muted whatever tensions existed among the diverse group of princes serving under him. Although rumors of opposition abounded, particularly in the early years, Faysal ruled with justice.[16] Moreover, preparations for succession after Faysal were in the works for several years, and as early as 1972 it was clear that Khalid would become king, while his younger half brother, Fahd, would follow. Hours after the death of King Faysal, a group of senior princes met in Riyadh and proclaimed Khalid ruler. The official announcement identified the family "leaders" as 'Abdallah bin 'Abdul Rahman ('Abdul 'Aziz's eldest surviving brother) and the princes Muhammad, Nasir, Sa'ad, and Fahd ('Abdul 'Aziz's oldest sons in order of age). Immediately following his ascension, Khalid nominated Fahd as his heir apparent; and two older half brothers, Nasir and Sa'ad, who were passed over in the line of succession, formally renounced their claims to the throne.

Second, collective leadership ended even if multiple power centers existed. Compared with Sa'ud's rule, the pattern of family politics was sharply different under Faysal, and the connection between politics and policy became blurred. Under Sa'ud, the inherent dilemmas facing Saudi Arabia in domestic and foreign policy issues were polarized as the power struggle escalated. Consequently, Saudi behavior was often erratic and contradictory. Under Faysal, in contrast, these same dilemmas were balanced under his central control.[17] Economic development, for example, had received scant attention throughout the 1950s, whereas Faysal adopted long-range development plans. If promises of political reforms had been inflammatory in the 1950s and early 1960s, under Faysal they were carefully handled after the mid-1960s. Similarly, in foreign policy, the inconsistency of Sa'ud's reign was replaced with a strategy that effectively combined the Arab and American connections of Saudi Arabia.[18] In the later years of his reign, Faysal's many successes in both the domestic and foreign policy arenas greatly strengthened his political influence in family affairs. Without a doubt, the overshadowing presence of Faysal helped to smooth the transition when, on March 25, 1975, the monarch was assassinated by a "deranged" nephew, Faysal bin Musa'id bin 'Abdul 'Aziz.[19]

Third, technocrats emerged within the Al Sa'ud ruling family. As grandsons and great-grandsons of the founder reached political maturity, Faysal harnessed their talent. The advent of King Faysal's own sons, followed by the progeny of the Al Fahd, meant that new alliances could be established. Naturally, this exponential increase of talented and ambitious young princes also meant that rivalries would emerge, fueled by powerful fathers who positioned their offspring as needed. This was not just nepotism but a case in which genuinely talented individuals would be recruited to reinforce existing or emerging alliances.[20] In fact, Faysal encouraged such promotions to better serve both crown and country, as several royals were encouraged to assume additional official responsibilities covering the entire gamut from civilian to military posts.[21] It would be facile to conclude that Faysal approached key family issues from narrow perspectives to favor one group of leaders over others, but, in fact, his appointments and promotions illustrated how careful his methodology was and how attuned he remained to existing factions. That he managed senior appointments with distinction certainly set a precedent for his successors, who, invariably, drew succor from the acute sense of justice displayed by their brother. Still, how Faysal managed family affairs was as critical as the personalities he supervised, for his primary task was to remake the Kingdom of Saudi Arabia after years of neglect.

Remaking Saudi Arabia

Faysal transformed the kingdom from a patriarchal backwater into a modern country as an estimated eight million Saudis were catapulted into the twentieth century. Mass education systems, advanced communication facilities, including radio and television, and air, sea, and land transportation networks were all erected to serve an increasingly enthusiastic population eager for more. Slowly but surely, the monarch demoted feudal lords and promoted educated leaders (both royals and commoners) with degrees from European or American universities. He rapidly upgraded various ministries and technical departments to better serve crown and country. In fact, internal reforms—starting with the armed forces—were so extensive that few recognized the nation by the end of his reign. The kingdom was remade into his image, proud of its many accomplishments but humbled to serve God.

Overhauling the Armed Forces

Under King Faysal, the Al Sa'ud family refined and articulated two major security goals. First, to maintain custodianship over the holy cites of Makkah and Madinah because that was the ultimate source of legitimacy (*raison d'état*). Second, to preserve the ruling family's custodianship role over holy sites because that was the family's *raison d'être*. Both, it was carefully posited by the ruler, ensured justice.

Historically, the Al Sa'ud united whenever faced with threats. Differences were quickly resolved through negotiations, side agreements, and concessions, as appropriate. Above all, succession crises, which intruded on internal stability, were settled without jeopardizing existing accords. As discussed above, during each succession crisis, the Al Sa'ud chose the designated heir apparent as ruler. Yet, because succession was subject to a consensus decision, disagreements over a successor endangered existing alliances. Therefore, the Al Sa'ud diligently strove to ensure that the succession issue never escalated into an open struggle for power that would weaken the monarchy and lead to its collapse. Above all else, the Al Sa'ud were acutely aware that support for a particular monarch was very much a personal pledge (*bay'ah*) rather than an institutional commitment. Faysal set out to upgrade this phenomenon by ushering in loyal military leaders who blended the personal with the institutional.[22]

Once the succession issue was satisfactorily resolved, Faysal quickly turned his attention to key security institutions, enhancing the capabilities of the armed forces. To meet potential threats, Saudi Arabia built a series of military cities—Tabuk and Khamis-Mushayt in the first instance, which were later supplemented by massive facilities at King Khalid Military City—in the most sensitive parts of the country.[23] More important than facilities, Faysal devoted attention to military leaders, starting with top commanders. Although the king was commander in chief of the armed forces, the minister of defense and aviation was given operational control over the military. It was decided that the army, air force, and navy would primarily recruit from the settled and urban populations to ensure external security. In contrast, Faysal decreed that the National Guard, under the personal control of the ruler, would only recruit from among loyal tribes. At first, the guard's mission was to defend the monarch and senior members of the family, but as critical oil fields came on line, the guard was also entrusted with such defense duties as these facilities necessitated. Inevitably, because of clearly defined missions, rivalries over security perceptions emerged among senior leaders, who yielded to Faysal when substantive differences emerged.[24]

Given its family-oriented decision-making style, little was actually known about how Saudi officials devised and implemented their security policies under

King Faysal. Nevertheless, because Saudi Arabia occupied an increasingly critical role—both as a political stabilizer as well as the world's leading producer and exporter of crude oil—its intrinsic capabilities were almost always under strain. As the former secretary of state, Henry Kissinger, opined: "The Kingdom has to navigate among certain fixed poles: a deeply felt friendship for the United States, a profound sense of Arab loyalty; a consciousness of internal and external danger. It is not Saudi Arabia's fault that the requirements of these goals occasionally clash. In this sense the ambiguity of Saudi policy is imposed by events, not by preference."[25]

This assessment notwithstanding, and despite magisterial efforts to insulate itself from direct challenges, Saudi Arabia remained vulnerable to external threats. Not only did Riyadh lack the ability to respond to potential attacks from Egypt and Yemen, it also was vulnerable to possible internal uprisings. These threats remained a problem and the adversaries of Saudi Arabia were periodically implicated in conducting subversive activities within the armed forces (see below). Consequently, the Al Saʿud sought extra-regional, preferably non-Arab, forces to guarantee their security. More specifically, Riyadh looked to the United States for military protection, especially under King Faysal.[26] Given this penchant, it is imperative to assess how the monarch perceived and transformed the military, and how key members of the family perceived the emerging institutions' security roles.

Factionalism and Stability in the Armed Forces

Throughout modern Saudi history, the ruling family faced some discontent within the armed forces, which was linked to both internal and external causes. Although soldiers sought extended benefits as the armed forces developed, many officers were exposed to Arab nationalist ideologies that clashed with the Unitarian (Wahhabi) character of the kingdom. Over the years, but especially under Faysal's rule, young, discontented nationalist military personnel represented the most serious opposition in the kingdom as they sought to emulate military uprisings in neighboring countries. How Faysal addressed their concerns was nothing short of prodigious.

Uprisings in the 1950s

All regular Saudi military services were at their embryonic stages in the early 1950s when loyal Ikhwan troops were slowly modernized. To be sure, the nascent organizations lacked institutional prestige and, if for no other reason than to ensure internal stability, were carefully counterbalanced by established National

Guard companies.[27] In 1954, King Saʿud's hasty decision to invite an Egyptian military mission to replace American advisors intensified the threat of a coup.[28] Ironically, so-called Free Officers mounted a failed coup a few months later, as an anti-American movement emerged within the armed forces. By the spring of 1955, however, several ringleaders were arrested, tried, and executed. During the trials, it became apparent that numerous military commanders planned to oust the king and replace the monarchy with a republican government. This was not the only movement that emerged that concerned Prince Faysal, the heir apparent. Riyadh dispatched air force planes to subdue rebellions as Faysal—the faithful custodian of religious freedoms throughout Saudi history—was particularly offended by tribal shenanigans that purported to gain ground by threatening the regime.

To be sure, tribal disputes were not new, nor were rivalries within the ruling family. Still, the latter accelerated the emergence of competing factions within the armed forces, which, at least technically, were supposed to avoid such patterns. Nevertheless, the death of King ʿAbdul ʿAziz in 1953, coupled with increasing foreign threats to the Al Saʿud—principally from Egypt and Yemen—caused King Saʿud to build up the armed forces to protect his personal power from rival princes.[29] The 1954 coup attempt created something of a "double handicap" as military commanders became suspects, giving rise to suspicions and intrigue. Saudi nationalists in the armed forces, however, survived the purges that followed and managed to organize fresh anti-monarchical activities over the course of the next few years. Consequently, many officers, as well as some enlisted men, were arrested in 1962 for sedition and were investigated by interior ministry personnel. In response, Faysal appointed Prince Sultan minister of defense and relied on him as a principal military advisor.[30]

Royal Saudi Air Force Defections (1962)

Between 1958 and 1962, the establishment of the United Arab Republic persuaded many more Saudi officers and noncommissioned officers to join the "Free Officers" movement. When protests occurred in sympathy with Nasir among the military, Faysal introduced various incentives to win disgruntled officers back. Surprisingly, the Saudi military appeared to be more loyal to Nasir than to the kingdom, a phenomenon that did not escape an increasingly wary heir apparent. Between October 2–8, 1962, four Saudi aircraft crews defected to Egypt, carrying arms for rebel forces fighting on the Yemen front.[31] Faysal, seconded by Prince Fahd and Prince Sultan bin ʿAbdul ʿAziz, managed to persuade King Saʿud to ground the entire Royal Saudi Air Force, while Riyadh asked Washington to patrol Saudi airspace.[32] A repeat of these events occurred a month later although under more dangerous circumstances. In November 1962, palace guards discovered a conspiracy against the Saudi monarchy that involved "seven Saudi air force pilots, [all] minor members of the royal family," who apparently planned a coup d'état. Before the conspirators could be arrested, however, the pilots defected to Egypt. Once again, Saʿud quickly grounded the air force and ordered storage batteries from royal guard tanks removed.[33] No matter how generous the Al Saʿud were to senior officers, Faysal discovered that Saudi Arabia was not immune to upheavals elsewhere in the Arab world. These episodes clearly demonstrated that internal stability was linked to regional balance, which, in turn, required nuance and imagination with friends and foes alike.

Coup Plots (1969–1975)

As tensions grew throughout the region, conservative regimes in Libya, Sudan, and Somalia were overthrown by military officers. Without a doubt, Saudi Arabia was affected by these political changes, as Faysal carefully nurtured his regional foreign policies. In June and July 1969, military supporters of the Popular Democratic Front, the National Front for the Liberation of Saudi Arabia, and the Federation of Democratic Forces in the kingdom were all implicated in a new coup attempt.[34] This time, the plotters included dozens of air force officers and the director of the air force academy in Dhahran. Their plan called for an attack on the king and senior princes by bombing key royal palaces before proclaiming their contemplated "Republic of the Arabian Peninsula." A thorough investigation revealed that several former and active garrison leaders were involved and, consequently, hundreds of officers were arrested in the wake of this latest coup plot. Once again, the air force was grounded for over a month, and when flying resumed none of the aircraft were armed as munitions had been removed from all flying vehicles on orders of the king.[35]

Empowering Military Officers

To be sure, Faysal and Sultan were amply aware of the consequences that such matters raised in the country, having learned the lessons of the 1962 defections. To address this latest rebellion, Riyadh initiated an intensive program to refurbish its intelligence services and devoted special attention to the National Guard.[36] It also started to screen foreigners wishing to enter Saudi Arabia and encouraged the replacement of Arab expatriates with non-Arab Asians wherever possible. Significantly, the ʿulamah supported all Al Saʿud decisions, primarily goaded by Faysal to understand his specific reform initiatives.[37] Not surprisingly, the 1969 coup attempt ignited a serious debate within the ruling family over the very future of the armed forces as semi-independent institutions with increasing power. A vocal faction led by conservative elements opposed further modernization programs. Prince 'Abdallah bin 'Abdul 'Aziz championed the cause of the National Guard rather than the regular armed forces because of the proven loyalties of the latter. Faysal, along with Sultan and Fahd, in contrast, concluded that the coup attempts did not justify a total halt to the modernization and expansion of the armed forces. Faysal correctly perceived that Arab nationalist rhetoric was the primary incentive that spurred many of these officers to act the way they did. His preference was to professionalize the military, gradually empowering it and thus earning the loyalty of its members. The monarch reasoned that the kingdom required an effective military that would only emerge over time, and, toward that end, it behooved the Al Sa'ud to stand behind their own creations. His arguments gained momentum after the 1967 Arab-Israeli War, and especially after London announced its decision to withdraw from the Persian Gulf. Saudi military leaders, ably coached by Faysal, became amply conscious of the security vacuum that was about to be created in their own neighborhood.[38] The 1973 October War further galvanized Saudi forces, but the ensuing stalemate on the battlefields rekindled military modernization efforts throughout the region, especially in Saudi Arabia. Faysal was aware of the need to equip the kingdom with modern assets, and he instructed Sultan to embark on a steady buildup. As the military modernized, few dissenters within the armed forces could legitimately claim negligence given that the country was creating more effective and enduring capabilities. Moreover, and while the Saudi armed forces were not immune to future upheavals, the decision by Faysal to empower senior officers was largely beneficial for the kingdom. By the mid-1970s, non-royal officers were rising through the ranks as the armed forces gained in professionalism. A new breed of citizen-soldiers emerged that supplemented traditional tribal levies earmarked for the National Guard. The institutional memory of the country took another leap forward as Faysal slowly catapulted Saudi Arabia from its tribal environment. His was a modernizing legacy for the armed forces that served the kingdom well for the balance of the twentieth century.[39]

Constructing a Nation

Amply aware of internal needs, and as Saudi Arabia entered the modern era, Faysal devoted attention to his cabinet and boosted key ministries, starting on the weakest front—agriculture. Given the various necessities of the nascent country, the choice appeared wanting, although the monarch signaled how critical it was for Riyadh to gain control over its food production. Consequently, the budget of the ministry increased from 213 million riyals in 1960 to 382 million in 1970, a significant jump over a ten-year period. By 1975, agriculture was engaging about 40 percent of the population, and while it provided about 8.5 percent of real GDP, the kingdom was able to produce about half of its food requirements.[40] With a population standing around 8 million souls, Saudi Arabia was keenly aware of the need for water and agricultural goods. When French engineers discovered the large aquifer under Riyadh in 1957, Faysal quickly devoted a great deal of attention to this sector, aware of the enormous costs involved but determined to assume any burden that would translate into victory over severe living conditions. Simply stated, food production independence and adequate water sources were a national security matter, and Riyadh welcomed desert agriculturalists specializing in adapting their crops to severe climates. Irrigation canals, vast reclamation zones, piped water systems, and various other methods were employed to produce wheat, barley, lettuce, tomatoes, and other essential products. An estimated 3 million acres of land were primed for agricultural production between 1970 and 1975 alone to serve the basic requirements of the kingdom. In a country with an established nomadic tradition sedentary agriculture was new, but Faysal persisted. His gargantuan efforts paid off as Saudi Arabia ushered in long-term, even if very costly, designs to build farms and expand indigenous production facilities.

Goods produced at great cost on distant farms could not possibly reach consumers without a proper infrastructure that permitted their efficient distribution. Toward that end, highways and roads linked major cities with smaller boroughs. In fact, the infrastructure erected in Saudi Arabia was initiated before the 1974 oil boom and was unprecedented in the Middle East. Harbors and airports were on drawing boards in the late 1960s, and while most of the construction was completed after 1975, the authorizations to allocate necessary funds were almost entirely approved by Faysal.[41] By 1975, the kingdom boasted twenty-three airports, including two with international links, as well as an airline equipped with modern aircraft. Likewise, for a country that lacked a single telephone at the dawn of the twentieth century, Saudi Arabia fielded over one hundred thousand lines in 1975, despite strong religious injunctions that objected to its introduction. It took all of Faysal's imagination to persuade the 'ulamah that the invention was not the work of the devil to gain final approval before telephone lines could be laid. Millions of dollars were thus allocated to various communications projects before 1974 when revenues were certainly limited for a government under pressure to produce miracles over the shortest time possible.

It must be emphasized that for the monarch, modernization was not limited to gadgets that Saudis acquired or the ease with which they moved about. Rather, what Faysal considered the worthiest investments were those associated with education. Given the dearth of qualified Saudis to assume nation-building burdens, Riyadh dramatically increased the number of primary and secondary schools. In 1952, the kingdom counted 316 primary and secondary schools, but by 1973 there were 6,595 such institutions. Whereas 39,920 pupils attended school in 1952, 707,318 attended in 1973. To accommodate these students, 1,605 teachers throughout the country saw their rank expand to 15,232, even if most were expatriate workers from other Arab countries. Over a twenty-year period, this growth topped the 15,000 percent rate, a unique statistic in contemporary education annals. Several universities, including King Sa'ud in Riyadh, King Faisal in Hofuf (near Dhahran), King 'Abdul 'Aziz in Jiddah, and the prestigious University of Petroleum and Minerals established in 1963—and now known as the King Fahd University of Petroleum and Minerals—assembled an initial higher-education system second to none in the Middle East.[42] Naturally, education was free, and it gradually became compulsory for boys. Queen 'Iffat Al Thunayan, the sophisticated spouse of the monarch, encouraged education for girls as well, and toward that end she devised the establishment of specialized schools although more conservative Saudis frowned on the idea of sending their daughters for such instruction. It took the queen and king a good deal of effort—by setting the example of enrolling their own daughters—to create a worthy model for others to emulate. Over time, however, the archetype found a steady audience among all Saudis.[43]

Progress was also made in the health services. From 1960 to 1973, the number of hospitals and clinics jumped from 40 (3,668 beds) to 197 (10,156 beds). With only 280 physicians in 1960, the kingdom could provide a minimum level of care, but by 1973, 1,260 physicians—most of whom were Saudi citizens—welled the ranks. A similar level of growth was registered for nurses, as their numbers increased from 757 to 2,800. Although most of the nurses were expatriate workers from Arab and non-Arab countries, these initial groups laid out the foundations for the emergence of health-care professionals from among the indigenous population. Over a decade, the ministry of health budget went from 58 million riyals to 168 million (in 1970), a growth rate of 188 percent.[44] It is worth underlining that these expenditures preceded the 1974 oil boom, which, as discussed below, catapulted the overall financial position of the kingdom into heretofore unrecorded levels in Arab history.

Inasmuch as Faysal's vision for Saudi Arabia encompassed a remaking of the kingdom, his real accomplishments included a steady gain over illiteracy, poverty, and disease. His carefully charted reconstruction concentrated on the individual while preserving the intrinsic norms of Saudi society. Faysal did not abandon tribal values but consolidated them into an increasingly urbanized environment where basic services were ensured for all those who needed them. It was his rule that mobilized the educated technocrats of the kingdom who, in turn, applied learned skills to their environment. Such men quickly tackled difficult economic problems and delved into solutions considered too heterodox—all to ameliorate as quickly as possible the Saudi standard of living.[45]

To be sure, Faysal oversaw his vast enterprises throughout the kingdom with utmost care, often working long hours to attend to every detail. Yet, it would be inaccurate to assume that he accomplished everything without assistance. On the contrary, the monarch was fortunate to have strong-minded advisors, both religious and secular, among royals as well as commoners, all of whom shared their views and expertise with him. Naturally, most deferred to his final decisions, but he was not an autocrat in the traditional sense. Those who knew him well or who had the opportunity to work with him noted how closely he listened.[46] In the event, Faysal assembled a core group of senior advisors with whom he interacted on a regular basis. His foremost religious advisors included Shaykh Muhammad Al Harakan, who became the minister of justice, Shaykh Rashid bin Khunayn, his undersecretary at the same ministry, Shaykh Muhammad bin Jubair, the late head of the Majlis al-Shurah, as well as Shaykh 'Abdallah Al Musnad, who eventually chaired the Religious Studies Department at Imam Muhammad University and is now a member of the Higher Council of 'Ulamah. The four scholars visited Pope Paul VI at the Vatican on October 25, 1974 to participate in the Catholic Church's dialogue between Christians and Muslims.[47] Faysal the believer, who held impeccable Muslim credentials as a learned man in his own right, was keenly interested in acculturating the Muslim scholars of the kingdom with the rest of the world. Perhaps because of his many visits overseas starting after World War I, Faysal had developed a strong interest in other cultures and religions, choosing to engage in a dialogue with the world's primary Christian institution. It was important for him that his advisors listen to, understand, and assent to dialogue to better serve Islam, Saudi Arabia, and the Muslim world at large. Although revisionist discourse assigns King Faysal with extreme levels of intolerance, this was certainly not the case as far as "the people of the book" were concerned—Jews and Christians—since the Saudi followed Qur'anic admonitions to the letter.[48] Rather, and as discussed in the next chapter, Faysal distinguished the political from the religious even if his detractors saw no differences between the two.

If religious leaders almost always stood as Faysal's first line, several key secular advisors assumed unmitigated responsibilities too. Next to the founder, King 'Abdul 'Aziz bin 'Abdul Rahman, the individual who acted as a genuine aide to Faysal was Omar Saqqaf, who was the deputy at the Ministry of Foreign Affairs until his death in 1974. Rashad Pharaon, Fadil Qabbani, Ibrahim 'Abdallah Al Za'id, Kamal Adham, Shaykh Ahmad Zaki Yamani, and Shaykh Ahmad 'Abdul Wahhab (then chief of protocol), all assumed added responsibilities. Naturally, the monarch's brothers, including Muhammad, Khalid, Fahd, 'Abdallah, Sultan, Nayif, Salman, and others, welcomed their duties with glee. In time, the monarch's eight sons—'Abdallah, Muhammad, Khalid, Sa'ud, 'Abdul Rahman, Sa'ad, Bandar, and Turki—received specific assignments to serve crown and country.[49] All of these men, along with countless other hard-working Saudis, supported Faysal to remake the kingdom and transform it from a largely *badu* society into a modernizing country. By adopting strict work habits and through his own deeds Faysal instilled very high standards as well as a rare work ethic in a part of the world where such habits were uncommon. His archetype was not easy to emulate although other ruling family members, along with a slew of commoner technocrats, seized the challenge. If the Saudi monarch and his trusted men were often dismissed throughout the 1960s and early 1970s, few ventured to neglect them in the aftermath of Arab-Israeli War of late 1973 and early 1974 that ensued in an "oil crisis." Throughout this most critical period, Faysal demonstrated that he was a capable ruler, a worthy monarch, and a custodian of all of the kingdom's assets.

Oil Policy under Faysal

Among all of the actions implemented by Faysal, his firm decision to use the oil weapon in 1973 stood out because it was controversial, even if largely misunderstood. In fact, while he may well have been "convinced of his country's strength, [and] decided to support the idea of using oil as a political weapon," he was not entirely sure how useful its application would be.[50] To be sure, the embargo decision in 1973 by the Organization of Arab Petroleum Exporting Countries (OAPEC) awakened nationalist sentiments among Arab leaders, perhaps even sparked latent notions of effectiveness, but Faysal correctly appraised its short- and long-term dangers. In the event, and while OAPEC did not actually adopt its embargo resolution until October 17, 1973—two weeks after hostilities were launched on October 6 between Egypt and Israel—its reverberations were rapidly felt in all industrialized countries. How were the kingdom's oil policies set and what motivated the king to act when he did with such determination?

The Oil Nexus

Vast petroleum resources, which were the core of the Al Sa'ud's privileged economic position in the world, allowed them to guarantee prosperity and to strengthen their custodianship over the two holy mosques in Makkah and Madinah. With this in mind, Faysal developed specific policies that were tied to the economic survival of Saudi Arabia and, equally important, prosperity. Relations with Iran, Iraq, and Yemen, as well as the repercussions of the Arab-Israeli conflict, regional unity in the Gulf, and Western support for the kingdom's military needs, were all somewhat tied to oil. At times, "petroleum policies" drove the security concerns of the kingdom, even if Faysal's vision for Saudi Arabia preceded vast improvements in revenues. Since oil was such a critical component of economic and political well-being, Faysal and his trusted advisors devised specific policy objectives to maintain and develop petroleum holdings. These included, (1) the application of moderate oil prices to ensure the long-term use of crude oil as a major energy source throughout the world; (2) the production of sufficient excess capacity to stabilize oil markets in the short term and secure a role for the kingdom as a permanent source to key Western importers over the long term; and (3) the accumulation of significant oil revenues to further develop the economy, which, in turn, would strengthen its political system.[51]

When Faysal acceded to the throne, Saudi Arabia held an estimated 64 billion barrels (bb) of oil, although these figures doubled by 1970. In 1960, the

Table 1. The Saudi Oil Juggernaught

Year	Daily Average	Cumulative	% Change in Average
1938	1.0	511	-
1953	845.0	1,606,630	2.4
1964	1,896.5	6,831,146	6.2
1965	2,205.3	7,636,080	16.3
1966	2,602.3	8,585,737	18.0
1967	2,805.0	9,609,562	7.8
1968	3,042.9	10,723,264	8.5
1969	3,216.2	11,897,177	5.7
1970	3,799.1	13,283,848	18.1
1971	4,768.9	15,024,497	25.5
1972	6,016.3	17,226,462	26.2
1973	7,596.2	19,999,075	26.3
1974	8,479.7	23,094,166	11.6
1975	7,075.4	25,676,687	-16.6

Data includes share of production from Neutral Zone (with Kuwait).

Source: "Saudi Arabia--Cumulative Crude Oil Production (1,000 b), Table 38," in *OPEC Annual Statistical Bulletin 2004* (Vienna): Organization of Petroleum Exporting Countries, 2005, 59.

country produced 481 million barrels of oil, or about 1.3 million barrels per day (mbpd), a capacity that rose to 1.74 million barrels per day in 1965. Per capita income stood around $200 per year in the mid-1960s. By 1975, the estimated proven reserves of petroleum jumped to 141 billion barrels, with probable reserves closer to 175.[52] Annual production reached 2,582 million barrels or about 7 million barrels per day.[53] These computations represented a quarter of the world's proven reserves, although Riyadh seldom emphasized its claims. In 1960, the petroleum sector accounted for approximately 55 percent of budget revenues, 40 percent of GDP, and almost all export earnings. Not surprisingly, these figures expanded throughout the 1960s and early 1970s, and by 1975 petroleum accounted for 75 percent of GDP.[54] Per capita income jumped to $833 in 1973 and $7,920 in 1975.[55] Petrochemicals accounted for another chunk of manufacturing value-added, petroleum refining accounted for an additional 5 percent, and the balance was in other manufacturing sectors. Because of its unique capabilities, Saudi Arabia became the most influential member of both the Organization of Petroleum Exporting Countries (OPEC) and OAPEC. Riyadh's oil strength led to substantial financial reserves and holdings in Western institutions, and by 1975 it boasted the largest economy in the Arab world. Concurrently, it also became one of the most important consumers of foreign goods between Western Europe and Southeast Asia. Whenever the kingdom decided to spend, save, or invest, it competed with Western countries because Riyadh's voice was heard in the highest councils of world economic chambers. Faysal transformed Saudi Arabia to such a degree that one of his successors would be invited to occupy a permanent seat on the board of executive directors of the International Monetary Fund (IMF).[56] It thus became the only non-G-8 country with its own permanent representative on the IMF board, which was a distinct recognition of the Saudi financial potential.

With a GDP of about $35 billion (SR 110 b), a high living standard, and a per capita income close to $8,000 in 1975, Saudi Arabia was among the twenty-five largest economies in the world and the most voluminous in the Arab world. After 1975, its per capita gross national product would surpass every African and Latin American state and, in Asia, was only exceeded by those of Japan, Singapore, and Hong Kong. Industry developed in line with the nature of the kingdom's resources, as a new focus emerged, primarily centered on manufacturing activities, which aimed to take the economy away from its heavy dependence on oil. What Faysal and his team of economic advisors planned early on was to develop the non-oil manufacturing sector.[57] In fact, these policies eventually succeeded, as Saudi Arabia established one of the most active construction markets in the developing world and possessed a growing conviction that its industry was poised to win regional and even international businesses.[58]

Still, it was not always like this because the kingdom ran huge budget deficits under King Sa'ud. In fact, deficits represented close to 10 percent of gross domestic product in 1962, nearly twice the comparable figure for most developed countries.[59] Emerging bottlenecks in utility supplies, the commitment to expanding sustainable oil production capacity, the overriding priority attached to defense, and the rising private demand for new buildings continued to plague the economy between 1970 and 1975, and even beyond. Faysal tightened the economic noose and managed to finance inevitable deficits through direct borrowing by the state, primarily from government-supported corporations and major local banks. Budget and current account deficits, which bled the economy, were severely curtailed by adopting strict spending rules. Faysal devised appropriate policies and adopted a new decision-making structure to better streamline vital resources.

The Decision-Making Structure in the Oil Industry

While oil wealth transformed Saudi foreign policy at both the regional and international levels, as it empowered Faysal to influence Arab and world affairs, his primary objective was to harvest this energy to create permanent institutions for the kingdom. He forged an industry out of thin air but, his objectives notwithstanding, petroleum income ignited political tensions within the country.[60] Although this inherent problem existed before the 1973 oil boom, it nevertheless galvanized opposition figures, some of whom disputed how the oil wealth of the kingdom was actually distributed. Which segments of society received the greatest benefits was an important question that determined the stability of Saudi Arabia for the balance of the twentieth century. How Faysal addressed these issues, and how he, as well as his successors, perceived the industry within the framework of national policies, illustrated his political genius.

Key Power Brokers in the Oil Industry

In addition to the Al Sa'ud ruling family, several institutional organizations participated in oil industry decision making that, not surprisingly, illustrated the vast changes that occurred immediately after the 1973 oil boom. Even if the institutional edifices were not apparent until the late 1970s and early 1980s, most were established under Faysal, who, more than any other Saudi, envisioned an overall framework.

Ruling Family Personalities

Decision making in the oil industry rested primarily in the hands of the Al Saʿud ruling family. On issues requiring their attention, the king, the heir apparent, and the second deputy prime minister were the ultimate decision makers, although the monarch retained a final say. He regularly issued decrees pertaining to the organization of Saudi oil companies, proclaimed incentives for their development, and chaired key institutions. In addition to these three powerful men, an undetermined number of prominent princes participated in the decision-making process. With large personal fortunes and their own patronage networks, over time many of these individuals created their own "oil clearinghouses." For the better part of modern Saudi history, members of the ruling family had the capability to approach the king or the heir apparent and ask to sell oil to a particular customer. Often, the monarch approved such deals to keep peace within the establishment since several members were also major investors in industrial and service companies.[61]

According to reliable press reports, several prominent examples preoccupied Faysal as well as his successors who were opposed to such practices. Yet, to maintain ruling family harmony, successive monarchs tolerated the custom. A prime example was Prince Muhammad bin ʿAbdul ʿAziz, the elder brother of King Fahd, who was passed over for the throne in 1975. Because of his seniority within the family, Muhammad bin ʿAbdul ʿAziz was allowed by his younger brothers to seek special payments (through a group of agents) for up to five hundred thousand barrels of oil a day.[62]

Riyadh moved cautiously in curbing these activities even before they became popular because members of the ruling family were too well entrenched in the system and could have created a real political dilemma for any official who tried to limit or eliminate such commission revenues. In many ways, this practice had the potential to undermine the kingdom itself, since it focused attention on corruption within the family. Because of such concerns, King Faysal had earlier imposed certain controls, but he was always wary of moving too fast lest past accusations of fiscal parsimony return.[63] If Faysal was lenient with some of these practices, King Fahd would impose a much stricter rule in 1983, when all oil income was channeled to the state treasury.

The Supreme Petroleum Council

In addition to the members of the ruling family, and starting in the late 1960s and early 1970s, the Al Saʿud recognized the need to include more commoners in their debates on long-term oil-related projects in the kingdom. Commoners with expertise in industry and commerce were brought into the decision-making process as Faysal appointed his chief oil advisors to the newly created Supreme Petroleum Council (SPC). Chaired by the monarch, the SPC included two royals and four technocrats—Khalid, the heir apparent; Fahd, the second deputy prime minister; Musa'id bin 'Abdul Rahman, the minister of finance; Ahmad Zaki Yamani, the minister of petroleum and mineral resources; Hisham Nazer, the minister of planning; 'Abdul 'Aziz Al-Qurayshi, the governor of the Saudi Arabian Monetary Agency (Central Bank)—and two businessmen. Although the ruling family would expand the SPC membership in the 1990s—to include the president and chief executive officer of ARAMCO, and several representatives of leading banks and private sector companies—the expansion reflected a change in Saudi petroleum priorities to better address monetary deficiencies.[64] Naturally, Faysal and his advisors could not fully foresee the dramatic changes of the post–oil boom era, but the institutions they helped create were capable of adapting to changing circumstances as necessary.

Since the inception of the SPC, members have had the unique opportunity to articulate divergent views to the Al Sa'ud and, consequently, persuade the king to decree changes in Saudi Arabia's oil policies as warranted. If the petroleum minister argued that the kingdom should slow oil production, for example, central bank officials would counter by adjusting financial reserves. And although SPC proceedings appeared to be highly informal, as there were no regularly scheduled meetings and decisions were reached through consultation and consensus, genuine expertise was available to senior decision makers. This expertise sought to balance the various needs and interests of the government.[65] To be sure, only the king and senior Al Sa'ud family members discussed and decided on the most sensitive matters, but the SPC ensured that the ultimate decisions were made after all options had been carefully laid out in front of the ruler. Consequently, it was increasingly more difficult to reach decisions by fiat, and this too was a direct consequence of preferences envisioned and implemented by Faysal.

The Ministry of Petroleum and Mineral Resources

Of all the agencies and organized bodies of the Saudi government, the Ministry of Petroleum and Mineral Resources was the most potent. The ministry derived its power directly from the ruling family, as well as the SPC, and was divided into three main branches concerned with the business and scientific affairs surrounding petroleum extraction and distribution: Finances and Administration, Mineral Resources, and Technical Affairs.[66]

In the 1960s and 1970s, Shaykh Ahmed Zaki Yamani, who was highly valued by Faysal, directed the oil affairs of the kingdom. Yamani influenced OPEC policies when crucial decisions were made in the aftermath of the 1973–74 oil crisis and the 1986 price crash.[67] Although Yamani was ousted from power in 1986—ostensibly because he was responsible for the significant financial chaos that resulted after prices collapsed—he nevertheless left his mark on the institution. His successor, Hisham Nazer—another commoner who served as deputy petroleum minister for several years—was chosen because of his expertise as planning minister on the SPC.[68] His familiarity with the numerous financial needs of Saudi Arabia made him an ideal choice for the post.

In the 1950s, 'Abdallah Tariki played a key role in oil affairs after Faysal appointed him as director-general of petroleum and mineral affairs in the new Ministry of Finance and National Economy in 1956.[69] Tariki, a Najdi geologist with a degree from the University of Texas, was a true Arab nationalist who envisaged an eventual constitutional monarchy for Saudi Arabia.[70] He also foresaw a day when oil would be used as a political weapon. In fact, Tariki pushed for a nationalization of ARAMCO, although Faysal was too savvy to miscalculate the repercussions of such an initiative. Tariki, who was a principal advisor on energy matters, became an opponent of Faysal in 1961 and was dismissed in 1962.[71] The monarch was disappointed even if he moved more cautiously than his advisors, who, for a variety of reasons, may have preferred far more nationalistic approaches.

PETROMIN and SABIC

In addition to the Ministry of Petroleum, several other bodies that contributed to the oil policies of Saudi Arabia were envisaged by Faysal and his team. Up until 1994, the General Petroleum and Minerals Organization—or PETROMIN—fell under the purview of the ministry.[72] King Faysal first ordered the establishment of PETROMIN in 1962, and it was staffed mostly by Western-educated Saudi technocrats who had direct access to the monarch.[73] PETROMIN's contacts with the government concentrated on funding critical petroleum research and analysis projects, the implementation and administration of public petroleum and mineral projects, importing raw materials, and the conduct of petroleum and mineral operations such as exploration, production, refining, transportation, and distribution.[74] In 1975, PETROMIN was viewed as "the cornerstone of the Kingdom's strategic industries . . . [that] within the next few years will make the country among the leading industrial nations."[75]

When King Faysal was assassinated in 1975, the resulting political crisis affected the emerging oil industry in general and PETROMIN in particular. Riyadh quickly created the Ministry of Industry and Electricity in October 1975 to assume responsibilities for all technical matters, save for the production, refining, and marketing of oil and gas. A year later, Riyadh established the Saudi Arabian Basic Industries Corporation (SABIC) to assume responsibility for the burgeoning petrochemical industries because Riyadh concluded that separate entities would be easier to manage.[76] The break-up of PETROMIN illustrated how tensions within the ruling family affected the government. In the event, the company would not become the superministry that Faysal had envisaged—supervising all of the oil resources of the kingdom—because it fell victim to various bureaucratic machinations. In fact, the smaller companies essentially meant that multiple bureaucratic layers would be added to the emerging maze to the delight of those who benefited from such arrangements.

ARAMCO and SAMAREC

Of course, the ARAMCO story was far more pertinent to contemporary Saudi Affairs, but it was not a wholly owned Saudi company until 1982. In 1933, four Western oil companies (Exxon Corporation, Mobil Corporation, Standard Oil Company of California, and Texaco Inc.) formed the Arabian-American Oil Company (ARAMCO) to ensure a steady supply of high quality oil from Saudi Arabia. Western oil companies, for the most part, controlled all industrial subsections within the organization. In the upstream portion, for example, ARAMCO commanded all exploration, development, and production decisions, and it managed oil fields, pipelines, and crude oil export facilities.[77]

During the 1970s and early 1980s, however, Saudi Arabia slowly gained full ownership of its petroleum industry through arbitration and stock exchanges. There was little doubt that Riyadh was keenly interested in gaining full control over its own resources. Indeed, Faysal warned ARAMCO of unilateral action as early as 1972 should the four partners fail to make satisfactory progress toward the conclusion of participation agreements.[78] In time, a general agreement was reached between the government and ARAMCO, which was supplemented with a more specific, graduated accord in 1974. Under Faysal's direct supervision, Riyadh purchased one-quarter of ARAMCO outright and, as specified in the 1974 agreement, pursued an annual 5 percent increase that would give it a majority stake by 1982. The two sides agreed that 100 percent Saudi ownership should occur no later that 1977, but numerous delays, including lack of Saudi training combined with Western apprehension, hampered full Saudi ownership. Still, Faysal was keen in his single-minded approach—*to purchase ARAMCO at a cost exceeding $2 billion*—rather than nationalizing the company.[79] It is worth underlining that the full purchase of an oil company exploiting the natural resources of the kingdom stood in direct contrast to Iranian and Iraqi behavior in the Persian Gulf region. In both of those instances, revolutionary governments nationalized foreign-owned assets. In the Iranian case, ironically, the pro-Western Muhammad Reza Shah did not renege policies espoused by Prime Minister Mohammed Mossadegh—who authorized the nationalization of the Anglo-Iranian Oil Company on March 15, 1951—when the dejected ruler was goaded by Britain and the United States to reclaim his throne in 1953.[80]

In the event, Faysal pushed for the acquisition and, by insisting on its implementation, set the course for later developments. When in March 1989, King Fahd appointed a new ARAMCO board of directors, he was the only ruling family member to have a seat on it. Still, the absence of other royals indicated how far along the technocratic operation had progressed, as the vision of King Faysal—to empower private sector representation to run day-to-day operations—materialized.[81] By November 1989, ARAMCO had assumed complete control over oil rights and assets from the original four Western companies. At the same time, the king ordered ARAMCO to "Saudize" its operations, relying on fewer and fewer expatriate workers wherever possible. Some 75 percent of the ARAMCO work force was defined as "Saudi" by 1993, less than two decades after Faysal first envisaged "Saudi ARAMCO."[82]

Upon the "acquisition," Riyadh transformed ARAMCO into a powerful state-owned oil company. In the words of the petroleum minister Hisham Nazer: "In less than four years we have overhauled and restructured the entire oil industry of Saudi Arabia. This has been done with a view to both enhancing our ability to respond to short-term market fluctuations as well as to gear up the oil sector to meet the long term challenges."[83]

The statement was backed with solid action. In a second merger in 1993, ARAMCO took control of all remaining PETROMIN assets in order to develop a centralized decision-making apparatus over downstream investments as well.[84] Riyadh began to invest heavily abroad—to fulfill King Fahd's strategy of global integration—which gave ARAMCO a major position in U.S. refining and a minor grasp of the oil market in the Far East—but this was nothing out of the ordinary. The kingdom was seeking contracts with European and Japanese refining interests with a view to match and ultimately surpass large companies such as Exxon and Royal Dutch/Shell in downstream operations.[85] Whether these long-term goals were devised in the early 1980s or whether they were first envisaged in the early 1970s is difficult to appraise. Still, the overall direction of Saudi petro-industries, to diversify while adopting nationalist objectives, was certainly set by Faysal and his team.

The result of these efforts meant that ARAMCO subsidiaries were spread throughout the United States, Europe, and the Far East, thereby creating a greater interdependence between Saudi Arabia and powerful world economies. This was one of the primary objectives of King Faysal, for he understood the necessity of long-term alliances with consuming societies. One of the most active subsidies was ARAMCO Services Company in Texas, which provided a range of services to the parent company in Dhahran. This included the administration of major engineering design project teams in Houston, evaluation of vendors, the procurement of materials, contract administration and controls, and recruitment and training. The ARAMCO Overseas Company B.V. in Leiden, the Netherlands, had similar responsibilities in Europe. The Saudi Petroleum International Inc., and the Saudi Petroleum Overseas Limited in London and Tokyo were marketing companies that scheduled, loaded, stored, and arranged transportation for the large amounts of Saudi crude oil destined for North America, Europe, and the Far East.[86] The ultimate goal was to convert ARAMCO into a global business enterprise with permanent connections to Western economies that could not be broken. In this manner, Saudi Arabia achieved its security needs by creating an interdependent economic system that ensured its long-term prosperity. Faysal's vision proved to be the correct one.

The OPEC and OAPEC Instruments

In the late 1950s, the Al Sa'ud realized that international oil companies reaped significantly larger profits from petroleum exploitation than did the kingdom. To reverse the trend, Riyadh concluded that an association of Arab oil-producing countries would strengthen the bargaining position of the Arab world with Western oil companies. Consequently, the Arab Petroleum Congress was held in April 1959, and non-Arab oil- producing states were invited to send delegates. Not surprisingly, Western consuming states (and companies) reacted negatively to the congress, dragging oil prices even lower than they already were. Faced with possible additional price reductions, representatives of Iran, Iraq, Kuwait, Saudi Arabia, and Venezuela met in Baghdad on September 14, 1960 and established OPEC. Based in Vienna, the main objectives of OPEC were to ensure stable oil prices as well as to gain control over oil extraction and flow. In an epoch-making statement, King Faysal announced in 1964 that Riyadh demanded direct participation in the production and marketing of oil from the kingdom, and that OPEC was the best venue to enforce such demands.[87]

As few improvements occurred between 1964 and 1967, Saudi Arabia determined that it had to make a stronger effort to unite the Arab petroleum-producing countries in order to bargain with a single voice with Western oil companies. Toward that end, Saudi Arabia submitted a proposal to both Kuwait and Libya for the establishment of OAPEC to counter Western dictates on petroleum demands—at least from Arab states. In the wake of the 1967 Six-Day War, representatives from the three countries met in Beirut and signed an agreement on January 9, 1968 to create OAPEC.[88] Although its formation signaled Saudi intentions to be a leader in the Arab world, over the years the venue proved to be far less effective than OPEC. OAPEC fell victim to festering disputes within the Arab world from which it never recovered.[89]

By 1971, both OPEC and OAPEC had succeeded in making significant inroads in the pricing and production mechanisms devised and implemented by Western oil companies. On February 14, 1971, for example, the six Persian Gulf members of OPEC and leading international oil company representatives signed the Teheran Agreement, in which all pricing duties were transferred to producing states.[90] With this agreement, Saudi Arabia and other oil producers gained more control over the flow of their oil, and, at least as an internal matter within OPEC, it meant that members had to acknowledge the growing Saudi position—the producer with the largest reserves. Until the 1971 Teheran Agreement, Iran was the leading actor in the area, but the balance of economic power was clearly shifting to Saudi Arabia, particularly as Riyadh's share of the market grew in size.

What the actual support of King Faysal for OPEC and OAPEC illustrated was that the Al Saʿud desired to form an economic and political tool to protect their wealth and to oppose undue Western influences on their internal affairs. By the mid-1970s, however, OPEC had become a political tool. In fact, a basic divergence in views between Saudi Arabia and its partners emerged after the Teheran Agreement not only on proposed pricing mechanisms but also on the putative utility of the organization as a political instrument. In the aftermath of the 1973–74 oil crisis, Saudi Arabia took a lead in creating its own production schedule, whereas a majority of OPEC producers complained at the OPEC Doha Conference in 1976 that this was a blatant attempt to control oil markets. Fahd, the heir apparent, objected, clearly linking Saudi policy with the health of the international economy, leading to further alienation between the kingdom and its neighbors. According to Fahd: "[Saudi oil policy was] an effective instrument for the promotion of stability and economic development throughout the world and for the fight against inflation which is a worldwide problem. . . . In the past, we used to go along with positions that we were not altogether convinced of. Now, we will do what we consider to be appropriate for our own interests and the interests of the world economy."[91]

This was the pragmatism that Faysal instilled in his brothers, who applied their predecessor's recommendations in the interest of the kingdom. Yet, political difficulties within OPEC began to take their toll as several members sided against Riyadh. With Iran and Iraq locked in battle throughout the 1980s, Saudi Arabia led OPEC even as it faced intransigence from other members over production ceilings. By 1983, Shaykh Yamani declared that there were two reasons for the breakdown within the organization, and that both were almost permanent in nature. According to Yamani:

> Interests within OPEC differed more than hitherto and certain members continued [their independent posturing to] impose their short-term interests on [Saudi Arabia whose] . . . patience was exhausted; and,

> That the output to be shared is very small, and some members reached a stage of financial suffocation while others exercised radical arrogance. . . .[92]

These explanations notwithstanding, the kingdom achieved its long-term objectives within OPEC because, at home, it assumed full ownership and control over ARAMCO without nationalizing the company. This was the policy of King Faysal, which, without a doubt, was carefully implemented by his successors. Moreover, the Al Sa'ud demonstrated that pricing and selling strategies—adopted since 1975—allowed them to support a truly independent policy. Faysal's initiatives proved to be correct as Saudi Arabia became the most critical oil producer in contemporary history.

Oil and Security Issues: The Internal Dimension

Undeniably, between 1973 and 1975 Faysal ruled the kingdom with the added capability of vast oil resources as a tool to meet political, economic, and security needs. Several factors, including the country's vulnerability, internal politics, impact on society, expectations, infrastructure, and technical issues, further complicated how he determined the national security of the country. The resulting balancing act, which increased the dependence of Saudi society on government largesse, required constant adjustments. Of course, he did not live long enough to make them, but his immediate successors implemented policies that were vintage Faysal. It is worth noting that the 1973–74 oil crisis, and how the monarch maneuvered through it, represented permanent blueprints for Khalid and Fahd, the kings who followed him.

Policy disagreements demonstrated how fluctuations in production or prices left their impact on the ruling family after 1973. In turn, Faysal balanced his intrinsic need to maintain order with potential disruptions that Saudi policies ushered into the world economy. Lower production and higher prices or overproduction at cheaper rates were the choices he faced. Above all else, Faysal recognized that he could not squander the resources of the nation and needed, therefore, to steer a course between specific political objectives and rapid economic development. Simultaneously, he was aware of the need to adhere strictly to the national heritage of Saudi Arabia, which, it must be underscored, was based on traditional norms that rejected innovation. In short, Faysal faced a key question: how to allocate expenditures to avoid inflation yet spend enough to insulate against instability.

Among his many preoccupations, he considered the security of Saudi oil installations in the Eastern Province, where an important Shiʿah community played a key role in the oil industry, with utmost care. This concern was made urgent by the reality of religious and political activities that influenced Shiʿah workers at ARAMCO in the 1970s.[93] Shiʿah riots in the Eastern Province in 1979 and 1980, combined with the fervor in Iran as well as the 1981 attempted coup in Bahrain, would vindicate Saudi anxieties that were first identified by the monarch in the 1960s. Riyadh therefore carefully assessed this presence in the oil-rich region, where Shiʿahs constituted a sizable force within ARAMCO.[94] To be sure, Faysal was also aware that ARAMCO's influence within the kingdom was far greater than many acknowledged and, consequently, he adopted steps to mitigate any renewed disturbances.[95]

Aware of potential difficulties, Faysal authorized several opinion polls to gauge how the Saudi people perceived his government. Although no public opinion polls were known to have been published in Saudi Arabia while Faysal ruled, security services monitored public attitudes toward the issue of oil production and government expenditures. According to one official, opinion was divided among those who had never traveled outside Saudi Arabia (and therefore could only compare the situation to the pre-oil era), and those with firsthand knowledge of the international arena. For the former, it was unthinkable to be anything but grateful for what oil revenues achieved, and for the latter Saudi Arabia needed to reformulate its pricing strategy not to sell oil too cheaply.[96] The feeling among Saudi technocrats, as well as some senior policymakers, was that Saudi Arabia helped the West in general and the United States in particular—despite the 1973–74 crisis—at some political cost to itself. In short, the overall perception in the mid-1970s was that Saudi Arabia reaped little benefits in return for its accommodation. Because of such sentiments, Faysal and his successors maintained that surveying public opinion—even if such results were seldom published—was necessary to defend the country against potential challenges.

While the kingdom sharply increased its oil investments after 1973—both to diversify a growing industrial base as well as vastly expand its educational system, transportation infrastructure, and communication grids—most of these policies were adopted by Faysal in the late 1960s. In short, Saudi Arabia moved from being a Third World country to one that was on the threshold of joining the ranks of developed nations, all in less than a few decades. These dramatic developments brought with them rapid social changes as well as economic dislocations. Indeed, given a conservative social structure—largely based on tribalism—Riyadh faced the potential for serious internal upheavals as the values developed by and for the emerging middle class became endangered. In fact, these values tended to be somewhat different from those of the establishment and a majority of Saudis interpreted the behavior of elites in negative terms. There was thus unanimous agreement that wealth had greatly accelerated economic growth while barely affecting the entire population. Moreover, the impact of this wealth on the traditional *badu* was devastating.[97]

Much of these social changes were directly tied to oil-generated income. Often, production levels were set by political considerations rather than economic ones. In a May 1991 speech delivered at the Harvard Business School, Minister Hisham Nazer amplified the outlook of the kingdom on short-term prices and its ability to produce for another fifty years:

> As owners of at least a quarter of the world's oil reserves, we have to take the long term view, for Saudi Arabia will be producing oil when many other fields would have gone dry. Short-term aberrations in the oil market will spring forth every now and then. One has to be flexible and efficient enough to meet them head on. Saudi Arabia is not distracted by them to lose sight of the long term goal of market stability and a comprehensive integration of the oil industry.[98]

This declaration, while uttered in 1991, was nevertheless ingrained in established Saudi perceptions, which had evolved over decades and were widely understood. In fact, the statement clearly illustrated a keen awareness of long-term expectations not only to provide for the growing financial needs of the Saudi population, but also to look after the welfare of the country over the long term. In other words, Saudi officials deemed it prudent to consider long-term revenues as an essential part of ruling family objectives, a concept that was first articulated by Faysal in 1974 when he outlined the central role of oil in Saudi strategy.[99]

Oil and Security Issues: The External Dimension

The idea of using oil as a political weapon predated the Arab-Israeli conflict. In fact, Arab nationalists first raised the issue when discussing intrinsic capabilities against imperialist (mainly Western) powers after World War I, when most experienced colonial rule. Because the 1917 Balfour Declaration coincided with this colonial onslaught, fervent nationalists eventually added the Israeli presence in the Middle East to their anti-imperialist struggle. An equally troublesome feature was the growing role of oil companies, which literally dominated ruling establishments. Although ruling families of the Arabian Peninsula did not object to their nascent alliances with Western oil companies or leading colonial powers, sensitized and awakened Arab leaders lent a careful ear to nationalist voices. It was only after an association was made between an oil company and a foreign power seeking domination that nationalist sentiments began to change. What clearly tipped the balance were post–World War II realities as Arab leaders finally realized that few of the many promises made by Western governments would ever be implemented. On the contrary, Arab officials were left high and dry, having lost out on various concession agreements—by granting producing companies a lion's share of income over long periods of time—as well as in the political arena—after the creation of Israel in 1948 and subsequent wars. The "raw materials" weapon was therefore well ingrained and was quickly utilized in 1948, 1956, and 1967, with little impact.

The politics of the Middle East changed in 1970 when Gamal ʿAbdul Nasir died. Simultaneously, British colonial rule had waned in the Persian Gulf, as the conflict between Arab nationalists and monarchists lost its earlier value. Still, perceived Soviet and Israeli threats remained. To balance the rising influence of the Soviet Union in several Arab countries, King Faysal opted to enhance the tempo of Saudi-American cooperation as the two countries shared a similar objective: to deny any gains to Communism in the Middle East.[100] Until mid-1972, Faysal actually believed that oil and politics should be kept separate in order to maintain a healthy economic relationship between the kingdom and its Western allies. In fact, and as late as July 1972, Faysal had categorically rejected Egyptian calls to use the oil weapon against Washington. Faysal declared:

> I recall that such a suggestion was made by some at the Rabat (Arab Summit) Conference, but it was opposed by Gamal ʿAbdul Nasir on the grounds that it would affect the economies of the Arab countries and interfere with their ability to support Arab staying power; at the same time such a measure would not affect America because America does not need any of our oil or

other Arab Gulf oil before 1985. Therefore my opinion is that this proposal should be ruled out, and I see no benefit in reviving its discussions at this time.[101]

Early Failures of the Oil Weapon

Faysal was probably prompted to reach this conclusion by various political challenges, perhaps even errors, plaguing the region. In the 1950s and 1960s, the Saudis supported the use of petroleum as a weapon to influence blatant American support of Israel. Many thought that they could use oil as a "unifying weapon" between Arabs and Persians against the West. This logic failed to take into account oil produced in other parts of the world. Shaykh Yamani defined the oil weapon during the 1956 and 1967 wars as "injudiciously used [which caused it to lose] much if not all of its importance and effectiveness."[102]

The first failure occurred in the aftermath of the 1956 joint invasion of Egypt by Britain, France, and Israel. At the time, Saudi Arabia supported the Egyptian decision to close the Suez Canal. Riyadh further supported the Arab position on halting Western access to oil, and although two-thirds of Middle Eastern exports to Europe were rerouted, the embargo had a minor impact because of abundant supplies. Clearly, Saudi Arabia suffered from this embargo because the country was dependent on oil revenues and, for a brief period of time, recorded a slight decrease in actual income.

In 1967, several Arab states used oil as a political weapon after oil workers went on strike throughout the Middle East to protest U.S. military support of Israel. Crude oil production practically came to a halt in Saudi Arabia, Iraq, and Kuwait. Other Arab producers subsequently launched an embargo on oil exports to the United States, Britain, and West Germany. In this instance as well, the embargo did not hold because the market was well supplied. For Washington—which then relied on Middle Eastern sources on a limited basis—the embargo was an opportunity to increase sales to targeted states.[103] In this instance as well, Saudi Arabia felt an economic pinch as it could not handle the resulting financial losses. "Saudi Arabia was the first to feel the pinch acutely . . ." King Faysal was informed by his finance minister, ". . . there was no more money in the till and . . . for once ARAMCO was unable to help."[104] Riyadh failed to secure alternative income in 1967, which, in turn, made the American and Western European resolve far stronger. The putative Arab effort to act unanimously, and thus send a clear message to consuming countries, would not be repeated vowed Faysal. Toward the end of the 1960s, external developments became far more difficult to handle as a rise in Palestinian terrorism galvanized Arab masses against entrenched governments.

Still, the linkage between oil and security would only gain prominence until the 1973 Arab-Israeli War.

In the event, Faysal's pragmatism was enhanced by successful negotiations between oil producers and Western oil companies that resulted in a substantial loss of influence for the latter. Throughout the late 1960s, a larger number of indigenous personnel were trained to manage Saudi facilities. Shaykh Yamani went a step further and proposed a bilateral agreement with Washington whereby the United States would be ensured steady oil supplies at stable prices in return for technology and development assistance. Yamani even suggested that surplus Saudi revenues from oil sales could be invested in downstream oil refining and marketing activities throughout the United States.[105] The offer was not accepted.

The Oil Weapon in 1973–1974

Political negotiations notwithstanding, Saudi Arabia sought a new arrangement with Washington that would guarantee additional income as well as ensure the security of the kingdom. The United States, in contrast, was not willing to commit itself, fearing that such an arrangement might limit its options in the Middle East. Once again, the American relationship with Israel proved embarrassing to Faysal. As a result, he altered his policy and, for the first time in modern Saudi history, directly linked oil to politics. In April 1973, Faysal dispatched Yamani to Washington to inform American officials that it would be impossible for Riyadh to work against the interests of its Arab neighbors if Washington continued to arm Israel indiscriminately.[106] Yamani, who was accompanied by Sa'ud al-Faysal, the deputy oil minister, "publicly linked oil and Israel for the first time" as he ruled out an expansion of Saudi production "unless the United Stated change[d] its policy toward Israel."[107] A disappointed Faysal reluctantly concluded that U.S. foreign policy in the Middle East was failing and that little or no efforts were under way to salvage it.[108] Increasingly, however, the mercurial Faysal appreciated the growing dependence of the United States on Arab oil and, likewise, the crucial position of Saudi Arabia as a global oil supplier. On May 23, 1973, Faysal cautioned that U.S. interests in the world in general, and Saudi Arabia in particular, were suffering as a result of unequivocal American backing of Israel. He warned that America risked "los[ing] everything" and told ARAMCO leaders in the kingdom that he was "not able to stand alone much longer" in the Arab world, where pressures were accelerating for the use of oil as a weapon.[109] American officials dismissed these warnings because, the assumption went, Saudis would not dare alienate themselves from the Western powers that ultimately protected them. What Western analysts failed to note, however, was the reality that Riyadh had a far greater control over oil markets than it did in 1956 or even in 1967.

Faysal and Yamani formed a solid team to improve the posture of Saudi Arabia vis-à-vis ARAMCO. When in early 1972 "the chairman of Exxon, on behalf of the ARAMCO four, contacted President Nixon to see if he'd intervene with King Faysal," Nixon duly send a note to the monarch. Nixon's message to Faysal was simple: "Yamani is taking an unreasonable position which will ultimately hurt the interests of Saudi Arabia."[110] According to Jeffrey Robinson, Faysal was irate to receive such a note from the American head of state, and he informed Yamani of his displeasure. "Nixon says you are too harsh," Faysal reportedly told Yamani before adding, "No, I am the one who is too harsh."[111] Allegedly, Riyadh then notified several oil executives that Saudi Arabia would cooperate to reach an agreement but that "unspecified actions would be taken in case of failure." Whether such a blatant statement was made could not be verified, but it appeared to be wishful thinking because Faysal was too steeped in diplomacy to insult a sitting head of state, especially a friendly one. Moreover, Saudis never threatened nationalization, and such a boast at this juncture would have been totally out of character.

By August 1973, however, the Egyptian president Anwar al-Sadat and the Syrian president Hafiz al-Asad had visited King Faysal in Riyadh, where the viability of the oil weapon was seriously discussed within the framework of a future war.[112] Faysal accepted the idea of using oil as a weapon—or as an instrument of pressure—even if a future military confrontation threatened to be a lengthy one. By September, both Faysal and his son Sa'ud were calling for the use of oil as a weapon. Sa'ud al-Faysal was clear:

> Oil is not an artillery shell, but an enormous weapon. All economic weapons need study and time for their effectiveness to appear. Talk of using the oil weapon . . . makes it sound as if we were threatening the whole world, while it is understood that our purpose is to bring pressure to bear on America . . . but America would be the last to get hurt, because the U.S. will not depend on Arab oil before the end of the 1970s, whereas Japan and Western Europe depend on it now. . . .[113]

Such pronouncements—in reality a combination of pleas and warnings—became moot a month later when Cairo crossed the famous Bar-Lev line in the Sinai and launched the October 1973 War. Faysal was on his Rubicon as the time came to act.

The October 1973 War

The breakout of the October War gave Saudi Arabia, as well as the Arab oil-producing states, a rare opportunity to use the oil weapon effectively. OAPEC quickly sought to castigate countries that transformed themselves into more than allies of the Jewish state, specifically the United States and the Netherlands. Indeed, OAPEC's purpose was to encourage those that were leaning toward Israel, or that preferred neutrality, to adopt pro-Arab policies. On October 17, 1973, OAPEC met in Kuwait, where a decision was made to cut back oil production and exports by 5 percent from September levels. This benchmark of 5 percent was to be duplicated each month Israel failed to withdraw from occupied Arab lands. King Faysal ordered a 10 percent reduction in Saudi exports, and while Riyadh led OAPEC countries, the decision was not a unanimous one, as Iraq balked, insisting on harsher restrictions. Indeed, Baghdad refused to participate in the embargo, allegedly because the proposed plan failed to achieve its purported objectives.[114] As the original purpose of OAPEC was to keep the oil question out of politics, Saudi arguments—to reduce production by 5 percent every month the conflict continued—fell on deaf ears. More than any other leader, however, Faysal understood the failures of earlier embargoes when petroleum was available in large quantities from non-Arab sources. In fact, Faysal sought to prolong the embargo to secure a settlement of the Arab-Israeli conflict, but he welcomed a modification when extremist forces threatened the Arab political balance of power. The decision placed the kingdom at odds with other oil-producing states, which was the first divergence of views between Saudi Arabia and OAPEC, and which sowed further discord.[115]

Moreover, while the kingdom kept detailed information and maintained strict controls over oil leaving its ports, it was committed, at least theoretically, to sabotaging its oil fields if Washington, or any other power, were to forcefully occupy them. Threats to seize Saudi oil fields were common and the Al Sa'ud took them very seriously indeed. What Riyadh was keenly interested in was a test of the bounds of the Washington-Riyadh relationship.[116] It may be worth repeating that Faysal knew that his country's long-term interests could only be safeguarded by a close relationship with Washington even if his interlocutors in the United States took him for granted. In other words, for Faysal, the gradual embargo was a test to gauge whether Washington expressed any reciprocal interests toward the kingdom. This was the case because Saudi Arabia voluntarily remained aloof of Arab affairs and, more directly, isolated itself from core Arab issues. Moreover, Riyadh was not in a position to challenge Washington, as the latter looked to the Middle East through a Cold War strategic prism. Instead, it opted to devise concrete economic policies that would seal the relationship in permanent dependency. It must also be emphasized that the kingdom was producing 8.5 million barrels per day in September 1973 and had an actual capacity of 9.2. Before the war started, Riyadh had authorized ARAMCO to produce 8.76 million barrels per day for October 1973 and 9.1 for November. Both of these targets were dropped after hostilities were launched and, especially, after the oil question took on an entirely political dimension.

As tensions grew throughout the summer of 1973, Faysal reiterated the linkage between oil and politics. On August 31, he spoke on the American television network NBC, and in September he gave an interview to *Newsweek*, in which he emphasized that "Saudi Arabia would use its oil as a political weapon if the United States continued to support Israel's policy of aggression against the Arab World."[117] In the event, and despite these warnings, Faysal failed to affect American policy even though back-channel negotiations never stopped.[118] When war actually broke out, Washington systematically ignored the public warnings issued by the Saudi monarch as well as private pleas that, not surprisingly, chagrined Faysal.

Challenging the Embargo

OAPEC reconvened in Kuwait on December 4, 1973 and it decided to expand the production cutback to 25 percent to further increase Arab pressure on key Western powers. Friendly countries, including Britain, France, Spain, India, and Pakistan, among others, were exempted.[119] A livid Nixon administration responded with an even more blatant challenge on October 19 when Washington granted a $2.2 billion military grant to Israel. The farcical Nixon assertion that Israel needed military assistance "to maintain a balance of forces and thus achieve stability" was Machiavellian because Israel enjoyed military superiority against all Arab countries combined. It was this final act that triggered a full Arab embargo against the United States on October 20, which resulted in near panic buying and long lines at gas stations. According to Yamani, Faysal "was never anxious to impose an embargo against the United States. But Nixon didn't leave him any choice."[120] Naturally, after the embargo, prices skyrocketed, mostly for psychological reasons since oil was still flowing. In fact, it may be worth repeating that there was little doubt that the embargo was mostly symbolic in nature because oil continued to gush through Saudi and other oil-exporting countries' ports. Given that producers had no control over the movement of tankers once laden with crude and on the high seas, Faysal's announcement that "the Kingdom of Saudi

Arabia has decided to halt all oil exports to the United States of America" needed to be placed in perspective lest one ascribed unimaginable motives to Saudi diplomacy.[121]

Still, Faysal was politically cornered because he did not wish to embark on this dangerous course, as demonstrated by specific instructions—which were fully applied—to ease production cuts. On October 18, Riyadh announced that it was limiting its OAPEC-mandated export reductions to 2 percent (instead of the obligatory minimum of 5 percent and his preferred 10 percent initiative), and actually delayed the proclamation of its embargo. Both King Faysal as well as Minister Yamani posited that a gradual reduction in oil production would actually enhance Arab interests at least in three areas. First, neither the king nor the oil minister was eager to confront Washington in an all-out showdown. Second, their approach contained a certain flexibility to adjust production rates as needed, quickly restoring lost output if warranted. Third, the preference distinguished friendly or neutral countries from those adopting belligerent policies. Faysal's methodological preferences notwithstanding, he was infuriated by various diplomatic and military steps taken by Secretary of State Henry Kissinger, and he ordered additional cutbacks for November 1973. In fact, Riyadh slashed production by 30 percent in November 1973, whereas most OAPEC states honored the agreed upon 25 percent benchmark.[122]

What transpired between the October 18–22 was illustrative of a collision of wills between Faysal and Kissinger (see chapter 5). Kissinger may well have won tactically, but Faysal emerged as a strategic victor of this battle of wills because resulting price increases permanently altered the balance of power between industrialized and oil-producing countries.

Oil Prices Skyrocket

With the exception of Iran, Gulf oil producers prodded OPEC to raise prices by 70 percent on October 16, 1973. The fifty-fifty parity that was negotiated under Iranian leadership in 1971 gave way to a more robust collective decision that shocked privileged oil company executives and unsettled consumers. Over a very short period of time, the price of oil per barrel jumped from $1.87 (January 1971) to $2.60 (January 1973) to $11.60 (January 1974). These were posted prices—not the royalties that producing countries received. In 1973, royalties were fixed at 12.5 percent for Saudi Arabia, which meant Riyadh collected $0.32 for every $2.60 sale. In addition to these earnings, Saudi Arabia levied taxes (at 55 percent) that brought in another $1.20 per barrel, for a grand total of $1.52 for every $2.60 sale.

Given that production costs were estimated at $0.10 per barrel in January 1973, oil companies were making $0.98 in profits for every barrel extracted from the kingdom.

Faysal's strategic gains, clearly a financial windfall directly associated with the oil embargo, itself triggered by the war, in fact translated into one of the largest transfers of funds from one set of countries to another. It was a magisterial outcome even if the monarch never entertained—as far as it is known—such ambitions. The frugal Faysal was not motivated by pecuniary gains. Rather, what propelled him to action was his conclusion that Arab pleas for evenhandedness were always ignored, and that Arabs were entitled to protect their interests as they saw fit. Although the word justice and the lack thereof in the Arab-Israeli arena, was used with greater frequency, Faysal the realist knew that the best he and others throughout the region could accomplish was to sensitize American officials to fair play.

In addition to the political loss that the West in general and the United States in particular experienced, the intransigence of the Nixon administration ushered in long-term constraints. Washington was now confronted with an "energy" crisis, one that would endure for decades. While excessive pressures would eventually be placed on oil-producing countries to recycle their petrodollars into Western economies, a psychological gap emerged when importers were made to reconsider who actually "owned" the oil, and whether Arab custodians would relinquish their control over what some considered to be theirs by virtue of power status. "Our" oil under "their" sand was a frequently heard comment even if everyone knew that it was Arab oil under Arab soil. A conscious effort was therefore made to manage the 1973–74 energy crisis, as higher prices affected lifestyles. This and

Table 2. Oil Prices 1973 versus 1974

	January 1973	January 1974
Posted Price	2.591	11.651
Royalty (12.5%)	0.324	1.456
Production Cost	0.100	0.100
Taxes	1.192	5.552
Revenues	1.516	7.008

Note: Taxes were levied at the 55 percent rate of posted price and costs.

Sources: Jean-Marie Chevalier, *The New Oil Stake* (London: Penguin, 1975), 61.

subsequent energy crises seriously affected a certain way of life, not to mention political schisms that emerged within the Atlantic Alliance and between developing and industrialized countries.

European Community members called for restraint, urging Israel to respect international law and withdraw to the 1967 de facto borders. Even Japan, which had maintained a fairly pro-Israeli stance for decades, rescinded past policies. On December 23, 1973, Tokyo abandoned its neutrality and followed European calls for Israeli withdrawal from the latest occupied territories. With dwindling petroleum stockpiles (at one point standing at around fifty-nine days worth of crude under Japanese control), Japan opened a new chapter in its ties with the Arab world.[123]

By December 1973, the Saudis were faced with a test of wills and displayed their strength within OPEC and OAPEC by enacting a key role in moderating Iraqi and Iranian demands. The OPEC decision to introduce higher prices at the conclusion of its December 22–23, 1973 meeting in Teheran may have influenced OAPEC to call for production cutbacks on December 25.[124] Yet, Yamani was cornered by the shah, who insisted on the higher price levels because of significant Iranian financial needs. In the event, Yamani, who failed to clear the matter with Faysal—allegedly Iranian telephone networks were down—guessed that higher prices could always be reduced. When Yamani returned to Riyadh, Faysal remarked that he would have opposed the hike to $11.65.[125] Saudi Arabia faced a dilemma. While Riyadh supported the embargo, it did not want to anger Western powers, which might, in turn, resort to military action. Moreover, Saudi economic interests dictated that the Al Sa'ud not accelerate a Western economic collapse because that would have certainly affected Riyadh's economic welfare too.

Following confidential negotiations with Washington in early January 1975, Saudi Arabia restored exports to the United States. Faysal was eager to return to prewar production levels, especially after he "demonstrated" his political strength when Secretary of State Henry Kissinger embarked on his shuttle diplomacy to advance the moribund peace process.[126] In fact, the kingdom lifted the embargo as disengagement negotiations started between Israel and its Arab protagonists, although Riyadh was convinced that the foundations on which Saudi-American relations were based had been permanently altered.[127]

Secretary of State Henry Kissinger was not necessarily persuaded that the long-standing relationship was perpetually modified. He called for an energy conference in Washington on February 11, 1974, which identified the schism that existed between several European countries and the United States. Led by

France, European Community members rejected the American proposal for a joint effort to confront looming energy emergencies. Washington advanced the idea that a defensive consumer organization would protect oil-importing industrialized countries from the vagaries of commercial and financial arrangements. While a collective approach—to negotiate *en bloc* with OPEC—was not ruled out, the American perspective in early 1974 was to lead oil-importing states. This was precisely what France objected to. Foreign Minister Michel Jobert refused to subscribe to the Washington scheme because he perceived that, beyond the craftsmanship, American officials desired to curtail European as well as Japanese independent negotiations. In other words, Washington wanted to coerce its allies to assume collective responsibilities for what were largely bilateral blunders. The French further argued "that the consumer organization the Americans advocated would antagonize the oil producers and could very well be counter-productive."[128] Again, with the exception of France, conference attendees adopted various plans to streamline energy consumption. These included conservation measures, sharing scarce resources during emergencies, developing alternative sources, and cooperating on international research methods.[129]

Faysal was not opposed to these recommendations for he valued a healthy relationship with oil-importing economies. Yet, the Kissinger conference failed because it overlooked the critical roles that oil companies played in the industry, as few were ready to surrender hard-earned monopolies to governments. Within weeks, bilateral agreements were signed between exporting and importing countries, all brokered by powerful companies. Ironically, while the United States strenuously criticized European administrations for entering into bilateral arrangements, it signed its own reciprocal accord with Saudi Arabia on June 8, 1974.[130] According to the "Statement on Co-Operation," the two countries would usher in a Joint Commission that would "promote programs of co-operation . . . in the field of industrialization, trade, manpower training, agriculture, and science and technology."[131] This was a marked departure from previous exchanges as the relationship took on more concrete expression.

Not surprisingly, Michel Jobert in Paris and other European ministers lambasted this Washingtonian inconsistency, vindicated perhaps by their earlier premonition—that the search for energy security was a pretext—turned out to be accurate. Although the United States denied that its bilateral agreement with Saudi Arabia intended to secure specific supply commitments, senior American officials had few illusions. Starting in early 1974, subtle nuances appeared in speeches and interviews delivered by political and military officials, warning of the dangers of blackmail. A less noticeable contention, but one that was certainly calculated by Treasury Department mandarins, was the huge transfer of wealth under way.

What the Oil Weapon Meant

For Faysal, the oil weapon was not a sentimental ace in his hand but a basic tool that he sought to use because major Western powers were too cavalier with fundamental Arab rights. Faysal politicized oil even if his overall pro-American attitude should have prevented him from penalizing the United States. His respect for, perhaps even belief in, American ideals, compelled him to act. Whether he succeeded in "neutralizing" American positions toward Israel, as suggested by Nasir, Sadat, and Mohammed Heikal after the 1967 Six-Day War, was less relevant than his willingness to give notice.[132]

President Anwar al-Sadat of Egypt was even more persuaded by the veracity that America should adopt neutral policies. It was toward that objective that Sadat embarked on his successful rapprochement with Faysal, for whom Nasir's enmity was legendary. To be sure, Sadat needed the financial support of Saudi Arabia but, equally important, Egypt needed the growing clout of King Faysal. To his credit, Faysal grasped the full meaning of what a relatively small country like his could add to the political battlefield. While successive American and European leaders expressed their concerns about the conflict and labored to limit the regional conflagration from spilling over into the international arena, it was Faysal's bold risk that transformed the meaning of their oft-repeated language of "peace and stability." While Faysal would not live to hear Kissinger change his prose, Kissinger adopted words that would have pleased Faysal. Speaking at a function in Atlanta in June 1975, Kissinger renewed the necessity for an active American role in the Middle East but added several new elements to his evolving vision. After identifying Washington's "moral commitment to the survival and well-being of Israel," he acknowledged that 150 million Arabs "sitting astride the World's largest oil reserves" represented "important interests."[133] He posited that "the eruption of a crisis in the Middle East would severely strain [American] relations with . . . allies in Europe and Japan" and warned that a putative U.S.-Soviet confrontation should be avoided at all costs. These comments were as close to a full-fledged recognition of the impact that Faysal had had on American foreign policy as Kissinger was willing to concede. Even after Faysal's death, it was not possible to ascertain fully whether Kissinger was willing to welcome the rising star of Faysal to the firmament of world leaders who left their mark on their societies. In the event, his reluctant efforts to genuinely improve Saudi-American relations clashed with the firm stand that Faysal held on crucial policies after Kissinger introduced a new twist in his arguments in 1974. For the erudite American policymaker, regional stability in the Middle East could only be achieved when moderate regimes with firm political bases were able to claim a stake in a peaceful settlement. In other words, Saudi leaders had to understand and accept that the kingdom's own long-term stability was directly linked to a peaceful resolution of the Arab-Israeli conflict, regardless of actual details toward the establishment of an independent Palestinian state. This was a subtle departure from previous pronouncements that excluded Arab rights in any outcome. Without admitting to a linkage, this evolution in American policies was duly noted. It was the premonition of such changes that led King Faysal to instruct Ahmad Zaki Yamani, the oil minister, to reach an accord on energy prices in the aftermath of the 1973–74 oil crisis.

5

Divergences from the United States

Because of its emerging oil wealth, Saudi Arabia faced direct threats to its security that required the adoption of new ventures, both to prevent as well as to deter potential foes, especially after 1974. The kingdom thus ventured into the world of "petro-politics" to balance various tactics to survive and prosper. Even before the critical 1970s, Riyadh extended generous—and sometimes undeserved—financial support to regimes that opposed it in order to accomplish many of its objectives. In hindsight, several of these initiatives produced negative results, although Faysal bin ʿAbdul ʿAziz Al Saʿud was persuaded of their long-term value. What proved to be very costly was Saudi support of Egyptian and Palestinian causes that, for very complex reasons, encompassed regional and international dimensions beyond the actual control of any Arab official.

When Faysal acceded to the throne, he confronted this intrinsic problem head on and, in the aftermath of the 1973–74 oil crisis, revamped Riyadh's approach. He quickly realized that the need to placate Western oil-consuming countries was to be balanced with the necessity of accommodating the powerful neighbors of the kingdom, especially Iran and Iraq. As a consummate Arab nationalist, he further deduced that his pro-Arab agenda needed a pro-business slant because only then could the kingdom generate the healthy income to fulfill many of its obligations. Yet, Faysal was acutely aware that appeasement added little or no value to Saudi foreign policy and, toward that end, opted to reposition his long-term vision within a legitimate Islamic field.

What were the primary factors that compelled the powerful Saudi monarch to embark on this epoch-making change, and how did he accomplish stated goals? What were the developments that influenced him and persuaded him to devise and adopt a new vision? To better address these questions and, because so much of the ruler's views were perceived through the prism of the 1973 crisis, the critical repercussions of the oil predicament are analyzed in some detail. How Faysal dealt with its chief interlocutor, ally, and protector—the United States—contained useful lessons for his successors. These preferences notwithstanding, Faysal firmly believed that Saudi Arabia would find solace in the unity of the Muslim Ummah and, toward that end, relied on the country's custodianship of two of Islam's holiest shrines as a legitimizing tool. Beyond a physical affinity to unite by all legitimate means, however, Faysal adopted a judicious logic—that true revolution was the one that the Prophet himself introduced—which, for the ruler, started in Makkah and Madinah.[1]

U.S. Perceptions of the Middle East in the 1960s and 1970s

For Westerners in general and the United States in particular, the Middle East was a low-profile policy arena until the 1967 Six-Day War. To be sure, the entire "Middle East was boiling over with conflict and hatred," as so accurately anticipated by George W. Ball, the undersecretary of state under President John F. Kennedy, but neither Kennedy nor his successor, Lyndon B. Johnson, considered it a priority. In fact, Western preoccupations were with repeated crises in Eastern Europe—the Soviet invasions of Hungary and Czechoslovakia as well as the Berlin Wall calamity—along with the Cuban Missile Crisis, the Chinese Cultural Revolution, and other Cold War catastrophes. It would therefore be fair to state that European and American leaders viewed the Middle East through the East-West prism. Local developments were deemed peripheral to more weighty concerns even if revolutionary movements toppled established regimes with increased frequency. In fact, at first Washington considered the Egyptian revolutionary government as a benign addition to regional affairs, with limited consequence to Western interests. It even envisaged a close working relationship with revolutionary Egypt although Nasir acquired power through a coup d'état. Still, it only altered its perceptions of President Gamal 'Abdul Nasir, "America's spoiled child [*al-walad al-mudalal*] in Faysal's own terms"—after Nasir entered into a devastating alliance with Moscow.[2] Nasir's meteoric rise on the Arab scene and, more important, his repeated gaffes, ensured that the United States would surely need to rely on more reliable Arab allies before long.

Johnson and the 1967 War

As discussed above, Washington developed unique insights of the developing world in general and the Middle East in particular, which were perhaps best articulated by President Johnson. For Johnson, the early 1960s "revealed a pattern of serious advances [in the region], sparked in large part by emotions generated in the Arab-Israeli confrontation and including the active expansion of Soviet sea power and missile capability."[3] This was, of course, only part of the story, but it was the only part that interested the United States. Nasir annoyed Johnson, who maintained that "substantial [U.S.] aid to Egypt, mainly wheat to feed the people in its teeming cities," persuaded Nasir to pursue an "imperial dream."[4] Where Johnson was completely mistaken was in his assessment that "Nasser's prestige in the Arab World declined" after the 1967 defeat. On the contrary, Nasir soared in stature and legitimacy, but Johnson, Secretary of State Dean Rusk, and presumably the Congress of the United States were all in agreement "that the Arabs should not be permitted to drive the Israelis into the sea."[5] This was vintage Johnson, long on hyperbole and short on facts because the combined Arab military capability in 1967 did not add up to anything resembling a credible threat to the Jewish state.

When the Israelis came out victorious in the Six-Day War, the entire Arab world, including Saudi Arabia, was left humiliated and demoralized. The Johnson administration dragged the cease-fire process but, in November 1967, accepted a British initiative at the United Nations Security Council—Resolution 242. That famous resolution, which established no more than a framework for a permanent settlement, provided for "withdrawal of Israeli armed forces from territories occupied in the recent conflict." It further provided for the "termination of all claims of states of belligerency and respect for and acknowledgment of the sovereignty, territorial integrity and political independence of every State in the area, and their right to live in peace within secure and recognized boundaries free from threats or acts of force." Although Resolution 242 was incomplete and lacked the tough initiatives required for a permanent settlement, it did not recognize the acquisition of territory by military means as a legitimate act. Since there was no independent Palestinian state, its creation remained a theory, to the chagrin of the hapless Palestinians, as well as most Arabs, including Saudis. Although the Arab world was condemned for the infamous 1967 "No" Summit in Khartoum, the fait accompli that Israel created gained in legitimacy in Western political views. Yet, and although Israel gloated in its amazing performances on the battlefield, the 1967 victory proved Pyrrhic because, within a period of five years, a new war shattered its leaders' complacency.

The End of the Nasir Era

Nasir died of a massive heart attack on September 28, 1970, and was succeeded by his vice president, Anwar al-Sadat. A few weeks later, Hafez al-Asad overthrew Shukri al-Quwatli in Damascus and established a regime that became a classic example of authoritarian rule. In late 1970, educated analyses opined that both Sadat and Asad would be interim figures on the political scene, but, to the surprise of most, the two military officers outmaneuvered opponents and changed in their respective ways the course of contemporary Arab history.[6]

Of the two, Sadat was lionized because he signed a peace treaty with Israel in 1979, recognizing the Jewish state as a legitimate political entity. By doing so, he fulfilled a pivotal American objective in the Middle East, even if the Palestinian question lingered. If Nasir was a dreamer who lacked the means to change the Arab world, Sadat was a pharaoh willing to accept new covenants in order to fulfill his perceived legacy for Egypt. Indeed, Sadat was an astute student of Nasir, but he quickly concluded that he needed Washington to accomplish long-term regional stability. Toward that end, he first shed his country's Soviet noose, even if it was of the self-inflicted variety. Being anti-Soviet had paid off handsomely for Israel, Sadat correctly surmised, and it should work for Egypt as well. This was also an effective selling point to conservative Gulf Arabs, including the Saudis, whose support Egypt depended on. Moreover, the astute Sadat observed how Henry Kissinger, the American secretary of state, moved on the world arena, and he opted to imitate the Kissinger mantra for interim agreements. Nasir mistakenly championed a comprehensive settlement whereas Sadat was eager to adopt set-by-step initiatives. Finally, Sadat realized that, for all their support, the Soviets could not match American wealth. In a way, the Egyptian president became a Mikhail Gorbachev long before the latter emerged on the world scene and applied the same treatment to the Soviet Union.

Sadat Goes to War

Although President Anwar al-Sadat would, in time, be hailed as a peacemaker, he was, nevertheless, a warrior. The process that transformed him, a mixture of pride and clever public relations, was meticulously managed by a slew of seasoned advisors who crisscrossed the globe. The effort paid off even if few wanted the Egyptian to become a sphinx. In other words, much sacrifice would be asked of Sadat, but he would have to accept conditions set to satisfy American and Western interests. Naturally, Sadat could and did play the devil's advocate just as well, and to make his point—that he did not favor interminable negotiations—he signed a Friendship Treaty with the Soviet Union on May 27, 1971. Given that Sadat was an excellent student of contemporary Middle Eastern history, he concluded that the Israelis would not sign an agreement—not even of the interim variety—unless Egypt forced their hand. For a Sadat in search of peace, war was inevitable and for that Egypt still needed the Soviet Union.

Like everyone else, therefore, King Faysal was surprised when in July 1972 Sadat expelled all Soviet troops—estimated at around sixteen thousand—stationed in Egypt.[7] This epoch-making decision offered Kissinger unique opportunities to engage in back-channel diplomacy—to manipulate as much as to innovate fresh policies. The Soviets had provided their Arab allies just about all of the military hardware they could afford either to sell or to give away, and Sadat knew that he could not receive any more. Furthermore, he realized that a war would have to be quickly followed up with political accords, which necessitated a high-level coordination with oil-producing countries such as Saudi Arabia. Whether he fully trusted his Soviet allies, especially Foreign Minister Andrei Gromyko, was also highly doubtful. For despite the existence of a working back-channel with Kissinger—first established in April 1972—Sadat was miffed with the Soviet Union when Moscow and Washington in a summit communiqué brushed aside almost cavalierly the Arab-Israeli conflict.[8] As National Security Council advisor to President Richard M. Nixon, Henry Kissinger was a prime mover and prided himself that he submitted Sadat to his "three-tiered diplomacy" treatment. The latter encompassed exchanging messages through a secret channel, receiving the Soviet version of the discussions between the United States and the Soviet Union, and being exposed to State Department overtures to win Egyptian agreement to enter the proximity talks. But it was not entirely clear whether the confusion was not on the American side. The Nixon White House pleaded ignorance that certain steps taken by the State Department, for example, "a conversation between [Assistant Secretary Joseph] Sisco and Prince Sultan of Saudi Arabia in June [1972]—in which Sisco sought to engage Sultan's help in persuading Egypt to agree to [proximity] talks"—occurred without its knowledge.[9] Perhaps preoccupation with the Watergate crisis in Washington explained this confusion even if visionary policies pursued by Sadat meant that war was imminent. In fact, on October 6, 1973, at the height of the holy day of Yom Kippur in Israel and in the middle of the holy month of Ramadan, Sadat launched the war that restored Arab pride. A modern sphinx was on the move, and he would alter the way Arabs dealt with the rest of the world, and the way the rest of the world was accustomed to dealing with an increasingly critical part of the international community. Few Westerners, especially in the United States, anticipated the profound changes that were about to be unleashed on world affairs. Even fewer Arabs then realized that some of their leaders could coordinate and make joint decisions with long-lasting consequences for the region as well as the international community.

Henry Kissinger and Faysal

Whether the Soviets moved faster than American officials during the October 1973 War remained open for debate. At a time when détente shaped Soviet-American relations, Moscow relied on conflicting interpretations of détente itself as well as "peaceful coexistence," by escalating the confrontation level. Unprecedented military air bridges to Cairo and Damascus literally changed the landscapes and determined the conduct of hostilities. Equally important, although Soviet leaders knew that Sadat would go to war a few days before the fighting actually started, they chose not to inform Washington. According to Mohammed H. Heikal, Sadat notified the Soviet ambassador to Cairo on October 1, 1973 of the Egyptian decision to launch an attack on Israel. On October 4, Moscow replied that the timing was up to Sadat but asked for additional time to withdraw remaining Soviet personnel.[10] In the event, Egyptian troops crossed the Suez Canal on October 6 and scored impressive victories for several days before Cairo essentially froze its advances. It was not long before the Egyptian 3rd Army was encircled in the Sinai and Israeli troops recrossed the canal. As negotiations for a cease-fire accelerated, so did superpower threats to escalate and even intervene.

The diplomat responsible for shaping much of this period was Henry Kissinger, who entered the scene with gusto and whose architecture fashioned ties with key countries for decades hence. Yet, his own perceptions of the Arab world were formed long before the 1973 confrontation.

A View of the Middle East

For Henry Kissinger, the Middle East was a "maddening, heroic, and exhilarating region" that was virgin territory to the erudite university professor holding a perch at Harvard University.[11] To be sure, the National Security Council advisor formed most of his perceptions of the Middle East in general and of Arabs in particular long before he assumed high office. Yet, Kissinger opined that he understood the "tenuous quality of [Israel's] statehood," with "implacable adversaries on all its frontiers," but sympathized with the reality that "the territories occupied in 1967 [were or represented] an assurance of the security that it had vainly sought throughout its existence."[12] In a exceptional moment of candor, however, Kissinger instinctively concluded that the Jewish state "strove for both territory and recognition, [while it was] reluctant to admit that these objectives might prove incompatible."[13] More important, Kissinger was aware, even in the late 1960s, that the importance of the Middle East was closely tied to oil. Beyond the rhetoric of a "crossroads of continents and civilizations," the eminent Harvard scholar perceived Soviet intentions and actions toward the area, while he sharply focused his lens on what was clearly in the American national interest. Still, Kissinger had a distinct agenda—as well as a desire to make Middle East policy—save for Nixon's own views, which were not always identical to his own.[14] WhileNixon may well have entrusted the Middle East portfolio to Secretary of State William Rogers, ostensibly because he wanted to insulate the White House from potential policy failures, Kissinger had a loyal presence on Rogers's staff—Joseph Sisco, the assistant secretary of state for Near Eastern and South Asian affairs —who worked very closely with the White House staff. Sisco, a man who had never served overseas in any official capacity, was a rare Middle East expert—he knew everything that others acquired through hard work—save for the feel of the region. More important, Kissinger found him to be a useful mediator between Rogers and himself and, eventually, the two men became good friends.[15]

The Late 1960s

When Nixon and Kissinger came to power in 1968, the Middle East was simmering, as a war of attrition between belligerents kept the kettle hot. Regular clashes in the Sinai, the West Bank, and in Lebanon meant deaths on all sides. Guerilla skirmishes against Israel and Israeli retaliations were constant, with a spectacular attack against the civilian Beirut International Airport on December 28, 1968. Although not state-sanctioned, the burning of the Al-Aqsah Mosque by a deranged Australian Jew in August 1969 had equally devastating effects. Naturally, career diplomats, who would be despised by the Nixon White House, were eager to test the resolve of the new president. They pushed for an early involvement to frustrate Soviet gains in Egypt and Syria in particular, but also to make up for the gross negligence that—they rightly concluded—the United States had practiced under President Lyndon B. Johnson.[16]

Initially Kissinger did not favor a hands-on policy because he did not see any merit in putting "pressure [on] an ally on behalf of countries, which, with the exception of Jordan, had broken relations" with Washington after the 1967 Six-Day War. He advised that the United States wait and see "what concessions the Arabs would make."[17] For Kissinger, everlasting delays were to become bread and butter, arguably to "demonstrate even to radical Arabs that [the United States was] indispensable to *any* progress and that it could not be extorted from us by Soviet pressure."[18] Form, not substance, was important because Kissinger wanted all Arabs—but especially the so-called radicals—to earn their contemplated friendships with America. If that meant delays or failures along the way, that was just fine with a major power that cherished procedure over substance, and which was certainly not in a hurry to record any permanent progress that was not of its own making. This was so as long as wobbly Arab regimes, undetermined European states, and the ostracized and ossified Soviet leadership realized that alliances were nurtured by compromise.

Nevertheless, mired in the tragic escalation of Vietnam, Nixon genuinely desired to come to terms with Moscow on this critical issue. Senior White House officials wanted a linkage with the Middle East if one could be devised that served American interests without appearing to have established a linkage. To be sure, Washington entertained a *discussion* over the Middle East once Moscow cooperated on Vietnam. Such an objective was desirable even if Kissinger argued that "the Middle East was not ready for a comprehensive American initiative" in early 1968.[19]

If little progress was achieved throughout early 1968, it was, according to Kissinger, due to Nasir's desire "to deal with us by blackmail but [he] had nothing to threaten us with."[20] Unlike the Kennedy and even the Johnson administrations (the latter until the 1967 War), the Nixon White House perceived Nasir's inflexibility as the main source of all obstacles to a more active American role in the area. Allegedly, Nasir was an anti-American who favored the Soviet Union and, under the circumstances, Kissinger was not ready or willing to assist a foe. Of course, Nasir was anything but anti-American, even if his sympathies were seldom recognized.[21] Moreover, in the aftermath of the Aswan Dam fiasco, Nasir distanced himself from Washington, although his pro-American preferences were long-standing.[22] For Kissinger, the "stuff of Middle Eastern politics" was either "independent action or blackmail."[23] It would, therefore, be an understatement to conclude that the National Security Council of the time would not trust the Nasirs of the Arab world and would look askance at other—especially conservative Saudi—leaders.

Perceptions of Saudi Arabia

Saudi leaders were naturally pro-American by long-standing habit. Their credentials were well-established and the Al Sa'ud were well-known to successive American government representatives in the kingdom as well as senior officials in Washington. In other words, there was an institutional memory buttressing the premise that the Al Sa'ud were partial to the United States, favored and encouraged close ties with America, and considered their own survival closely tied to that of the United States throughout the world. Simply stated, Saudi Arabia was in the American camp.[24] It was against this backdrop that fundamental shifts were recorded in the perceptions of Riyadh especially as the attrition war between

Egypt and Israel gained momentum. Likewise, the August 1969 attack on the Al-Aqsah Mosque prompted King Faysal—in a quote reproduced by Kissinger—to call "for a holy war to liberate Jerusalem,"[25] a long sought objective of the pious Saudi monarch.

Kissinger, America's strategic maestro, stood his ground and repeatedly argued that the Saudis had nowhere else to turn to. For his part, Nixon leaned heavily on both Egypt and Israel, underlining that military aid would require flexibility in future negotiations. A similar message was send to Riyadh, where Washington's preferences were duly noted. The Arab despair at the growing radicalization of the Middle East, with a September 1969 coup in Libya that brought into power Colonel Mu'ammar al-Qaddhafi as the latest salvo, fell on deaf ears. For their part, the Israelis chose to ignore Nixon because the latter was enmeshed in problematic domestic impediments. For the beleaguered American president, the Vietnam War and the extrication of the United States from Southeast Asia remained a priority; for Kissinger, not offering any meaningful solutions and delaying everything at every conceivable opportunity would add to American credibility. He was, in his own terms, "always opposed to comprehensive solutions."[26] Delays, according to Kissinger, would further disillusion Arabs from the Soviet Union. By the end of 1969, Washington was persuaded that Riyadh was not prepared for peace with Jerusalem, an objective—no matter how putative—that mattered to the history-conscious Kissinger. The rest was taken for granted. Predictably, wait and see interpretations festered successive Middle Eastern crises, which gained momentum and longevity. In 1970, the Soviets moved additional weapons to Egypt, and the United States was further traumatized by an escalation of the Southeast Asian war—this time in Cambodia. Kissinger, proud of his abilities to handle multiple crises simultaneously, certainly faced a full plate: Vietnam and Cambodia, the Allende crisis in Chile, Soviet incursions in Egypt and Cuba, a looming civil war in Jordan, and, among others, a serious tug of war with Secretary of State William Rogers over American foreign policy.

For the Nixon White House, the crisis in Jordan was the direct result of the "the Soviet military thrust into Egypt and its incitement of radical Arabs."[27] In the event, the Jordan crisis was chiefly a Palestinian attempt to overthrow King Hussein, who, not surprisingly, intended to survive in power. It was no longer possible to pretend any notions of "Arab solidarity" when regular raids and counter-raids between Palestinians and Israelis resulted in many deaths. The Palestinians, rightly or wrongly, perceived Hussein of Jordan as a usurper and fought to topple the Hashemite throne. They failed miserably in what became known as Black

September when the Jordanian military unleashed its forces against Palestinian irregulars. To be sure, the Syrian mini-intervention into Jordan, from September 20–23, 1970, was an invasion, but whether it was the result of a calculated and coordinated effort against a monarchy was difficult to determine. Kissinger, with considerable Israeli assistance (overflights, reconnaissance, intelligence, and so forth), stood by the "Plucky Little King" as so many American officials were fond of referring to the Jordanian monarch.[28] The Syrians, and not the Iraqi Army contingent that was then stationed in Jordan, were the ones who moved. They may have done so with full Soviet support, but that was a moot issue. Nixon, who perceived almost all foreign policy behavior through the East-West prism, was more than happy to conclude that Syria, a regional mischief maker, was dealt a harsh blow. Equally important, Nixon was delighted that Moscow, even if indirectly, lost one. In the meantime, and as expected, Saudi Arabia stood by King Hussein, but Faysal was concerned that lack of progress in ongoing but haphazard negotiations had precipitated the Jordan crisis and that similar crises would rise elsewhere throughout the region.

This was the overall background in which the United States introduced the "Nixon Doctrine," whereby "friends and allies would be given massive aid and armaments as an invitation to participate more fully in regional security tasks deemed necessary by the United States."[29] In the Persian Gulf, the identified "friend" was the shah of Iran, whose long-standing pro-American and anti-Soviet positions were legendary.

Kissinger and the Shah of Iran

Kissinger considered the shah of Iran, Mohammed Reza Pahlavi, a friend of the United States. He admired the "authoritarian ruler," since authoritarianism was "in keeping with the traditions, perhaps even the necessities, of his society."[30] For the Nixon White House, the shah was "progressive" because he sought to "industrialize his society" even if "he modernized too rapidly" and "did not adapt his political institutions sufficiently to the economic and social changes he had brought about."[31] This last point was critical because Kissinger concluded that the shah "was not farsighted enough to create new political institutions or to enlist new loyalties to sustain political stability,"[32] even if the shah thought otherwise.[33] It must be made amply clear that Kissinger did not perceive Iranian arms purchases, which Washington encouraged with a vengeance, as diverting the country's "resources from economic development." A classic response for pushing such large sales was that similar weapons would be alternatively available from Britain and

France. Moreover, it was also thought that selling arms added value to American political leverage.

Equally important for Kissinger, the shah possessed "a sure grasp of the importance of both the global and the regional balance of power," accepting the notion that whatever dangers lurked against the Gulf region hailed from the north. According to Kissinger, "the Shah of Iran chose friendship with the United States" over the many options available to Teheran.[34] In reality, this was the least the shah could do since Washington had restored him to the Peacock throne in 1953. Whatever else one may say about the shah, he was certainly loyal and grateful. But he could also spot opportunities that would advance his grandiose visions, even if these were mired in illusions. The shah could comfortably be anti-Soviet, play the role of policeman of the West in the Gulf, introduce a balance of power with Iraq and Pakistan, and stand up to radicalism as long as Washington catered to his never-ending appetite for arms.

These details notwithstanding, Kissinger attributed additional values to the friendship that the shah expressed toward the United States. In fact, according to Kissinger, who was then the National Security Council advisor, "Israel aside," Iran stood "alone among the countries of the region" to make "friendship with the United States the starting point of its foreign policy."[35] This perception certainly came as a rude awakening to Saudi Arabia and other Arab Gulf monarchies that were under the impression that their friendships were pivotal to painstakingly developed ties with Washington. In fact, Saudi leaders were livid to read in Kissinger's memoirs that the shah of Iran "never used his control of oil to bring political pressure, [and] never joined any oil embargo against the West or Israel."[36] Part of that statement was of course correct because Iran was not an OAPEC member and therefore could not join the oil embargo against the United States and the Netherlands in the aftermath of the October 1973 Arab-Israeli War. Yet, the first part of the statement etched by Kissinger was hollow because the shah persuaded his American friends to encourage higher oil prices, which would in turn allow Iran to pay for American arms.[37] There was no need for political pressure but, in reality, plenty of hints floated in the stratosphere of the American-Iranian sky. Iranian oil needed protection from the Soviet Union after all. That said it all, even if the terminology was not of the "political pressure" variety.

Interestingly, however, Kissinger recognized that the shah pushed for higher oil prices even as Iran pushed for an entirely new formula starting in 1971. At the time, Iran was eager to assist Israel—since the two countries were on good terms and Iran was meeting Israel's as well as South Africa's oil requirements—which, naturally, enhanced the prestige of the shah with Kissinger.

In May 1972, Nixon and Kissinger traveled to Teheran on their way back from Moscow. It was an important visit because the Americans were eager to reach an understanding with the shah over the latter's growing role in the Gulf. A power vacuum, created by the British withdrawal from the Lower Gulf region in 1971, could not be left unfilled. Even after the shah had invaded and occupied territory of the United Arab Emirates—the three islands of Abu Musa, the Greater Tunb, and the Lesser Tunb more precisely—on December 1, 1971 (a day prior to the United Arab Emirates' independence from Britain), he successfully persuaded Washington that Saudi Arabia, the United Arab Emirates, and the other Gulf shaykhdoms were under threat from a hegemonic Soviet Union and therefore in need of Iranian protection. The Arabian Peninsula, argued the wily shah, was being encircled and he offered his good services to deny Moscow any access to any part of it.[38]

Nixon and Kissinger knew that American military capabilities were overstretched—mostly mired in Vietnam or poised in Europe. Arguably, assigning military units to the Persian Gulf would not be feasible, at least in the early 1970s. Luckily for the United States, "Iran was willing to play this role" and, in one of the most convoluted foreign policy initiatives ever devised, the British vacuum "would be filled by a local power friendly" to Washington.[39] Moreover, the move would further discourage Iraq from adventures against the Lower Gulf states, or against its foes in Jordan and Saudi Arabia. Nixon thus "persuaded" the shah to become the policeman of the West during his celebrated May 1972 visit to Iran. For rendering such valuable services, and as a clear linkage to his preferred policies, the shah was rewarded with eighty top of the line F-14 aircraft and assorted equipment sold at rack rates.

What the Nixon-Kissinger-Shah rapprochement indicated was a sharp turn in how Washington perceived Saudi Arabia. Between 1968 and 1972, and despite the kingdom's undeniable role in bringing stability to oil prices, America opted to place a local policeman to monitor regional conduct. Aside from the historical differences that existed between Saudi Arabia and Iran, this shift illustrated the erosion of the value that Saudi Arabia represented in American eyes, especially as the Nixon "Twin Pillar" policy armed one of the mainstays while holding the other one in check. Ironically, the sale of truly large quantities of weapons to Iran required the presence of a significant American military presence—in the form of advisors and technicians—throughout the country, with profound consequences for the stability of the peacock throne. None of this escaped the sharp eyes of King Faysal, although his warnings fell on deaf ears.

Kissinger and the 1973 War

In the frantic morning hours of October 6, 1973, Kissinger dispatched an urgent cable to Faysal asking Saudi Arabia "to intervene immediately with Presidents Sadat and Asad and urge that no such attack be launched on their part."[40] Kissinger "had little hope" because "if the attack was premeditated," Saudi Arabia "could not halt it" and, to Kissinger's disappointment, "Faisal emphasized Arab solidarity" when he responded.[41] By attacking Israel in an unprovoked move, Egypt and Syria clarified specific objectives, including a strong desire to break the impasse that both countries had reached in their negotiations. In early 1973, the Egyptian president Anwar al-Sadat in particular concluded that the superpowers seemed committed to the status quo, which, remarkably, he wished to alter.[42] Given the element of surprise and very careful planning, both Egyptian and Syrian forces made significant headway during the first week of hostilities. The supposedly impregnable Bar-Lev Line, built after the 1967 occupation of the Sinai and manned by electronic sensors, was overrun by Egyptian troops, who constructed pontoon bridges across the Suez Canal. Even the heralded Israeli Air Force could not establish its accustomed superiority during the first week of fighting. Clearly the 1967 humiliation was erased as Arab forces reconquered some of their lost territories. Amazingly, rather than push ahead in the Sinai, the Egyptians stood their ground near the canal under Sadat's direct orders. On the Golan Heights as well, Syrian troops reoccupied territory lost in 1967 with no plans for invading Israel. The respite allowed Israeli forces to regain their strength, regroup, and launch counterattacks quite effectively. Still, by the second week of fighting, Israeli casualties increased. From an Arab point of view, the carefully nurtured idea of Israeli invincibility proved to be a myth, as frantic messages kept world chancelleries busy. Tensions escalated between Washington and Moscow, as both sought to outmaneuver each other before cooler heads lowered tensions.

As far as Saudi Arabia was concerned, a conscious effort was made to inform King Faysal that his concerns were "being heard" in the hope that he would "not become more actively involved in the hostilities."[43] Presumably, Washington was privy to news that the Saudis might do so, which prompted the cautionary dispatch. A message of October 12, 1973 from the White House to Faysal clarified that American "policy at this time [wa]s not one-sided." Nixon reminded Faysal that Washington was "neither pro-Israel[i] nor pro-Arab" but that it was "pro-peace."[44] There were no indications that Faysal doubted Nixon's pledges but neither were there any hints that he trusted them. Because the war was increasingly conducted as a Soviet-American proxy confrontation, the actual hostilities—as well as most diplomatic maneuvers—were assessed through the classic Cold War prism. Kissinger feared for his cherished détente policy, but expectations that this war would take less than a week—as in 1967—turned to naught. When Soviet transport aircraft started an airlift to Syria on October 10, in part as a response to the October 7 American airlifts to Israel, the die was cast. An escalation was therefore inevitable. Washington objected and launched a massive airlift that was, qualitatively as well as quantitatively, superior to anything deployed by the Soviet Union.

On October 14, 1973, Kissinger wrote an explanatory telegram to Faysal, seeking Saudi understanding that the U.S. airlift to Israel was "not intended as anti-Arab."[45] Rather, Kissinger clarified, it was a reaction to the "200" Soviet flights—then estimated by U.S. intelligence services—that allegedly intended to "exploit the situation to their own advantage in the Arab World."[46] Kissinger was determined not to let Moscow "take advantage of the situation." He promised Faysal that Washington was prepared to stop its own "airlift promptly, provided the Soviets did the same," and after "an effective cease-fire" was achieved.[47]

The caveats were eye-popping even if Kissinger's tone was firm. Furthermore, Kissinger did not encourage an urgent delivery of this last message, opining that it could wait until "the opening of business local time—[on] Monday, October 15," specifying that "earlier delivery [was neither] required [n]or desired." Naturally, he did not provide Faysal with a qualitative assessment of how the Soviet and American airlifts compared, although the Saudis received detailed data from Egypt, indicating significant technical advantages for Israel. Faysal was distraught that his pleas fell on deaf ears in Washington. On October 16, the American ambassador in Riyadh, James Akins, wrote to Kissinger that Saudi Arabia expressed "no visible anger at US announcements [concerning U.S. arms to Israel], but rather genuine expression of sorrow that USG [United States Government] move had set course for inevitable divergence of interests of US and SAG [Saudi Arabian Government]."[48]

The Aftermath of the Airlifts

According to Kissinger, in 1973 Omar Saqqaf, the Saudi minister of state for foreign affairs, declared to President Richard M. Nixon in the Oval Office that "Israel [wa]s not being threatened by the Arabs with annihilation" and explicitly affirmed that Israel had a right to exist, albeit within its 1967 frontiers. Saqqaf apparently summarized a collective regional point of view by stating that the Arabs "want[ed] no more than a return to the 1967 borders and respect for the rights of refugees to return to their lands or be compensated for what they have lost. This would be enough to guarantee the stability and integrity of Israel."[49] Nixon responded by pledging to work within United Nations Security Council Resolution 242, without promising a withdrawal, allegedly because Israel would not return to previous frontiers when the 1973 War was imposed on it. This critical caveat notwithstanding, it was a modest promise given the Nixon preoccupation with putative impeachment proceedings in the aftermath of the Watergate scandal. Nixon committed the task to Kissinger despite his "Jewish origin," to which Saqqaf retorted: "We are all Semites together."[50] Speaking to reporters after the White House meeting, Saqqaf displayed diplomatic confidence in Washington's vows and expressed his faith in Kissinger when he announced, "The man who could solve the Vietnam war, the man who could have settled the peace all over the World, can easily play a good role in settling and having peace in our area of the Middle East."[51]

Elated by such support, Kissinger concluded that the American airlift in 1973 "perhaps enhanced" the "Arab conviction that the United States was the key to a peace settlement,"[52] and later stated that Washington desired "the most massive Arab defeat."[53] In the minds of its leaders, Washington was indispensable and would use its influence because there were no substitutes to America. Moreover, Kissinger was persuaded that Arab armies should not win the war and, consequently, would need to vacate whatever gains they may have achieved—especially breaching the Bar-Lev Line—to allow for a proper diplomatic settlement. Toward that end, Kissinger insisted that the United States "keep the stuff going into Israel," as this was deemed useful. "We have to pour it in until someone quits," underlined Kissinger, allegedly because the airlift was having a salutary effect on diplomacy. On October 17, 1973, the State Department was confident that its guarantees to mediate, as reflected in the mood of Arab ministers, "seemed to confirm that there would be no immediate oil embargo."[54] Apparently, Nixon sought a winning position in the negotiations before a cease-fire could be reached, in order to buttress several Arab leaderships—including that of Saudi Arabia—that feared "being left at the mercy of the Soviet Union." He concluded that the war was "bigger than the Middle East," and that Washington could not possibly "allow a Soviet-supported operation to succeed against an American-supported operation. If it does, our credibility everywhere is severely shaken."[55]

To the surprise of most Washington officials, before the evening was out, the OAPEC meeting in Kuwait announced an immediate oil production cutback. Simultaneously, Iran and the Arab Gulf producers increased the price of oil unilaterally by 70 percent, from $3.01 to $5.12 a barrel. Both of these developments caught the Nixon administration by total surprise, although before the day was out Kissinger informed the Israelis that they "should base . . . military operations on [the] assumption that [the United States] would not be able to stall a cease-fire more than forty-eight hours after [it] w[as] approached."[56] Kissinger was furious, perceiving the OAPEC decision as another example of intolerable Arab "blackmail" and, important, worthy of a bitter diplomatic response, even of a brutally nasty bickering. What upset Washington most was the Arab insistence that United Nations Security Council Resolution 242 be applied in full as Saudi, Egyptian, and Kuwaiti leaders remained adamant on this crucial point of principle: the absence of a direct linkage to Resolution 242 meant no lifting of the embargo. Moreover, Arab leaders and commentators underscored, given that successive American presidents had repeatedly promised full implementation of the resolution, a commitment to honor it should pose no dilemmas.

The Effectiveness of the Oil Weapon

The oil weapon proved effective in 1973 because it dramatically affected subsequent diplomatic initiatives. President Nixon revealed in his memoirs that his major concern was to end the Arab oil embargo "from the moment [it] began."[57] Within days, and after Israeli forces had successfully expanded territories under their control on both the Egyptian and Syrian borders, the major powers brokered a cease-fire at the United Nations. On October 22, 1973, Resolution 338 passed the Security Council, clearly because the oil weapon proved its effectiveness.[58] In the midst of the Watergate scandal, Washington was eager to find a way out, just as Moscow was eager to see neither Egypt nor Syria fully defeated on the battlefield. Although all fighting should have stopped on October 23, Israeli forces advanced toward Suez, west of the Canal, to completely isolate the Egyptian Third Army, which was trapped east of the Canal. Cairo called for assistance and Moscow responded by placing some of its forces on nuclear alert. Washington reciprocated for reasons that have not yet been fully revealed although Secretary of State Henry Kissinger claimed that Nixon—faced with the consequence of the infamous "Saturday Night Massacre" of Watergate fame that nearly brought his government down then and there—had an incentive to paint the crisis . . . in the darkest possible terms."[59] Nixon allegedly "obtained information . . . that the Soviet Union was planning to send a very substantial force into the Mideast, a military force," which, according to Kissinger, was unacceptable to the United States. In the event, a United Nations Emergency Force was dispatched to the area—at kilometer 101 on the Suez-Cairo road—to enforce a disengagement plan. It took the efforts of world powers several months, from January 18 to May 31, 1974 precisely, to work out more or less definitive disengagement accords to separate forces. By the end of 1973, the war entered a new phase, as Washington shifted attention to oil-producing countries. Kissinger was about to meet Faysal in a new face-off.

Face to Face in Riyadh

Kissinger arrived in Riyadh on November 8, 1973, having been prodded by an embattled Nixon to produce tangible foreign policy successes, if for no other reason than to buttress shattered White House credibility. In fact, Nixon wanted Faysal by his side in Washington to announce whatever progress could be achieved on the oil issue. Toward that end, an invitation to Faysal was contemplated, although Kissinger thought that the idea was tantamount to "total insanity." For him, a visit by Faysal "so soon after the war was absolutely inconceivable," as "it would defeat the entire thrust of Saudi strategy, which had been to build credit with radical Arab regimes."[60] This was a mistaken reading of Saudi strategy or of Faysal's motives, but what was undeniable was Kissinger's accurate report to Alexander Haig at the White House that such an invitation "would be interpreted throughout Arab World as U.S. collapse."[61] Kissinger further cautioned that Faysal's tête-à-tête with Nixon "would magnify, not reduce, Arab incentives to keep pressure on U.S. via [the] oil weapon." In the event, Faysal was not particularly accommodating, even if Saudi leaders "felt friendship for the United States" in Kissinger's words.[62] At this juncture, the Saudi monarch placed Arab loyalty above all else not only because he correctly assessed domestic and regional dangers, but because he genuinely identified with the Arab cause.[63] If Washington perceived Saudi policy as being ambiguous, it was the result of American preferences, not necessarily Saudi behavior. Still, Kissinger recognized that his intrinsic abilities to score "dramatic breakthroughs" in Riyadh would come to naught, as Faysal and the Al Sa'ud adopted an opaque built-in resistance to eloquence and to threats.[64]

Traveling to the kingdom and entering a Saudi palace for the first time in his life, Kissinger broke bread with Faysal, as he reflected on "what strange twists of fate had caused a refugee from Nazi persecution to wind up in Arabia as the representative of American democracy."[65] The majesty of the moment quickly gave way to Kissinger's ire toward "Faisal's standard speech." "Its basic proposition," lamented the reflective envoy, "was that Jews and Communists were working now in parallel, now together, to undermine the civilized world as we knew it. Oblivious to my ancestry—or delicately putting me into a special category—Faisal insisted that an end had to be put once and for all to the dual conspiracy of Jews and Communists. The Middle East outpost of that plot was the State of Israel, put there by Bolshevism for the principal purpose of dividing Americans from the Arabs."[66]

Kissinger reportedly changed the subject since he did not know "where to begin" to answer "such a line of reasoning." Yet, by his own admission, and as he came to know the Saudi monarch, Kissinger concluded that Faysal "was a man of rare quality, highly intelligent, formidable and yet wise enough never to display his strength. The imperatives of conviction and tactical expediency merged, so that he both believed in what he was doing and did what served his purposes."[67] This appraisal was justified even if Kissinger refused to hear or accept those principles that defined Faysal. Faysal was a pro-American, anti-Communist, pro-Arab, pro-Palestinian nationalist.[68] Although Westerners rejected such a compilation, the perspectives were entirely compatible with Arab intentions and, more important, were consistent with religious convictions.

Still, while Kissinger believed that Faysal felt deeply about his position on Communism and Zionism, he compartmentalized Faysal's logic. Faysal's "strident anti-Communism helped reassure America," Kissinger opined, while "his virulent opposition to Zionism reassured radicals and the PLO and thus reduced their incentives to follow any temptation to undermine the monarchy domestically."[69] Again, this was a mistaken reading of the Saudi ruler for at least two reasons. First, Riyadh had established impeccable pro-American credentials for some four decades and, therefore, was confident that its policies did not require any reassuring.[70] Second, Faysal was secure in the knowledge that the Al Saʿud, despite periodic internal unrest, were masters of their own destinies. If outsiders perceived dangers—as a cottage industry anticipated the demise of the Al Saʿud as early as 1932—Faysal knew that he, in particular, was a legitimate ruler in the full meaning of the term.[71] The monarch was at ease in his rule because of his established record. Moreover, Faysal genuinely believed that Communism and Zionism represented equal threats to the Arab and Muslim worlds even if most Westerners refused to believe him. In fact, Faysal and leading Arab leaders have declared for decades that the Palestinian cause—itself the result of injustices committed against the hapless people—was a core concern to the entire Ummah, only to be dismissed by interlocutors eager "to change the subject."[72]

The deeply religious Faysal was cohesive, cogent, and consistent. He was not easily blackmailed because his reputation for piety, according to Henry Kissinger, "combined exaltation and anonymity, great influence and aloofness from the fray."[73]

Faysal fascinated Kissinger. For the American secretary of state, the enigmatic

Saudi monarch clothed his greatness in anonymity and generally "delivered more than he promised."[74] What Washington wanted from Riyadh was the lifting of the oil embargo because the United States was hurting, at least diplomatically. Yet, no matter how insistent Kissinger was, Faysal did not alter his innermost perceptions and, equally important, his decisions. He conceded to the shuttling diplomat that "peace with Israel was possible—an unusual acknowledgment for Faisal—but he immediately qualified the statement by making it conditional on Israeli withdrawal to the 1967 frontiers and the return of *all* Palestinian refugees to their homes, which in practice would mean an influx of over a million Arabs into pre-1967 Israel."[75] These conditions were eminently logical to Faysal although Kissinger perceived them as an attitude rather than a program. Why Washington opted to reject these conditions was left unanswered. One possible explanation was the preference for a drawn-out process rather than a permanent settlement. In the event, Kissinger also rejected the emphasis on Israeli dependence and how Israel acquiesced to the United States whenever Washington linked its putative plans to specific goals.

Nixon's Messages to Faysal

After Kissinger failed to persuade King Faysal, President Nixon wrote a personal letter to the Saudi monarch on January 25, 1974, in which he made this crucial statement:

> In earlier messages to Your Majesty I have said that events have proven the wisdom of your counsel over the years. My Government is now embarked upon and committed to a course of action that can, I am convinced, bring a just and durable peace to the Middle East. The first fruits of that commitment are reflected in the agreement on the disengagement of forces signed last Friday, under which Israel forces will withdraw into Sinai as a first step toward a final settlement in accordance with Security Council Resolutions 338 and 242.[76]

Three days later, on January 28, the CIA station chief in Saudi Arabia, Raymond Close, "received an urgent privacy-channel message from Kissinger explaining in confidence that Nixon was becoming desperate." Kissinger inquired whether the Saudi monarch would permit the president of the United States "to announce to the American people in his State of the Union address two days later that the oil embargo would soon be lifted?" According to Close, Sa'ud and Turki al-Faysal reported that their father gave his approval on two conditions.

First, Nixon would be welcome to announce in his speech that he had received assurances from "friendly leaders" in the Middle East that an urgent meeting would be called to discuss lifting of the embargo. Second, the president's announcement should include unequivocal linkage to full implementation of a Middle East peace settlement based on Resolution 242. The explicit enjoinder conveyed by King Faisal was that Nixon should employ in his State of the Union speech precisely the same phraseology that he had used in his personal letter to Faisal just three days before: that the recent disengagement in Sinai was only the "first step" toward full implementation of resolutions 242 and 338.[77]

In effect, the Saudis were eager for Nixon to confirm his oft-repeated private promises to Faysal to seek a just and lasting peace for the Palestinians. Close recalled "an observation made that evening by Prince Turki, a young man of 27 at the time," who "remarked that by asking the U.S. president to employ the same words that he himself had just written in a personal letter to a fellow head of state," Riyadh "could be confident that no one, not even Henry Kissinger, would dare to portray the request as an unreasonable 'demand' on the part of the Saudi king."

On January 30, 1974, Nixon delivered his speech to Congress, in which he recognized the values of Resolutions 242 and 338. According to the president:

The first step in the process is the disengagement of Egyptian and Israeli forces which is now taking place. Because of this hopeful development, I can announce tonight that I have been assured, through my personal contacts with friendly leaders in the Middle Eastern area, that an urgent meeting will be called in the immediate future to discuss the lifting of the oil embargo. This is an encouraging sign. However, it should be clearly understood by our friends in the Middle East that the United States will not be coerced on this issue.[78]

Remarkably, Nixon, perhaps on Secretary of State Henry Kissinger's recommendation, did not "honor the true spirit of the agreement" he reached with Faysal. The added sentence—"it should be clearly understood by our friends in the Middle East that the United States will not be coerced on this issue"—was a direct threat. Close concluded that its insertion "probably reflected the resentment that Kissinger felt at having been outmaneuvered."[79] When briefed on the speech, Faysal concluded that the credibility of the United States was lost, but that cooperation with Washington should and would continue.

Linkages and Stalled Negotiations

A linkage between oil and politics existed long before the 1973 War as successive American governments, starting in the early 1930s, looked to the Middle East with heightened interest. But with the most recent crisis, Richard M. Nixon explicitly drew a parallel on September 5, 1973 when he chastised Congress for failing to act on his energy proposals. Responding to a question about American influence with Arab oil producers, Nixon declared:

> With regard to Saudi Arabia, perhaps the relations which the United States has with Saudi Arabia might lead to more influence there. [But,] in a broader context, the answer to the problem of oil that we presently depend upon in the Mideast—we depend on it not, of course, nearly as much as Europe, but we are all in the same bag when you really come down to it—the problem that we have here is that as far as the Arab countries are concerned, the ones involved here, is that it is tied up with the Arab-Israeli dispute. That is why, in talking with Dr. Kissinger both before I nominated him and since, that we have put at the highest priority moving toward making some progress toward the settlement of that dispute.[80]

The acknowledgment—a perfect illustration of linkage even if everyone involved denied it—shocked generally unassuming reporters. Within a month, and barely two weeks after Henry Kissinger had moved from his National Security Advisor perch to lead the State Department, Anwar al-Sadat launched the Ramadan War in October 1973. Even if American policy could not change under duress, two fundamental features preoccupied the State Department. First, the new secretary of state was already drawing the broad outlines of his détente policy with the Soviet Union and, therefore, did not cherish the idea of a confrontation. Second, and perhaps more important, Washington did not wish to erect a separation wall with increasingly critical Arab countries such as Saudi Arabia. Yet, because the war was perceived as a classic proxy clash with the Soviets, and because of dire military conditions on the battlefield, Nixon authorized a military airlift to Israel. The ultimate purpose of that choice was to further boost the Jewish state's technical advantages while promoting disengagement talks to achieve a cease-fire without, it was hoped, pushing the Arab regimes to impose an oil embargo. In the event, several miscalculations led to the conflict, as Kissinger himself acknowledged: "The conditions that produced this war were clearly intolerable to the Arab nations and . . . in a process of negotiation it will be necessary to make substantial concessions."[81] Whether this shift conveyed a new American initiative—to be even-handed—was then too early to determine, but the secretary of state conceded the idea of conceding. What remained was to find the appropriate "partners" to whom a superpower could concede without appearing doing so. While Sadat and to a lesser extent Asad of Syria as well as Palestinian forces that participated in the fighting certainly deserved much of the credit for the change, Kissinger had the oil producers in mind, Faysal in particular. The willingness of the Saudi monarch to use his oil weapon forced an evolution of American Middle East policies. Rather than be limited to the preservation of Israel, after 1973–74 Washington was compelled to consider the perspective of Arab oil producers as well. To be sure, the United States still looked at the Middle East through the Soviet prism, but it was now committed to a process that, over time, would try and solve the Arab-Israeli dispute. As little as that represented in real terms, it was nevertheless a huge victory for Faysal, who, single handedly, earned Washington's attention. What would not stand, however, was the defiance over oil because no power could tolerate the perception of economic "strangulation."

Nixon Visits Faysal

Unsurprisingly, negotiations stalled throughout the first few months of 1974 when a frustrated Nixon, perhaps to reduce pressure on the home front, decided to visit the region. After an enthusiastic stop in Cairo—with a media savvy Sadat acting as the perfect host—and before visiting Syria, Israel, and Jordan, Nixon and his party made a short stop in Saudi Arabia. On June 14, 1974, Faysal welcomed Nixon in a sweltering Jiddah for what were surely extremely serious talks between the two men and their advisors. From the American perspective two primary issues stood out: the impact that high oil prices were having on global economies and the substantial financial support allocated by the kingdom to front-line states.[82] Faysal was perceived with suspicion even if Nixon recognized his worth. An incredulous Nixon believed that the king "saw Zionist and Communist conspiracies around him."[83] Surely, and with this limited logic, one could be safely opposed to Communism, but having differing views on Zionism automatically categorized one to the "conspiracy" bin. Apparently, Faysal "even put forward what must be the ultimate conspiratorialist notion: that the Zionists were behind the Palestinian terrorists."[84] These views notwithstanding, Nixon aimed to alter policies pursued by the Saudi monarch by encouraging him to moderate oil prices. This was really one of his main objectives in stopping in Jiddah, and while Faysal did not concede he played to Nixon's weakness rather well. Aware of Nixon's myriad Watergate problems, Faysal bade his American guest farewell by declaring:

> Anybody who stands against you, Mr. President, in the United States or outside the United States of America, or stands against us, your friends in

this part of the world, obviously has one aim in mind, namely, that of causing the splintering of the world, the wrong polarization of the world, by
bringing about of mischief, which would not be conducive to tranquility
and peace in the world. Therefore, we beseech Almighty God to lend His
help to us and to you so that we both can go hand in hand, shoulder to
shoulder in pursuance of the noble aims that we both share, namely, those
of peace, justice, and prosperity in the world.[85]

Nixon was elated but a decision on the business at hand—lower oil prices—
was postponed. He moved on to Syria, where he met his match in the person of
Hafez al-Asad. According to Nixon, while Faysal "was one of the wisest leaders in
the entire region," Asad had "elements of genius, without any question."[86] In Damascus, the United States and Syria reestablished diplomatic relations—broken
after the 1967 War—and Asad paid his guest the ultimate Arab compliment by
kissing Nixon on both cheeks during departure ceremonies.

If Nixon left Jiddah with only a promise, he soon landed in Israel, where an
eager Yitzhak Rabin was "bluntly anxious to know how much more aid he could
depend on from us." An irritated President did not mince his words, and while
the White House recommended that Congress allocate generous aid packages to
Israel, Nixon also expected that the Israelis would play "a sincere and serious part
in maintaining the momentum of the peace negotiations" that Kissinger had initiated with his famous "shuttle" diplomacy.[87] As he revealed in his memoirs, Nixon
emphasized that the American relationship with Israel was difficult, at times even
problematic.

The "Journey to Peace" ended with a brief stop in Jordan, where Nixon met
King Hussein, who "impressed" Nixon "by the charm and intelligence" he usually displayed.[88] Nixon reflected on how much "the Arabs really want[ed] to be
friends of the Americans."[89] He further opined that "with the exception of some
arrogant Americans, particularly in the foreign service and some business types,"
most Americans would reciprocate.[90] The friendship theme, of course, was abun-
dantly discussed in Saudi Arabia except that it was unclear whether anyone other
than Nixon shared these views.

The Kissinger Threat

Nixon's visit did not produce immediate results as high oil prices unsettled world
markets throughout the summer of 1974 and as negotiations on the peace process stalled. Moreover, little progress was achieved because antagonists as well as
mediators lambasted each other. Simultaneously, successive OPEC and OAPEC
meetings produced little relief, which, not surprisingly, drew the ire of major par-

ticipants. In a calculated interview with *Business Week*, Kissinger raised the possibility of American attacks on Saudi oil fields in case of an economic "strangulation." He considered a new war to be very dangerous and dismissed the military option as an automatic selection because it was "easier to get into a war than to get out of it." He underlined, however, that exceptional conditions could force Washington to act when he declared, "I am not saying that there's no circumstance where we would not use force. But it is one thing to use it in the case of a dispute over price; it's another where there is some actual strangulation of the industrialized world."[91]

Even before Kissinger's "strangulation" statement, Faysal did not fully trust him because he had "lied to him," , according to James Akins, the American ambassador to Riyadh. "Before Kissinger first came out [to Saudi Arabia]," Akins recalled, "Faisal was very apprehensive. I talked to the king at length and said, look, he's the American foreign minister. He has a sense of history. He'll be doing all the things that will advance America's interests, not Israel's interests. You can deal with him. I was probably more responsible than anybody else for getting a reasonable relationship between Kissinger and the king. Then Kissinger started playing fast and loose with the truth."[92]

Needless to say, Akins did not last long in Riyadh as Kissinger dismissed him from the ambassadorship because, allegedly, he did not follow orders. Yet, as Akins was not a Saudi, he was not inclined to back Faysal willy-nilly. Rather, he may well have reasoned that long-term American interests required a modicum of honesty and cooperation with the Saudi monarch, who, like most world leaders, appreciated a little candor.

The Last Faysal-Kissinger Meeting

A few months after this threat, Faysal and Kissinger met for the last time on February 14, 1975. As the Saudi deputy foreign minister had just passed away, Faysal asked Ahmad Zaki Yamani to receive Kissinger at the airport on behalf of the Saudi government. Kissinger, who was eager to conclude a second disengagement agreement in his shuttle diplomacy, came to Riyadh to secure the monarch's accord. He explained to Faysal why it was essential to conclude a second accord between Egypt and Israel, but Faysal rejected Kissinger's rationale, insisting that Kissinger frame the second disengagement to include one between Israel and Syria.[93] According to Yamani, a long session of back-and-forth argumentation ended without any understanding when Kissinger reiterated his preferred method—Egypt first then Syria—and Faysal declaring his opposition.[94] What Faysal really objected to was Kissinger's cunning plan to isolate Egypt from the Arab camp. It may be fair to state that the Saudi monarch read the American diplomat through and through as he insisted on an overall scheme that addressed all protagonists. By this time Kissinger fully understood how critical Faysal's word was because it had become clear that every step taken by Sadat was with the full consent of Riyadh.[95] Naturally, the opprobrium was too evident, and the second disengagement accord—between Egypt and Israel—would only be signed on September 1, 1975, several months after Faysal was assassinated.

To be sure, the Arab-Israeli dispute was not resolved in 1975, even after Faysal and his allies relied on the oil weapon to shake the momentum. Simply stated, Kissinger (both under the Nixon and Ford administrations) was far more interested in piecemeal accords than an overall settlement. Shuttle diplomacy was inherently a piecemeal approach that dealt with a disengagement here, a partial withdrawal there, or a commitment to delegate attention. It was vintage Kissinger diplomacy but, in truth, the American could not deliver more.[96]

The Consequences of the Oil Embargo

Throughout the 1973–74 oil crises, Riyadh maintained that its contribution to the stability of Western economies was essential for its own survival as well, and that it would not jeopardize carefully tailored ties with the United States for short-term gains. By calling for moderate prices and flooding the market whenever shortages loomed, Saudi Arabia concretely demonstrated to major powers that its policy was indeed consistent with their own interests in the Persian Gulf region even if policy differences remained. As early as the 1970s, King Faysal expressed his concern for the worldwide recession that the 1973–74 oil crisis caused when he argued that the economic downturn might so seriously destabilize Western economies as to lead to a Communist takeover in Italy and France.[97] In 1974, Yamani argued—most likely with the full approval of King Faysal—that Saudi economic growth was directly linked to U.S. energy needs when he stated:

> Our priority is to industrialize Saudi Arabia and to diversify its economy. Investment by Saudi Arabia towards achieving its end will benefit the United States from whom we will need to import capital goods and technical expertise. . . . The need for oil in the United States and the need for technological expertise in Saudi Arabia provides a natural starting point towards intensified cooperation aimed at serving the best interests of both countries . . . which would reflect not only a marked benefit to our individual economies but also to the world and its stability as a whole.[98]

Yamani revisited the issue in 1975 when he declared:

The security and stability of the oil-producing countries is of the utmost importance not only to the producers themselves but to the world at large. The security of oil supplies, so important to consumer countries[,] is totally dependent on the security and stability of the oil producing states. . . . The countries of the world, be they oil suppliers or consumers, have a common vested interest in the security and continuity of oil supplies. Therefore their cooperation in combating any threat to peace in the Middle East is an absolute and constant necessity.[99]

Over the years, Yamani reaffirmed this view—on how Saudi oil policy was intimately linked to the West—with some consistency, even if he cautioned his audiences. In 1981, for example, he declared that Saudi Arabia was "concerned over the international economy because [of its] interest[s] in it." He further underlined that the kingdom was "temporarily investing its money in the West," and that were the international economy to collapse, Saudi Arabia's own "investments w[ould] erode away." Yamani concluded by declaring that the "concern over the international economy arose from [Riyadh's] desire to industrialize," something that would not be possible "if the international economy" were to collapse.[100] Such cautionary notes notwithstanding, the Al Sa'ud recognized the main dangers of their dependence on the West. If Saudi production came under physical attack, an immediate exodus of American and European technicians—who were essential to manage oil fields—would occur. Such an exodus happened in 1967 after a mob attacked ARAMCO housing.[101] Smaller withdrawals also occurred during the October 1973 War and in subsequent conflicts. Given the high uncertainty levels, and starting in the 1960s, Riyadh sought to secure oil fields in such a way that a potential exodus would not cripple its production and export capabilities. In fact, security equipment, as well as adequate manpower to keep the fields pumping, received priority. Simultaneously, the Al Sa'ud recognized that oil was a double-edged political sword that must be branded with utmost care. Because the kingdom used the oil weapon against the United States and the Netherlands during the 1973 Arab-Israeli War, it drew specific lessons and insisted that its past behavior did not preclude full cooperation with Washington. Indeed, Riyadh embarked on an elaborate reconciliation policy with Washington following the 1973 OAPEC embargo. Recognizing the value of petroleum to Western economies, and aware of their limited capabilities to defend a country as large as Saudi Arabia, the Al Sa'ud acknowledged the need for a special relationship with the United States. Although King Faysal and senior members of the family argued for a more even-handed approach—Faysal positing that Britain and France be given equal importance to the United States—the debate was finally settled after the Iranian Revolution, when epoch-making revolutionary ideas affected the entire region.

Because of its vast oil wealth, Saudi Arabia faced direct threats to its security and, to prevent or deter potential foes, ventured into a world not of its making in the 1970s. Toward that end, King Faysal developed and implemented a unique outlook predicated on the use of his strategic weapon—oil—to serve Saudi, Arab, and Islamic interests. In 1971, he proposed that Saudi Arabia provide all the energy needs of the United States in return for a commitment to solve the Palestinian problem. In 1972, He entrusted his son Sa'ud with this most sensitive offer—in the form of a formal proposal—to Kissinger, with no response. This was followed by a similar mission entrusted to the petroleum minister, Yamani, who made another trip to Washington for the same purpose, with similar results. When faced with such rejections, Faysal engaged in a media blitz to promote the idea to the American public, as he engaged newspaper and television personalities with rare interviews. The extraordinary frequency and, at times, bluntness of his message were carefully vetted to emphasize the quid pro quo, to no avail.

Therefore, and to survive as a state, Saudi Arabia assumed various Arab political mantles as it provided billions of dollars to key Arab and Muslim allies in what came to be known as its petro-political portfolio. Yet, the pragmatic Faysal realized that neither petro-politics nor alliances with key Western powers—especially the United States—guaranteed permanent solace. As an alternative, he encouraged the formulation of intrinsic and more genuine options, which resulted in his magisterial Islamic vision. Whatever security would hence come to the Arabian Peninsula would do so through the Organization of Islamic Conference (OIC). A long-standing but authentic foresight germinated in Faysal's mind long before the 1973–74 crisis confirmed his innermost fears. The best way to serve Saudi interests, Faysal knew, was by shaping Saudi Arabia's own destiny.

6

A Modernizing Vision for an Emergent Kingdom

Rather than become a victim of his encounters with the West in general and the United States in particular, the pious Faysal bin ʿAbdul ʿAziz Al Saʿud sought salvation in his faith as he articulated a modernizing vision for the emergent Kingdom of Saudi Arabia. Without a doubt, this was his greatest challenge because its complex ideological features germinated in his mind over decades. Moreover, Faysal probably knew that this vision could not be achieved within a single lifetime, given necessary variations and subtleties. As time went on, his fears materialized, although the attempt to empower his nation with a defining image of itself allowed successive generations to embark on epoch-making reforms that literally transformed a *badu* society into a modern country.

Even before Faysal acceded to the throne, he confronted various problems, though few paralleled the consequences of the 1973–74 oil crises. In fact, what preoccupied Faysal most were domestic issues but also, *inter alia*, the quests for Arab leadership, critical developments concerning the Palestinian question, and regional stability in the aftermath of the British withdrawal from east of the Suez. The astute monarch realized that leaning toward the West ensured the latter's support of conservative Arab monarchies. He further understood that such alliances provided the wherewithal to establish a welfare state on the Arabian Peninsula. Yet, Faysal grasped the real meaning of ballooning oil income as nothing more than sudden wealth, which transformed Saudi Arabia and placed it on a collision course with modernization. It was, therefore, essential for the kingdom to devise its own intrinsic vision that would soften the impacts of modernization. Whether he wished to placate the West was less important that his search for long-term internal stability, even if that objective required various accommodations with powerful neighbors, especially Iran and Iraq.

As a consummate Arab nationalist, Faysal further deduced that his pro-Arab agenda needed a pro-business slant because only then could the kingdom generate the healthy income needed to fulfill many of its obligations. He was acutely aware that appeasement added little or no value to Saudi foreign policy and opted to reposition his long-term vision within a legitimate Islamic field. This was not a fallback position but the original goal because Faysal embedded piety in his political direction.

What were the primary factors that compelled the powerful Saudi monarch to embark on this exalted change and how did he accomplish his stated aspirations? What were the developments that influenced him and persuaded him to devise and adopt such a vision? Were his preferences engrained in any particular belief? How did Faysal articulate the Saudi quest for salvation? Was the unity of the Muslim Ummah a forgone conclusion and, if so, how did he rely on his custodianship of two of Islam's holiest shrines as a legitimizing tool? Was his quest limited to a physical affinity to unite the Muslim world or did he adopt a different logic to ensure the emergence of a legitimizing leadership? To better address these questions, this penultimate chapter examines the Saudi clash under Faysal with key Arab and Muslim powers before assessing the ideological gap with Communism. It concludes with a brief analysis of his vision for the Kingdom of Saudi Arabia.

Pan-Islamism and the Organization of Islamic Conference

Unlike Judaism or Christianity, the Islamic revelation enjoined believers to organize as a community where loyalty to the Creator was immediately followed by allegiance to society. Moreover, because there were no distinct lines separating church from state, Muslim clergymen historically supported rulers whose legitimacies derived from their application of Shari'ah. Naturally, Muslim rulers were commanded to be just, with specific provisions to rebel against them in case of injustice. Sadly, Muslims have failed to empower strong communities that could lead to the formal establishment of a united Ummah, at least until now. Internecine warfare, the rise of an unbearable Ottoman Empire, and, more recently, colonialism, among other reasons, were responsible for this fundamental catastrophe. Still, it was an Ottoman sultan, 'Abdul Hamid II, who turned to a Muslim philosopher for advice as he attempted to salvage what was left of his disintegrating empire. Jamal al-din Al Afghani, a Persian thinker and politician who promoted the concept of Muslim unity—chiefly against British rule—called for true solidarity among the faithful. His message influenced the rise of the Egyptian nationalist movement, propelled the Ottoman Tanzimat reforms, and, perhaps most important, mobilized the masses for constitutional and religious revolutions in Iran.[1]

Buoyed by such ideas, various Muslim leaders called for the formal establishment of the World Muslim Congress, which first convened under 'Abdul 'Aziz bin 'Abdul Rahman Al Sa'ud in 1926.[2] Six follow-up conferences assembled over the next few years but with mixed results. In fact, the last gathering of the original World Muslim Congress in 1967 was a non-event, especially as the Six-Day War of 1967 overshadowed it.[3] At the height of the Arab Cold War, Faysal lamented the state of the institution and vowed to turn it around. It was his assessment that the tragedy that befell Arabs, peoples and leaders alike, was due to a systematic neglect of fundamental ideological precepts that were included in Islam. He understood that Nasir would squander what was truly precious to Egyptians and all Arabs by submitting to alien dogmas whereas the only worthy salvation was readily available to leaders and subjects alike in Islam. In short, it was the Arab Cold War that prompted Faysal to reinvigorate the World Muslim League under Saudi leadership. For Faysal bin 'Abdul 'Aziz, the only true revolution was the one that the Prophet himself introduced— which, for the ruler, started in Makkah and Madinah.[4]

The Quest for Arab Leadership

As discussed throughout this volume, the most severe strain in Saudi-Egyptian relations occurred between 1957 and 1967, when Gamal 'Abdul Nasir was president of Egypt and the unchallenged hero of Arab nationalism. The charismatic Nasir thrived on his autonomist rhetoric, which included widely publicized denunciations of the Al Sa'ud as corrupt rulers and subservient puppets of the United States. Over the years, Cairo supported numerous revolutionary groups opposed to the Saudi regime and its regional allies, and Riyadh believed that Nasir was involved in major political upheavals, such as the military overthrow of monarchies in Iraq (1958), Yemen (1962), and Libya (1969). At first, King Sa'ud supported Nasir, but in 1956 he realigned the Kingdom of Saudi Arabia with the Hashemite rulers of Jordan and Iraq.[5] Sa'ud further opposed the 1958 union between Egypt and Syria—as the United Arab Republic—and rejected Nasir for his putative pan-Arabism programs. When, in September 1962, pro-Nasir revolutionaries in Yemen deposed the new imam and declared that kingdom a republic, Sa'ud, along with Hussein bin Talal of Jordan, agreed to the decision of Faysal, the heir apparent, to aid the royalist camp. Consequently, Saudi relations with Egypt were severed in 1962. In fact, Saudi-Egyptian ties worsened further after Nasir sent a large number of troops to bolster the newly established Yemen Arab Republic.[6] Saʿud and Faysal were genuinely surprised when Washington recognized the new republic, but that decision did not stop them from increasing their financial and military assistance to Yemeni royalists. In an effort to portray Egypt as the champion of progressive, even democratic, values throughout the Arab world, Nasir excoriated Saudi Arabia (and Jordan) as "reactionary," worthy of being overthrown like the deposed Yemeni imamate.[7] As discussed earlier, subsequent Egyptian attacks on Saudi border towns and villages in Najran and Jizan propelled Riyadh to call on Washington to protect it from this blatant attack.

To better address Nasir's condemnations of Arab leaders allegedly failing to don the Arab nationalist mantle, Faysal sponsored an international conference in Makkah, whose primary objective was to place radicalism and secularism in their proper perspectives. Senior religious authorities accepted the invitation of May 1962 and, as a rebuke to radical nationalist mobilizations, declared: "Those who distort Islam's call under the guise of nationalism are the most bitter enemies of the Arabs whose glories are entwined with the glories of Islam."[8] The delegates revitalized the World Muslim Congress by approving the establishment of a new institution known as the Rabitat al-ʿAlam al-Islami (Muslim World League).

Faysal and the assembled authorities that created the Muslim World League (MWL) were primarily interested in a religious organization that protected Arabs from alien ideologies. The MWL was not—and is not—a political organization even if its writ allowed for coordination with opinionated bodies.[9] Still, Faysal knew that the MWL could be a powerful tool in his clash with Nasir and, consequently, spared no efforts to fully fund it for propagation purposes. The Saudi leader accepted that the MWL was well situated to oppose secularism, socialism, and nationalism given that Nasir was literally proposing these as the only available "isms." Over time, Faysal would expand his notions of pan-Islamism—the actual promotion of political unity for Muslim countries—but the initial rivalry between Faysal and Nasir was fought on purely religious grounds. It was a foregone conclusion that Faysal, who had a legitimate religious upbringing, would prevail on this front.

Nevertheless, it was not sufficient for Faysal and Al Saʿud family members to triumph over Nasir on a selective basis. Nasir's popularity throughout the Arab and developing worlds was significant. Many saw him as a shining light to redress decades- and centuries-old failures. Western governments, including that of the United States, welcomed the Egyptian revolution even if few understood its long-term consequences. In time, however, President John F. Kennedy perceived Nasir as a far greater threat than originally believed, especially after the Yemeni insurrection gained momentum. Washington finally concluded that Nasir was not necessarily interested in Yemen but considered its presence in Sana'a as a foothold on the entire Arabian Peninsula.[10] Kennedy further believed that spill-over effects on Saudi Arabia could only be avoided if Riyadh engaged in internal economic and political reforms—as well as stopping its support of Yemeni royalist forces—and, toward that end, increased pressure on Sa'ud and Faysal to accelerate their reforms.[11] Once Riyadh committed to such reforms, Kennedy unleashed American help to protect Saudi Arabia and to mediate the volatile Egyptian-Saudi tensions. Faysal was cornered, even if he quickly recognized a need for tangible American support. What truly upset him were American innuendoes about possible instability in Saudi Arabia. He was indignant, perhaps even vexed, but the pragmatic prince was too sophisticated to be sidetracked by insinuations. Kennedy understood from Ambassador Ellsworth Bunker, a distinguished former diplomat and businessman, that mediation was useful up to a point. At stake were far bigger contentions, including emerging leadership roles, which pitted conflicting ideologies. Tragically, the 1963 assassination of President Kennedy—perhaps as a forerunner to King Faysal's own murder in 1975—ended the search for effective Arab leadership. Faysal endured as the clash of titans bruised both contenders on the Arab scene.

The years that followed heightened the frustration of the Saudi ruler since the tragedy in Yemen drained valuable resources. As a primarily religious organization, the MWL could only introduce spiritual reforms, which were seldom objective. Once in power, Faysal mobilized his energies and called for the adoption of political unity. Toward that end, he visited several conservative Muslim countries to better ascertain prospects. He began his tours in Iran in December 1965 to emphasize his universal quest lest he be accused of dividing Arabs from Muslims. This important first stop was followed by visits to Jordan, Sudan, Pakistan, Turkey, Morocco, Guinea, Mali, and Tunisia, which lasted until September 1966.[12] In Karachi, Pakistan, Faysal spoke of the bond that united all Muslims and called for genuine cooperation to defeat radicalism since "brotherhood and love . . . [are] derived from the spiritual teachings of Islam . . . that can bind human beings together. . . . It is in these moments, when Islam is facing many undercurrents that are pulling Muslims left and right, East and West, that we need time for more co-operation and closer ties to enable us to face all the problems and difficulties that obstruct our way as an Islamic nation, believing in God, His Prophet and His Laws." He concluded by stating that "however hard some people try to distort the call of Islam, Islam will remain a clear and straight path that needs no alteration or amendment. . . .[13] This was a new and important message that resonated well. Several countries, including Pakistan and Iran, endorsed Faysal and his call for a pan-Islamic alliance. Predictably, Egypt and Syria disapproved, opting to engage in yet another disinformation campaign to discredit Saudi Arabia. Cairo, seconded by its Damascus acolytes, "reviled Faisal as a traitor to the Arab cause, and argued that the Islamic alliance was an American-British conspiracy aimed at dividing the Arab world and undermining Arab hopes for unity."[14] While this was not surprising, the accusations misread Saudi motivations, which were in search of a broader alliance than a mere Arab umbrella. How could Faysal be in cahoots with American or British governments when he clearly identified Zionism, Communism, and imperialism—classic Western "isms"—as enemies of his pan-Islamic alliance? How could Faysal address hundreds of thousands of people in at least a dozen countries and convince most unless he was consistent? Why would Riyadh engage in such duplicity when its primary opposition to Arab nationalism, as practiced or recommended by Nasir, was not even a secret? In the event, Nasir's futile attempts to sabotage Faysal met a different destiny after Cairo fell into the 1967 war trap. It was a tragic end, for the opportunistic policy crashed along with most of the then known Arab air forces.

'Abdul Nasir resigned on June 9, 1967 after the Arab catastrophe (Nikbah) that led to an outright Israeli military victory and the loss of the Sinai Peninsula, the Golan Heights, and the West Bank, including East Jerusalem. Delirious Egyptian masses adjured the dejected leader, pleading with him not to abandon them. Nasir returned to power without much of a military and laden with immense financial debts. He even lost portions of the annual $200 million Suez Canal revenues as traffic through the waterway was halted. Swallowing his pride, the ever popular Egyptian leader attended the League of Arab States summit at Khartoum on August 29–September 2, 1967, even if his animosity toward the Sudanese leadership was well established. When Faysal landed in Khartoum, Nasir welcomed him and, after a few long minutes of silence, the two men embraced and walked hand in hand toward their vehicles. This was pan-Islamic unity par excellence, a notion that accounted for long-term objectives to better serve the interests of all Arabs and Muslims, and one that escaped those who talked of doing rather than actually doing it.

Faysal did not gloat in Khartoum for he knew that humiliating Nasir would produce little. Both men recognized, however, that the Saudi was right and that a new chapter needed to be opened to wary leaders eager to preserve what was left.

The conspiracy-laden Nasir needed Faysal and the Saudi grasped the gravity of the situation.

Nasir promised to end all interferences in intra-Arab affairs, sacrificed his adventure in Yemen (at the terrible cost of five thousand Egyptian dead and countless casualties on all sides), and sought to rebuild Egypt as the frontline state with much anticipated Arab financial assistance. It was a tour de force, but Faysal, advised by the United States, ignored his overtures. Nevertheless, the opportunity was also there for Faysal to place "Arab Socialism" into history's dustbin. Ignoring several American recommendations, he pledged an enormous aid package to Egypt and disregarded the goading to initiate peace talks between Arabs and Israelis. King Faysal was not ungrateful to the United States, as his next steps would amply illustrate, but on matters of principle, he stood apart from his American "friends." He recognized that the United States would continue to play a key role as a defender of Saudi Arabia, but he was disappointed that an equitable settlement of the Arab-Israeli conflict would not be forthcoming. He welcomed the U.S. Army Corps of Engineers to build an enormous military infrastructure in Saudi Arabia, but he relished in retaining his almost theocratic views on what separated the Muslim world from the rest.

In another moment of magnanimity in Khartoum, Faysal announced that Riyadh would heretofore assume 37 percent of all losses derived from the Suez Canal traffic. Over the years, these accumulated payments surpassed one billion U.S. dollars, on top of other grants made to Cairo.[15] For its part, Kuwait pledged to make up another 40 percent of canal losses, and Libya assumed the balance of 23 percent. Nasir was saved by Arab solidarity, but more important, he literally saved his rule due to the actions of Arab "monarchs." Cairo would thus be forced to curtail its inelegant and entirely gratuitous anti-monarchical rhetoric. Although the Khartoum Summit issued its "No" resolution of September 1, 1967—no to peace through, no to recognition of, and no to negotiations with Israel—in reality, the gathering sealed a Saudi victory over Egypt in the Yemen crisis. Egyptian troops returned home, having wasted thousands of lives and billions of dollars, as Cairo acknowledged that internal developments in Yemen fell entirely within the purview of its people and leadership.

To be sure, Faysal was victorious against Nasir, but his major dilemma over Palestine took on new dimensions. First, Jerusalem—the third holiest city in Islam—was lost, which became an injury that affected every Muslim; and second, confrontation states turned to the Arabian Peninsula for financial support. Not surprisingly, Israel insisted that Jerusalem was now a united city and would remain the eternal capital of the Jewish state. Against this onslaught, Faysal declared that one of his fondest wishes was to "live to see Jerusalem liberated from Zionist control and to pray in its holy shrine, [the] *al-Aqsa* Mosque."[16] This desire was repeated often enough to underscore its vital importance to Muslims as a religious issue and to garner wide support throughout the realm. By gaining backing on this critical problem, Faysal managed to unite Muslims behind an Arab cause. The strategy proved successful.

Likewise, Faysal's willingness to shift positions on the financial support extended to frontline states after the Israeli victory over Egypt, Jordan, and Syria in June 1967 accomplished concrete results. A formal agreement was concluded between the Saudi monarch and the Egyptian president, which incorporated a full Egyptian withdrawal from Yemen in exchange for Saudi largesse.[17] Saudi Arabia froze its assistance to royalist elements and, by 1970, resumed normal diplomatic contacts with the Yemen Arab Republic. Simultaneously, Riyadh gave Cairo and Amman over $140 million a year, in part to compensate for the devastations that the 1967 War had caused. These tangible initiatives enhanced the Saudi position in the Arab world and, after Britain declared its anticipated withdrawal from the Persian Gulf area, throughout the Muslim world as well. Ever the pragmatist, Faysal pursued friendship policies with Arab states as well as Iran in the first instance, and with other non-Arab Muslim countries in the second.[18]

Reluctantly, a crippled Nasir conceded to Faysal the rising leadership capabilities of Saudi Arabia, as Riyadh stood firm against Iranian expansion in the Lower Gulf. While Faysal encouraged the Arab shaykhdoms to form the United Arab Emirates, he was reluctant to accept Iranian hegemony over the Lower Gulf. This was a delicate maneuvering because Riyadh was eager to secure Iranian support within OPEC and, toward that end, did not wish to antagonize the shah unnecessarily. In a way, Saudi Arabia faced the Iranian colossus single-handedly, but after Anwar al-Sadat became president of Egypt in 1970, Faysal earned the backing of a strong advocate. Consequently, Saudi-Egyptian ties developed rapidly, without necessarily competing for primacy. Sadat, in particular, was secure in his power to tolerate, even encourage, the emergence of a second power pole on the Arab scene. In fact, the tacit alliance between Sadat and Faysal was far deeper than most realized, as Cairo—in large part at Saudi urging but without informing it of contemplated timing—expelled Soviet military advisers in 1972. In response to this nascent entente, Egypt froze its long-established assistance to revolutionary groups operating on and around the Arabian Peninsula and patched up strained relations with Syria, again at Faysal's goading.[19] The quest for leadership entered a more efficient phase after 1970, when Faysal mobilized Arab public opinion at the

Rabat Summit Conference, after Sadat came to perceive the kingdom as a genuine partner. Moreover, as devout Muslims, Sadat and Faysal shared closer principles than a more secularized Nasir ever could dream of communicating with the Saudi monarch. By 1972, the two countries had outlined a combined platform to tackle Arab concerns and, at Faysal's urging, the Muslim world's growing agenda for independence and prosperity.[20]

Faysal's agenda was immensely helped by yet another dramatic development. Between 1970 and 1973 new and somewhat less radical leaders came to power in several countries and most of them succumbed to Riyadh's message. In addition to Sadat in Egypt, Hafez al-Asad brought a semblance of order to Syria, Ja'afar al-Numayri successfully overcame a Communist coup in the Sudan, and Colonel Mu'ammar al-Qaddhafi discovered religion. Of course, these men were revolutionary at heart and acceded to power following coup d'états, but their radicalism lost much of their original impetus as Faysal rallied Arab and Muslim masses. None of them could challenge the Saudi who concentrated on core values espoused by millions throughout the region. In February 1972, foreign ministers of the Organization of the Islamic Conference (OIC) adopted a permanent charter and approved the establishment of the International Islamic News Agency (IINA), headquartered in Jiddah. With a reinvigorated momentum, Faysal placed various questions on the table, including the Jewish character of Jerusalem, solidarity "with the African struggle against colonialism and racism in Southern Africa," and OIC support for "the territorial integrity of Pakistan against the 1971 Indian invasion" of Bangladesh.[21] By 1973, only Algeria and Iraq—both of which maintained close ties with the Soviet Union—opted to distance themselves from the pan-Islamic movement.

During the October 1973 War, Saudi Arabia supported Egypt by taking the unprecedented step of initiating an embargo on oil shipments to the United States and the Netherlands, two countries that backed Israel militarily. Nevertheless, Riyadh also encouraged Cairo to participate in American mediations to secure phased Israeli withdrawals from occupied Egyptian and Syrian territories. The kingdom refused to recognize Israel even if Faysal would not rule out the existence of the Jewish state. To be sure, Riyadh conditioned such a recognition to the creation of an independent Palestinian state, though the pragmatic Faysal realized that the search for such statehood would be time consuming and diplomatically hazardous. Other members of the Al Sa'ud ruling family would eventually make bold initiatives—the 1981 Fahd peace plan and the 2003 'Abdallah initiative—but in 1973–74, the quest was subservient to the vagaries of the Cold War. Faysal would remain true to the Palestinian cause and aspire to pray at the Al-Aqsah

Mosque in Jerusalem even as Egypt began to distance itself from the Palestinian issue in 1975.

The Clash over the Palestinian Question

Saudi Arabia supported and defended the Palestinian cause, which for Faysal was a seminal affair, even before the conflict gained notoriety in the late 1960s. The "Palestine question" was at the center of the kingdom's concerns under 'Abdul 'Aziz bin 'Abdul Rahman and has remained so ever since. At every opportunity, Saudi Arabia emphasized that the peace sought was a just and comprehensive one based on UN resolutions and on international law, an amity that secured for the Palestinian people all of their rights on the basis of Resolutions 242 and 338, which, in turn, affirmed the right of Palestinians to self-determination and Israeli withdrawal from the occupied Arab territories.[22]

The question of Jerusalem, in the view of the Kingdom of Saudi Arabia, represented the very essence of the Palestinian cause and the core of the Arab-Israeli dispute. For Faysal, the whole peace process depended on the way in which this question was dealt with, which drew the ire of those who wished to sidestep their responsibilities.

Faysal approached the "Palestine question" through the Islamic unity prism. It was necessary, he concluded after the 1973 War, that Palestinian rights be defended not just by fellow Arabs but also by the Muslim world at large. Toward that end, he channeled significant efforts into gaining such collaboration. After 1973, the number of countries that actually extended support to various Palestinian movements rose, and not just because most felt the repercussions of higher oil prices or because they benefited financially from Saudi and other Arab Gulf largesse. In fact, several African countries broke diplomatic ties with Israel because they had concluded that serious injustices had been committed under international law. It may be worth repeating that while the anticipation of financial rewards from Saudi Arabia and other wealthy Arab oil producers may have tilted the balance, most leaders who voiced support genuinely sympathized with the Palestinians. A new spirit of unity surfaced as various countries improved contacts with Fatah and its leader, Yasir 'Arafat. Iran and Iraq signed their 1975 Shatt al-'Arab border accord and reestablished diplomatic relations. Libya's Colonel Qaddhafi visited Riyadh and Cairo to resolve differences with King Faysal and President Sadat. Saudi Arabia and the People's Democratic Republic of Yemen normalized ties, as did Syria and Jordan, after the latter broke all contacts in the aftermath of the September 1970 massacres. Likewise, King Hussein of Jordan welcomed President

Habib Bourguiba of Tunisia, and Pakistan recognized the formal independence of Bangladesh. Faysal was pleased with all of these positive changes in intra-Arab and intra-Muslim contacts, as he sensitized Muslim opinion to the plight of Palestinians at every opportunity that arose.

In February 1974, the OIC held its second summit in Lahore, Pakistan, where Faysal succeeded in gaining widespread Muslim backing for the Palestinian cause. Perhaps the most important decision reached in Lahore was to elevate the observer status of the Palestine Liberation Organization (PLO) to full membership and to accord Yasir 'Arafat the honors of a head of state. Not only were the thirty original members in attendance, but new OIC members joined in and, perhaps feeling its complete isolation, Iraq participated for the very first time.[23] Beyond rhetorical speeches, the OIC tackled the most important issue facing member-states, namely poverty and lack of fiscal growth. To alleviate the impact of high oil prices on fledgling economies, the OIC established the Islamic Solidarity Fund and provided financial assistance to those least well-off. Faysal accomplished a remarkable feat since no head of state boycotted the proceedings. It was a rare moment in contemporary Muslim history.

Indeed, the total Saudi aid to various Palestinian institutions and organizations, whether at the official level—from Riyadh to the PLO or to Fatah—or at the popular one—from Riyadh to charitable institutions such as the Red Crescent Society—amounted to billions of dollars. Yet, more important than the financial aid given by the kingdom to the Palestinians, was the legitimization of the question created by Faysal. With the support of the OIC, he squarely placed the plight of the stateless Palestinians in front of the United Nations, gaining necessary votes for the General Assembly to grant the PLO observer status. In time, the United Nations granted the Palestinians the right of self-determination, even if westerners balked at first. On November 10, 1975, the 30th General Assembly session adopted Resolution 3379—by a vote of 72 to 35 (with 32 abstentions)—which stated as its conclusion that "Zionism is a form of racism and racial discrimination."[24] The resolution further endorsed an August 1975 statement by the Conference of Ministers for Foreign Affairs of the Non-Aligned Movement, which "... severely condemned Zionism as a threat to world peace and security and called upon all countries to oppose this racist and Imperialist ideology."[25] Although the controversial resolution was finally revoked on December 16, 1991—by a vote of 111 to 25 (with 13 abstentions)— the Palestine question was no longer an imaginary problem. Through the pan-Islamic movement, Faysal had legitimized it and, in the process, gave the more than one billion Muslims of the planet an undeniable voice in international affairs. In fact, the OIC grew into a formidable political institution (with up to forty-three members after Nigeria joined in 1975), and it had a voice to be reckoned with. It was, to say the least, a Faysal legacy par excellence, which encompassed different cultures and societies.

As stated above, Faysal was not the first Saudi to espouse the Palestinian cause, since King 'Abdul 'Aziz bin 'Abdul Rahman, the founder of the modern kingdom, supported the idea of supplying the Palestinians with money and arms to enable them to defend themselves and their land. What Faysal added to this endorsement, however, surpassed the Saudi volunteers who extended a helping hand. If modest Saudi forces contributed to the preservation of the Arabism of the Gaza Strip and prevented its loss in the 1920s and 1930s, and if token troops were dispatched in every conflict since 1948, the more valuable contribution was the legitimacy granted Palestinians through concrete initiatives adopted by Faysal. He perceived the Israeli presence in the Middle East in ominous terms precisely because it was at the expense of an uprooted population with inalienable rights. When in 1972, he declared that "all countries should wage war against the Zionists, who are there to destroy all human organizations and to destroy civilization and the work which good people are trying to do,"[26] many categorized this pronouncement as yet another rhetorical speech. Hyperbole aside, Faysal believed that full reconciliation between Israelis and Arabs required an Israeli recognition of Palestine as an independent country, and of the Palestinians as an independent people. His perceptions never wavered, pitting Saudi Arabia against the most powerful actors in the international system, which, in turn, exerted a very heavy price for his intransigence.

The Search for Stability in the Gulf Region

An equally critical preoccupation for Faysal was the situation on and around the Arabian Peninsula, especially after London declared its desire to withdraw troops stationed in the Lower Gulf shaykhdoms by late 1971. A precipitous British withdrawal was expected to create a security vacuum that could entangle regional powers. Faysal was keenly determined to avoid a confrontation with Iran, the dominant military power in the area and, more important, a fellow Muslim state. Long before the late 1960s, however, Saudi perceptions of Iran were colored by Teheran's imperial ambitions.

Because Saudi Arabia viewed Iranian participation in the Baghdad Pact and its follow-up Central Treaty Organization (CENTO) with apprehension, relations between the two countries were almost always lukewarm. The Baghdad Pact, concluded in 1955 by Iraq, Iran, and Turkey, and acceded to by Britain and

Pakistan, frightened the Arab world in general and Saudi Arabia in particular. Although all members of the League of Arab States (LAS) and major Western powers concerned with security in the Middle East were invited to join, a strong anti-colonial wave among Arab masses, as well as antipathy among Arab elites toward Western incursions, precluded participation on a larger scale. Ideological clashes were thus inevitable even if Riyadh sought to accommodate the shah whenever possible.

Saudi leaders noted that Washington maintained a certain distance from the Baghdad Pact, which ensured that the Al Saʿud could rely on America for their security against putative Iraqi and/or Iranian threats. From the Saudi perspective, these sources represented far greater threats than any contemplated direct or indirect Communist challenges. In a rare diplomatic initiative, King Saʿud sought to persuade the shah of Iran that revolutionary Iraq posed a danger to both monarchies, and he pleaded with the shah to withdraw from the pact. He failed in this endeavor because the shah perceived the treaty as an opportunity to advance Iranian hegemonic interests in the area.[27] Saʿud's prescience proved correct after the Baghdad Pact withered in the aftermath of the Iraqi withdrawal following the 1958 Revolution. The new alliance—CENTO—that emerged was carved through an American initiative to provide security in the Middle East against Communist aggression as well as foster economic and social cooperation among such members as Britain, Iran, Pakistan, and Turkey. Washington, although never an official member, joined as an associate, concluded bilateral agreements with Teheran, Islamabad, and Ankara, and committed itself to defending alliance members against a Communist attack. Ironically, Iran would withdraw from CENTO after the 1979 Iranian revolution, when the Ankara-based organization ceased to exist formally. At the time, however, Faysal noted with apprehension both CENTO designs as well as the liberties the military institution granted the shah.[28] Again, from a Saudi perspective, CENTO empowered the shah to grant himself additional influence, even if his supremacist tendencies were largely illusory.

Ties with the Smaller Gulf States

In contrast to relations with Iran or Iraq, Saudi ties with the small Arab oil-producing states along the eastern flank were not always antagonistic. Riyadh favored the establishment of a large federation—to include Bahrain and Qatar—but, after three tortuous years, Manama and Doha opted for full independence. Even Ras al-Khaymah at first opted for independence but reversed its decision in 1972 to join the United Arab Emirates. After the 1973 rise in oil prices, the United Arab

Emirates was transformed from an impoverished region with primarily nomad settlements into a sophisticated state with one of the highest per capita incomes in the world and equipped with a broad social welfare system.

Although Riyadh supported independence for the Gulf shaykhdoms, the Kuwaiti experience increased overall regional anxiety due to hegemonic preferences advanced by Iran. Iran continued to make various claims on Bahrain and the United Arab Emirates, but by the end of 1971 those states were independent, leaving a bitter aftertaste to Teheran's regional aspirations. Lower Gulf leaders faced uncertainty about the form their states should take. Should they all band together in the largest entity possible? Or should they break up into nine separate entities, the smallest of which had little territory, few people, and no oil? With the exception of Oman, whose treaty relationship with Britain guaranteed the bulk of its borders, Riyadh favored the former solution.

Faysal promoted the Kuwaiti-Saudi settlement as a model for the Lower Gulf states. As the main concession for oil exploitation was held by a joint British-American firm until 1974, Kuwait took control of most of the operations with full Saudi acquiescence. A complete accord was reached over the neutral zone that divided all profits on a fully equal footing. A co-founder of OPEC, Kuwait channeled its oil revenues into various investment projects and provided sorely needed financial assistance to fellow Arab countries, including the Lower Gulf shaykhdoms. In fact, given the high coordination between Kuwaiti and Saudi policies—over the Palestinian cause, their pro-Western alliances, and Kuwait's diplomatic ties with the Soviet Union after 1963—Faysal wished that Bahrain, Oman, Qatar, and the United Arab Emirates would emulate these preferences. Differences aside, all of the conservative Arab monarchies on the Arabian Peninsula followed the Saudi penchant, which, admittedly, was in some measure due to Faysal's unique leadership qualities. When OAPEC imposed an oil embargo against the United States and the Netherlands, Arabian Peninsula shaykhdoms were fully supportive of the Saudi initiative.

The Iranian Seizure of the Abu Musa and Tunb Islands

Saudi Arabia and Iran then faced major security hurdles after Teheran invaded and occupied the Abu Musa and Tunb islands. In 1970, both countries faced the prospect of a military vacuum in the wake of the British withdrawal from the Persian Gulf. Simultaneously, Saudi Arabia faced a threat from Yemen and sought to quell any potential conflict in the south by quickly coming to terms with Iran on Abu Musa and the Tunbs. King Faysal sought an understanding with Muhammad Reza Shah Pahlavi on a division of "spheres of influence" in the area, but this was not agreed to. In fact, Faysal strove to secure for the United Arab Emirates the same conditions for independence as those he had lobbied for on behalf of Bahrain, with full Iranian recognition of the territorial integrity of the new state. London, perhaps with the assistance of the ruler of Sharjah, opted for a deal with the shah. Faysal even contemplated taking the case to the United Nations, but Shaykh Zayed and other shaykhs concluded that this might delay their quest for independence, and the king, reluctantly, dropped the issue. Nevertheless, Iran recognized a tacit Saudi sphere of influence to include the shaykhdoms, while Saudi Arabia acknowledged a primary role for Iran as guardian of the Persian Gulf. This agreement was reached despite disapproval among several Arab states of granting non-Arab Iran such a prominent role in regional affairs. Indeed, it may be argued that the kingdom entered into this arrangement because it had few alternative options.[29]

Teheran, in contrast, pursued a second agreement with London over Abu Musa. In this new agreement, signed in 1971, Iran gained the right to station troops on Abu Musa although similar provisions were provided for deployments on the Greater and Lesser Tunbs. Because Britain fashioned and implemented the foreign policies of the seven "Trucial States" that gained independence on December 2, 1971 to form the United Arab Emirates, this agreement with Iran could well have been valid. Consequently, when Iran captured the three islands by dispatching troops to them on December 1, 1971, the shah illustrated that the use of force prevailed in the region. Riyadh failed to anticipate, as well as understand, that Iran seized the islands to enlarge its sphere of influence. Through this act Teheran obliged Saudi Arabia to embark on a military purchase spree in Europe and the United States as regional perils concretized. At the time, Defense Minister Sultan bin ʿAbdul ʿAziz asserted that Riyadh had tried to arrange for Iran to lease the islands, whereas the shah responded by taking hostile action.[30] Given the preponderant Iranian military power in the area, the United Arab Emirates acknowledged, albeit reluctantly, the military occupation and Faysal acquiesced.[31] Still, to maintain its own legitimacy—how could it explain to its own population that Saudi Arabia, and Iraq a few years later, were more concerned with liberating occupied United Arab Emirates territory than Abu Dhabi—the United Arab Emirates adopted concrete policies to regain sovereignty over the islands, including a formal understanding with Saudi Arabia.

Diplomatic Ties with the United Arab Emirates

Shaykh Zayed bin Sultan Al Nahyan, the president of the United Arab Emirates, understood that a linkage was formally established between the "islands" status and the difficult relations between Abu Dhabi and Riyadh. What he could not foresee was the Saudi *raison d'état* after the formation of the United Arab Emirates in 1971. Abu Dhabi was clearly disappointed that it was not immediately recognized by Riyadh as the latter insisted on a clearly defined border agreement as a precondition. Inasmuch as the consequences of the long-standing Buraymi Oasis dispute lingered, diplomatic contacts between the two countries remained subservient to Arabian Peninsula vagaries, which, in turn, prevented the development of friendly ties.[32]

Chief among its objections, Saudi Arabia rejected the preponderant Iranian presence in the area, but "Riyadh was determined not to allow its territorial grievances to preclude" efforts to push the proposed union of the nine small emirates to a successful conclusion.[33] In time, however, and fearing Communist instigated tensions in Bahrain and the Lower Gulf, Riyadh placed its long-standing demands aside. Rather, it extended assistance to Ras al-Khaymah, whose ruler was holding off his acquiescence for purely tribal concerns. Inasmuch as this backing further encouraged Shaykh Saqr bin Muhammad Al Qasimi to adopt obscurantist positions—not to join the nascent federation—Zayed and his allies formed negative views of putative Saudi actions.[34] Such efforts were irritants that slowed down the development of relations between the two countries and it was not until July 29, 1974 that the United Arab Emirates finally reached a temporary agreement with Saudi Arabia over the Buraymi conflict. Among the many factors that influenced both sides to finally set their differences aside were the above discussed pan-Islamic efforts, the need to resolve internal and regional disputes to better concentrate on the spillover effects of the Arab-Israeli conflict, and the need to firmly address the slow but certain encroachment of the Soviet Union in the People's Democratic Republic of Yemen. In the end, both sides displayed magnanimity, in part because their newly found wealth—which went beyond anyone's expectations—allowed them to generate good will and generosity. Although hard-line elements in Saudi Arabia never abandoned their expansionist ambitions to rule over the entire Arabian Peninsula, Faysal was inclined to reach border agreements with his neighbors and, with Zayed at the helm in Abu Dhabi, felt confident that differences could be tackled peacefully. The United Arab Emirates was not ready or willing to concede any potential oil-rich areas on its disputed border with Saudi Arabia, but, as a fellow member of OPEC and OAPEC, it agreed to coordinate its oil policies with Saudi Arabia since both Zayed and Faysal understood that coordinated efforts would allow them greater freedoms to survive and to maneuver as they established viable economies.[35]

The Tense Relationship with the Shah

These problems notwithstanding, cooperation between Saudi Arabia and Iran was not totally lacking, which, in turn, helped maintain correct ties between the two monarchical regimes. Throughout the 1970s, several high-level discussions on regional security occurred, both in Riyadh and Teheran.[36] Omar Sakkaf, then Saudi deputy minister of foreign affairs, traveled to Teheran—ostensibly to mediate between Iran and Iraq over the Shatt al-'Arab estuary dispute—but in reality, to negotiate with Iranian authorities a modus vivendi on Gulf security. At the conclusion of one meeting, Sakkaf declared that Riyadh considered its role in the region as one of mediator and expressed his readiness to do whatever he could to help settle festering regional conflicts. In a revealing interview he identified "friendship with Iran [as] the cornerstone [of the kingdom's] foreign policy."[37]

The cooperation of the 1970s developed further despite major disagreements between the two countries. Differences over oil policy within OPEC, as well as over Iranian-sponsored Gulf security proposals, prevented them from achieving Saudi objectives. In fact, little was actually accomplished on regional security because Saudi Arabia feared Iranian hegemony in the area.[38]

The Ideological Conflict with Communism

Faysal perceived the Soviet Union as a genuine source of threat to Saudi security and stability. Although initial contacts were quickly established by King 'Abdul 'Aziz bin Abdul Rahman, principally after Faysal visited Moscow in 1932, Russian interests in a warm water port in the Persian Gulf were never forgotten. Moreover, after the 1958 Revolution in Baghdad, Saudi Arabia assessed various Iraqi-Soviet accords in negative terms.

When Faysal acceded to rulership in 1964, Anastas Mikoyan, then the president of the Supreme Soviet, forwarded a private congratulatory message. Simultaneously, *Pravda*'s Cairo correspondent was allowed to enter the country for a visit and interviews. He praised the monarch, identifying him as a reformist as well as a supporter of the Non-Aligned Movement. Faysal confided "that Saudi Arabia had no quarrel with the U.S.S.R. or prejudice against Russians, and that there were 'no obstacles' to improving bilateral relations."[39] *Pravda* further claimed that Faysal signed the key resolution of the Second Non-Aligned Conference, which met in Cairo in 1964. That, in turn, called for the closure of all foreign bases in the Middle East. Naturally, the reference was to the U.S. Air Force facility at Dhahran—which was closed in 1962—even if Faysal made no such outright references to it, especially after that date.

On the heels of this *Pravda* article, *Izvestiya*, the other major Soviet daily, scored a rare scoop when one of its correspondents spent ten days in the kingdom and was actually received by the king. In the published interview, Faysal reportedly told *Izvestiya* that "he did not intend to confine his country's relations exclusively to the Western Powers, and that the Saudis had no prejudices against the Russians."[40] The correspondent provided a generally accurate picture of the country, highlighting the progress recorded in public education and health, and of the financial discipline that royals and commoners alike were subjected to.

This overture closed as Moscow sided with Egypt in the latter's quest for Arab hegemony. After the 1967 Six-Day War and, more important, after Egypt entered the Yemen quagmire, Faysal lost interest in improving relations with the Soviet Union. In fact, Faysal never entertained a full entente with Moscow, even if Soviet arms helped Egypt in the 1973 war. Inasmuch as the Soviet Union was continuously involved on the Arabian Peninsula, chiefly in the People's Democratic Republic of Yemen and by providing assistance to Omani rebels opposing Sultan Qaboos, Saudi Arabia was not ready to foresee major improvements. For a brief moment after the 1973 War, political prognosticators anticipated the establishment of diplomatic relations between the two countries and, perhaps, even a new visit by Faysal. The source of this speculation was the monarch's congratulatory message to Nicolai Podgorny, then chairman of the Supreme Soviet, on the 1973 anniversary of the October Revolution.[41] In the event, this was probably a clever ploy by Faysal to add pressure on the United States, as the latter negotiated with Riyadh on lifting the oil embargo. Consistently, *Faysal rejected Communism as being anathema to what Muslims believe*. Ingrained ideological differences precluded any rapprochement even if the pragmatic Faysal could find merit in specific Russian or Soviet policies. In the end, his views of the Soviet Union and of Communism, perhaps neutral when he visited in 1932, clashed with his pan-Islamic vision and were not deemed worthy of serious consideration. The pious Faysal could not contemplate permanent partnerships with those who rejected the existence of a supreme being. Simply stated, for a believer, Communism and religion were like oil and water; they simply did not mix.

A Modernizing Vision

Faysal was above all a pious individual who perceived life through the brilliant prism of faith. His first introduction to Islam was carefully nurtured by his maternal grandmother, whereas his maternal grandfather, 'Abdallah bin 'Abdul Latif Al Shaykh, instilled in him values of piety and discipline. The elder Al Shaykh taught Faysal the scriptures and instilled a deep love and respect for his heritage. Shaykh 'Abdallah bin 'Abdul Latif wanted his protégé to be close to the people, to share values and dreams alike. Equally important, the erudite shaykh insisted that his young charge absorb modern skills, including reading and writing, since his father needed accomplished leaders to succeed him. These lessons proved essential as 'Abdul 'Aziz bin 'Abdul Rahman recognized his son's intrinsic capabilities. Advisors heard him declare how he wished he "had several Faysals."[42] Few outsiders realized the value that this prince added to the nascent kingdom, save, perhaps, for the founder himself.

As only a father can know his son, 'Abdul 'Aziz recognized that Faysal harbored strong beliefs and impeccable convictions. Faysal always kept his promises and, later on, reproached others whenever they failed to do likewise.[43] These attributes slowly shaped his character and, as the latter translated into policies, formed his nascent vision. In fact, these characteristics were demonstrated time and again regarding various concerns, ranging from his passionately pro-Arab views to his equally pro-Western proclivities. Seldom did Faysal waver even if his policies drew reprisals both by Arabs as well as westerners. Although outsiders criticized his support of the Palestinian cause as bordering on the obsessive, he was remarkably consistent in his pronouncements and, equally important, particularly attuned to views espoused by a vast majority of Saudis. In this context, endorsing Palestinian rights required an unbending opposition to Zionism, since doing otherwise would have meant contradiction. Likewise, Faysal maintained a thorough consistency on his perceptions of the role that great powers played in the international system, squarely placing Saudi Arabia with those who "rejoic[ed at] the collapse of the last stronghold of tyranny and oppression."[44] He was not miserly in his praise of leading American statesmen whom he perceived to be inherently fair minded. He admired their determination, appreciated their predicaments, and endorsed their planks, up to the point when he concluded that opportunists had hijacked those great ideals.

Faysal was not easily disappointed, but when President Harry Truman failed to honor his predecessor's assurances, he was "stunned and hurt."[45] In hindsight, and as discussed above, this letdown affected Faysal more than any other political event because he was made to re-examine the trust he had personally placed on American backing. This episode, perhaps coupled with his direct experience with Nasir, persuaded him to rely on his innermost beliefs. For Faysal, resolute political success derived from a firm reliance on intrinsic values, solid allegiances, and ironclad initiatives. The only source to fulfill those expectations was faith.

It may therefore be accurate to conclude that Faysal rejected alien "isms." Nationalism or Communism, two ideologies that appealed to so many after World War II, offered little to a believer's life. Moreover, Communism was a stranger dogma because it pretended to supplant established religious practices. Naturally, his own vision differed sharply from such vagaries, and while most of his ideas assumed more concrete identities after the establishment of the Muslim World League, his pan-Islamic vision was first enunciated in 1962. Still, Faysal did not just oppose his Communist or Arab nationalist enemies but offered an alternative to Saudis, Arabs, Muslims, and indeed to everyone who shared a similar outlook. In the end, he considered the fads of the 1950s and 1960s as nothing more that signs of inner weakness, which prevented real intra-state cooperation and, on the domestic front, the implementation of sorely needed socioeconomic reforms. Consistent throughout, his pan-Islamist vision was compatible with his Ten Points reform program of October 31, 1962 because the latter upheld the principles of the faith.[46]

To be sure, Faysal's strong character proved to be extremely useful, but the need for steadfast determination was equally necessary. At stake was the unity of Saudi Arabia, which the Yemen war, in particular, threatened. In fact, had that conflict spilled over inside the kingdom, Al Sa'ud rule would probably have ended and Saudi Arabia would have become a very different country. Faysal held it together through sheer determination, steadfast backing of enunciated principles, eminent consistency, and faith. The Saudi monarch, who "possessed a far more receptive and discriminating mind," refrained from superfluous games.[47] He drew lessons from the tragedy, including a conviction that success in regional affairs required close cooperation with like-minded believers. Toward that end, he rallied dozens of countries to back the formal establishment of the Muslim World League, perhaps his crowning accomplishment outside family affairs. He consistently emphasized Islam and linked Arab virtues to Islamic values. Remarkably, the Saudi monarch remained true to this mission, committing time and resources to accomplish what others only spoke of doing.

Likewise, he understood that Islam and free enterprise matched harmoniously, and that his choices served long-term Saudi interests rather well. In the end, his vision sidestepped symbolism, focusing instead on tangible progress, including a form of participatory democracy that concentrated on substance.[48] Faysal adopted policies that insured progress, stability, and relative prosperity. His vision was thus modest, consistent, and attuned to both earthly requirements as well as divine wisdom.

7

The Faysal Legacy

Faysal bin Abdul 'Aziz Al Sa'ud aspired to reign like the *Just Prince* who rules with an unwavering belief in God, displays the courage to conquer evil, exercises patience to persevere regardless of costs or consequences, submits to the will of God against hardships, and considers the burdens of rule with exuberance.[1] As discussed throughout this study, his numerous accomplishments for Saudi Arabia, as well as his genuine contributions to the advancement of Arab and Muslim interests, were legendary. Even if some of his policies were not universally praised, few could be indifferent to them, and even fewer could doubt his sincerity in advancing Saudi interests. World leaders who dealt with Faysal appreciated his keen sense of fairness because he could forgive his enemies. That, ultimately, was a characteristic of a great leader, one who understood that justice was a double-edged sword, that its exercise was seldom free of heavy costs, and that its permanence necessitated mercy. When contentions abounded, Faysal displayed magnanimity, relying on reason to promote specific issues and gentle persuasion when hotter heads collided. To be sure, he ruled with a strong hold, but he also governed with unparalleled evenhandedness. Few Al Sa'ud ruling family members could expect to receive preferential treatment unless their conduct was irreproachable. Many were not, which upset him more than was generally acknowledged, for he was plainly aware of the custodianship entrusted them. In fact, four decades after his untimely death, the Faysal legacy lives on because his policies have left an undeniable impact on the kingdom.

Death of a King

King Faysal celebrated the 1,405th birthday of the Prophet Muhammad on March 25, 1975 by offering early morning prayers. Unlike Levantine states, where the

Mawlad is a national holiday, Unitarian Saudis continued to work. Their stark ceremonies were limited to special prayers offered in memory of the Prophet—nothing more. As was his habit, Faysal arrived early at his office to start a routine day at his desk, delving into a voluminous correspondence with several world dignitaries. He dictated a few letters to a secretary to expedite matters, but, as a stickler for accuracy, he reread each one before signing them. Earlier in his life, he wrote most of his messages, but after he assumed the throne the sheer volume compelled him to delegate. As was also his practice, he received a slew of visitors, often several Arab or Muslim delegations each day, along with family members who sought an audience for a variety of reasons.

On his morning schedule on the Prophet's birthday in 1975 the Kuwaiti oil minister, Shaykh 'Abdul Mutalib al-Kazimi (accompanied by the Saudi minister of petroleum, Shaykh Ahmad Zaki Yamani), came with several experts who had been studying recent findings along the Saudi-Kuwaiti border area known as the Neutral Zone. According to his secretary, Faysal was seriously preoccupied that morning with the failed Kissinger negotiations in Jerusalem and was planning to communicate with President Sadat immediately after his audience with the Kuwaitis.

Among the throng of Saudis waiting with the Kuwaitis in the antechamber was twenty-seven-year-old Prince Faysal bin Musa'id bin 'Abdul 'Aziz Al Sa'ud, a nephew of the monarch. According to eyewitnesses, when the king recognized his nephew, he lowered his head so that the young Faysal could, according to tribal custom, kiss the ruler's shoulder. What followed, as narrated by several individuals present in the room, was sheer pandemonium. The young man reached under his cloak, pulled out a handgun, and shot the king at least three times.[2]

Palace guards quickly subdued the young man as the fallen ruler was transported to a hospital, where he passed away shortly thereafter. When the news was broadcast on local radio stations, shocked Saudis flocked to the palace in the thousands to seek additional details of their beloved leader. In a rare display of emotion, Saudis mourned their martyr, even if few comprehended the enormity of the loss. What followed was pure frenzy as hundreds of dignitaries expressed a desire to attend the funeral. It quickly became obvious that no burial would be possible before sunset. A brief ceremony was then scheduled for March 26 in the presence of over one hundred official delegations. As each head of state arrived in Riyadh, he was driven to the Nasiriyyah Palace, where Faysal's body lay in state, simply covered in his death shroud. Most recited prayers and were genuinely moved by the austere protocol surrounding the last rites conferred on the most powerful Arab leader at the time. Faysal lay on a bare stretcher covered by his *thawb*, which was returned to his family at the end of the ceremonies.

High-level dignitaries traveling from near and far attended the funeral at a time when such journeys were not as frequent as they would become. All Gulf rulers were present, led by Shaykh Zayed bin Sultan Al Nahyan from the United Arab Emirates, Sultan Qaboos bin Saʿid of Oman, Shaykh ʿIsa bin Salman of Bahrain, Shaykh Khalifah bin Hamad Al Thani of Qatar, and Shaykh Sabah al-Salim Al Sabah of Kuwait. Hundreds of other Gulf shaykhs made the journey, including Shaykh Saqr bin Muhammad Al Qasimi of Ras al-Khaymah, and countless others from throughout the Arabian Peninsula. Naturally, numerous Arab allies and incontestable foes were also present, ranging from Presidents Anwar al-Sadat of Egypt to Hafez al-Asad of Syria. Presidents Houari Boumedienne of Algeria and Habib Bourguiba of Tunisia were there. Ahmad Hassan Bakr of Iraq and Jaʿafar al-Numayri of Sudan were in attendance although both the Iraqi Baʿathist and his fellow Sudanese revolutionary loathed traditional monarchical regimes. King Hussein bin Talal of Jordan and Chairman Yasir ʿArafat of the PLO made the trip, as did Moulay ʿAbdallah and Muhammad bin Hassan, both of Morocco, along with a slew of delegates from Mauritania, Yemen, Libya, Lebanon, and Somalia. Presidents Zulfiqar ʿAli Bhutto of Pakistan and Muhammad Daud of Afghanistan, as well as Prince ʿAli Reza of Iran arrived to pay their respects. Idi Amin Dada of Uganda was so emotional—to the embarrassment of most Al Saʿud family members—that he "threw himself to the ground, seemingly in a paroxysm of grief."[3] Among Western leaders, David Rockefeller, the vice president of the United States, Yvon Bourges, the minister of defense of France, and King Juan Carlos of Spain were noticed. Dozens of ambassadors represented governments whose leaders simply could not make the trip on such short notice. At the time, this was one of the largest gatherings of world leaders, all moved by the tragic demise of Faysal bin ʿAbdul ʿAziz Al Saʿud.

At the end of the official ceremonies, the body was moved to the Riyadh Central Mosque, where an estimated one hundred thousand individuals attended Faysal's funeral service. According to eyewitnesses, the silence was deafening as his brothers and sons carried the body inside the mosque. Faysal was then buried in an unmarked grave according to the true Unitarian creed—no particular reverence is given to the powerful because all are equal before the Creator.

The Investigation

Although Faysal bin Musaʿid was beheaded for his crime on June 18, 1975, that is, eighty-five days after the murder, a careful investigation was followed by a religious trial to ascertain guilt. This was not a hurried affair as the assassin was not even aware that the monarch was dead for several weeks. In the event, the religious court found him guilty of murder and sentenced him after an exhaustive effort to determine whether the young man was mentally deranged.[4] Within hours of the verdict, he was led into a public square in front of the Great Mosque of Riyadh and decapitated. This was the first time that a member of the ruling family had been executed after Saudi Arabia declared its independence in 1932 and, interestingly, the trial concluded that the assassination was politically motivated. The assassin wished to avenge his fallen brother.

Faysal bin Musa'id's puritanical brother, Khalid, died in 1965 when police opened fire on a demonstration against the introduction of television into the kingdom. The conservative prince and his followers challenged the authority of the monarch to safeguard the faith and insisted that Riyadh acquiesce to the religious establishment. In fact, Faysal bin Musa'id believed that semi-theocratic rule was "standing in the way of the development of his country," and to remedy this perceived shortcoming he decided to murder his uncle. Whether the young man actually believed his own imaginary utopia or whether his zeal was the product of foreign travel and influence was impossible to determine.

As an Al Sa'ud, the prince benefited from the financial largesse bestowed on its members and was first enrolled at San Francisco State College at seventeen. He then transferred to the University of Colorado at twenty and returned to the University of California at Berkeley when he was twenty-two. While in Colorado, he was apparently arrested for selling illicit drugs in 1969, although some of his friends denied that he smoked marijuana. Photographs taken of him in Colorado illustrate that he kept his hair long, but that was a worldwide rage at the time. On a more ominous note, at Berkeley, Faysal bin Musa'id joined militant Arab students. This was certainly not typical of members of the ruling dynasty, who, in general, behaved with utmost discretion. Ironically, several of these young radicals believed that King Faysal stood in the way of progress, even if few of those students had ever set foot in Saudi Arabia or were aware of the political struggles that the monarch had encountered and overcame. Even more paradoxically, these same militants dismissed Faysal's proud role in the 1973 Arab-Israeli War and resulting oil embargo as mere theatrics.

Was the young Faysal bin Musa'id a lone assassin or was King Faysal killed by an organized machine to create instability in the Middle East? No evidence surfaced to buttress the conspiracy theories that gripped the Arab and Muslim worlds, although hard proof seldom emerges in any political assassination. Suffice it to say that Arab revolutionaries disliked Faysal, even if he forgave misguided officials. His abhorrence of godless Communism was legendary and Moscow never forgave him for the critical role he played in persuading President Sadat to expel the Russian military machine from Egypt in 1972. Likewise, his vital role in the October 1973 War and his even more essential deed in the OAPEC oil embargo against the United States and the Netherlands earned him scorn. The language used by the *Washington Post* editorial that marked his death summarized American perceptions. It claimed: "Feisal probably did more damage to the West than any other single man since Adolf Hitler," an entirely gratuitous soubriquet.[5] For it was erroneous to compare Faysal's actions to those of a mass murderer, except that 1973 was the year when beleaguered Western societies reignited their hunt for villains. As stated in the introduction, Faysal was perceived as a determined leader who was eager to advance the interests of his nation. Even at the height of the Cold War, when anti-Communism was much heralded by successive Western regimes, independent statesmen were understood to represent metaphysical threats to a certain "way of life."

Of course, the court that tried Faysal bin Musa'id did not delve into such questions, but it may be useful to recall that Secretary of State Henry Kissinger left the Middle East on March 24, 1975 after a failed chapter in his on-going shuttle diplomacy between Egypt and Israel. Faysal was apprised of key negotiations and planned to speak on the telephone with President Anwar al-Sadat after his audience with the visiting Kuwaiti delegation. Little of what transpired in court proceedings regarding the monarch's physical security, and whether any blame was apportioned to National Guard units entrusted with his safety, came out. Still, as Riyadh entrusted the security of senior members of the ruling family to an elite group of National Guardsmen that were trained by the American Vinnell Corporation, strict new rules were immediately implemented for his successor. Vinnell, which enjoyed a rather close association with the U.S. Department of Defense, trained Saudi National Guard units, armed them, and taught exceptional techniques—including parachute jumping from airplanes and helicopters—to ensure the safety of the monarch and his senior associates. In the aftermath of the assassination, the open *majlis* preferences that became legendary under Faysal were quickly replaced with carefully monitored audiences, among many such innovations. To be sure, access to the monarch and other senior princes was still possible, but vetting procedures carefully screened those who wished to enter the palace. It was unrealistic to expect anything less, as successor monarchs and heirs recalled with horror how a beloved, even if stern ruler, was slain.

Faysal left behind three major accomplishments. First were his offspring: six daughters and eight sons. His daughters played key roles in various charitable and educational institutions and spearheaded significant reforms that drew strength from their father's legacy. His sons, 'Abdallah, Muhammad, Khaled, Sa'ud, Sa'ad, 'Abdul Rahman, Bandar, and Turki, all excelled in government service, business, or charitable foundations.

Second, he established permanent institutions that solidified the country and allowed it to weather socioeconomic storms. His most enduring legacy was the systematic transformation of the nascent institutions of the kingdom into permanent structures. A tribal environment was gradually metamorphosed into an institutionalized state without reneging intrinsic values. Parochial groups coexisted with the Al Sa'ud, the critical Al Shaykh as well as other Unitarian religious leaders, and an increasingly educated intelligentsia that learned to accept the twin pillars that legitimized Saudi society while launching the country on the path of progress.

Third, Faysal secured the ruling family by limiting intra-family feuds. In fact, his most enduring work was related to the family itself, as he insisted on accountability. His decision to decree "that the royal family's take from oil exports should be capped at 18%," was a rule that analysts believed still applied in 2006.[6] Other reforms applied to family members included service to crown and nation in civilian as well as military fields. He elevated the notion of duty further than most and, in doing so, secured the throne for the Al Sa'ud, who could thus rule with the model of the *Just Prince*.

The Post-Faysal Evolution

As the peace process inched forward in the Middle East, and as access to energy sources continued to play a critical role in background developments to all negotiations, Saudi behavior evolved as well. With declining oil revenues in both 1976 and 1977, the Al Sa'ud simply could not meet their defense obligations while maintaining social commitments. Moreover, the Saudi quest for oil price stability translated into damaging inflation and economic gyrations that, in turn, added pressure on Riyadh. Then heir apparent Fahd explained:

> We believe that world economic stability is the most important pillar of world peace. . . . The spread of international economic crises distracts efforts to achieve peace in the Middle East. Accordingly, when the Kingdom of Saudi Arabia . . . decided on a 5 percent increase in oil price against the 10 percent recommendation of the other members of OPEC . . . it was only

taking into consideration the interests of the international community and world stability in the hope that peace would be returned to those regions that have been deprived of peace and most important, of course, to the Middle East. We are a part of the world, and we see our oil interests linked to the question of economic peace.[7]

Although Saudis perceived the need to coordinate economic and political interests, they did not favor separate peace treaties between Israel and the Arab states. As Washington championed the Camp David Accords, the U.S.-Saudi relationship suffered. Riyadh felt considerable annoyance at Washington for overtly promoting President Sadat's peace initiative at the expense of Saudi proposals. At the time, the Egyptian-Israeli agreement threatened to consolidate a radical Arab coalition and provided new opportunities to attack conservative regimes. To display their disapproval, the Al Sa'ud dropped daily production of oil by one million barrels in June 1979.[8] Moreover, they stopped pegging oil prices to the dollar because of the greenback's declining value. Despite these measures, Prince Fahd bin 'Abdul Aziz, the heir apparent, Shaykh Ahmad Zaki Yamani, and Shaykh 'Abdul 'Aziz al-Turki, the deputy minister of petroleum recognized that there was no substitute to the dollar over the short-term.[9] In an important interview with a Kuwaiti newspaper, Prince Fahd declared that Saudi Arabia believed "the dollar to be the most important currency, and . . . that the dollar will return to its former strength. . . ."[10] Even if the greenback never recovered its full potency, the statement was yet another indication of the dependence of Saudi Arabia on the United States.

After the Camp David Accords were signed, several Saudis—especially those who preferred to distance Riyadh from its overt dependence on Washington—argued for a production cut, but by December 1978 Saudi output was at an all time high of 10.4 million barrels per day. On January 20, 1979, Riyadh announced a ceiling for first-quarter production of 9.5 million barrels per day, although the decision may have reflected technical difficulties in producing at near maximum capacity. This policy change occurred in the aftermath of the Iranian Revolution, when OPEC agreed on a graduated pricing formula for 1979 that, in effect, drove spot prices sharply higher.[11] The short-term strategy was clear: increase revenues to purchase additional defensive equipment against this new threat. According to Shaykh Ahmad Zaki Yamani,

°if Faysal had lived, I don't think we would have seen the Camp David Agreements. He was so very respected by all the leaders in the Middle East that if he was against something they would not do it. He would go to an Arab summit conference and the minute he took the floor to speak, you could see everyone in the room paying great attention to what he was saying. His opinions were not challenged. Also, I don't think we would have seen a higher price of oil. What happened in 1979 might not have happened. There was pressure put on us to raise the price of oil in 1979 and I don't think Faysal would have succumbed to it. Inside, he was a very strong man, strong enough to resist those pressures.[12]

King Faysal may have adopted different policies, but what was certain, and amply evident under his successors, was the leadership role assumed by the kingdom. By associating Riyadh with core Arab causes, Faysal empowered Saudi rulers to defend Arab ideas, political parties, beleaguered governments, or disparate groups. He mediated whenever necessary to settle intra-state disputes, for example, between Morocco and Mauritania over the Sahara conflict and in the Lebanon Civil War, just to name two cases. This characteristic has been freely emulated by his three successors and may be said to have become a bedrock of Saudi foreign policy. Likewise, Faysal intervened to settle personal quarrels among Arab heads of states, several of whom took on legendary proportions during his lifetime. The animus that developed between Presidents Sadat of Egypt and Asad of Syria, Asad and 'Arafat of the PLO, and King Hussein of Jordan and 'Arafat were legendary and, in each instance, Faysal expanded both time and treasure to impose civility. Kings Khalid, Fahd, and 'Abdallah have continued this tradition, which has also evolved into a feature of Saudi diplomacy exercised with frequency and relative success.

In the end, Faysal's most enduring legacy was his successful defense of faith, which empowered Riyadh and legitimized the Al Sa'ud. It may be said that this characteristic of Saudi foreign policy featured both moral as well as pragmatic aspects. To be sure, and while it was true that Saudi rulers always relied on Islam to rule with justice, Faysal elevated the trait to new heights. Faith and its defense became the essence of his behavior and most of his policies. He lived the moral example and insisted that those around him conduct themselves impeccably. More specifically, it may be said that Riyadh experienced post- 'asabiyyah attributes under Faysal, in order to defend the Ummah materially as well as spiritually. As Ibn Khaldun's 'assabiyah (solidarity) implied group consciousness, under Faysal raising one's consciousness was no longer limited to blood relatives or narrow tribal outfits. In fact, Faysal insisted that new institutions be created to allow for a development of Muslim societies that encompassed a vast array of people spread over large distances in many countries. Muslims, led by Saudis, were called upon to truly "develop" and to better eliminate national, ethnic, and linguistic boundaries. Even if some of these preferences were idealistic, Faysal believed that they were essential for the Ummah, especially if the latter were to retain any meaning in the world at large. Remarkably, his three successors found merit in this vision of King Faysal's, as they undeniably benefited from the selection. That earned authority further secured the Saudi throne.

Appendix 1. Chronology

1720   Sa'ud bin Muhammad reigns as a local shaykh(ruler) around Dir'iyyah in central Arabia.

1744   Muhammad bin Sa'ud campaigns for religious piety and order with Muhammad bin 'Abdul Wahhab. The "first" Saudi state is initiated.

1818   The first Saudi state ends after most of Arabia falls to the Ottoman Empire. The great-grandson of Muhammad bin Sa'ud, 'Abdallah bin Sa'ud bin 'Abdul 'Aziz bin Muhammad bin Sa'ud, is executed by Ottoman conquerors.

1824   Turki bin 'Abdallah bin Muhammad bin Sa'ud, a grandson of Muhammad bin Sa'ud, seizes Riyadh from Egyptian forces, marking the beginning of the "second" Saudi state. The seventh Saudi ruler, and probably the most powerful in the nineteenth century, Turki rules until 1834. He is succeeded by his son Faysal, who is exiled to Cairo in 1837.

1843   Faysal bin Turki bin 'Abdallah escapes from his Cairo prison and returns to power to usher in a period of prosperity and stability. He unifies Riyadh and rules until 1865.

1916   The start of a two-decade-long Al Sa'ud family feud over succession matters; increasingly the Al Rashid dominate Riyadh and its surroundings.

1891   The "second" Saudi state ends when 'Abdul Rahman bin Faysal bin Turki flees to Kuwait. His eleven-year-old son, 'Abdul 'Aziz, escapes with him.

1902   'Abdul 'Aziz bin 'Abdul Rahman leads a small group of men in attack on Riyadh and seizes control.

1906   Faysal bin 'Abdul 'Aziz bin 'Abdul Rahman is born in Riyadh to 'Abdul 'Aziz bin 'Abdul Rahman and Tarfah bint 'Abdallah Al Shaykh. Faysal is born on the same day and the same hour as his half brother Muhammad, whose mother is Jawharah bint Musa'id bin Jiluwi. 'Abdul 'Aziz bin 'Abdul Rahman regains control of Hasah.

1912   Tarfah bint 'Abdallah Al Shaykh, Faysal's mother, passes away and the young prince is entrusted to his maternal grandmother. His maternal grandfather, 'Abdallah bin 'Abdul Latif Al Shaykh, is charged with his religious education. The Ikhwan, a religious brotherhood of tribesmen, is established to provide 'Abdul 'Aziz bin 'Abdul Rahman with shock troops.

1913   'Abdul 'Aziz bin 'Abdul Rahman gains control of the Gulf coast.

1916   Ikhwan fighters under 'Abdul 'Aziz control the region of Jabal Shammar. Winston Churchill and T. E. Lawrence (of Arabia) promote a "Sharifian solution," under which the Hashemite family would rule the Makkah region for Britain. Britain and France carve up Arabia and create Jordan under 'Abdallah; his brother Faisal becomes king of Iraq. France is given influence over Syria and Lebanon, while Jewish immigration is allowed into Palestine.

1919   Britain's King George V receives Faysal bin 'Abdul 'Aziz on October 30. The thirteen-year-old prince is representing his father in London at the post–World War I negotiations. Faysal visits Britain, Ireland, Belgium, and France as well as key World War I battlefields, including Verdun. Widespread rivalry and takeovers on the Arabian Peninsula occur throughout the 1920s.

1920   Faysal bin 'Abdul 'Aziz engages in 'Asir battles.

1926   Makkah, until June 10 under Turkish control, falls to an Arab force during the Great Arab Revolt.

1926   'Abdul 'Aziz bin 'Abdul Rahman gains control of Makkah and Madinah as well as all of the Hijaz (the western region of the kingdom). He declares himself king of the Hijaz. Faysal bin 'Abdul 'Aziz takes a second trip to Europe with stops in Britain, France, and Holland. Faysal is the viceroy of Hijaz (until 1953). The General Education Department is established. Primary and secondary education start in earnest.

1927   Ataturk forces the abolition of the caliphate; he bans all Kurdish schools, publications, and associations. The Ottoman Empire ends and the modern Middle East is created, although Iraq, Jordan, Lebanon, Saudi Arabia, and Syria are still partially under British and French control. Faysal bin 'Abdul 'Aziz struggles in the two-year long conquest of the Hijaz. 'Abdul 'Aziz bin 'Abdul Rahman declares himself king of the Hijaz and Najd.

1929   Rebellious Ikhwan forces are defeated.

1930   The Ministry of Foreign Affairs is established in Jiddah. Prince Faysal is appointed minister. He is his father's first minister and will hold the post until 1975, except for the period 1960–62.

1932   ʿAbdul ʿAziz bin ʿAbdul Rahman establishes the Kingdom of Saudi Arabia. Prince Faysal makes his third visit to Europe, which lasts six months with stops in Italy, Switzerland, France, Britain, Holland, Germany, Poland, and the Soviet Union, as well as Turkey, Iran, Iraq, and Kuwait. The Ministry of Finance is established.

1933   ʿAbdul ʿAziz bin ʿAbdul Rahman appoints his eldest son, Saʿud, heir apparent and declares that the next eldest, Faysal, will be heir apparent when Saʿud is king. Saudi Arabia gives Standard Oil of California exclusive rights to explore for oil.

1937   Oil is discovered in Saudi Arabia.

1939   Faysal returns to London for the Palestine Conference.

1943   Faysal makes his first visit to the United States of America.

1944   The Ministry of Defense is established.

1945   ʿAbdul ʿAziz bin ʿAbdul Rahman meets President Franklin D. Roosevelt on the USS *Quincy* in the Red Sea. An understanding is reached whereby Washington pledges security in return for preferred access to Saudi oil. Saudi Arabia is a founding member of the United Nations and a founding member of the League of Arab States.

1951   The Ministry of the Interior is established.

1952   Saudi Arabia occupies the Buraymi Oasis at the border of Oman and Abu Dhabi. The Saudi Arabian Monetary Agency (SAMA) is established and paper currency is introduced in the kingdom.

1953   The Council of Ministers is established. Saʿud, the heir apparent, heads the cabinet. ʿAbdul ʿAziz bin ʿAbdul Rahman dies. Saʿud succeeds him and Faysal is declared heir apparent. Faysal is regent (until 1964). ARAMCO workers go on strike in October. The General Education Department is transformed into the Ministry of Education. Fahd bin ʿAbdul ʿAziz is the minister of education.

1954   Faysal is appointed prime minister.

1956   ARAMCO workers strike. King Saʿud issues a royal decree banning strikes. Washington ships the first tanks sold to Saudi Arabia.

1957   The University of Riyadh (later King Saʿud University) is established.

1958   A military coup overthrows the Hashemite monarchy in Iraq. Riyadh suspects Egyptian interference. Faysal, the heir apparent, takes over executive powers after King Saʿud surrenders his authority under pressure from the ruling family. Serious internal disagreements on governance surface. Faysal is also minister of finance and commerce. Later, he will serve as minister of the interior and defense.

1960 Faysal resigns. King Sa'ud regains full executive powers. Prince Talal bin 'Abdul 'Aziz is appointed minister of finance and Shaykh 'Abdallah Tariqi is appointed minister of petroleum. Talal bin 'Abdul 'Aziz proposes constitutional reforms for the kingdom. Seven primary schools and three teacher training facilities for female students are established. Saudi Arabia is a prime mover in setting up OPEC along with Iraq, Iran, Kuwait, and Venezuela. Fuad Rouhani (1907–2004) of Iran serves as OPEC's first secretary-general.

1961 The government is shuffled in September. Talal bin 'Abdul 'Aziz leaves the cabinet. Faysal is appointed vice president of the Council of Ministers.

1962 A split in the ruling family leads to the rise of the so-called Liberal Princes. Princes Talal, Badr, and Fawwaz present themselves as liberal backers of King Sa'ud against the so-called conservatism of Prince Faysal, the heir apparent. Their "cause" is supported by President Gamal 'Abdul Nasir of Egypt. Faysal promises to establish a Majlis al-Shurah and to abolish slavery in the kingdom following the family contest. Shaykh Ahmad Zaki Yamani replaces Shaykh 'Abdallah Tariqi as minister of petroleum and mineral resources. The 'Alawi monarchy is overthrown by the military in Yemen in September. Riyadh suspects Egyptian interference. Egypt and the Soviet Union support the new revolutionary government. Faysal is named head of the Council of Ministers in October and announces a ten-point reform plan including the abolition of slavery. Saudi Arabia is a founding member of the Muslim World League in Makkah.

1963 The Egyptian Air Force, supporting Yemeni revolutionaries, initiates bombing raids on Saudi Arabia. King Sa'ud attempts to retake power against sustained family opposition. Fahd bin 'Abdul 'Aziz is minister of the interior.

1964 Members of the ruling family gain the support of senior 'ulamah (religious leaders) to force a change of power. Sa'ud is deposed after he is declared "unfit to rule" and Faysal is proclaimed king on November 2. Fahd bin 'Abdul 'Aziz is the second deputy prime minister.

1965 Khalid bin 'Abdul 'Aziz is named heir apparent. Faysal defies Islamist opposition and introduces women's education. Television is also introduced.

1966 A joint French-Saudi geophysical survey company is set up. Faysal embarks on a state visit to Jordan on January 27. The Abu Safah joint offshore oilfield between Bahrain and Saudi Arabia is officially opened. Faysal welcomes the ruler of Kuwait in Riyadh on February 8. In mid-February, the kingdom becomes the world's fourth largest oil producer, behind the United States, the Soviet Union, and Iran, but ahead of Kuwait. Faysal arrives in Khartoum on a state visit to Sudan on March 5. Faysal inaugurates the PETROMIN industrial area near Jiddah on April 8 and lays the foundation stone for a new steel rolling mill. Faysal arrives in Islamabad on a state visit to Pakistan on April 19. A major air defense project is signed on May 5 with the British Aircraft Corporation. Faysal receives the Qatari heir apparent, Khalifah bin Hamad Al Thani, in Jiddah on June 9. Faysal lands in Madrid on June 15 for a state visit to Spain. Faysal flies to the United States on June 20 for a state visit. A Saudi-Kuwait agreement on the partition of the Neutral Zone is ratified and exchanged on July 25. Faysal receives Adam 'Abdallah Osman, the president of Somalia, on a state visit starting on August 2. A treaty of friendship and cooperation is signed with Tunisia on August 23. Faysal arrives in Ankara on a state visit to Turkey on August 29. In Egypt Sayyid Qutb, the intellectual godfather of radical Islamism, is executed on August 29 under direct orders issued by Nasir. Qutb had earlier written: "A Muslim has no nationality except his belief." Faysal starts a state visit to Morocco on September 4. Faysal embarks on a state visit to Guinea on September 12. Faysal arrives in Bamako on a state visit to Mali on September 15. Faysal lands in Tunis for a state visit to Tunisia on September 18. Saudi Arabia and the U.S. Corps of Engineers announce a $130 million "soft vehicle" deal on September 27. On September 30, a new agreement is signed with ARAMCO that abolishes discounts on posted oil prices, which earns Saudi Arabia an additional $35 billion in annual revenues. The University of Petroleum and Minerals is established in Dhahran on October 29 (having been elevated from Petroleum College status and later to become King Fahd University of Petroleum and Minerals). The Muslim World League's eighth annual meeting of the Constituent Council convenes on November 1. Faysal inaugurates the eighth Arab Telecommunications Conference in Riyadh on November 7. Faysal receives Hamani Diori, the president of Niger, on a state visit starting on November 14. A Saudi-Jordanian economic agreement is signed in Riyadh on November 22. On November 23, Faysal places Saudi forces in Tabuk at the disposal of Jordan after an Israeli attack on the

Hashemite monarchy. Faysal receives Ismail Al Azhari, the president of Sudan, on a state visit starting on November 26. Saʿud bin ʿAbdul ʿAziz Al Saʿud, the former ruler, arrives in Cairo on December 18.

1967   Egyptian forces launch several attacks in Yemen on January 5. An undetermined number of Egyptians are arrested in Saudi Arabia, accused of sabotage activities under directives issued by Cairo. Egyptian air force units attack Najran on January 27. The first desalination plant is inaugurated in Jiddah on February 5. Cairo and Misr Bank branches are closed throughout the kingdom on February 9. Faysal receives King Hussein of Jordan on February 12. A telecommunications agreement is signed with France on February 23. Faysal inaugurates the Riyadh-Hijaz Highway on March 1. Seventeen Yemeni "saboteurs" are executed in Riyadh on March 17. Zayed bin Sultan Al Nahyan, the ruler of Abu Dhabi, visits Faysal on April 12. Faysal travels to London on a state visit to Britain starting on May 8. Egyptian air raids on Najran continue after May 11 and start on Jizan on May 14. Saudi armed forces go on alert on May 25; several units take up positions overlooking the Gulf of ʿAqabah on May 27. Faysal goes on a state visit to Belgium starting on May 29. Three explosive devices, one a car bomb, are set off in Jiddah: one is outside the U.S. embassy; another is at Grove International, an American construction company; and the last is at the U.S. Military Training Mission (June 2). Faysal visits General Charles de Gaulle, the president of France, in Paris on June 4. The Six-Day Arab-Israeli War is launched on June 5. Saudi forces move toward Jordan but stay out of the actual fighting. On June 7 Faysal calls upon all Muslims to fight a holy war against Israel. Riots in the Eastern Province temporarily stop oil production as well as exports, which resume on June 12 (except to the United States and the United Kingdom). On June 9, Riyadh rejects a UN Security Council resolution calling for a cease-fire. Faysal extends financial support but no military help to Egypt. Faysal receives King Hussein of Jordan on August 17. Faysal receives ʿAbdul Rahman ʿArif, the president of Iraq, on August 23. At the Khartoum LAS Summit, which starts on August 29, Faysal spearheads a program of Arab financial assistance to Egypt to overcome the economic effects of the 1967 loss. The oil embargo on the United States and the United Kingdom is lifted on September 2. Faysal is on a state visit to Somalia starting on September 20. Shaykh Saqr bin Muhammad Al Qasimi, the ruler of Ras Al-Khaymah, visits Faysal on September 30. Fahd bin ʿAbdul ʿAziz Al Saʿud, the minister of the interior, is appointed second deputy prime minister on October 1. Shaykh

Rashid bin Saʿid bin Maktoum Al Maktoum, the ruler of Dubai, visits Faysal on October 14. Shaykh Khalifah bin Salman Al Khalifah, the ruler of Bahrain, visits Faysal on November 6. Saudi Arabia and Romania agree to an oil-barter agreement on November 6. Charles Hélou, the president of Lebanon, visits Faysal starting on November 12. A trade agreement is renewed on December 10. ARAMCO production reaches nine billion barrels on November 22. After Britain grants independence to its former colony of Aden and the adjoining protectorate of South Arabia in November 1967, a self-proclaimed Marxist government gains control of South Yemen, now the People's Democratic Republic of Yemen. Saudi Arabia and Egypt resolve differences over the Yemen Arab Republic and normalize relations on November 1, which means that Riyadh accepts republican government in Sanaʾa as Cairo withdraws its troops.

1968 Shaykh Jasim bin Hamad Al Thani, then the Qatari minister of education, visits Faysal on January 6. Faysal receives King Hussein of Jordan on January 10. Shaykh Khalifah bin Salman Al Khalifah, the ruler of Bahrain, visits Faysal on January 15. Britain announces on January 16 that treaties with nine Arab emirates would be terminated by the end of 1971 when it plans a "withdrawal" from east of the Suez. Cevdet Sunay, the president of Turkey, visits Faysal on January 22. The shah of Iran, who was scheduled for a state visit, cancels his trip on January 29 as differences emerge on Gulf security issues (he will make a brief stop at the Jiddah airport on June 3 for a talk with Faysal). Defense Minister Sultan bin ʿAbdul ʿAziz signs a major military accord with France on February 14 to diversify arms acquisitions; Sultan visits France starting on February 19 and Belgium on February 26. Shaykh Ahmad bin ʿAli Al Thani, the ruler of Qatar, visits Faysal on April 1. Faysal is on a state visit to Kuwait starting on April 8. Faysal receives King Hassan II of Morocco on a state visit to Saudi Arabia starting on April 20. Faysal receives King Hussein of Jordan on April 21. Saudi Arabia agrees to disburse $25 million to Jordan on June 9. On July 17, the Baʿath party seizes power in Baghdad as Iraq embarks on a new *nahdah* (Arab Islamic renaissance) based on nonsectarian Arab nationalism. George Ball, the U.S. ambassador to the United Nations, visits Faysal on July 19 on a special mission. Saudi Arabia and the United States sign a cultural agreement on July 29. The Central Planning Organization signs a key agreement with Stanford University (Palo Alto, California). The latter's Research Institute will streamline the long-term planning initiatives of the kingdom. Saudi Arabia and Iran sign a cultural agreement on

August 6. Faysal issues a royal circular on September 9 instructing government officials to observe group prayers. Faysal receives King Hussein of Jordan on September 22. Shaykh Khalifah bin Hamad Al Thani, the heir apparent of Qatar, visits Faysal on October 13. Saudi Arabia and Iran sign a border agreement on October 24, delineating the continental shelf in the Persian Gulf. Faysal receives Muhammad Reza Pahlavi, the shah of Iran, on a state visit starting on November 9. ARAMCO tops 10 billion barrels (production level) on November 14. The first meeting of the Organization of Arab Oil Exporting Countries (OAPEC) is held in Riyadh on December 14.

1969   The French minister of defense, Pierre Messmer, visits Faysal on January 16 to discuss a new arms accord. Saudi Arabia and Iran ratify the Sovereignty Agreement over the Arabian and Farsi Islands and the Median Line in the Persian Gulf on January 29. Deposed King Sa'ud bin 'Abdul 'Aziz dies in exile in Greece on February 23. The news reaches Faysal as he is speaking to leaders of pilgrim delegations when he calls for a holy war to liberate Jerusalem. Faysal receives King Hussein of Jordan on March 18. A coup attempt within the Royal Saudi Air Force occurs. Hadhrami and Ghamidi tribal members are arrested. Purges follow as an undetermined number of officers are indicted over the course of several weeks. Tapline, the oil pipeline to Lebanon, is sabotaged by the Popular Front for the Liberation of Palestine on May 31. A military coup overthrows the Sanusi monarchy in Libya. Riyadh suspects Egyptian interference. Military clashes with South Yemen occur. Saudi Arabia signs a multimillion dollar contract with the British Hovercraft Corporation for the supply of hovercrafts to the Saudi Coast Guard. The accord is inked by Interior Minister Fahd bin 'Abdul 'Aziz on August 4. The Al-Aqsah Mosque in Jerusalem is set on fire on August 21. Faysal renews his call for a holy war to liberate Jerusalem on August 24. Faysal receives King Hussein of Jordan on August 29. Faysal attends the Organization of Islamic Conference Summit meeting in Rabat on September 21. South Yemeni forces attack and capture the Saudi frontier post at Wadi'ah. They are expelled by force on December 4. The grand mufti of the kingdom, Shaykh Muhammad bin Ibrahim Al Shaykh, dies on December 3. Faysal attends the Rabat LAS Summit on December 20. Faysal is treated for schistomiasis in Paris in late December 1969 and early January 1970.

1970   Israel attacks Safi and Fifa islands in Saudi Arabia on January 20. One Saudi soldier is killed. Yasir 'Arafat, the head of Fatah, is received by Faysal on March 9. Faysal receives Joseph P. Sisco, the U.S. assistant secretary of state for Near Eastern and South Asian affairs, on April 23. Zayed bin Sultan Al Nahyan, the ruler of Abu Dhabi, visits on May 2. The Trans-Arabian Pipeline (Tapline) is damaged on May 3. Shaykh Rashid bin Saʿid bin Maktoum Al Maktoum, the ruler of Dubai, visits Faysal on May 9. Saudi Arabia and Kuwait sign an agreement to partition a Neutral Zone between the two countries and to share its resources equally. Khalid bin ʿAbdul ʿAziz has a heart attack on May 21. Faysal embarks on state visits to Malaysia (June 7–10), Indonesia (June 10–13), Afghanistan (June 13–16), and Algeria (June 16–20). Faysal meets with U.N. secretary general U Thant in Geneva on July 4 while on a private visit to Switzerland. Faysal recognizes the Yemen Arab Republic on July 22. He attends the LAS Cairo Summit meeting on September 23. Gamal ʿAbdul Nasir dies on September 28 in Cairo. Anwar al-Sadat is the new president of Egypt. Faysal is in Geneva for medical treatment so Saudi Arabia is represented at Nasir's funeral services by Prince Fahd bin ʿAbdul ʿAziz. Faysal receives King Hussein of Jordan on December 1. Nawwaf bin ʿAbdul ʿAziz, along with Omar Saqqaf and a delegation of senior foreign ministry officials, join Fahd bin ʿAbdul ʿAziz in London for comprehensive Anglo-Saudi talks on the Persian Gulf. Faysal receives Yasir ʿArafat, the head of Fatah, on December 18.

1971　William Luce, the British political resident in the Gulf between 1961 and 1972 (before assuming the position of personal representative for Gulf affairs for the foreign and commonwealth secretary), visits Faysal on January 24. Faysal receives the Omani goodwill mission headed by Shaykh Saʿud Al Khalili, the sultanate's first minister of education, on January 26. Ahmad bin ʿAbdul ʿAziz is appointed deputy governor of Makkah on January 12. The first five-year economic plan is introduced on February 25. On March 1, Sir Alec Douglas-Hume, the British foreign secretary, announces in the House of Commons that Britain will terminate its defense treaty obligations with nine Arab shaykhdoms by the end of the year. Faysal receives U.S. Secretary of State William Rogers on May 1. Faysal receives William Luce on May 12. Faysal arrives in Taiwan (then Formosa) on a state visit to the Republic of China on May 17–20. He then flies to Tokyo on a state visit to Japan on May 20–25. Faysal reaches San Francisco before starting a state visit in Washington, D.C. He also stops in Williamsburg, Virginia on what will be his last trip to the United States (May 27–30). Muhammad bin Faysal, a son of the king, is appointed the director of saline water conversion in the Ministry of Agriculture and Water in late May. Faysal receives ʿAbdul Rahman Al ʿIryani, the president of the Yemen Arab Republic, in Jiddah on May 11–16. Faysal visits Cairo on a state visit on May 19–26. The OIC Summit Conference meets in Jiddah on May 21–23). Vice President Spiro Agnew of the United States visits Saudi Arabia on July 8–9. Faysal receives King Hussein of Jordan on July 25. Faysal appoints Hisham Nazir president of the Central Planning Organization on July 25. Bahrain gains its independence from Britain on August 14. Faysal congratulates the Al Khalifah on August 15 and extends formal diplomatic recognition. Anwar al-Sadat, then vice president of Egypt, visits on August 21. Qatar gains its independence from Britain on September 3. Faysal agrees to exchange ambassadors with Doha on October 12. Faysal arrives in Beirut on a state visit to Lebanon on September 27–October 2. Faysal receives Sayyid Mukhtar Walad Dada, the president of the Islamic Republic of Mauritania, on October 17. Faysal welcomes Jaafar Muhammad Numayri, the president of Sudan, on November 15. Faysal receives Muhammad Siad Barre, the president of Somalia, on November 28. The shah of Iran threatens to forcibly take the three islands of Abu Musa and the Greater and Lesser Tunbs, which belong to the emirates of Ras al-Khaymah and Sharjah but are under British protection. On December 1, Iranian troops invade and occupy the islands of Abu Musa and the Greater and Lesser Tunbs. On December 2, six of the Trucial States (Abu Dhabi, ʿAjman, Dubai, Fujayrah, Sharjah, and Umm al-Qiwayn) proclaim themselves as separate shaykhdoms and, as a federated state within the United Arab Emirates, sign a ten-year treaty of friendship with Britain. Shaykh Zayed bin Sultan Al Nahyan, the ruler of Abu Dhabi, is elected president for a five-year term. Shaykh Rashid bin Saʿid Al Maktoum, the ruler of Dubai, is elected vice president. Saudi Arabia does not extend diplomatic recognition to the United Arab Emirates until 1974. Ahmad Khalifah Al Suwaydi, the foreign minister of the United Arab Emirates and the principal advisor to Shaykh Zayed bin Sultan Al Nahyan, meets Faysal on December 12. Sultan Qaboos of Oman visits Saudi Arabia to meet Faysal on December 11–14. Saudi Arabia recognizes the independence of the Omani sultanate on December 15. The Arab Socialist Union between Egypt, Syria, Sudan, and Libya, fails.

1972 Riyadh demands accountability from oil companies operating in the kingdom. For the first time in its history, it gains control of a proportion (20 percent) of ARAMCO, lessening American control, as the government purchases 25 percent of the company. Washington delivers the first of 114

F-5 fighters to the Royal Saudi Air Force. Anwar al-Sadat expels Soviet advisors from Egypt.

1973 The October Arab-Israeli War occurs. King Faysal supports the oil embargo of the Organization of Arab Petroleum Exporting Countries (OAPEC) (which Iraq refuses to honor) against the United States and the Netherlands after an arms resupply air bridge is opened between the United States and Israel (via the Netherlands). The People's Democratic Republic of Yemen provides active support for the Dhuffar rebellion against Sultan Qaboos of Oman. Riyadh supports Qaboos.

1974 Riyadh purchases 60 percent of ARAMCO in June. Saudis control the company for first time ever. Saudi-American relations improve after a cease-fire agreement is brokered between Israel and Egypt as well as Israel and Syria (both mediated by Henry Kissinger, the U.S. secretary of state). President Richard M. Nixon of the United States becomes the first American head of state to visit the kingdom when he arrives in Jiddah on June 14.

1975 Faysal bin 'Abdul 'Aziz is assassinated on March 25 by Faysal bin Musa'id bin 'Abdul 'Aziz. The king's American-educated nephew has a history of mental illness. He is tried, found guilty, and executed on June 18, 1975. The heir apparent, Khalid bin 'Abdul 'Aziz, is proclaimed king after his older brother, Muhammad, renounces his place in the line of succession. Fahd bin 'Abdul 'Aziz becomes the heir apparent. The latter decision skips over Princes Nasir and Sa'ad, both of whom step aside as well. Fahd assumes additional responsibilities to manage the government. Sa'ud al-Faysal, a son of the late monarch, is appointed foreign minister.

Sources: Foreign Broadcast Information Service—Middle East and Africa, 1960–1975; Kechichian, *Succession in Saudi Arabia*, 161–68.

Appendix 2. Vital Speeches

First Address to the United Nations

Today marks the end of this great historic occasion in which many nations, struggling for the establishment and support of peace, have participated. We have finished today what may be called the Charter of Justice and Peace, after hard work, long discussions, and deliberations in order to put this Organization in the most effective form to safeguard peace and justice for the future world.

This Charter does not represent perfection as visualized by the small states. Nevertheless, it is doubtless the best ever produced by people representing fifty states, many of which have suffered much in their struggle for liberty, the defense of humanity, and its liberation from slavery, which only God knows how long would have lasted, or when we would have been saved from its tragedies and calamities, had injustice prevailed.

We have seen the powers of tyranny succeed in Europe and threaten the Near and Middle East. But, with God's help, these powers have been completely defeated. We, the sons of the Near and Middle East and particularly of the Arab Nations, are filled with happiness and joy at the collapse of these powers of evil. We look forward with rejoicing to the collapse of the last stronghold of tyranny and oppression. Indeed, the whole world is indebted for its survival to the Allied Nations, which engaged themselves in war, sacrificing the best of their youth and the wealth of their resources for their security and for the security of mankind.

In such a moment as this we should not forget the resolute efforts of the late Franklin Delano Roosevelt in the cause of peace and his farsighted action in initiating this conference. By having achieved these purposes, we have given credit to his memory. We must also pay our tribute to President Truman for his noble efforts for the achievement of peace and security through this Conference.

No doubt this Charter will lead toward prosperity and happiness for all nations, great and small. We have all done our best here to fulfill our obligations to humanity. As long as we are united together in a spirit of cooperation, the hand of Almighty God will lead us. We shall always have His aid insofar as we help one another.

I wish to thank the people of this beautiful city, the pride of the Pacific, for their hospitality, kindness and friendship. From now on, indeed, San Francisco should be called the City of Peace.

Let that faith which led the Conference guide our future footsteps. Let us practice and preserve the principles which we have here put down on paper. Once and for all, let us put an end to selfishness, greed, persecution, tyranny, and oppression. Let this Charter be the solid foundation upon which we shall build our new and better world.

Source: "Address by the Chairman of the Delegation of Saudi Arabia to the Inaugural Plenary Session, 25 April 1945," in *United Nations Documents*, vol. 1 (San Francisco: Conference on International Organization, 1945).

I Am a Servant

Brothers,

Peace be upon you and God's mercy and blessings.

It gives me the greatest pleasure to extend to you my warmest thanks, my appreciation for all that you have said and the feelings of pure love which I have sensed. I pray God to give me strength and make me worthy of the trust you put in me.

Brothers,

I have not the slightest doubt in my heart about what my feelings are towards your love and loyalty; I have the same feelings for you. I feel bound to repeat to you now what I have said before, namely that I feel myself to be one of you, both a brother and a servant of yours at one and the same time.

Brothers,

I give you my word that in all my dealings I will look to God for guidance, and in serving you I pledge you my loyalty. I will be fair to great and small alike, for, as far as justice is concerned, whichever of you is farthest removed from me is equal to him who is nearest to me. I ask God that by His strength I may be trustworthy, that I may be loyal to God and just in my dealings with my family, nation and brothers. I ask you all to help me bear this responsibility by being loyal to God, by treating yourselves and your state honestly and, through this very loyalty and honesty, to help the Government in its work. Help the reformer carry out his reform and set yourselves against anyone who would spoil his work.

The State should serve the people. Indeed, it is the duty of the State to seek the good of its people and nation, and to strive for anything which can be to the people's advantage. The people, on the other hand, should help the State with their loyalty and trust: they should openly tell the benefactor that what he has done is good; and equally tell the malefactor that what he has done is harmful. You should be a support for reformers and a scourge to those who would spoil or ruin such work. It is, of course, not meant by this that anyone should avail himself of these sentiments of this trend of thought to do his will in the name of the public good. What it does mean is that the reformer should come and face the malefactor and present his case; for at the same time we have to impose justice on those who try to avoid it.

Brothers,
There is one small remark I would like to make. I keep hearing repeated the words "Your Majesty" and "seated on the throne" and such like. I beg you, brothers, to look upon me as both brother and servant.

Brothers,
"Majesty" is reserved for God alone, and "the throne" is the throne of the God of the Heavens and the Earth. These words and these attributes are foreign to our religion and to our language. When I say this I am not deceiving you: I only tell you what I feel. For when I hear the words "Your Majesty" or "seated on the throne" if affects me deeply because I am only human and every human being should be a slave of God who is seated on His throne. It is only the fact that you have entrusted me with this responsibility that differentiates you from me. I pray God to help me shoulder the burden I carry (to lead me along the right path) and to allow me to serve you until I die. If what I do is good, then it is due to the grace of God. If what I do is wrong, then the action is mine. I wish you all a happy future and good luck.
Peace be upon you and God's mercy and blessings.

Source: Address delivered in Riyadh on 19–7–1384AH (November 8, 1964), responding to popular support after his inauguration as the ruler, in Kingdom of Saudi Arabia, *Faisal Speaks* (Riyadh: Ministry of Information, n.d.), 16–17.

Institutions to Serve Religion and Nation

Friends and brothers,
It is a splendid occasion for me to participate in the opening and inauguration of this great Institute. The least we can say about this Institute is that it represents one aspect of our scientific, economic and industrial progress. I am delighted to see in this Institute Saudi and Algerian students, side by side, representing great strides towards our hopes of bringing the Arab world to the forefront among the nations of the worlds—nations that accept their responsibilities, serve their people and provide a bright future for them.

A few years ago, this Institute was just a big dream. We used to look around and find ourselves unable to compete with other nations in various aspects of progress. But God has helped us and in less than two years, we find ourselves with this Institute already functioning. In my opinion, this is a record.

The opening of institutes and colleges and the celebration of their inauguration is not in itself important. But what is important is that we serve our religion and nation. And I pray to God that this will be only a beginning, leading to the building of other institutes and not the end of the road.

It is my pleasure to thank the body of this Institute, professors, administrators and students, for the progress they have demonstrated which will be to the benefit of all. I would also like to say how pleased I am to see the people's appreciation of the work carried out by the Government. This is very encouraging for us and will help us pursue our course of action in the service of our people in all honesty and sincerity.

May God support our actions for the good of everyone.

Source: Address delivered in Dhahran on 8–10–1384H (September 2, 1965), at the inauguration of the Petroleum College, in Kingdom of Saudi Arabia, *Faisal Speaks* (Riyadh: Ministry of Information, n.d.), 30–31.

Islamic Solidarity

Your Excellency Mr. President, Gentlemen,
It is my pleasure at this moment to thank you for all the hospitality you have shown. This reception shows the charitable Islamic spirit that is the quality of the President of Pakistan, its Government and people.

Your Excellency,
What you have explained about the ties that bind this country to mine, based on

brotherhood and love and derived from the spiritual teachings of Islam, is the best ideology that can bind human beings together. This makes it easier for me to explain and emphasize to Your Excellency the feeling, which the Kingdom of Saudi Arabia, its people and government share with you and its hopes of fostering with you a link based on spiritual ideology.

The sentiments and relationship that derive from a pure ideology, transcending material interests, are the right basis for co-operation between peoples and governments. It is in these moments, when Islam is facing many undercurrents that are pulling Muslims left and right, East and West, that we need time for more co-operation and closer ties to enable us to face all the problems and difficulties that obstruct our way as an Islamic nation, believing in God, His Prophet and His Laws.

However hard some people try to distort the call of Islam, Islam will remain a clear and straight path that needs no alteration or amendment. For what Islam calls for is brotherhood, co-operation, peace and the love of man for his fellow men. This opposition to our faith will not change the basic principles of Islam. And when we call for our brothers in Islam for more co-operation between each other, we seek no enmity or aggression, but only to defend ourselves from all aggression.

We seek peace and we want understanding so that we may work towards co-operation. But that does not mean we are willing to sacrifice our principles and beliefs in Islam in order to reach that peace or that understanding.

Your Excellency, Gentlemen,
We have been accused, I am sorry to say, by certain Muslims, of trying to establish pacts, treaties, or certain privileged relationships with non-Muslim powers or foreign countries beyond those agreements approved by international councils. I would like to assure you that we have no such intentions and our only aim is to promote Islam, support the religion of God and bring all Muslims closer together to enable them to discuss between themselves the affairs of their religion and life.

We are carrying on with our message despite any opposition we may encounter and despite the distortion that some people will inflict us with. But we still persist in welcoming all our brothers in all Islamic countries to co-operate with us for the benefit of our religion, the good of their own people and of the world. And I sincerely hope that they will follow the will of God and their religion, which is the religion of truth, strength, knowledge, progress and peace.

There is everything in our religion and our laws to dispense us from importing inferior ideologies made by mere mortals, because Islam is the Law of God revealed to His Prophet, and God knows best the interests of his creation. Therefore, Your Excellency, in the name of the Kingdom of Saudi Arabia, and, on behalf of its Government and people, I thank you for all the wonderful hospitality you have shown us, and for your sincere co-operation which, we hope, will prosper and flourish in the years to come. And, Your Excellency, if we have shown some brotherly feelings and co-operation in this Islamic country, it is because this is the least of what our religion and belief demand from us.

I hope that this good and generous country will prosper under your wise leadership and your sincere devotion to your people, that it may give the greatest example to all the world of how a Muslim can lead his country to progress and peace.

I thank you again, Your Excellency, as I thank the Government and the people of Pakistan, for all they have shown us of their good hospitality and for the true Islamic spirit we have encountered in this beloved land. I hope that God will keep with you the blessings of Islam and will support us in our endeavor to serve His religion and laws, as well as our nations and countries and all humanity.

Source: Address delivered at arrival ceremonies at Karachi Airport in Pakistan on April 19, 1966, in response to President Ayub Khan's welcoming remarks, in Kingdom of Saudi Arabia, *Faisal Speaks* (Riyadh: Ministry of Information, n.d.), 52–54.

Prosperity, Integrity and Security

Your Excellency,
Allow me to assure Your Excellency of my profound pleasure at your kind hospitality and at your good intentions that I felt throughout the talks we had together today, as well as for the impression I got of your fine personality and your desire to serve your country and the whole world.

You reminded me, Your Excellency, when you mentioned the beginnings of relations between our two countries by those two great men: Franklin D. Roosevelt and His Majesty King 'Abdul 'Aziz, of the phases through which this relationship has passed in the last twenty-one years. It is fortunate that this relationship, which the two great men had started, is progressing from good to better. If an occasional misunderstanding has occurred during that period, it is only natural that differences of opinion should exist but these do not affect the solid bases of a relationship that is built on loyalty to common ideals or the sincerity we have shared in carrying out the good work for the benefit of all, irrespective of these differences of opinion and without in any way damaging the roots of these bases.

Your Excellency,

I greatly appreciate your assurance of co-operation between our two countries to the benefit of our people. This co-operation includes the efforts that are being made to remedy the shortage that my country, and part of your country, suffers from, namely water. As the Qur'an has said: "And we have created from water everything that is living." So, without water, there is no life.

We find it very difficult, Your Excellency, to execute certain projects in our country owing to this shortage of water. For the climate and topography of our country are such that this important source of life is lacking.

If we co-operate together, there is excellent hope of solving this vital problem for the people of Saudi Arabia and, for that matter, for the people of the United States as well, and of providing them with a splendid life.

Your Excellency,

After I got to know your desire, plans and work for the good of this people and their future, I look up to you with even more admiration. For when you work for the good of society, you work for your own good and the good of all individuals.

And when Your Excellency mentioned what we have done for our country and our people, we were representing the very outlook that you have explained, in the hope that God would help us to provide everyone with his needs in dignity and peace.

I thank Your Excellency for giving me this opportunity to meet the different distinguished personalities and institutions that are working for the good of this country. I would like to reiterate my thanks and my gratitude for the excellent care you have taken of me and for the good intentions you have shown.

I thank you Mr. President and all those present here.

Source: Address delivered in response to President Lyndon B. Johnson at a White House state dinner, Washington, D.C., June 21, 1966, in Kingdom of Saudi Arabia, *Faisal Speaks* (Riyadh: Ministry of Information, n.d.), 60–62.

Interference and Harm

It gives me great pleasure to express my gratitude to the Secretary of State for his generous speech that reflected his loyal and noble sentiments. I was very gratified to hear you referring to the ties of friendship and co-operation which exist between our two countries and peoples, based on right, a sense of justice and a desire for the prosperity and happiness of the people.

Mr. Secretary,
We have no intention to be aggressors, nor do we seek to swallow up the rights of any individual or group of persons. But, at the same time, we will not willingly allow ourselves to become targets for aggression: our desire for peace and reform does not mean that we will flinch at the threat of danger.

The reforms we are carrying out in our country, and the founding of public services that you mentioned are considered our most sacred duty. And, inasmuch as we claim to serve our people and country loyally, they are the least we can offer them. I am quite convinced that if in any country the leaders or those in authority attended to the affairs of the people and concentrated on reforming the country and raising the standards of living, they would be too busy to interfere in other people's affairs or to harm anyone.

Mr. Secretary,
In our country we are kindly disposed to this friendly people as well as to all other peoples. We hope that these relations will benefit our country and all mankind. We also hope that we will set an example to others who are working for good objectives, who have no evil intentions and no desire to encroach on the sacred rights and interests of other people.

Mr. Secretary,
In our call for Islamic solidarity between the Muslim peoples we have no hostile intentions against non-Muslims, nor do we seek personal interest or some hollow form of leadership. Above all else, our aim is to serve our religion and to affirm our belief in God the Almighty. Indeed, we call upon all men of other religions to co-operate with their Muslim brothers for the good of humanity and the world, at a time when subversive trends pull people in various directions, wreck their economies, undermine their morale and cheat them of the personal dignity and right to work which is their inheritance from God.

Mr. Secretary,
While I am speaking on this subject, I would like it to be known that our call only aims at the good of our nation and the good of others. We ask God Almighty to preserve this gift for us; the gift of serving our religion, nation and

people and help us to bring them to that advanced state of progress that we so greatly need.

I reiterate my thanks to you for your warm words of welcome, which express the wish of the friendly American people, that the cordial relations which exist between our two peoples and countries should continue to flourish. We sincerely hope that these relations will bear fruit, not only, as I have said, for our benefit, but, by the strength of God, for the benefit of all mankind.

Source: Address delivered in response to Secretary of State Dean Rusk in Washington, D.C., June 22, 1966, in Kingdom of Saudi Arabia, *Faisal Speaks* (Riyadh: Ministry of Information, n.d.), 64–65.

American-Saudi Relations

Gentlemen,

It gives me great pleasure to express my thanks to the senior members of the press, who have provided me with this opportunity to meet all these people and get to know them as friends. I am also delighted to be able to express my deepest gratitude and appreciation to President Johnson, who, ever since we arrived, has accorded us his hospitality and affection. I feel that the time I spent with President Johnson during our meeting represents some of the happiest hours of my life. I extend my deepest thanks to the friendly American people for the wonderful reception they gave me, for the abundance of friendly feelings and noble sentiments the individual American has at heart.

I am very pleased to be able to speak at this moment, about the relations, which exist between the Kingdom of Saudi Arabia and the United States. These relations are not the child of the hour, nor are they the product of a particular set of circumstances: they have no secret interests or hidden aims as their object. They are founded on the basis of free friendship, and on those fundamental aims that the two peoples have in common, to love freedom and to cling to a firm belief in themselves which binds all nations which believe in this principle. Despite the fact that the United States and the Kingdom of Saudi Arabia do have mutual interests, their relations are not built on this alone—they are built on the principles I have just enumerated.

Perhaps the brothers present would like me to clarify some points about Saudi Arabia. The Kingdom of Saudi Arabia is made up of a people who believes in its God, loves freedom and aspires to a prosperous future. We are on the way to reforming our country. We do not claim to have achieved the impossible or to have worked miracles: we strive to the best of our abilities.

Our plans aim to raise our people and bring them to the position they deserve and to which they aspire.

The land area of Saudi Arabia is one million square miles. Although there has been no accurate census, the population, according to our estimate, is between seven and eight million people. Furthermore, it is apparent from what one hears on the news that there is a widespread belief that the Kingdom of Saudi Arabia is one of the richest countries in the world. We thank God that we do indeed have resources in abundance; but this is not sufficient for our needs, nor is it enough to enable us to carry out our duty towards the country. For a country that has had to start from scratch is in need of everything.

We are greatly concerned to spread education and culture over our country. We have opened schools, established colleges and sent students to study abroad at the State's expense. Education at every stage in the Kingdom of Saudi Arabia is free; and in some cases students are paid. As for health, we are seeking to make health services embrace the whole country; no village or town is without a hospital or clinic. Health services and medicines are provided free for all the people and, in addition, any patient who cannot be treated inside the country is sent for treatment to any country abroad at the Government's expense.

As far as building is concerned, the State is above all interested in constructing modern roads to link up the various parts of the Kingdom and to facilitate the transportation and movement of people and materials. A five or ten-year plan has been drawn up to build 10,000 kilometers of paved roads. On the social side, the State has established a Ministry of Social Affairs, one of whose tasks is to open social education institutes, as well as institutes and houses for the needy and handicapped who cannot earn their own living. There is also in existence what we call the social security system whereby the State guarantees the livelihood of each person who is incapable of work or who has no source of income.

I do not want to go into long explanations, my friends, because time is precious to us all. However, statements and statistics can be obtained from the Saudi Embassy in Washington for those who require further explanations or greater detail. I would also like to add that in Saudi Arabia we have sixteen airports for domestic and international aircraft, as well as other un-surfaced airstrips.

I apologize for mentioning this, but I was afraid that the Minister of Defense would have remonstrated with me if I had failed to do so. He is responsible for it.

Speaking more generally, the Kingdom of Saudi Arabia has peace and stability as its aims, for without stability and without peace, no country can rise and prosper.

I again repeat my thanks for these moments I have been able to spend with you. My colleagues in the delegation would second that also, for they have the same sense of duty towards our friends as I do myself.

Source: Address delivered to the National Press Club in Washington, D.C., June 22, 1966, in Kingdom of Saudi Arabia, *Faisal Speaks* (Riyadh: Ministry of Information, n.d.), 66–69.

Appendix 3. Documents

Message from Kissinger to Faysal and Hussein of Jordan, October 6, 1973

DECLASSIFIED
Authority *E O 12958*
By MB NARA Date 06/05/02

73 War

******* T O P S E C R E T *******S COPY

FLASH   /OP IMMED
DE RUEHC #9583 2791244
Z O 061233Z OCT 73 ZFF6
FM SECSTATE WASHDC

TO AMEMBASSY AMMAN FLASH 4863
AMEMBASSY JIDDA FLASH 2929

INFO USINT CAIRO NIACT IMMEDIATE 4596
AMEMBASSY MOSCOW NIACT IMMEDIATE 5487
AMEMBASSY TEL AVIV NIACT IMMEDIATE 7938
AMEMBASSY BEIRUT NIACT IMMEDIATE 1033
USMISSION USUN NEW YORK IMMEDIATE 3761

Secretary's message to Faisal & Hussein

T O P S E C R E T STATE 199583

TOSEC 141
E.O. 11652: -XGDS
SUBJ: MESSAGE FROM SECRETARY TO KING FAISAL AND KING
HUSSEIN

1. PLEASE SEND FOLLOWING ORAL MESSAGE TO KING FAISAL
AND KING HUSSEIN FROM SCRETARY OF STATE KISSINGER:
QUOTE:
YOUR MAJESTY:
WE HAVE JUST RECEIVED THE REPORT FROM THE ISRAELIS THAT
EGYPTIAN AND SYRIAN FORCES ARE PLANNING A.COORDINATED
ATTACK WITHIN THE NEXT SEVERAL HOURS. WE HAVE URGED
THE ISRAELIS NOT TO LAUNCH ANY OREEMPTIVE ATTACK. I
HAVE SPOKEN WITH THE EGYPTIAN FOREIGN MINISTER TO URGE
THAT HIS GOVERNMENT REFRIAN FROM LAUNCHING ANY ATTACK
WHICH COULD LEAD TO SERIOUS CONSEQUENCES. WE HAVE
ALSO DISCUSSED THIS MATTER ON A MOST URGENT BASIS WITH
THE SOVIETS.
I ASK YOU MAJESTY TO INTERVENE IMMEDIATELY WITH PRESIDENTS
SADAT AND ASSAD AND URGE THAT NO SUCH ATTACK BE LAUNCHED
ON THEIR PART. WE BELIEVE THIS IS A TIME FOR RESTRAINT,
NOT ONLY BECAUSE OF THE OBVIOUS DANGERS THAT ARE IN-
VOLVED BUT BECAUSE IT IS IMPORTANT TO MAINTAIN CONDITIONS
WHICH WILL MAKE IT POSSIBLE IN THE DAYS AHEAD TO
PURSUE A PEACEFUL RESOLUTION OF THE ARAB-ISRAELI
CONFLICT. UNQUOTE. RUSH
BT

Proposed Presidential Message to King Faysal, October 12, 1973

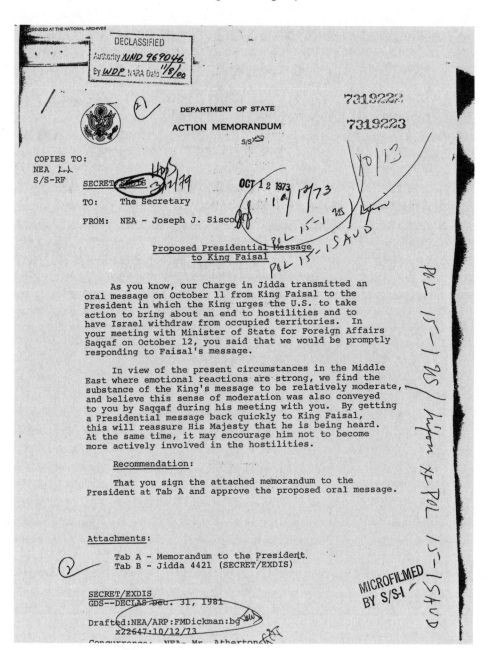

DECLASSIFIED
Authority *NND 969046*
By *WDP* NARA Date *11/8/00*

7319223

DEPARTMENT OF STATE

ACTION MEMORANDUM

S/S

7319223

COPIES TO:
NEA
S/S-RF

SECRET/EXDIS

OCT 12 1973

TO: The Secretary

FROM: NEA - Joseph J. Sisco

Proposed Presidential Message
to King Faisal

As you know, our Charge in Jidda transmitted an
oral message on October 11 from King Faisal to the
President in which the King urges the U.S. to take
action to bring about an end to hostilities and to
have Israel withdraw from occupied territories. In
your meeting with Minister of State for Foreign Affairs
Saqqaf on October 12, you said that we would be promptly
responding to Faisal's message.

In view of the present circumstances in the Middle
East where emotional reactions are strong, we find the
substance of the King's message to be relatively moderate,
and believe this sense of moderation was also conveyed
to you by Saqqaf during his meeting with you. By getting
a Presidential message back quickly to King Faisal,
this will reassure His Majesty that he is being heard.
At the same time, it may encourage him not to become
more actively involved in the hostilities.

Recommendation:

That you sign the attached memorandum to the
President at Tab A and approve the proposed oral message.

Attachments:

Tab A - Memorandum to the President.
Tab B - Jidda 4421 (SECRET/EXDIS)

SECRET/EXDIS
GDS--DECLAS Dec. 31, 1981

Drafted:NEA/ARP:FMDickman:bg
x22647:10/12/73
Concurrence: NEA- Mr. Atherton

MICROFILMED
BY S/S-I

Reply to Faysal's Oral Message, October 12, 1973

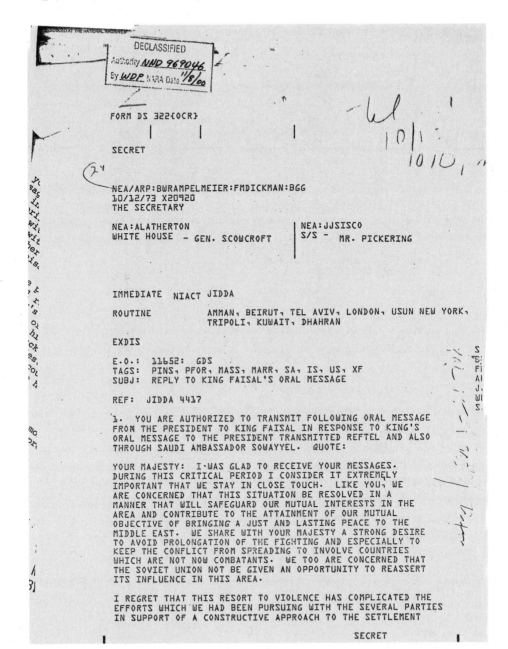

FORM DS 322(OCR)

SECRET

NEA/ARP:BWRAMPELMEIER:FMDICKMAN:BGG
10/12/73 X20920
THE SECRETARY

NEA:ALATHERTON
WHITE HOUSE - GEN. SCOWCROFT

NEA:JJSISCO
S/S - MR. PICKERING

IMMEDIATE NIACT JIDDA

ROUTINE   AMMAN, BEIRUT, TEL AVIV, LONDON, USUN NEW YORK,
             TRIPOLI, KUWAIT, DHAHRAN

EXDIS

E.O.: 11652: GDS
TAGS: PINS, PFOR, MASS, MARR, SA, IS, US, XF
SUBJ: REPLY TO KING FAISAL'S ORAL MESSAGE

REF: JIDDA 4417

1. YOU ARE AUTHORIZED TO TRANSMIT FOLLOWING ORAL MESSAGE
FROM THE PRESIDENT TO KING FAISAL IN RESPONSE TO KING'S
ORAL MESSAGE TO THE PRESIDENT TRANSMITTED REFTEL AND ALSO
THROUGH SAUDI AMBASSADOR SOWAYYEL. QUOTE:

YOUR MAJESTY: I WAS GLAD TO RECEIVE YOUR MESSAGES.
DURING THIS CRITICAL PERIOD I CONSIDER IT EXTREMELY
IMPORTANT THAT WE STAY IN CLOSE TOUCH. LIKE YOU, WE
ARE CONCERNED THAT THIS SITUATION BE RESOLVED IN A
MANNER THAT WILL SAFEGUARD OUR MUTUAL INTERESTS IN THE
AREA AND CONTRIBUTE TO THE ATTAINMENT OF OUR MUTUAL
OBJECTIVE OF BRINGING A JUST AND LASTING PEACE TO THE
MIDDLE EAST. WE SHARE WITH YOUR MAJESTY A STRONG DESIRE
TO AVOID PROLONGATION OF THE FIGHTING AND ESPECIALLY TO
KEEP THE CONFLICT FROM SPREADING TO INVOLVE COUNTRIES
WHICH ARE NOT NOW COMBATANTS. WE TOO ARE CONCERNED THAT
THE SOVIET UNION NOT BE GIVEN AN OPPORTUNITY TO REASSERT
ITS INFLUENCE IN THIS AREA.

I REGRET THAT THIS RESORT TO VIOLENCE HAS COMPLICATED THE
EFFORTS WHICH WE HAD BEEN PURSUING WITH THE SEVERAL PARTIES
IN SUPPORT OF A CONSTRUCTIVE APPROACH TO THE SETTLEMENT

SECRET

CRET | 2

OF THE DISPUTE BETWEEN ISRAEL AND ITS ARAB NEIGHBORS.
SECRETARY KISSINGER HAD ALREADY BEGUN EXPLORATORY TALKS
WITH THE PARTIES INVOLVED IN NEW YORK PRIOR TO THE OUT-
BREAK OF HOSTILITIES ON OCTOBER 6. IN HIS MEETING SHORTLY
BEFORE WITH YOUR MINISTER OF STATE FOR FOREIGN AFFAIRS,
MR. SAQQAF, THE SECRETARY HAD INDICATED OUR INTENTION TO
PURSUE ACTIVELY THE SEARCH FOR PEACE AND OUR DESIRE FOR
SAUDI ARABIA'S HELP IN THIS ENDEAVOR. THIS CONTINUES TO
BE OUR INTENTION.

YOUR MAJESTY, I CAN ASSURE YOU THAT THE UNITED STATES
GOVERNMENT IS DOING ALL THAT IT POSSIBLY CAN TO BRING
HOSTILITIES TO AN EARLY END. WE STRONGLY BELIEVE,
HOWEVER, THAT THIS MUST BE DONE IN SUCH A WAY THAT THE
PROCESS OF DIPLOMACY CAN ONCE AGAIN TAKE HOLD AND THAT
GENUINE PROGRESS TOWARD A LASTING PEACE CAN BE OBTAINED.

AS SECRETARY KISSINGER EXPLAINED TO MINISTER SAQQAF IN
THEIR MEETING OCTOBER 12, THE OBJECTIVE OF THE US IS TO
BRING ABOUT AN END TO HOSTILITIES AND LAY A BASIS FOR
ACHIEVING A JUST SETTLEMENT. IT IS PARTICULARLY IMPORTANT
DURING THIS CRITICAL TIME TO CONDUCT OURSELVES IN SUCH
A WAY THAT IT WILL NOT BE IMPOSSIBLE FOR THE US TO PLAY
A HELPFUL ROLE ONCE THE FIGHTING IS OVER. I UNDERSTAND
AND APPRECIATE THE DELICATE POSITION IN WHICH SAUDI
ARABIA FINDS ITSELF. I FIND ENCOURAGING THAT YOUR
MAJESTY'S STATESMANSHIP IS BEING MADE FELT ON THE SIDE OF
MODERATION AND GOOD SENSE.

LET ME REASSURE ALSO YOUR MAJESTY THAT OUR POLICY AT
THIS TIME IS NOT ONE-SIDED. AS I SAID ON SEPTEMBER 5,
THE U.S. IS NEITHER PRO-ISRAEL NOR PRO-ARAB: IT IS
PRO-PEACE. CONSEQUENTLY, IN THE DIFFICULT HOURS AND
DAYS AHEAD, I BELIEVE IT IS ESSENTIAL THAT WE CONTINUE
TO WORK TOGETHER TO HELP BRING ABOUT A RESTORATION OF
AN ATMOSPHERE IN WHICH WE CAN RENEW EFFECTIVELY THE
SEARCH FOR A JUST AND LASTING POLITICAL SETTLEMENT.

IN CLOSING I WANT TO TELL YOU HOW MUCH I PERSONALLY
APPRECIATED MINISTER SAQQAF'S ASSURANCES CONVEYED TO
SECRETARY KISSINGER THAT SAUDI ARABIA CONTINUES TO DESIRE
CLOSE RELATIONS WITH THE US. THIS TOO IS MY GOVERNMENT'S
POLOIC
POLICY AND ONE WHICH I INTEND TO PURSUE VIGOROUSLY.
END QUOTE.

44

Message from Kissinger to Faysal, October 14, 1973

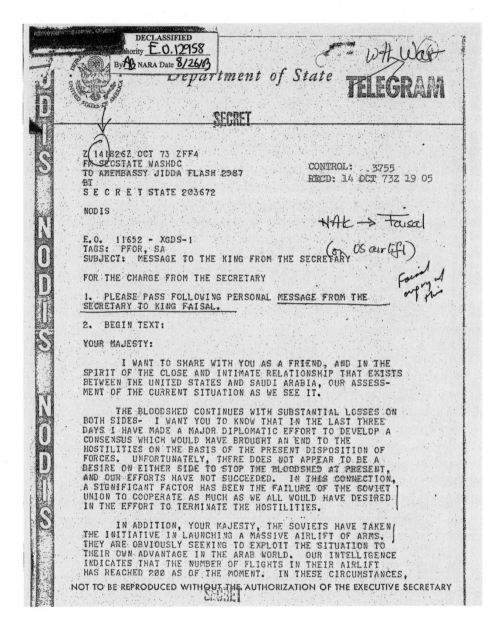

DECLASSIFIED
Authority E.O.12958
By AB NARA Date 8/26/03

Department of State TELEGRAM

SECRET

Z 141826Z OCT 73 ZFF4
FM SECSTATE WASHDC
TO AMEMBASSY JIDDA FLASH 2987
BT
S E C R E T STATE 203672

CONTROL: 3755
RECD: 14 OCT 73Z 19 05

NODIS

HAK → Faisal
(on US airlift)

E.O. 11652 - XGDS-1
TAGS: PFOR, SA
SUBJECT: MESSAGE TO THE KING FROM THE SECRETARY

Faisal enjoyed this

FOR THE CHARGE FROM THE SECRETARY

1. PLEASE PASS FOLLOWING PERSONAL MESSAGE FROM THE
SECRETARY TO KING FAISAL.

2. BEGIN TEXT:

YOUR MAJESTY:

I WANT TO SHARE WITH YOU AS A FRIEND, AND IN THE
SPIRIT OF THE CLOSE AND INTIMATE RELATIONSHIP THAT EXISTS
BETWEEN THE UNITED STATES AND SAUDI ARABIA, OUR ASSESS-
MENT OF THE CURRENT SITUATION AS WE SEE IT.

THE BLOODSHED CONTINUES WITH SUBSTANTIAL LOSSES ON
BOTH SIDES. I WANT YOU TO KNOW THAT IN THE LAST THREE
DAYS I HAVE MADE A MAJOR DIPLOMATIC EFFORT TO DEVELOP A
CONSENSUS WHICH WOULD HAVE BROUGHT AN END TO THE
HOSTILITIES ON THE BASIS OF THE PRESENT DISPOSITION OF
FORCES. UNFORTUNATELY, THERE DOES NOT APPEAR TO BE A
DESIRE ON EITHER SIDE TO STOP THE BLOODSHED AT PRESENT,
AND OUR EFFORTS HAVE NOT SUCCEEDED. IN THIS CONNECTION,
A SIGNIFICANT FACTOR HAS BEEN THE FAILURE OF THE SOVIET
UNION TO COOPERATE AS MUCH AS WE ALL WOULD HAVE DESIRED
IN THE EFFORT TO TERMINATE THE HOSTILITIES.

IN ADDITION, YOUR MAJESTY, THE SOVIETS HAVE TAKEN
THE INITIATIVE IN LAUNCHING A MASSIVE AIRLIFT OF ARMS.
THEY ARE OBVIOUSLY SEEKING TO EXPLOIT THE SITUATION TO
THEIR OWN ADVANTAGE IN THE ARAB WORLD. OUR INTELLIGENCE
INDICATES THAT THE NUMBER OF FLIGHTS IN THEIR AIRLIFT
HAS REACHED 200 AS OF THE MOMENT. IN THESE CIRCUMSTANCES,

NOT TO BE REPRODUCED WITHOUT THE AUTHORIZATION OF THE EXECUTIVE SECRETARY

SECRET

DECLASSIFIED
Authority E.O.12958
By AB NARA Date 8/26/13

Department of State TELEGRAM

SECRET

-2-STATE 203672, OCT 14

WE HAD NO ALTERNATIVE BUT TO BEGIN OUR OWN AIRLIFT.
IT IS EQUALLY IMPORTANT TO NOTE THAT IT WAS ONLY AFTER
THE SOVIET SUPPLY EFFORT HAD REACHED MASSIVE PROPORTIONS
THAT OURS BEGAN.

    I HOPE, YOUR MAJESTY, YOU WILL UNDERSTAND THAT OUR
AIRLIFT IS NOT INTENDED AS ANTI-ARAB. IT BECAME
INEVITABLE WHEN THE SOVIETS MOVED TO TAKE ADVANTAGE
OF THE SITUATION INSTEAD OF USING THEIR INFLUENCE TO
WORK FOR A CEASEFIRE WHICH WOULD END THE FIGHTING AND
IT BECAME NECESSARY IF WE ARE TO REMAIN IN A POSITION
TO USE OUR INFLUENCE TO WORK FOR A JUST AND LASTING
PEACE.

    I WANT TO ASSURE YOU THAT AS SOON AS AN EFFECTIVE
CEASEFIRE HAS BEEN ACHIEVED, WE ARE PREPARED TO STOP
OUR AIRLIFT PROMPTLY PROVIDED THE SOVIETS DO THE SAME.

    I HOPE, YOUR MAJESTY, THAT IN OUR COMMON INTERESTS,
YOU WILL MAKE EVERY EFFORT TO SHARE WITH YOUR ARAB
BROTHERS THIS EXPLANATION OF OUR PRESENT ACTIONS.

            SINCERELY,

                HENRY A. KISSINGER

END TEXT.

3. CHARGE SHOULD DELIVER THE MESSAGE AT THE OPENING OF
BUSINESS LOCAL TIME MONDAY, OCTOBER 15. EARLIER DE-
LIVERY IS NOT REQUIRED OR DESIRED. PLEASE INFORM WHEN
DELIVERY COMPLETED. KISSINGER
BT
#3672

DRAFTED BY: NEA:JJSISCO
APPROVED BY: THE SECRETARY

SECRET

U.S. Arms to Israel: Saudis Sorrowful; King May Send Another Message, October 16, 1973

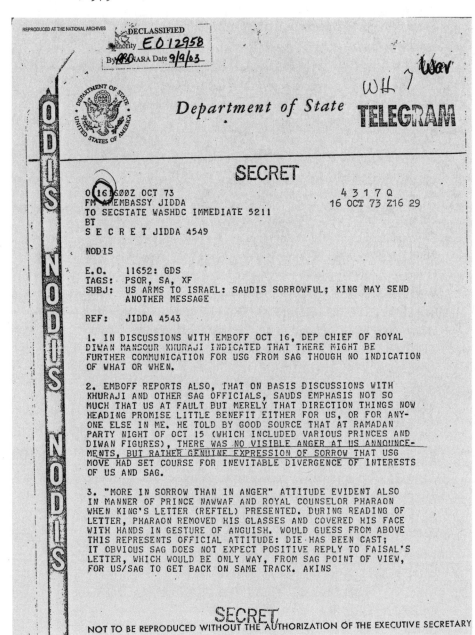

DECLASSIFIED
Authority *E O 1 2 9 5 8*
By ARO NARA Date *9/9/03*

WH 7 war

Department of State TELEGRAM

SECRET

O 16 1600Z OCT 73
FM AMEMBASSY JIDDA
TO SECSTATE WASHDC IMMEDIATE 5211
BT
S E C R E T JIDDA 4549

4 3 1 7 Q
16 OCT 73 Z16 29

NODIS

E.O.   11652: GDS
TAGS: PSOR, SA, XF
SUBJ: US ARMS TO ISRAEL: SAUDIS SORROWFUL; KING MAY SEND
       ANOTHER MESSAGE

REF: JIDDA 4543

1. IN DISCUSSIONS WITH EMBOFF OCT 16, DEP CHIEF OF ROYAL
DIWAN MANSOUR KHURAJI INDICATED THAT THERE MIGHT BE
FURTHER COMMUNICATION FOR USG FROM SAG THOUGH NO INDICATION
OF WHAT OR WHEN.

2. EMBOFF REPORTS ALSO, THAT ON BASIS DISCUSSIONS WITH
KHURAJI AND OTHER SAG OFFICIALS, SAUDS EMPHASIS NOT SO
MUCH THAT US AT FAULT BUT MERELY THAT DIRECTION THINGS NOW
HEADING PROMISE LITTLE BENEFIT EITHER FOR US, OR FOR ANY-
ONE ELSE IN ME. HE TOLD BY GOOD SOURCE THAT AT RAMADAN
PARTY NIGHT OF OCT 15 (WHICH INCLUDED VARIOUS PRINCES AND
DIWAN FIGURES), THERE WAS NO VISIBLE ANGER AT US ANNOUNCE-
MENTS, BUT RATHER GENUINE EXPRESSION OF SORROW THAT USG
MOVE HAD SET COURSE FOR INEVITABLE DIVERGENCE OF INTERESTS
OF US AND SAG.

3. "MORE IN SORROW THAN IN ANGER" ATTITUDE EVIDENT ALSO
IN MANNER OF PRINCE NAWWAF AND ROYAL COUNSELOR PHARAON
WHEN KING'S LETTER (REFTEL) PRESENTED. DURING READING OF
LETTER, PHARAON REMOVED HIS GLASSES AND COVERED HIS FACE
WITH HANDS IN GESTURE OF ANGUISH. WOULD GUESS FROM ABOVE
THIS REPRESENTS OFFICIAL ATTITUDE: DIE HAS BEEN CAST;
IT OBVIOUS SAG DOES NOT EXPECT POSITIVE REPLY TO FAISAL'S
LETTER, WHICH WOULD BE ONLY WAY, FROM SAG POINT OF VIEW,
FOR US/SAG TO GET BACK ON SAME TRACK. AKINS

SECRET
NOT TO BE REPRODUCED WITHOUT THE AUTHORIZATION OF THE EXECUTIVE SECRETARY

Saudi Ban on Oil Shipments to the United States, October 23, 1973

Document:
Saudi Ban on Oil Shipments to the United States
23 October 1973
STAMP AFFIXED ON TOP OF EACH OF THE FIVE PAGES OF DOCU-
MENT:
Declassified
Authority: EO12958
By: RBO NARA Date: 9/9/03
   *******CONFIDENTIAL*******E COPY

[HAND-WRITTEN NOTES ON MARGIN: WAR, 23 OCT, OIL. WQ,
HS.]
DP IMMED
ESA138RAA522
DE RUESRA #4663/1 2961030
D 230935Z OCT 73
FM AMEMBASSY JIDDA
TO SECSTATE WASHDC IMMEDIATE 5275
INFO AMEMBASSY ABU DHABI IMMEDIATE 147
AMEMBASSY AMMAN IMMEDIATE 2020
AMEMBASSY BEIRUT IMMEDIATE 4651
AMCONSUL DHAHRAN IMMEDIATE 6048
AMEMBASSY KUWAIT IMMEDIATE 2044
AMEMBASSY LONDON IMMEDIATE 2693
AMEMBASSY PARIS IMMEDIATE 838
AMEMBASSY ROME IMMEDIATE 461
AMEMBASSY TEHRAN IMMEDIATE 1329
AMEMBASSY TEL AVIV IMMEDIATE 678
AMEMBASSY TOKYO IMMEDIATE 79
AMEMBASSY TRIPOLI IMMEDIATE 599
USMISSION EC BRUSSELS IMMEDIATE 127
USMISSION OECD PARIS IMMEDIATE
   C O N F I D E N T I A L SECTION 1 OF 2 JIDDA 4663
DEPT PASS CAIRO
BEIRUT ALSO FOR BAGHDAD
E.O. 11652: GDS
TAGS: ENRG, SA, XF

SUBJECT: SAUDI BAN ON OIL SHIPMENTS TO U.S.

REF: A) JIDDA 4621; B) JIDDA 4615; C) JIDDA 4616

   D) JIDDA 4630; E) JIDDA 4600: F) JIDDA 4620

SUMMARY: SAUDI DECISION TO CUT OFF OIL SHIPMENTS TO U.S. ATTRIBUTABLE TO KING'S OWN DECISIONS; KING ANGRY AT ANNOUNCEMENT OF LARGE U.S. MILITARY GRANT PROGRAMS TO ISRAEL AND PROBABLY FELT THAT ANY LETTER RESPONSE WOULD LEAVE SAUDI ARABIA UNCOMFORTABLY ISOLATED IN ARAB WORLD. U.S. MISSION CONTACTS WITH HIGH-LEVEL SAG [SAUDI ARABIA GOVERNMENT] OFFICIALS, HOWEVER, INDICATE SAG WISHES TO MINIMIZE DAMAGE THAT PRESENT CRISIS MAY DO TO US-SAG RELATIONS. JOINT US-USSR RESOLUTION IN SECURITY COUNCIL POTENTIALLY A RADICALLY POSITIVE STEP; BUT IF IT DOES NOT SUCCEED SAG MAY FEEL COMPELLED TO INCREASE PRESSURE ON U.S. INTERESTS IN MILITARY, COMMERCIAL, ENERGY AND FINANCIAL

PSN:015361 PAGE 01   TDR:296/11:13Z DTG:230935Z OCT 73
                 *******CONFIDENTIAL*******E COPY

AREAS. EMBASSY IS STRESSING WITH SAG NEED THAT CHANNELS OF COMMUNICATION REMAIN OPEN, AND THAT EACH SIDE GIVE OTHER MAXIMUM ADVANCE NOTICE OF ANY MEASURES IT IS CONTEMPLATING. END SUMMARY.

   1. THERE IS LITTLE DOUBT THAT SAG DECISION TO BAN PETROLEUM EXPORTS TO U.S. STEMMED FROM KING FAISAL HIMSELF. DISCUSSION BETWEEN HIGH-RANKING SAG OFFICIALS AND AMBASSADOR (REF B AND E) IN 24 HOURS PREVIOUS, HAD NOT INDICATED SAG ON VERGE OF TAKING SUCH BIG STEP.

   2. SOURCES IN ROYAL DIWAN OCT 21 HAVE CONFIRMED TO EMBASSY THAT DECISION TAKEN BY KING, AND WAS PRINCIPALLY MOTIVATED BY U.S. PROPOSAL TO PROVIDE ISRAEL WITH 2.2 BILLION DOLLARS OF GRANT MILITARY AID. WE TOLD BY CHIEF OF ROYAL DIWAN, AHMAD ABDUL WAHAB A WELL-ADJUSTED PRO-AMERICAN FIGURE) THAT KING WAS AS FURIOUS AS HE HAD EVER SEEN HIM AND THAT HM [HIS MAJESTY] TOOK PARTICULAR UMBRAGE AT WHAT HE CONSIDERED TO BE DIFFERENCE BETWEEN REASSURING TONE OF VARIOUS COMMUNICATIONS HE HAD RECEIVED FROM USG [UNITED STATES GOVERNMENT], AND U.S. ANNOUNCEMENT OF "INCREDIBLE" AMOUNT OF AID

TO GOI [GOVERNMENT OF ISRAEL]. KING'S SUBSEQUENT CALL FOR JIHAD (FBIS KYRENIA 210810Z OCT 73) CAN ALSO BE AS-CRIBED TO KING'S DISPLEASURE. KING'S MOOD EMPHATICAL-LY REFLECTED ALSO BY ABLE, NATIONALIST MINISTER HISHAM NAZER, HEAD OF CENTRAL PLANNING ORGANIZATION.

3. WE SHOULD NOT, HOWEVER, OVERSTRESS THE CAUSATIVE EFFECT OF PURE EMOTION IN KING'S DECISION TO CUT BACK OIL SHIPMENTS TO U.S. A NUMBER OF ARAB COUNTRIES HAD ALREADY TAKEN STEP OF BANNING SUCH SHIPMENTS, AND YA-MANI HAD INFORMED AMBASSADOR THAT OTHERS WOULD PROBABLY FOLLOW (REF B). AS IMPACT OF U.S. AID DECISION MADE ITSELF FELT IN ARAB WORLD, KING MAY HAVE FELT THAT SAG WOULD OCCUPY EXPOSED SALIENT IF IT—ALONE AMONG ARAB OIL PRODUCERS—CONTINUED TO PROVIDE OIL TO U.S.
BT
PSN:015361 PAGE 02 OF 02 TDR:296/11:13Z DTG:230935Z OCT 73
*******CONFIDENTIAL*******E COPY
*******CONFIDENTIAL*******E COPY

DP IMMED
ESA151RAA523
DE RUESRA #4663/2 2961045
D 230935Z OCT 73
FM AMEMBASSY JIDDA
TO SECSTATE WASHDC IMMEDIATE 5276
INFO AMEMBASSY ABU DHABI IMMEDIATE 0148
AMEMBASSY AMMAN IMMEDIATE 2021
AMEMBASSY BEIRUT IMMEDIATE 4652
AMCONSUL DHAHRAN IMMEDIATE 6049
AMEMBASSY KUWAIT IMMEDIATE 2045
AMEMBASSY LONDON IMMEDIATE 2694
AMEMBASSY PARIS IMMEDIATE 0839
AMEMBASSY ROME IMMEDIATE 0462
AMEMBASSY TEHRAN IMMEDIATE 1330
AMEMBASSY TEL AVIV IMMEDIATE 0679
AMEMBASSY TOKYO IMMEDIATE 0080
AMEMBASSY TRIPOLI IMMEDIATE 0600
USMISSION EC BRUSSELS IMMEDIATE 0128
USMISSION OECD PARIS IMMEDIATE

CONFIDENTIAL SECTION 2 OF 2 JIDDA 4663
DEPT PASS CAIRO
BEIRUT ALSO FOR BAGHDAD

4. EMBASSY CONTACTS ELSEWHERE IN SAG, MOREOVER, TEND TO CONFIRM OUR ASSESSMENT THAT SAG WISHES MINIMIZE DAMAGE THAT PRESENT CRISIS COULD CAUSE TO US-SAUDI RELATIONS. DCMIS [DEPUTY CHIEF OF MISSION] DISCUSSION WITH DIRECTOR OF PUBLIC SECURITY FOR WESTERN REGION OCT 20 MADE CLEAR SAG'S GREAT CONCERN WAS SECURITY, WELL-BEING, AND GOOD MORALE OF AMCITS [AMERICAN CITIZENS] IN SAUDI ARABIA (REF F). ALSO, DURING MEETING OCT 21 BETWEEN CHIEF OF U.S. MILITARY TRAINING MISSION (GUSMTM), GENERAL HILL AND DEPUTY MODA [MINISTRY OF DEFENSE AND AVIATION] (AND KING'S BROTHER) PRINCE TURKI, PRINCE STATED "WE HAVE HAD TO TAKE CERTAIN PO-LITICAL DECISIONS DURING THE WAR JUST AS YOU HAVE, BUT THAT MUST BE KEPT ENTIRELY SEPARATE FROM RELATIONSHIPS BETWEEN MOSA AND USMTM." PRINCE IN SOMBER MOOD, BUT WAS AT ALL TIMES COURTEOUS AND FRIENDLY TO GENERAL HILL AND HIS STAFF.

5. FURTHER SAUDI REACTIONS WILL BE DETERMINED PARTLY BY

PSN:015366   PAGE 01   TDR:296/11:20Z DTG:230935Z OCT 73
                      *******CONFIDENTIAL*******E COPY
                      *******CONFIDENTIAL*******E COPY

WHAT WE DO AND SOME BY COURSE OF ARAB/ISRAELI FIGHT-ING. JOINT US-USSR RESOLUTION IN SECURITY COUNCIL PO-TENTIALLY RADICALLY POSITIVE STEP; BUT IF PROGRESS NOT FOLLOWING ON IMPLEMENTATION AND IF THE ARABS THEN FACE PROSPECT OF SERIOUS MILITARY SETBACK OR IF A CEASE-FIRE IS NOT RAPIDLY FOLLOWED BY ISRAELI WITHDRAWAL FROM AT LEAST SOME ARAB LANDS; SAUDIS WOULD RESPOND MUCH AS WOULD THEIR NEIGHBORS AND CAST ABOUT FOR WAYS TO PRESSURE/PUNISH U.S. AND WESTERN EUROPEANS. AMONG THE MEASURES THEY COULD TAKE MIGHT BE AC-CELERATED USE OF OIL WEAPON (FURTHER CUTS IN PRODUC-TION OF NATIONALIZATION OF U.S. ASSETS), TERMINATION OF U.S. MILITARY OVERFLIGHTS (WHICH NUMBER CIRCA 20 EACH

WEEK), OR USE FINANCIAL RESOURCES TO APPLY PRESSURE ON DOLLAR. (AMBASSADOR HAS ALREADY POINTED OUT TO MINISTER YAMANI THIS WOULD BE COUNTERPRODUCTIVE—REF C, AND WE ARE TOLD BY RELIABLE SOURCE THAT DIRECTOR OF MONETARY AGENCY ANWAR ALI OPPOSES SUCH A STEP). WE MIGHT ALSO EXPECT CALLY [CALL?] BY SOME RADICAL OF COMBATANT ARAB NATION FOR MEETING OF FOREIGN MINISTERS OR CHIEFS OF STATES, AND THAT SOME PRETTY NEGATIVE RECOMMENDATIONS RE OUR MIDDLE EAST INTERESTS WOULD ENERGE FROM ANY SUCH GATHERING.

6. SAG ACTION COULD ALSO DELIVER A SETBACK TO IMPORTANT U.S. COMMERCIAL AND MILITARY SALES; SAG HAS GROWN TO BE ONE OF LARGEST MARKETS FOR AMERICAN PRODUCTS BETWEEN EUROPE AND JAPAN, WITH SALES RUNNING AT MORE THAN A THIRD OF A BILLION DOLLARS THIS YEAR. OUR MILITARY SALES PROGRAMS MOREOVER HAVE IN PAST THREE YEARS EXCEEDED 500 MILLION DOLLARS, AND THERE ARE GOOD PROSPECTS FOR FMS [FOREIGN MILITARY SALES] CASH SALES OF A SIMILAR ORDER TO BE CONCLUDED WITHIN THE NEXT TWO YEARS. WE SHOULD REMEMBER THAT EUROPE, PARTICULARLY FRENCH AND BRITISH SOURCES, ARE MORE THAN PREPARED TO PICK UP THE FALLOUT FROM THE AMERICAN DILEMMA IN THE MIDDLE EAST CONFLICT.

[HAND-WRITTEN NOTE ON MARGIN TO PARAGRAPH 6: RIVALS ARE THINKING OF BANNING US PRODUCTS].

7. IN MEANTIME, AMBASSADOR HAS PASSED WORD TO CHIEF OF ROYAL DIWAN THAT IT [IS] ESSENTIAL FOR CHANNELS OF COMMUNICATION BETWEEN HIM AND SAG TO REMAIN OPEN AT ALL TIMES. AMBASSADOR ALSO SAID THAT IN ORDER TO MINIMIZE STRAIN OF CURRENT DEVELOPMENTS ON OUR RELATIONS, IT [IS] IMPORTANT THAT EACH SIDE BE GIVEN MAXIMUM POSSIBLE NOTICE OF STEPS OTHER MIGHT BE CONTEMPLATING; DIALOGUE MUST GO ON. AMBASSADOR MAKING SAME POINT ALSO TO MINPET [MINISTER OF PETROLEUM] YAMANI WHO [IS] BASICALLY WELL DISPOSED TO SAG'S WESTERN CONNECTION, AND MIGHT THUS BE USEFUL IN A SEMI-PRIVATE ROLE.

8. FINALLY, WITH REGARD TO SAUDI ACTIONS AGAINST U.S. OIL AND OTHER INTERESTS, WE SHOULD AVOID ACRIMONIOUS

PSN:015366   PAGE 02   TDR:296/11:20Z DTG:230935Z OCT 73
                *******CONFIDENTIAL*******E COPY
                *******CONFIDENTIAL*******E COPY
COMMENTS, SINCE THESE TEND TO KEEP AN UNHELPFUL DIA-
LOGUE GOING.
AKINS
BT
PSN:015366 PAGE 03 OF 03 TDR:296/11:20Z DTG:230935Z OCT 73
                *******CONFIDENTIAL*******E COPY

Source: United States of America, Department of State, "Saudi Ban on Oil Shipments to the United States," October 23, 1973; declassified September 9, 2003.

Notes

Introduction

1. For two particularly aggressive assessments, see Posner, *Secrets of the Kingdom*; and Gold, *Hatred's Kingdom*. Posner alleges that "Henry Kissinger was among those who received a copy of the Protocols [of Zion] from the king [Faisal]," (45) even if no evidence exists to buttress this claim.

2. Kean and Hamilton, *The 9/11 Commission Report*. See also Strasser, *The 9/11 Investigations*, 170; and *9/11 and Terrorist Travel*, 73.

3. In addition to Gold and Posner cited earlier, several other books advance this logic, including Baer, *Sleeping with the Devil*; and Schwartz, *The Two Faces of Islam*.

Chapter 1

1. This section draws on Kechichian, *Succession in Saudi Arabia*, especially 1–65. What follows is a summary of key developments rather than a comprehensive narrative.

2. For a good discussion of the Al Sa'ud ruling family, see Holden and Johns, *The House of Saud*.

3. Howarth, *The Desert King*, 42–52.

4. Philby, *Sa'udi Arabia*, 265–91; see also Kostiner, *The Making of Saudi Arabia*, 10, 185–88.

5. On the 1744 alliance between the Al Sa'ud and Al Shaykh families, see al-Yassini, *Religion and State*, 21–37. See also 'Abdul Ghafur, *Muhammad bin Abdul Wahhab*, 1979. The use of "Unitarian," rather than "Wahhabism," is not intended to equate the religious creed to its Christian namesake. Rather, the preference for "Unitarian" is to avoid perpetuating any pejorative connotations associated with Wahhabism in some Western sources.

6. Rentz, "Wahhabism and Saudi Arabia," 57.

7. Lambton, "Law and the State, 422.

8. 'Abdul Al Uthaymin, *Tarikh al-Mamlakah*, 1: 105–13. See also Samore, *Royal Family Politics*, 19, 483.

9. 'Abdul Al Uthaymin, *Tarikh al-Mamlakah*, 1: 151–207.

10. Ibid., 1: 219–24.

11. Ibid., 1: 232–34.

12. The details of this particular change in leadership are rather complex because Faysal was away campaigning in Bahrain. In the event, his eventual return was "accelerated," perhaps by the British, who by then were fully aware of the need for stability in the area. See ibid., 1: 237–41.

13. Ibid., 1: 242–49.

14. Troeller, *The Birth of Saudi Arabia*, 15–19.

15. Philby, *Sa'udi Arabia*, 160–68.

16. Philby, *Sa'udi Arabia*, 253–81; see also Al Rasheed, *Politics in an Arabian Oasis*, 150–58; and Samore, *Royal Family Politics*, 26–28.

17. For the history of the Ikhwan and their participation in the recreation of the Saudi kingdom, see Habib, *Ibn Sa'ud's Warriors of Islam*.

18. Lewis, "Politics and War," 163.

19. Kishk, *Al Sa'udiyyun Wal Hal Al-Islami*, 313–416. 20. Holden and Johns, *The House of Saud*, 107–8.

21. Ibid., 135–38.

22. See E. Wilson, *Decision on Palestine*.

23. King Sa'ud's controversial rule cannot be adequately analyzed here because so much of what actually occurred is either unknown or anecdotal. No reliable Saudi sources exist and most Western data are inadequate. This section aims to highlight key developments that emerged from his rule in order to draw better comparisons between his and Faysal's rules. For a detailed assessment of Sa'ud's rule, see Samore, *Royal Family Politics*, 74–229. See also Vassiliev, *The History of Saudi Arabia*, 354–68.

24. For the full text of the ten-point program, see De Gaury, *Faisal: King of Saudi Arabia*, 147–51.

25. Importantly, Faysal himself flew to Jiddah on March 14 to conduct business as usual. His main concern was to let the 'ulamah and the senior princes reach an independent decision. See Samore, *Royal Family Politics*, 185.

26. "Document: Transfer of Powers from HM King Sa'ud to HRH Amir Faysal." The *fatwah* issued by the 'ulamah was signed by twelve leading clerics; in turn, the religious decree was ratified by sixty-eight senior Al Sa'ud family members.

27. De Gaury, *Faisal*, 130–40; Faysal's own views on the engineered coup are reproduced from his first interview to the Beirut newspaper *Al-Hayat* in De Gaury, 136–38.

28. Al-Jawwad, *Al-Tatawwur al-Tashri'i fil-Mamlakah*, 39–42; for the text of the constitution of 1926, see Davis, *Constitutions, Electoral Laws*, 248–58.

29. For a discussion of the first nine meetings of the Majlis al-Shurah, see Hamzah, *Al-Bilad al-'Arabiyyah al-Sa'udiyyah*, 98–111.

30. For a history of the ministries and the growth of their functions, see ibid., 157–78 (finance), 113–56 (foreign affairs), and 248–60 (defense). See also Sharabi, *Governments and Politics*, 231.

31. 'Ali, *Al-Nizam al-Idari al-Su'di*, 24–31.

32. The audit office was headed by a controller-general appointed by the king and directly responsible to him. His extensive powers included a right to lodge complaints against the highest officials and dignitaries. The office was not filled until June 1957 when Sa'ud trusted it to his princely uncle Musa'id bin 'Abdul 'Aziz bin 'Abdul Rahman Al Sa'ud (whose son would assassinate King Faysal in 1975), who was, simultaneously, the head of the Grievances Office. Arguably, since the audit office was supposed to monitor state funds, and since the monarch was its largest spender, the authority of the audit office was sharply limited so as not to reveal the monarch's extravagant spending habits.

33. Shakir, "Saudi Arabia," 5.

3. For the text of Royal Decree 380, dated 22 Shawwal 1377 (May 11, 1958), and translated by H. St. John B. Philby, see Philby, trans., 320–23.

35. Holden and Johns, *The House of Saud*, 198–222.

36. Ibid., 210.

37. De Gaury, *Faisal*, 89–102.

38. Hanbali Islam represents the smallest Islamic school in Sunni theology. The school, one of four, was substantially weakened under Ottoman rule when *qadis* (judges) loyal to the Ottoman Porte dominated the vast Islamic realm. The Hanbali school was reinvigorated in the eighteenth century when Muhammad bin 'Abdul Wahhab, a pious cleric, rekindled the teachings of one of Arabia's great religious scholars, Taqidin Ahmad Ibn Taymiyyah, and aligned himself with Muhammad bin Sa'ud. See 'Abdallah Al-'Uthaymin, *Al-Shaykh Muhammad bin 'Abdul Wahhab*.

39. 'Abdul Wahab, *Al-Usul Al-Thalathah wa 'Adillatuhah*.

40. It must be emphasized that Faysal authorized informal Shurah gatherings throughout his tenure even if the institution was not officially established until 1992. For additional details, see Al Dhahrani, *Masirat al-Shurah fil-Mamlakah*, 319–49.

41. As quoted in Ansari, *The Islamic Boomerang in Saudi Arabia*, 7.

Chapter 2

1. Other meanings in Arabic for Faysal are sword and judge because whoever is entrusted with a sword must administer justice among men.

2. De Gaury, *Faisal*, 8.

3. The King Faisal Center for Research and Islamic Studies in Riyadh is painstakingly collecting parts of this vast correspondence for ultimate use by researchers.

4. Habib, *Ibn Sa'ud's Warriors of Islam*, 105–61.

5. It is often assumed that such skills are only attributable to tribal politics, an assumption that is certainly valid. Yet, several Arab political treatises were also available, for those

who linked their authority with the application of religious norms. For one illustration, Muhammad Ibn Zafar al-Siqilli's *Sultan al-Muta' fi 'Udwan al-Atba'* [Consolation for the ruler during the hostility of subjects], see Kechichian and Dekmejian, *The Just Prince*, 227–64.

6. Kostiner, *The Making of Saudi Arabia*, 49–55.

7. Benoist-Méchin, *Fayçal, Roi d'Arabie*, 30–31.

8. De Gaury, *Faisal*, 26–27.

9. Ibid., 28.

10. Ibid., 30.

11. Benoist-Méchin, *Fayçal, Roi d'Arabie*, 37.

12. De Gaury, *Faisal*, 40–41. See also al-Tahawih, *Al Malik Faysal wal-'Ilaqat al-Kharijiyyah al-Sa'udiyyah*, 18–21.

13. Al-Tahawih, *Al Malik Faysal wal-'Ilaqat al-Kharijiyyah al-Sa'udiyyah*, 31–32.

14. Benoist-Méchin, *Fayçal, Roi d'Arabie*, 43.

15. Kostiner, *The Making of Saudi Arabia*, 101.

16. Ibid., 146.

17. Bligh, *From Prince to King*, 26–29.

18. "Mission of Emir Feisal to The Hague; Despatch of U.S. Minister, The Hague, 19 October 1926," in al-Rashid, *Documents on the History of Saudi Arabia*, 2: 96–97.

19. "Visit of Faisal as Saud to Baghdad; Despatch of U.S. Ambassador, Baghdad, 13 July 1932," in al-Rashid, *Documents on the History of Saudi Arabia*, 3: 125–29.

20. Al-Rashid, *Documents on the History of Saudi Arabia*, 3: 127.

21. Richard, "Le Premier Voyage en France du Futur Roi Fayçal (1926)," 103–5.

22. Three men in particular, Mr. Cameau, Charles Puyraimond, and Mr. Chassagnon, assisted by Arab and Italian foragers, accomplished the second Saudi miracle—discovering water aquifers—in 1956. See ibid., 105.

23. "Documents on the Diplomatic Relations between the Kingdom of Saudi Arabia and the Soviet Union, 1926–1932," in al-Rashid, *Documents on the History of Saudi Arabia*, 3: 214–24, especially 223.

24. Naumkin, *Emir Faisal in Russia*, 4.

25. For a firsthand assessment of such meetings, albeit from a Dutch perspective, see Van Der Meulen, *The Wells of Ibn Sa'ud*.

26. Gerald De Gaury maintains that Faysal met with both Stalin and Molotov although there is no evidence that he met the Soviet strongman. See De Gaury, *Faisal*, 74.

27. Somehow, Iraqi sources heard of this request, probably from a member of the Saudi delegation, and passed it on to Ambassador Sloan. In the event, the rumors were not substantiated, although various authors referred to them.

28. De Gaury, *Faisal*, 15–23. See also "Documents on the Diplomatic Relations between the Kingdom of Saudi Arabia and the Soviet Union, 1926–1932," in al-Rashid, *Documents on the History of Saudi Arabia*, 3: 214–24, especially 223–34.

29. Kostiner, *The Making of Saudi Arabia*, 151.

30. Al-Tahawih, *Al Malik Faysal wal-'Ilaqat al-Kharijiyyah al-Sa'udiyyah*, 46–48.

31. Kostiner, *The Making of Saudi Arabia*, 147. See also al-Tahawih, *Al Malik Faysal wal-'Ilaqat al-Kharijiyyah al-Sa'udiyyah*, 46.

32. De Gaury, *Faisal*, 49.

33. Lacey, *The Kingdom*, 256–60.

34. Holden and Johns, *The House of Saud*, 133–35.

35. Eddy, *F. D. R. Meets Ibn Sa'ud*, 29–32.

36. Wilson, Decision on Palestine, 147..

37. Eddy, F.D.R. Meets Ibn Sa'ud, 37; see also Hart, *Saudi Arabia and the United States*, 41–42.

38. Wilson, *Decision on Palestine*, 66, 133–37.

39. Benoist-Méchin, *Fayçal, Roi d'Arabie*, 57.

40. De Gaury, *Faisal*, 69.

41. U.S. Department of State (Office of the Historian), *Foreign Relations of the United States, 1943*, 4: 840–52.

42. Hart, *Saudi Arabia and the United States*, 19.

43. Ibid., 28.

44. It must also be emphasized that Faysal and Khalid, who had returned home via London—where they met King George and the wife of Prime Minister Winston Churchill (who was away)—and Algiers (where they met the French general Charles de Gaulle), were keenly aware of the rising American power vis-à-vis its traditional Western allies.

45. Benoist-Méchin, *Fayçal, Roi d'Arabie*, 59.

46. De Gaury, *Faisal*, 63.

47. Benoist-Méchin, *Fayçal, Roi d'Arabie*, 61.

48. De Gaury, *Faisal*, 73.

49. Al-Tahawih, *Al Malik Faysal wal-'Ilaqat al-Kharijiyyah al-Sa'udiyyah*, 89–92.

50. Ibid., 92–98.

51. De Gaury, *Faisal*, 74.

52. It may indeed be argued that access to Gulf oil was and remained the primary objective of both Britain and the United States throughout the twentieth century as policies were developed toward Saudi Arabia.

53. Lacey, *The Kingdom*, 294–95.

54. Truman, *Memoirs*, 2: 136.

55. For an authoritative assessment of 'Abdul 'Aziz and his reign, see Howarth, *The Desert King*. See also Hamzah, *Al-Bilad al-'Arabiyyah al-Sa'udiyyah*.

56. Badeeb, *The Saudi-Egyptian Conflict over North Yemen*, 8–25.

57. On Saudi-Egyptian ties under Nasir, see Lacey, *The Kingdom*, 310–17; and Holden and Johns, *The House of Saud*, 198–222.

58. Abir, *Saudi Arabia in the Oil Era*, 70.

59. For a full discussion of these vital border accords, see Wilkinson, *Arabia's Frontiers*, 61–109.

60. Safran, *Saudi Arabia*, 45.

61. Wilkinson, *Arabia's Frontiers*, 144–46.

62. Safran, *Saudi Arabia*, 78.

63. Al-Tahawih, *Al Malik Faysal wal-'Ilaqat al-Kharijiyyah al-Sa'udiyyah*, 124.

64. Safran, *Saudi Arabia*, 74–75, 78.

65. Badeeb, *The Saudi-Egyptian Conflict over North Yemen*, 18–20.

66. Twitchell, *Saudi Arabia*, 102.

67. De Gaury, *Faisal*, 59–60.

68. "Appointment of Prince Saud as Lawful Successor to King Ibn Saud as Ruler of the Kingdom of Saudi Arabia; Despatch of U.S. Consul, Aden, 31 July 1933," in al-Rashid, *Documents on the History of Saudi Arabia*, 3: 174–79.

69. Ibid., 3: 178.

70. In the words of a former American ambassador, Faysal "could out-'Ulamize the 'Ulamah." Interview with Ambassador Herman Eilts, Wellesley, Massachusetts, October 27, 2005.

71. Robinson, *Yamani*, 150.

72. The White Army was so-titled because its members wore traditional Arab dress rather than military uniforms. See Yizraeli, *The Remaking of Saudi Arabia*, 147–64.

Chapter 3

1. De Gaury, *Faisal*, 78.

2. King Sa'ud's controversial rule cannot be adequately analyzed because so much of what actually occurred is either unknown or anecdotal. No reliable Saudi sources exist and most Western data are inadequate. This section aims to highlight key developments that emerged from his rule the better to draw patterns. For a detailed Western assessment of Sa'ud's rule, see Vassiliev, *The History of Saudi Arabia*, 354–68. See also Lacey, *The Kingdom*, 318–57; and Holden and Johns, *The House of Saud*, 198–222.

3. Dissatisfaction grew over wasteful expenditures, the lack of development of public projects and educational institutions, and the low wages for the growing labor force. See Lackner, *A House Built on Sand*, 57–68.

4. Powell, *Saudi Arabia and Its Royal Family*, 230–32.

5. Yizraeli, *The Remaking of Saudi Arabia*, 63–64.

6. "Visit to the Department of State by Prince Faisal; Memorandum of Conversation, U.S. Department of State, Washington, 3 March 1953," in al-Rashid, *Documents on the History of Saudi Arabia*, 3: 92–94.

7. For a full discussion of detailed intra-Gulf disputes over the Buraymi, see Cave Brown, *Oil, God, and Gold*, 198–214.

8. Ibid., 208–9.

9. For a detailed analysis of military ties between Saudi Arabia and the United States, see Long, *The United States and Saudi Arabia*, 33–40.

10. Ibid., 108–12.

11. Ibid., 112.

12. Ibid., 39.

13. Holden and Johns, *The House of Saud*, 193.

14. De Gaury, *Faisal*, 83.

15. Ibid., 88.

16. Ibid., 90.

17. Holden and Johns, *The House of Saud*, 196–97.

18. De Gaury, *Faisal*, 92.

19. Yizraeli, *The Remaking of Saudi Arabia*, 69–70.

20. De Gaury, *Faisal*, 93.

21. For details on the kingdom's financial situation in early 1958 and beyond, see Holden and Johns, *The House of Saud*, 206–10; and Lacey, *The Kingdom*, 324–27.

22. This was confirmed by Ambassador Eilts. Interview with Ambassador Herman Eilts, Wellesley, Massachusetts, October 27, 2005.

23. The literature on this period is rich and amply documented. For a thorough documentary discussion, see U.S. Department of State (Office of the Historian), *Foreign Relations of the United States, 1955–1957*, 16: 212–447.

24. Katz, *Russia and Arabia*, 134.

25. It should be emphasized that the coalition was never a homogeneous body and that the Saudi attachment to this alliance was tenuous at best. King Saʿud saw himself as part of the alliance but at the same time refrained from taking any steps that would expose the monarchy to subversive Egyptian activities. See Podeh, "The Struggle over Arab Hegemony after the Suez Crisis," 103.

26. Abir, *Saudi Arabia in the Oil Era*, 81.

27. Khadduri, *Republican Iraq*. See also Kerr, *The Arab Cold War*.

28. Sullivan, "Saudi Arabia in International Politics," 448.

29. Abir, *Saudi Arabia in the Oil Era*, 82.

30. Albaharna, *The Arabian Gulf States*, 40–46, 250–58.

31. Ibid., 250.

32. For additional details on the invasion and deployment of League troops, see MacDonald, *The League of Arab States*, 234–40; for specific details on Western military operations, see Koburger, "The Kuwait Confrontation of 1961," 42–49.

33. Long, "King Faisal's World View," 173–83.

34. Wenner, *Modern Yemen*, 193–228.

35. Ibid., 200–5.

36. Badeeb, *The Saudi-Egyptian Conflict over North Yemen*, 51.

37. Benoist-Méchin, *Fayçal, Roi d'Arabie*, 76.

38. Badeeb, *The Saudi-Egyptian Conflict over North Yemen*, 13–14.

39. When these air strikes failed to achieve their intended goals—to cripple the kingdom—Nasir turned to subversion. Egypt trained and infiltrated Yemeni terrorists into the

kingdom and set off a series of bombs throughout the country—even during the annual Hajj (pilgrimage). See ibid., pp. 39–40.

40. In August 1962, Nasir believed that the Saudi ruling family was on the verge of collapse when a rogue movement, led by Prince Talal, called for the adoption of a formal constitution. In the event, Talal was first dissuaded of his ill-advised actions, then exiled to Egypt when his vituperative arguments caused alarm. For further details, see Holden and Johns, *The House of Saud*, 198–222.

41. O'Ballance, *The War in the Yemen*, 78–79; see also Sullivan, "Saudi Arabia in International Politics," 441.

42. De Gaury, *Faisal*, 163.

43. Badeeb, *The Saudi-Egyptian Conflict over North Yemen*, 74.

44. Ibid., 56.

45. These measures were in response to Egyptian attempts to sabotage Saudi interests. For example, Egypt disrupted the 1966 Hajj with terrorist attacks and allowed the deposed King Saʿud to broadcast anti-Faysal propaganda on Cairo Radio in January 1967. See Gause, *Saudi-Yemeni Relations*, 69–70.

46. In 1965 and 1966, Faysal requested and received a military package worth several hundred million dollars from the United States and obtained from President Lyndon B. Johnson assurances of continued support for the security of the kingdom. See chapter 4.

47. Stookey, *Yemen*, 247; see also Badeeb, *The Saudi-Egyptian Conflict over North Yemen*, 81.

48. Yizraeli, *The Remaking of Saudi Arabia*, 203.

49. Ibid., 204.

50. Talal, the first member of the Al Saʿud family to write a public exposé, later felt that Saʿud was misrepresenting the country and its people and, eventually, fled to Cairo along with several air force officers. See Al Saʿud, *Risalah ilal-Muwatin*.

51. Although several Al Saʿud family members urged Faysal to take control of the government and the country, he at first declined, citing a promise he had made to his father to support Saʿud. Instead of just taking over, Faysal became prime minister, named Khalid the deputy prime minister, and formed a new government. He took command of the armed forces and quickly restored their loyalty and morale. This step proved to be a turning point. See De Gaury, *Faisal*, 93–94.

52. Ibid., 100.

53. For the full text of the ten-point program, see ibid., 147–51.

54. Importantly, Faysal himself flew to Jiddah on March 14 to conduct business as usual. His main concern was to let the *ʿulamah* and the senior princes reach an independent decision because he wanted the process to be as transparent as possible. See Samore, *Royal Family Politics in Saudi Arabia*, 483, 185.

55. Yizraeli, *The Remaking of Saudi Arabia*, 186–87.

56. Ibid., 194–95.

57. Hart, *Saudi Arabia and the United States*, xvii.

58. Bass, *Support Any Friend*, 89–95, 104–5.

59. Long, *The United States and Saudi Arabia*, 40–44.

60. Hart, *Saudi Arabia and the United States*, 94.

61. Bass, *Support Any Friend*, 104.

62. Hart, *Saudi Arabia and the United States*, 114, emphasis added.

63. Bass, *Support Any Friend*, 104.

64. McMullen, *Resolution of the Yemen Crisis*, 9–10, 13, 20.

65. Bass, *Support Any Friend*, 177–80.

66. Hart, *Saudi Arabia and the United States*, 145–50.

67. Robins, *A History of Jordan*, 114–16.

68. Public Record Office/Foreign Office, "Annual Review of Saudi Arabia for 1962," January 1, 1963, *FO 371/168867*.

69. As quoted in Bass, *Support Any Friend*, 109.

70. Hart, *Saudi Arabia and the United States*, 157–62.

71. Ibid., 166–68; see also Bass, *Support Any Friend*, 129.

72. Hart, *Saudi Arabia and the United States*, 168–69.

73. Ibid., 176.

74. Ibid., 176–78.

75. Ibid., 191.

76. Bass, *Support Any Friend*, 100–101.

77. Hart, *Saudi Arabia and the United States*, 192–94.

78. Ibid., 195–200.

79. Stookey, *Yemen: The Politics of the Yemen Arab Republic*, 484–85. At the time of the Yemen crisis, Stookey was U.S. chargé d'affaires in Sana'a.

80. Gause, *Saudi-Yemeni Relations*, 57–74.

81. Hart, *Saudi Arabia and the United States*, 222.

82. Ibid., 229–32.

83. Ibid., xvii, 236.

Chapter 4

1. De Gaury, *Faisal*, 130

2. Ibid., 133.

3. It is difficult to ascertain where this meeting occurred. Some sources insist that there was no encounter because Faysal was driving from Jiddah to Riyadh and Sa'ud was in Riyadh. Others maintain that the encounter did in fact occur even if the details are enveloped in secrecy.

4. As quoted in De Gaury, *Faisal*, 136.

5. For a detailed discussion of these key philosophical precepts, see Kechichian and Dekmejian, *The Just Prince*.

6. As quoted in De Gaury, *Faisal*, 138.

7. Huyette, *Political Adaptation in Saudi Arabia*, 57–77.

8. Bligh, *From Prince to King*, 76–77.

9. Prince Fahd, who would later become king, pressed for King Saʿud's abdication. See Holden and Johns, *The House of Saud*, 201.

10. Aburish, *The Rise, Corruption, and Coming Fall of the House of Saud*, 68 and passim.

11. Bligh, *From Prince to King*, 84–90.

12. Holden and Johns, *The House of Saud*, 249–52.

13. Ibid., 237. See also Bligh, *From Prince to King*, 86–87.

14. King Faysal provided for his deposed half brother's substantial expenses, although hard data are unavailable. He was quoted to have said: "Saʿud is our brother and we shall do our best to ensure his comfort." See Holden and Johns, *The House of Saud*, 240. It may also be useful to note that King Saʿud's estate was divided among 108 individuals, including 105 sons and daughters, two wives, and his mother. The estate was relatively small since Saʿud had "loaned" several million dollars to the Egyptian government. See "Confidential Jedda Minute by Mr. W. Morris, 22 April 1969–King Saud's Estate," in Burdett, *Records of Saudi Arabia*, 4: 111. In an attempt to ensure that the late monarch's estate was distributed equitably and according to Shariʿah, Faysal invited all of King Saʿud's sons to return to Saudi Arabia, and all did so save for Khalid bin Saʿud. See "Confidential Jedda Minute by Mr. W. Morris, 12 March 1969, Concerning the late King Saud," [FC08/1164], in Burdett, *Records of Saudi Arabia*, 4: 362–64.

15. For a good analysis of how Faysal brought stability to the process, see "Confidential Foreign Office Research Department Minute, 21 November 1968, the Succession to the Saudi Throne," [FC08/1209/1], in Burdett, *Records of Saudi Arabia*, 3: 111.

16. Though many of these rumors were clearly hostile to Saudi Arabia—especially in the Egyptian press—the consistency of several rumors is striking. For example, Egyptian sources reported throughout 1966 and 1967 that Interior Minister Fahd, supported by his full brothers Salman (governor of Riyadh) and Sultan (defense minister), intended to replace ʿAbdallah as commander of the National Guard but was opposed by both Faysal and Prince Khalid, the heir apparent. Even if exaggerated, the factions and tensions currently ascribed to family politics may be traced to the Faysal period. For a flavor of these rumors, see Burdett, *Records of Saudi Arabia*, 4: 98–99, 119.

17. It is remarkable that senior American officials failed to see this dramatic shift, mistakenly ascribing the style as being "oblique and persistent, reticent and assertive." In the words of Henry Kissinger, the U.S. secretary of state, "Saudi Arabia obscures its vulnerability by opaqueness and hides its uncertainty about the motivations of outsiders by an aloof pride." This may indeed have been the case under Saʿud's rule, but no objective political assessment can advance such an assertion about Faysal. See Kissinger, *Years of Upheaval*, 658–59.

18. Long, *The United States and Saudi Arabia*, 134–45; see also Hart, *Saudi Arabia and the United States*, 237–47.

19. Holden and Johns, *The House of Saud*, 377–79. See also Henderson, *After King Fahd*, 12–13.

20. Kechichian, *Succession in Saudi Arabia*, 71–89.

21. Ibid., 45–48.

22. For an overall assessment with rare insights on this subject, see Al Saʿud (with Seale), *Desert Warrior*.

23. The military cities appeared to be an extension of ʿAbdul ʿAziz's Ikhwan encampments. See Knauerhase, "Saudi Arabia," 36.

24. For an assessment by Brigadier A. Donaldson, the head of the British military mission to the Saudi Arabian National Guard, see his "Secret Despatch No. 10/2/3 from Mr. W. Morris, Jedda, to Mr. A. A. Acland, Arabian Department, Foreign Office, 3 February 1971," [FCO8/1755], in Burdett, *Records of Saudi Arabia*, 6: 358–70.

25. Kissinger, *Years of Upheaval*, 659.

26. Numerous dispatches to and from Saudi Arabia address military questions and how Washington could meet Riyadh's various needs. See U.S. Department of State (Office of the Historian), *Foreign Relations of the United States, 1964–1968,*21: 424–612.

27. For background on the Ikhwan, see Habib, *Ibn Saʿud's Warriors of Islam*.

28. Abir, *Saudi Arabia in the Oil Era*, 77.

29. Safran, *Saudi Arabia*, 104.

30. For an example of Sultan's hands-on approach, see "Confidential Telegram No. 534 from Jedda to Foreign Office, 26 September 1966, Saudi Air Defence Scheme," [FO371/185499], in Burdett, *Records of Saudi Arabia*, 1:704–5.

31. Gause, *Saudi-Yemeni Relations*, 60.

32. Abir, *Oil, Power and Politics*, 53–54.

33. Powell, *Saudi Arabia and Its Royal Family*, 247–48.

34. For various confidential telegrams from British diplomats to Whitehall discussing the plot and subsequent arrests, see Burdett, *Records of Saudi Arabia*, 4:35–85.

35. Avi Plascov maintains that about 300 officers were arrested in 1969; see Plascov, *Security in the Persian Gulf*, 96. J. B. Kelley, in contrast, argues that 135 soldiers (officers and enlisted men in the army and air force) were sentenced to death and 305 to life imprisonment. Another 752 officers, soldiers, and civilians received sentences ranging from ten to fifteen years imprisonment; see Kelley, *Arabia, the Gulf, and the West*, 271. Finally, William Powell asserts that the whole plot was uncovered when Saudi Special Security Forces infiltrated the organizations, thereby touching off numerous arrests throughout Saudi Arabia and as far away as England; see Powell, *Saudi Arabia and Its Royal Family*, 349–50. See also Abir, *Saudi Arabia in the Oil Era*, 116.

36. Khalid, "The Situation in Saudi Arabia and the Horizons for Development," 15.

37. Abir, *Saudi Arabia in the Oil Era*, 119.

38. Ibid., 119–20.

39. For an assessment of the kingdom's early military capabilities, see Cordesman, *The Gulf and the Search for Strategic Stability*, especially 122–92.

40. Benoist-Méchin, *Fayçal, Roi d'Arabie*, 100. See also, El Mallakh, *Saudi Arabia*, 26, 77–104.

41. El Mallakh, *Saudi Arabia*, 138–62.

42. Benoist-Méchin, *Fayçal, Roi d'Arabie*, 103. See also Presley, *A Guide to the Saudi Arabian Economy*, especially, 114–22.

43. For an authoritative discussion of women's issues in Saudi Arabia, see Doumato, *Getting God's Ear*.

44. As is well known, manpower needs in the health field tend to take years to develop, and the efforts devoted to the creation of an indigenous sector were a large financial burden on the fledgling economy. See Benoist-Méchin, *Fayçal, Roi d'Arabie*, 104.

45. Rugh, "Emergence of a New Middle Class in Saudi Arabia," 7–20.

46. This was confirmed by a former American ambassador who had extensive contacts with the king before and after his rule and who knew Saudi Arabia as well as any westerner living in the kingdom at the time. Interview with Ambassador Herman Eilts, Wellesley, Massachusetts, October 27, 2005.

47. The visit of the four religious officials was not a coincidence as it followed a carefully laid out dialogue between Muslims and Christians. In February 1973, the organization MAE Medici signed a cultural, scientific, and technical exchange agreement in Riyadh, and in June of that same year, King Faysal visited Rome, where the Islamic Cultural Center received approval for construction. Impressed by this progress, Pope Paul VI approved a request by the Italian government in 1974 to allow the building of a mosque as well as the Centro Culturale Islamico. On April 24, 1974 in Riyadh, Faysal received Cardinal Pignedoli, the president of the Vatican Office of Non-Christian Affairs, who conveyed "the regards of His Holiness, moved by a profound belief in the unification of Islamic and Christian worlds in the worship of a single God, to His Majesty King Faisal as supreme head of the Islamic World." See *Le Monde*, April 25, 1974. See also Benoist-Méchin, *Fayçal, Roi d'Arabie*, 111.

48. For two recent studies on the genre, see Gold, *Hatred's Kingdom*; and Schwartz, *The Two Faces of Islam*. For a more serious examination of Faysal's religiosity, see Al-Manjad, *Falsafat Faysal fil-Tadamun al-Islami*; and Idem, *Ahadith 'an Faysal wal-Tadamun al-Islami*.

49. Kechichian, *Succession in Saudi Arabia*, 181–82.

50. Al-Sowayyegh, "Saudi Oil Policy during King Faisal's Era," 202–29, especially 207.

51. Metz, *Saudi Arabia*, 142.

52. El Mallakh, *Saudi Arabia*, 53, 55. In 2006, proven reserves were estimated at around 260 billion barrels.

53. Ibid., 53. By the late twentieth century, daily production averaged 8.5 million barrels per day, and according to ARAMCO, a 5–10 percent improvement in oil recovery by application of horizontal drilling technology translated into a 12–25 billion barrel increase in reserves in its fields. See Aalund, "Horizontal Drilling Taps More Oil in the Middle East," 47. Saudi Arabia held the world's largest single oil field, at Ghawar, as well as the

world's largest offshore field, at Safaniyyah. Eleven additional fields were also operational: Manifah, Qatif, Najd, Zuluf, Marjan, Barri, Khurays, Abu Hadriyyah, Harmaliyyah, Abqa'iq, and Shaybah. An increase of capacity to 10.8 million barrels per day by 2007 as well as modernizing and expanding energy-related industries were under discussion; see *The Saudi Arabia Report* 55 (2005),19–24.

54. El Mallakh, *Saudi Arabia*, 28–30.

55. Globalis, Global Virtual University, UNEP/GRID-Arendal [United Nations Environmental Program], http://globalis.gvu.unu.edu/indicator.cfm?IndicatorID=19&Year=1975&Country=NO.

56. Saudi Arabia joined the IMF in 1957 with a single vote. Over the years, this voting strength increased to 1.74 percent in 1974 and 3.5 percent by March 1981. See El Mallakh, *Saudi Arabia*, 400.

57. "MEED Special Report on Saudi Arabia," 36.

58. "MEED Special Report on Construction," 20.

59. Gerth, "Saudi Stability Hit by Heavy Spending over Last Decade," A1.

60. According to Ahmad Zaki Yamani, a legal advisor to the oil ministry and a minister without portfolio until his 1962 appointment as minister of petroleum and mineral resources, his early push to create a petroleum institute was rejected by ARAMCO. Even the decision to establish PETROMIN, favored by Faysal, proved problematic. World Bank officials counseled Faysal to abandon the scheme, but he rejected their counsel. See Klayb, "Ziyarat Khasat ma' Ahmad Zaki Yamani," episode 1, 1–3.

61. Naturally, the system evolved over several years, but it was already in existence in early 1974. See Ignatius, "Some Saudi Princes Pressure Oil Firms for Secret Payments," 23.

62. Subsequently, Muhammad bin 'Abdul 'Aziz allegedly established a worldwide network of personal agents who sold his own oil reserves to the highest bidder using his name and personal seal. Embarrassed Saudi officials canceled several such "agreements" whenever they became public. In the case of the Italian and Thai government enterprises that participated in such arrangements, major scandals erupted, resulting—in the Thai case—in the resignation of the prime minister Prem Tiusulanonda's government in 1981. Another example was Prince Muhammad bin Fahd, who secured the spot-market oil concession during the 1980–81 oil shortage as key companies, including Petromonde, channeled significant commissions to his private accounts. See Ignatius, "Some Saudi Princes Pressure Oil Firms for Secret Payments," 1, 23; see also Ignatius, "Royal Payoffs," 1, 21; Islami and Kavoussi, *The Political Economy of Saudi Arabia*, 80; and Field, *The Merchants*, 102.

63. Starting in March 1983, King Fahd would direct the Ministry of Petroleum and Mineral Affairs to retain exclusive rights on all future sales. See "Ministry Statement Forbids Oil Middlemen," *FBIS-MEA-83-058*, March 24, 1983, C1.

64. "Saudi Arabia," 42.

65. Long, "Saudi Oil Policy," 85. For a more recent analysis of this issue, see Obaid, *The Oil Kingdom at 100*.

66. Al-Farsy, *Modernity and Tradition*, 83, 105–33.

67. See Klayb, "Ziyarat Khasat ma' Ahmad Zaki Yamani."

68. Hisham M. Nazer was also the kingdom's chief delegate to OPEC. He was chairman of the board of ARAMCO, PETROMIN, and SAMAREC, and a member of the Supreme Petroleum Council. Nazer began his career in the Saudi oil industry in 1961, when he was chosen to represent Saudi Arabia on the OPEC Board of Governors. He subsequently played a role in the development and industrialization of Saudi Arabia. In 1970 he was charged with setting the direction and pace of Saudi Arabia's economic and social development with the first Five-Year Plan (1970–75). The industrial cities of Jubayl and Yanbu were the result of his vision. See "Saudi Arabia," 40.

69. Abir, *Saudi Arabia in the Oil Era*, 82–83.

70. Ibid., 83.

71. Whether Faysal reflected on Tariki's vision is subject to interpretation. See Cave Brown, *Oil, God, and Gold*, 151–53.

72. In 1994, ARAMCO absorbed PETROMIN.

73. De Gaury, *Faisal*, 151.

74. Islami and Kavoussi, *The Political Economy of Saudi Arabia*, 21.

75. Braibanti and Al-Farsy, "Saudi Arabia," 29.

76. "Petromin," 12. See also Al-Farsy, *Modernity and Tradition*, 111–12.

77. For additional discussions on ARAMCO, see Lippman, *Inside the Mirage*; Cave Brown, *Oil, God, and Gold*; and Nawwab, Speers, and Hoye, *ARAMCO and Its World*.

78. Ahrari, *OPEC*, 103.

79. Braibanti and Al-Farsy, "Saudi Arabia," 29. The interest in creating a robust oil industry has been best illustrated by Saudi ARAMCO's achievements since the late 1980s. As with other petroleum decision-making bodies in the kingdom, the Saudi monarch assumed chairmanship of the company in 1988. By gaining control over ARAMCO, the Al Sa'ud could supervise the primary source of income and could direct their investments and profits in areas best suited to ensure their security objectives. Simultaneously, the Al Sa'ud created the Saudi Arabian Refining and Marketing Company (SAMAREC) to manage all downstream operations formally supervised by PETROMIN. The former was given responsibility for domestic refining and distribution, all joint-venture refinery stakes, and international refined product marketing. These steps were made possible because of policies adopted in 1974.

80. For a detailed analysis of the Shah's foreign policy preferences towards and after Mossadegh, see Ramazani, *Iran's Foreign Policy, 1941–1973*. See also the seminal autobiography of Farmanfarmaian and Farmanfarmaian, *Blood and Oil*.

81. "New ARAMCO Supreme Council Includes Five Private Businessmen," 15–16.

82. "Saudi Arabia," 47. It might also be important to note that Faysal's inclinations to move in the direction of full ownership were reported as early as 1971. See, for example, "Confidential Despatch, No. 12/5 from Mr. W. Morris, Jedda to Mr. R. H. Ellingworth,

Oil Department, Foreign Office, 23 June 1971, ARAMCO: Conversations with ARAM-CO," [FCO67/598] in Burdett, *Records of Saudi Arabia*, 6: 648–49.

83. "Excerpts from an Address by Hisham Nazer," 5.

84. ". . . Saudi ARAMCO Merges for a Second Time," 16.

85. Benedict, "Saudi Oil Policy Changes Still Evolving," 2; see also "Saudi Arabia," 38.

86. "Saudi Arabia," 47.

87. Knauerhase, *The Saudi Arabian Economy*, 173.

88. Al-Farsy, *Modernity and Tradition*, 126–28.

89. Maachou, *L'OPAEP et le Pétrole Arabe*.

90. Knauerhase, *The Saudi Arabian Economy*, 167–68, 172.

91. Seymour, *OPEC*, 167.

92. "Saudi Oil Minister on OPEC Policies," 4.

93. Abir, *Saudi Arabia in the Oil Era*, 126.

94. Shaw and Long, *Saudi Modernization*, 98. Because the kingdom's main oil loading facilities were less than 150 miles from Iran and 300 miles from Iraq—easily within reach of combat aircraft—Saudi oil fields and oil-producing facilities were highly vulnerable to attack. At a minimum, substantial revenues needed to be devoted to defending these vital assets, as well as the Saudi population in toto. However, the prime danger of an external strike from Iran or Iraq was not just the damage that such an attack could yield, but actually the threat that one would occur at all. To protect itself from such potential circumstances, in 1988 Saudi Arabia launched a massive training program to upgrade security at its pipeline networks and other facilities. See "Kuwait, Saudi Arabia Upgrade Defenses against Sabotage of Trans-Peninsula," *Platts Oilgram News* 66, no. 87 (May 5, 1988): 2.

95. During the 1967 Arab-Israeli War, for example, company officials photographed Saudi students demonstrating against the conflict and used these as anti-Western fodder in their various negotiations with King Faysal. At the time, the ruler sacrificed the director of the Petroleum Institute, although, according to Yamani, the man was innocent of any instigation. See Klayb, "Ziyarat Khasat ma' Ahmad Zaki Yamani," episode 2, p. 4.

96. It was not clear when these polls were actually taken or by which government agencies. Still, the idea was intriguing. See Pickett, "Young Saudis Worry about Oil Policy, Rapid Change," 4.

97. For several incisive studies on the impact of modernization on Saudi society, see Cole, *Nomads of the Nomads*; and Lackner, *A House Built on Sand*.

98. "Excerpts from an Address by Hisham Nazer," 5.

99. Cave Brown, *Oil, God, and Gold*, 281–302.

100. Akins, "The Oil Crisis," 467.

101. Seymour, *OPEC*, 110.

102. Sheikh Rustum Ali, *Saudi Arabia and Oil Diplomacy*, 106.

103. Ahrari, *OPEC*, 112–13.

104. Mosely, *Power Play*, 343.

105. Quandt, "U.S. Energy Policy and the Arab-Israeli Conflict," 282–83.

106. According to Yamani, Henry Kissinger was quite upset and warned him not to discuss the matter with anyone else in the U.S. administration, but it was too late. Several members of the Saudi delegation had already conducted extensive briefings. See Klayb, "Ziyarat Khasat ma' Ahmad Zaki Yamani," episode 2, p. 7.

107. Al-Sowayyegh, "Saudi Oil Policy during King Faisal's Era," 208.

108. Ahrari, *OPEC*, 115.

109. Seymour, *OPEC*, 111; see also Sheikh Rustum Ali, *Saudi Arabia and Oil Diplomacy*, 108.

110. Klayb, "Ziyarat Khasat ma' Ahmad Zaki Yamani," episode 2, p. 5.

111. Faysal received the Nixon démarche, which lobbed a complaint against Yamani. Allegedly, the oil minister wanted cooperation (*musharakah*) with ARAMCO, even if the intent was assistance in the decision-making process. The king quizzed Yamani as to whether this was important for Saudi Arabia and, persuaded in the affirmative, authorized Yamani to write a communiqué for the king that was broadcast on the radio: Saudi Arabia would henceforth protect its long-term interests. See ibid., episode 2, p. 5; and Robinson, *Yamani*, 66.

112. Seymour, *OPEC*, 110.

113. Sheikh Rustum Ali, *Saudi Arabia and Oil Diplomacy*, 108.

114. On June 6, 1973, Iraq nationalized U.S. (Exxon and Mobil) as well as Dutch (Shell) interests in the Basrah Petroleum Company.

115. Abir, *Saudi Arabia in the Oil Era*, 128. For more on the successes and failures of the embargo, see Feith, "The Oil Weapon De-Mystified," 19–39.

116. Ahrari, *OPEC,* 125.

117. As quoted in al-Sowayyegh, "Saudi Oil Policy during King Faisal's Era," 208.

118. Cave Brown, *Oil, God, and Gold*, 293–302.

119. While no countries were identified as "friendly," Saudi Arabia actually published a list of countries that the embargo overlooked: France, the United Kingdom, Spain, all League of Arab States except the PDRY, Turkey, Pakistan, Malaysia, India, Brazil, and African countries that had severed diplomatic relations with Israel. Embargoed countries were specifically identified as the United States, Holland, Portugal, South Africa, Rhodesia, and the People's Democratic Republic of Yemen. *The Petroleum Economist*, January 1974, 5; also *International Herald Tribune*, June 30, 1974.

120. Robinson, *Yamani*, 94.

121. Ibid.

122. Al-Sowayyegh, "Saudi Oil Policy during King Faisal's Era," 211.

123. Momoi, *The Energy Problems and Alliance Systems*, 26.

124. Iran did not initially wish to increase oil prices, but it changed its policy in 1973, when Henry Kissinger persuaded the shah to become the "policeman of the Gulf." Simply stated, Teheran needed the added revenues to pay for its massive military purchases. See Klayb, "Ziyarat Khasat ma' Ahmad Zaki Yamani," episode 2, p. 5.

125. Robinson, *Yamani*, 116.

126. Turner and Bedore, "Saudi Arabia," 409.

127. Quandt, *Saudi Arabia in the 1980s*, 129.

128. Al-Sowayyegh, "Saudi Oil Policy during King Faisal's Era," 217.

129. United States Department of State, *Washington Energy Conference Communiqué*, February 13, 1974 (Washington, D.C.: U.S. Government Printing Office), .

130. Gwertzman, "Milestone Pact Is Signed by U.S. and Saudi Arabia," 1, 2.

131. United States Department of State, "Text of Joint Statement on Co-Operation," June 8, 1974 (Washington, D.C.: U.S. Government Printing Office).

132. Heikal, *The Road to Ramadan*, 115.

133. Quoted in Al-Sowayyegh, "Saudi Oil Policy during King Faisal's Era," 220–21.

Chapter 5

1. Benoist-Méchin, *Fayçal, Roi d'Arabie*, 72.

2. This oft-repeated soubriquet was confirmed by both U.S. Ambassador Eilts and U.S. Secretary Murphy. Interview with Ambassador Herman Eilts, Wellesley, Massachusetts, October 27, 2005; and interview with Assistant Secretary of State Richard W. Murphy, New York, October 27, 2005.

3. Johnson, *The Vantage Point*, 288.

4. Ibid., 290.

5. Ibid., 291.

6. For useful perspectives on both men and their regimes, see El-Sadat, *In Search of Identity*; and Seale, *Asad of Syria*.

7. Lacey, *The Kingdom*, 393–94.

8. El-Sadat, *In Search of Identity*, 229.

9. Kissinger, *White House Years*, 1295.

10. Heikal, *The Road to Ramadan*, 24, 34.

11. Rather than quote from his many detractors, this study relies on Kissinger's own memoirs to situate his evolving views. See Kissinger, *White House Years*, 341.

12. Ibid., 343.

13. Ibid.

14. For a good comparison, see Nixon, *RN*.

15. For details on the Kissinger-Sisco friendship and the esteem felt by the National Security Council advisor, see Kissinger, *White House Years*, 348–49.

16. For a flavor of interdepartmental skirmishes between the White House and the State Department, see Hanhimäki, *The Flawed Architect*, especially, 68–115.

17. Kissinger, *White House Years*, 351.

18. Ibid., 354, emphasis in the original.

19. Ibid., 357.

20. Ibid., 361.

21. Nasir's pro- or anti-American sentiments are beyond the scope of this study, but he was careful not to lock himself in an ideological straight jacket. For an illustration of his preferences, see Ambassador Raymond G. Hare's "Telegram from the Embassy in the United Arab Republic to the Department of State, March 20, 1958," in U.S. Department of State (Office of the Historian), *Foreign Relations of the United States, 1958–1960*, 13: 435–36, and passim.

22. "Despatch from the Embassy in the United Arab Republic to the Department of State, March 27, 1960," in U.S. Department of State (Office of the Historian), *Foreign Relations of the United States, 1958–1960*, 13: 582–86. For a thorough examination of the role that the Aswan Dam played in Nasir's search for legitimacy, see Dekmejian, *Egypt under Nasir*, especially chapters 6 and 13.

23. Kissinger, *White House Years*, 362.

24. See Cave Brown, *Oil, God, and Gold*; Hart, *Saudi Arabia and the United States*; Lippman, *Inside the Mirage*; and Long, *The United States and Saudi Arabia*.

25. Kissinger, *White House Years*, 368.

26. Ibid., 1279.

27. Ibid., 594; see also Robins, *A History of Jordan*, 129–32.

28. Robins, *A History of Jordan*, 88.

29. Buheiry, "From Truman to Kissinger," 206.

30. Kissinger, *White House Years*, 1259.

31. Ibid. For two comprehensive assessments of the shah's legacy, see Ramazani, *Iran's Foreign Policy, 1941–1973*; and Bill, *The Politics of Iran*.

32. Kissinger, *White House Years*, 1260.

33. Pahlavi, *Mission for My Country*.

34. Kissinger, *White House Years*, 1261.

35. Ibid., 1262.

36. Ibid. 1262.

37. Ramazani, *The United States and Iran*, 47–53. See also Klayb, "Ziyarat Khasat ma' Ahmad Zaki Yamani," episode 2, p. 6.

38. For a carefully written Saudi perspective on this critical issue, see Badeeb, *Saudi-Iranian Relations, 1932–1982*, 62–68.

39. Kissinger, *White House Years*, 1264.

40. See Appendix 49–Department of State, "Message from Secretary to King Faisal and King Hussein," NPMP, NSCF, Box 1174, *1973 Middle East War*, October 6, 1973, File Number 9; telegram declassified on June 5, 2002 and posted by the National Security Archive at http://www.gwu.edu/~nsarchiv/NSAEBB/NSAEBB98/index.htm/document12.

41. Kissinger, *Years of Upheaval*, 454.

42. El-Sadat, *In Search of Identity*, especially 232–70.

43. See Appendix 59–Department of State, "Proposed Presidential Message to King Faisal," RG 59, SN 70–73, POL 15–1 U.S./Nixon; declassified on 8 November 8, 2000 and

posted by the National Security Archive at http://www.gwu.edu/~nsarchiv/NSAEBB/
NSAEBB98/index.htm/document28.

44. See Appendix 69–Department of State, "Message to the King from the Secretary," NPMP, NSCF, Box 1174, 1973 Middle East War, October 14, 1973, File Number 9;
telegram declassified on August 26, 2003 and posted by the National Security Archive at
http://www.gwu.edu/~nsarchiv/NSAEBB/NSAEBB98/index.htm/document29 A.

45. See ibid.

46. For comprehensive assessments of these deliveries, see Shazly, *The Crossing of Suez*;
and Quandt, *Soviet Policy in the October 1973 War*.

47. Shazly, *The Crossing of Suez*.

48. See Appendix 79–Department of State, "U.S. Arms to Israel: Saudis Sorrowful;
King May Send Another Message," NPMP, NSCF, Box 1174, 1973 Middle East War, October 16, 1973, File Number 11; telegram declassified on September 9, 2003 and posted by the
National Security Archive at http://www.gwu.edu/~nsarchiv/NSAEBB/NSAEBB98/
index.htm/document29B.

49. Kissinger, *Years of Upheaval*, 534.

50. Ibid., 535.

51. Ibid.

52. Ibid.

53. Quoted in "Document: Kissinger Memorandum," 24.

54. Kissinger, *Years of Upheaval*, 536.

55. Ibid. See also Nixon, *RN*, 574, 941–43, 1061.

56. Kissinger, *Years of Upheaval*, 538.

57. Nixon, *RN* 986.

58. Buheiry, "From Truman to Kissinger," 208–9.

59. Kissinger, *Years of Upheaval*, 606.

60. Ibid., 657.

61. Ibid.

62. Ibid., 659.

63. Buheiry, "From Truman to Kissinger 208, 212.

64. Kissinger, *Years of Upheaval*, 659.

65. Ibid., 660.

66. Ibid., 661.

67. Ibid., 661–62.

68. For a measured assessment of Faysal's ideology, see al-Husayn, *Faysal bin ʿAbdul
ʿAziz Al Saʿud*, 241–344.

69. Kissinger, *Years of Upheaval*, 662.

70. Al-Tahawih, *Al Malik Faysal wal-ʿIlaqat al-Kharijiyyah al-Saʿudiyyah*; see also
Hart, *Saudi Arabia and the United States*, especially xvii and passim.

71. Concerns notwithstanding, Washington was confident of the kingdom's internal
stability. See Eilts, "Saudi Arabia," 56–88.

72. Kissinger, *Years of Upheaval*, 661. For a detailed examination of Faysal's views of the Palestinian question, see below, and Al-Tahawih, *Al Malik Faysal wal-'Ilaqat al-Kharijiyyah al-Sa'udiyyah*, 185–206.

73. Kissinger, *Years of Upheaval*, 662.

74. Ibid., 662–63.

75. Ibid., 663–64.

76. As reported by Close, "Nixon and Faisal."

77. Ibid.

78. Richard M. Nixon, "1974 State of the Union Address," online at http://www.janda.org/politxts/State%20of%20Union%20Addresses/1970–1974%20Nixon%20T/RMN74.html.

79. Close, "Nixon and Faisal."

80. John Wooley and Gerhard Peters, "Richard Nixon—The President's News Conference of September 5th, 1973," The American Presidency Project (online), Santa Barbara, Calif. hosted by the University of California, at http://www.presidency.ucsb.edu/ws/?pid=3948.

81. Daniel, "Nixon-Kissinger Policy."

82. It was important to note, however, that King Faysal turned Yasir 'Arafat down in early 1975 when the latter requested a training camp in Tabuk, Saudi Arabia. See Klayb, "Ziyarat Khasat ma' Ahmad Zaki Yamani," episode 3, p. 6.

83. Nixon, *RN*, 1012.

84. Ibid.

85. Nixon, *RN*, 1013.

86. Ibid., 1012, 1014.

87. Ibid., 1016.

88. Ibid., 1017.

89. Ibid., 1018.

90. Ibid., 1015.

91. "Interview: Kissinger on Oil, Food, and Trade," *Business Week*, January 13, 1975, 66. Another useful discussion is Brown, "The Oil Weapon," 301–18.

92. As reported by Robinson, *Yamani*, 118–19.

93. Faysal toured Syria, Jordan, and Egypt in January 1975 and followed up these stops when he received several high-ranking Arab leaders before Kissinger's arrival. It would therefore be eminently logical to conclude that some coordination existed among Arab officials. For Faysal's exchanges with Kissinger, see Kissinger, *Years of Upheaval*, 1061–69.

94. Robinson, *Yamani*, 121.

95. For a useful examination of the overall Saudi-Egyptian coordination, see Heikal, *The Road to Ramadan*, especially 266–67. See also Buheiry, "From Truman to Kissinger," 208.

96. For additional details on the process, see Kissinger, *Years of Renewal*, 422–59.

97. Seymour, *OPEC*, 148.

98. Dawisha, *Saudi Arabia's Search for Security*, 7.

99. Ibid., 7–8.

100. "Interview with Minister of Petroleum and Mineral Resources Shaykh Ahmad Zaki Al-Yamani," 49–52..

101. Shaw and Long, *Saudi Arabian Modernization*, 9.

Chapter 6

1. Al Afghani was born in Asadabad, Iran, in 1838 and died in Istanbul, Turkey, on March 9, 1897. For a thorough assessment of his influence on the rise of the Ummah as well as contemporary revolutionary movements, see Keddie, *An Islamic Response to Imperialism*. See also Young, "Pan-Islamism in the Modern World," 194–95.

2. For a report on the first congress, see Toynbee, "The Proclamation of Sultan Abdul-Aziz bin Saʿud as King of the Hijaz and the Islamic Congress at Mecca (1926)," 309–19.

3. For additional details on the various congresses, see Gibb, "The Islamic Congress at Jerusalem in December 1931," 99–109; Halem, "The Baghdad World Muslim Conference," 169–76; Khan, "The Moʾtamar Al-ʿAlam Al-Islami," 27–29; and Kramer, *Islam Assembled*.

4. Benoist-Méchin, *Fayçal, Roi d'Arabie*, 72.

5. Kelidar, "The Arabian Peninsula in Arab and Power Politics," 145–59.

6. As discussed above, when Faysal met with Kennedy in Washington, he advised Kennedy to delay recognition of the republican regime in Yemen until the situation became clearer. Kennedy wanted to extend recognition immediately after the republic was declared. At the time, nobody knew whether the imam had been killed, as the Egyptians asserted; and, sure enough, within a couple of weeks, the imam appeared, alive and well, in the northern Yemeni city of Saada. Kennedy deferred recognition for a few months, but then recognized the new regime, probably on the advice of State Department mandarins.

7. Sindi, "King Faisal and Pan-Islamism," 184–201.

8. Quoted in "Islam Against Nationalism," 903.

9. The Muslim World League is headquartered in Makkah, Saudi Arabia, and has various branches and affiliates throughout the world. Its international reputation is well established as it achieved a nongovernmental organization status with the United Nations. For additional details, see its web page at http://www.themwl.org/

10. Copeland, *The Game of Nations*, 266.

11. Long, *The United States and Saudi Arabia*, 113–16.

12. At each of these stops, Faysal delivered useful speeches—often impromptu as he preferred to speak from the heart—to the delight of large masses that welcomed him. For a sampling of these addresses, see Kingdom of Saudi Arabia, *Faisal Speaks*.

13. Kingdom of Saudi Arabia, *Faisal Speaks*, 52.

14. Sindi, "King Faisal and Pan-Islamism," 188.

15. Benoist-Méchin, *Fayçal, Roi d'Arabie*, 93.

16. Sindi, "King Faisal and Pan-Islamism," 190.

17. Salameh, *Al-Siyasah al-Kharijiyyah al-Sa'udiyyah munzu 'am 1945*, 470–82.

18. Al-Husayn, *Faysal bin 'Abdul 'Aziz Al Sa'ud*, 239–328. See also Al-Tahawih, *Al Malik Faysal wal-'Ilaqat al-Kharijiyyah al-Sa'udiyyah*, 167–203.

19. "Confidential Despatch No. 3/18 from Mr. I. S. Winchester, Chargé d'Affaires, Jedda, "The Saudi/Egyptian Honeymoon: Assessment of the Recent History, Current State and Future Prospect of the Saudi/Egyptian Relationship FCO8/1739," in Burdett, *Records of Saudi Arabia,* 6: 191–98.

20. For additional details on the 1970 rapprochement at the Rabat Islamic Summit, see Sindi, "King Faisal and Pan-Islamism," 190–93.

21. It must be emphasized that Faysal was not entirely satisfied with this particular issue, as he wanted India and Pakistan to fulfill their OIC responsibilities. He championed India's membership in the Muslim World League but relented after Pakistani delegates walked out. To be sure, Indian-Saudi ties suffered after the 1967 War—because New Delhi supported Nasir within the larger Non-Aligned Movement—but this was a momentary setback, for Faysal was keenly aware of the role that India could play in the Muslim world. In the event, he did not allow differences to affect overall ties and, toward that end, maintained friendly ties with various Indian officials. I thank the Indian Vice President, then ambassador Muhammad Hamid Ansari for clarifying these issues. Interview with Muhammad Hamid Ansari, Doha, Qatar, December 3, 2005. See also Sindi, "King Faisal and Pan-Islamism," 193; and Al-Sayegh, *Ziyarat Al-Malik Faysal Li-Afriqiyah.*

22. Salameh, *Al-Siyasah al-Kharijiyyah al-Sa'udiyyah munzu 'am 1945*, 192–96, 539–34, and passim.

23. The Lahore conference welcomed eight new members to the OIC. Bangladesh, Cameroon, Gabon, Gambia, Guinea-Bissau, Uganda, and Upper Volta became full members along with the thirty founding countries. See *Pakistan Horizon* 27, no. 1 (1974): 29–49.

24. General Assembly, 30th Session, "Resolution 3379: Elimination of All Forms of Racial Discrimination," November 10, 1975, at http://daccess-ods.un.org/TMP/7250293.html.

25. United Nations, General Assembly, Thirtieth Session, "Resolution Adopted by the General Assembly, 3379 (XXX), Elimination of all Forms of Racial Discrimination," 10 November 1975.

26. Speech delivered in Uganda on November 16, 1972 as quoted in *The Daily Star*, November 17, 1972.

27. Abir, *Saudi Arabia in the Oil Era*, 78.

28. Badeeb, *Saudi-Iranian Relations, 1932–1982*, 52–62.

29. Safran, *Saudi Arabia*, 136.

30. Abir, *Saudi Arabia in the Oil Era*, 120.

31. Ironically, it was Iraq that rekindled an interest in Abu Musa and the Greater and

Smaller Tunb Islands after Saddam Hussein vowed to liberate all occupied Arab lands in 1980. Because the islands were less pressing than the raging war on its borders with Iran, Iraq limited its anti-Iranian calls on the islands to verbal assaults.

32. "Confidential Telegram No. 969 from Jedda to Foreign Office, 29 December 1971, Suggested Message from Prime Minister to King Faisal Concerning Anglo-Saudi Relations and the Gulf FCO8/1741," in Burdett, *Records of Saudi Arabia*, 4: 97–101.

33. Khalifa, *The United Arab Emirates*, 148.

34. Al-Alkim, *The Foreign Policy of the United Arab Emirates*, 116–18.

35. Ibid., 126–29.

36. Salameh, *Al-Siyasah al-Kharijiyyah al-Sa'udiyyah munzu 'am 1945*, 579–95.

37. *Kayhan International*, December 12, 1982, 1.

38. It may be worth noting that in the months preceding the fall of the Shah on January 16, 1979, when Iran underwent severe internal upheavals, Saudi authorities dreaded for the stability of their country, especially after their own Shi'ah population in Hasah province proclaimed support of the Iranian regime.

39. Katz, *Russia and Arabia*, 135.

40. De Gaury, *Faisal*, 75.

41. Yodfat, *The Soviet Union and the Arabian Peninsula*, 8.

42. Khadduri, *Arab Contemporaries*, 88–105, especially, 94. See also De Gaury, *Faisal*, 78, where the remark is quoted as "I only wish I had three Faysals."

43. Khadduri, *Arab Contemporaries*, 104.

44. "Address by the Chairman of the Delegation of Saudi Arabia to the Inaugural Plenary Session. See appendix 2.

45. Alireza, "The Late King Faisal," 218.

46. Khadduri, *Arab Contemporaries*, 98–99. See also De Gaury, *Faisal*, 147–51.

47. Khadduri, *Arab Contemporaries*, 90.

48. See the interview with Brady, "Saudi Traditions Relaxing Slowly," 5.

Chapter 7

1. These five precepts for just rule draw on Muhammad ibn Zafar al-Siqilli, the twelfth-century philosopher who advised a threatened monarch in his celebrated *Sulwan al-Muta' fi 'Udwan al-Atba'* (Consolation for the ruler during the hostility of subjects). See Kechichian and Dekmejian, *The Just Prince*.

2. This section draws on several sources. Benoist-Méchin, *Fayçal, Roi d'Arabie*, 257–70; al-Husayn, *Faysal bin 'Abdul 'Aziz Al Sa'ud*, 339–44; and Holden and Johns, *The House of Saud*, 379–83. Reportedly, Faysal bin Musa'id knew Shaykh 'Abdul Mutalib al-Kazimi from their sojourn in the United States. Because both were students at the University of Colorado, several sources implied that the young Faysal took advantage of the audience to gain access to the monarch's *majlis*, although this could not be verified independently. Still, it was entirely possible because the king conducted a fairly open *majlis* to members of

the ruling family, and it was not particularly difficult to see him. The coincidence was duly noted after the assassin was interrogated, but nothing further was said about the linkage.

3. Holden and Johns, *The House of Saud*, 381–82.

4. Under Shari'ah, mental insanity would have spared the life of an assassin, and the sick individual would have been allowed to live the rest of his life under house arrest with full medical attention. Another explanation for the lengthy trial, of course, was to ascertain whether there were any accomplices or a foreign plot to cut down the ruler. In the event, Faysal bin Musa'id was found to be mentally sane and reportedly confessed to his crime.

5. As quoted in Holden and Johns, *The House of Saud*, 382.

6. Rodendeck, "A Long Walk," 5.

7. Dawisha, *Saudi Arabia's Search for Security*, 8.

8. Samore, "The Persian Gulf," 68.

9. "Disappointing Diplomacy," 3.

10. "Support for Oil Price Increases," 5.

11. Quandt, *Saudi Arabia in the 1980s*, 130.

12. Quoted in Robinson, *Yamani*, 150.

Bibliography

Authors with last names beginning with the particles Al, al-, El, or de are alphabetized under the name immediately following the particle. For example, Al Dhahrani is alphabetized under the Ds.

Aalund, Leo. "Horizontal Drilling Taps More Oil in the Middle East." *Oil and Gas Journal* (June 21, 1993): 47.

'Abd al-Majid, Faruq. "The Saudi-Yugoslav Flirtation." *Al-Musawwar* 3118 (July 13, 1984): 35–38.

Abd Al-Muttalib, Fikri. "Clandestine Opposition Movements in Saudi Arabia." *Al-Yaqzah Al-Arabiyah* (Cairo) (December 1987): 27–39.

'Abdul Ghafur, Ahmad. *Muhammad bin 'Abdul Wahhab*. Makkah: Muassasat Makkah Lil-Nashr, 1979.

'Abdul-Hay Gazzaz, Hassan. *Al-Amn Allazi Na'ishuha* [The security we enjoy]. 2 vols. 3rd ed. Jeddah: Dar Al-'Ilm Printing and Publishing Co., 1993. (A one-volume summary was published in English under the same title in 1992.)

'Abdul Wahab, Muhammad. *Al-Usul Al-Thalathah wa 'Adillatuhah* [The three principles and their proofs]. Cairo: Dar Al-Tiba' Al-Yusufiyyah, n.d.

Abir, Mordechai. *Oil, Power, and Politics*. London: Frank Cass, 1974.

———. *Saudi Arabia in the Oil Era: Regime and Elites; Conflict and Collaboration*. Boulder, Colo.: Westview Press, 1988.

AbuKhalil, As'ad. *The Battle for Saudi Arabia: Royalty, Fundamentalism, and Global Power*. New York: Seven Stories Press, 2004.

Aburish, Said K. *The Rise, Corruption, and Coming Fall of the House of Saud*. London: Bloomsbury, 1994.

"Address by the Chairman of the Delegation of Saudi Arabia to the Inaugural Plenary Session, 25 April 1945." *United Nations Documents*. Vol. 1. San Francisco: Conference on International Organization, 1945.

Ahrari, Mohammed E. *OPEC: The Falling Giant*. Lexington: University Press of Kentucky, 1986.

Akins, James E. "The Oil Crisis: This Time the Wolf is Here." *Foreign Affairs* 51, no. 3 (April 1973): 460–75.

Alangari, Haifa. *The Struggle for Power in Arabia: Ibn Saud, Hussein, and Great Britain, 1914–1924*. Reading, U.K.: Ithaca Press, 1998.

Albaharna, Husain. *The Arabian Gulf States: Their Legal and Political Status and their International Problems*. Beirut: Librairie du Liban, 1978.

Algar, Hamid. *Wahhabism: A Critical Essay*. Oneonta, N.Y.: Islamic Publications International, 2002.

Algosaibi, Ghazi A. *Arabian Essays*. London: Kegan Paul International, 1982.

'Ali, Gaafar 'Abdul Salam. *Al-Nizam al-Idari al-Su'udi* [The administrative law in Saudi Arabia]. Cairo: Al-Salfiyat, 1977.

Ali, Sheikh Rustum. *Saudi Arabia and Oil Diplomacy*. New York: Praeger, 1976.

Alireza, Marianne. *At the Drop of a Veil: The True Story of an American Woman's Years in a Saudi Arabian Harem*. Costa Mesa, Calif.: Blind Owl Press/Mazda Publishers, 2002. First published in 1971 by Houghton Mifflin.

———. "The Late King Faisal: His Life, Personality and Methods of Government." In *Conference on the Kingdom of Saudi Arabia: 100 Years*, 201–36. Riyadh: January 1999.

al-Alkim, Hassan Hamdan. *The Foreign Policy of the United Arab Emirates*. London: Saqi Books, 1989.

Ambah, Faiza Saleh. "Crown Prince Popular with Saudis." The Associated Press, July 31, 1999.

Anderson, Irvine H. *Aramco, the United States, and Saudi Arabia: A Study of the Dynamics of Foreign Oil Policy, 1933–1950*. Princeton, N.J.: Princeton University Press, 1981.

Ansari, M. Hamid. *The Islamic Boomerang in Saudi Arabia: The Cost of Delayed Reforms*. New Delhi: Samskriti in association with the Observer Research Foundation, 2004.

Armstrong, Harold C. *Lord of Arabia: Ibn Saud, an Intimate Study of a King*. London: Arthur Barker, Ltd., 1934.

Askari, Hossein. *Saudi Arabia's Economy: Oil and the Search for Economic Development*. Greenwich, Conn.: JAI Press, 1990.

Ayoub, Mouna. *La Vérité: Autobiographie*. Paris: Michel Lafon, 2000.

Azydan, Hamad. "The Economic and Political Situation in Saudi Arabia and the Effect of the Iranian Revolution." *Al-Hurriyyah* (Beirut), June 4, 1979, 36–37.

Badeeb, Saeed M. *The Saudi-Egyptian Conflict over North Yemen, 1962–1970*. Boulder, Colo.: Westview, 1986.

———. *Saudi-Iranian Relations, 1932–1982*. London: Centre for Arab and Iranian Studies and Echoes, 1993.

Baer, Robert. *Sleeping with the Devil: How Washington Sold Our Soul for Saudi Crude*. New York: Crown, 2003.

Barzin, Saeed. "Iran: Evolving New Axis?" *Middle East International* 600 (May 21, 1999): 13–14.

Basbous, Antoine. *L'Arabie Saoudite En Question: Du wahhabisme à Bin Laden, aux origines de la tourmente*. Paris: Perrin, 2002.

Bass, Warren. *Support Any Friend: Kennedy's Middle East and the Making of the U.S.-Israel Alliance*. New York: Oxford University Press, 2003.

Beling, Willard A., ed. *King Faisal and the Modernisation of Saudi Arabia*. London: Croom Helm; Boulder, Colo.: Westview, 1980.

Benedict, Roger. "Saudi Oil Policy Changes Still Evolving as Nazer Develops International Ties." *The Oil Daily*, May 27, 1992, 2.

Benoist-Méchin, [Jacques]. *Fayçal, Roi d'Arabie: L'Homme, le Souverain, sa Place dans le Monde (1906–1975)*. Paris: Albin Michel, 1975.

———. *Le Loup et le Leopard: Ibn-Seoud ou la naissance d'un royaume*. Paris: Albin Michel, 1955.

Bill, James Alban. *The Politics of Iran: Groups, Classes and Modernization*. Columbus, Ohio: Charles E. Merrill, 1972.

Bin Ladin, Carmen. *Inside the Kingdom: My Life in Saudi Arabia*. New York: Warner, 2004, 2005.

Bligh, Alexander. *From Prince to King: Royal Succession in the House of Saud in the Twentieth Century*. New York and London: New York University Press, 1984.

de Borchgrave, Arnaud. "Undercutting Fahd." *Newsweek*, April 23, 1979, 51–52.

de Bouteiller, Georges. *L'Arabie Saoudite: Cité de Dieu, Cité des Affaires, Puissance Internationale*. Paris: Presses Universitaires de France, 1981.

Brady, Thomas F. "Saudi Traditions Relaxing Slowly: Customs on Women Persist Despite Modern Trend." *New York Times*, May 31, 1966, 5.

Braibanti, Ralph, and Fouad Abdul-Salem Al-Farsy. "Saudi Arabia: A Developmental Perspective." *Journal of South Asian and Middle Eastern Studies* 1, no. 1 (fall 1977): 3–43.

Brown, William R. "The Oil Weapon." *Middle East Journal* 36, no. 3 (summer 1982): 301–18.

de Briganti, Giovanni. "Cash-Strapped Saudis Proceed on 3 French Contracts." *Defense News* 9, no. 5 (February 7–13, 1994): 36.

Buheiry, Marwan R. "From Truman to Kissinger: American Policy-Making and the Middle East." In *The Formation and Perception of the Modern Arab World: Studies by Marwan R. Buheiry*, ed. Lawrence I. Conrad, 189–214. Princeton, N.J.: Darwin Press, 1989.

Bulloch, John. *Reforms of the Saudi Arabian Constitution*. London: Gulf Centre for Strategic Studies, 1992.

Burdett, Anita L. P., ed. *Records of Saudi Arabia, 1966–1971*. London: Archives Editions, 2004.

Byrd, Robert C. *Child of the Appalachian Coalfields*. Morgantown: West Virginia University Press, 2005.

Canard, Marius. "Fatimids." In *Encyclopaedia of Islam*, new ed., vol. 2, 850–62. Leiden: E. J. Brill, 1960.

Cave Brown, Anthony. *Oil, God, and Gold: The Story of Aramco and the Saudi Kings.* Boston: Houghton Mifflin Company, 1999.

Champion, Daryl. *The Paradoxical Kingdom: Saudi Arabia and the Momentum of Reform.* New York: Columbia University Press, 2003.

"Change Is Inevitable in Saudi Arabia." *Al-Quds Al-Arabi*, April 16, 1998, reproduced in *Mideast Mirror*, April 17, 1998.

Chevalier, Jean-Marie. *The New Oil Stake.* London: Penguin, 1975.

Citino, Nathan J. *From Arab Nationalism to OPEC: Eisenhower, King Sa'ud, and the Making of U.S.-Saudi Relations.* Bloomington and Indianapolis: Indiana University Press, 2002.

Close, Raymond. "Nixon and Faisal: If Arabs Mistrust America, There's Good Reason." *International Herald Tribune*, December 19, 2002, 4. Available online at http://www.iht.com/articles/2002/12/19/edray_ed3__o.php.

Cole, Donald Powell. *Nomads of the Nomads: The Al Murrah Bedouin of the Empty Quarter.* Arlington Heights, Ill.: Harlan Davidson, 1975.

Conrad, Lawrence I., ed. *The Formation and Perception of the Modern Arab World: Studies by Marwan R. Buheiry.* Princeton, N.J.: Darwin Press, 1989.

Copeland, Miles. *The Game of Nations: The Amorality of Power Politics.* New York: Simon and Schuster, 1969.

Cordesman, Anthony H. *The Gulf and the Search for Strategic Stability: Saudi Arabia, the Military Balance in the Gulf, and Trends in the Arab-Israeli Military Balance.* Boulder, Colo.: Westview, 1984.

———. *Saudi Arabia: Guarding the Desert Kingdom.* Boulder, Colo.: Westview, 1997.

———. *Saudi Arabia Enters the Twenty-First Century: The Military and International Security Dimensions.* Westport, Conn., and London: Praeger, 2003.

———. *Saudi Arabia Enters the Twenty-First Century: The Political, Foreign Policy, Economic, and Energy Dimensions.* Westport, Conn., and London: Praeger, 2003.

"Crackdown on Opposition Feared after Alleged Attack." *Al-Quds Al-Arabi*, September 17, 1993, 1.

Dakroub, Hussein. "Gulf States May Form Joint Military Unit." *Washington Times*, December 22, 1993, 15.

Daniel, Clifton. "Nixon-Kissinger Policy; Negotiation Instead of Confrontation Still Working Despite No Small Odds; Kissinger Clearly Dismayed; Unanimous Recommendation." *New York Times*, October 26, 1973, 1.

Al-Darwis, Idris. "We Make Educated, Devout Fighters: Interview with Col. Mitab Bin Abdallah, Commander of the King Khalid Military Academy." *Al-Yamamah*, January 23, 1985, 14–19.

Davis, Helen Miller. *Constitutions, Electoral Laws, Treaties of States in the Near and Middle East.* 1st ed. Durham, N.C.: Duke University Press, 1947.

Dawisha, Adeed I. "Internal Values and External Threats: The Making of Saudi Foreign Policy." *Orbis* 23, no. 1 (spring 1979), 129–43.

———. *Saudi Arabia's Search for Security.* Adelphi Paper Number 158. London: International Institute for Strategic Studies, 1979.

Dekmejian, R. Hrair. *Egypt Under Nasir.* Albany: State University of New York Press, 1971.

———. *Islam in Revolution: Fundamentalism in the Arab World.* Syracuse, N.Y.: Syracuse University Press, 1985, 1989.

———. "The Rise of Political Islamism in Saudi Arabia." *Middle East Journal* 48, no. 4 (autumn 1994): 627–43.

———. "Saudi Arabia's Consultative Council." *Middle East Journal* 52, no. 2 (spring 1998): 204–18.

Delong-Bas, Natana J. *Wahhabi Islam: From Revival and Reform to Global Jihad.* Oxford and New York: Oxford University Press, 2004.

Al Dhahrani, 'Abdul Rahman bin 'Ali. *Masirat al-Shurah fil-Mamlakah* [The Shurah legacy in the kingdom]. 3rd ed. Riyadh: Majlis Al-Shurah, 2002.

Dickson, H. R. P. *The Arab of the Desert.* London: N.p., 1949.

"Differences Still Seen Within Ruling Family." *Al-Nida Al-Usbu* (Beirut), May 27, 1979, 1.

"Disappointing Diplomacy." *Quarterly Economic Review Saudi Arabia.* London: The Economist Intelligence Unit, Ltd., 2 (1978), 8.

"Document: Kissinger Memorandum: To Isolate the Palestinians, June 15, 1975." *MERIP Reports* 96 (May 1981), 24.

"Document: Transfer of Powers from HM King Sa'ud to HRH Amir Faysal." *Middle East Journal* 18, no. 3 (summer 1964): 351–54

Dorsey, James. "After Mecca, Saudi Rulers Provide a Channel for Dissent." *Christian Science Monitor,* March 14, 1980, 7.

Doumato, Eleanor Abdella. *Getting God's Ear: Women, Islam, and Healing in Saudi Arabia and the Gulf.* 2nd ed. New York: Columbia University Press, 2000.

Eddy, William. *F.D.R. Meets Ibn Sa'ud.* New York: American Friends of the Middle East, 1954.

"18 Preachers Banned in Riyadh." *Arabia Monitor* 2, no. 2 (February 1993): 7.

Eilts, Herman. "Saudi Arabia: Traditionalism versus Modernism—A Royal Dilemma." In *Ideology and Power in the Middle East,* ed. Peter J. Chelkowski and Robert J. Pranger, 56–88. Durham, N.C.: Duke University Press, 1988.

Emerson, Steven. *The American House of Saud: The Secret Petrodollar Connection.* New York: Franklin Watts, 1985.

Engel, Richard. "Saudi Succession Issues Unresolved." *Washington Times,* April 22, 1998, A1.

"Excerpts from an Address by Hisham Nazer, Saudi Arabian Minister at the Harvard Business School." *The Oil Daily,* May 9, 1991, 5.

Fandy, Mamoun. *Saudi Arabia and the Politics of Dissent.* New York: St. Martin's, 1999.

Farmanfarmaian, Manucher, and Roxane Farmanfarmaian. *Blood and Oil: Memoirs of a Persian Prince*. New York: Random House, 1997.

Al-Farsy, Fouad. *Modernity and Tradition: The Saudi Equation*. London and New York: Kegan Paul International, 1994.

———. *Saudi Arabia: A Case Study in Development*. New York: Routledge, Chapman, and Hall, 1986.

Feith, Douglas J. "The Oil Weapon De-Mystified." *Policy Review* 15 (winter 1981): 19–39.

Feuillet, Claude. *Le Système Saoud*. Paris: Editions Pierre-Marcel Favre, 1983.

Field, Michael. *The Merchants: The Big Business Families of Saudi Arabia and the Gulf States*. Woodstock, N.Y.: Overlook Press, 1985.

Finnegan, Philip. "Iran Navy Buildup Stirs U.S.-Arab Response." *Defense News* 8, no. 49 (December 6–12, 1993): 28.

Foulquier, Jean-Michel. *Arabie Séoudite: La Dictature Protégée*. Paris: Albin Michel, 1995.

de Gaury, Gerald. *Arabia Phoenix: An Account of a Visit to Ibn Saud, Chieftain of the Austere Wahhabis and Powerful Arabian King*. London: G. G. Harrap, 1946.

———. *Faisal: King of Saudi Arabia*. New York: Praeger, 1967.

———. *Rulers of Mecca*. New York: AMS Press, 1954.

Gause, F. Gregory, III. *Oil Monarchies: Domestic and Security Challenges in the Arab Gulf States*. New York: Council on Foreign Relations Press, 1994.

———. *Saudi-Yemeni Relations: Domestic Structures and Foreign Influence*. New York: Columbia University Press, 1990.

Gerth, Jeff. "Saudi Stability Hit by Heavy Spending Over Last Decade." *New York Times*, August 21, 1993, A1.

Gibb, H. A. R. "Al-Mawardi's Theory of the Caliphate." In *Studies on the Civilization of Islam*, ed. Stanford J. Shaw and William R. Polk, 151–65. Princeton, N.J.: Princeton University Press, 1982.

———. "The Islamic Congress at Jerusalem in December 1931." *Survey of International Affairs*, 1934, 99–109, London: Royal Institute of International Affairs.

Globalis, Global Virtual University, UNEP/GRID-Arendal [United Nations Environmental Program], http://globalis.gvu.unu.edu/indicator.cfm?IndicatorID=19&Year=1975&Country=NO.

Gold, Dore. *Hatred's Kingdom: How Saudi Arabia Supports the New Global Terrorism*. Washington, D.C.: Regnery, 2003.

Goodarzi, Jubin. "Behind Iran's Middle East Diplomacy." *Middle East International* 608 (September 17, 1999): 21–23.

Graham, Douglas F. *Saudi Arabia Unveiled*. Dubuque, Iowa: Kendall/Hunt, 1991.

Grayson, Benson Lee. *Saudi-American Relations*. Washington, D.C.: University Press of America, 1982.

"Growing Regional Influence of Kingdom Discussed." *Al-Majallah* 83 (September 12–18, 1981): 12–19.

Gwertzman, Bernard. "Milestone Pact Is Signed by U.S. and Saudi Arabia; Acclaimed by Kissinger." *New York Times*, June 9, 1974, 1, 2.

Habib, John S. *Ibn Sa'ud's Warriors of Islam: The Ikhwan of Najd and Their Role in the Creation of the Sa'udi Kingdom, 1910–1930*. Leiden: E. J. Brill, 1978.

Halem, A.B.A. "The Baghdad World Muslim Conference." *Pakistan Horizon* 15, no. 3 (1962): 169–76.

Hammed, Mazher A. *Arabia Imperiled: The Security Imperatives of the Arab Gulf States*. Washington, D.C.: Middle East Assessments Group, 1986.

Hamzah, Fu'ad. *Al-Bilad al-'Arabiyyah al-Sa'udiyyah* [The Kingdom of Saudi Arabia]. 2nd ed. Cairo: Maktabat al-Nasr al-Hadithat, 1968.

———. *Fi Bilad 'Asir*. Cairo: N.p., 1951.

Hanhimäki, Jussi. *The Flawed Architect: Henry Kissinger and American Foreign Policy*. Oxford: Oxford University Press, 2004.

Hart, Parker T. *Saudi Arabia and the United States: Birth of a Security Partnership*. Bloomington and Indianapolis: Indiana University Press, 1998.

Heikal, Mohammed H. *The Road to Ramadan*. London: Collins, 1975.

Heim, Pierre. "After the Shock." *Remarques Arabo-Africaines* (Brussels)527 (1980): 10–12.

Heisbourg, Francois. "France and the Gulf Crisis." In *Western Europe and the Gulf*, ed. Nicole Gnesotto and John Roper, 17–38. Paris: Institute for Security Studies-Western European Union, 1992.

Helms, Christine Moss. *The Cohesion of Saudi Arabia: Evolution of Saudi Arabia*. Baltimore and London: Johns Hopkins University Press, 1981.

Henderson, Simon. *After King Fahd: Succession in Saudi Arabia*. Policy paper number 37. 2nd ed. Washington, D.C.: Washington Institute for Near East Policy, 1995.

Herb, Michael. *All in the Family: Absolutism, Revolution, and Democracy in the Middle Eastern Monarchies*. Albany: State University of New York Press, 1999.

Holden, David. "A Family Affair." *New York Times Magazine*, July 6, 1975, 8–9, 26–27.

Holden, David, and Richard Johns. *The House of Saud: The Rise and Rule of the Most Powerful Dynasty in the Arab World*. New York: Holt, Rinehart, and Winston, 1981.

Howarth, David. *The Desert King: The Life of Ibn Saud*. London: Quartet Books, 1965, 1980.

al-Husayn, 'Abdul Rahman bin 'Abdul 'Aziz Sulayman. *Faysal bin 'Abdul 'Aziz Al Sa'ud: Wujuhuhu fil-Qadayah al-'Arabiyyah wal-Islamiyyah (1906–1975)* [Faysal bin 'Abdul 'Aziz Al Sa'ud: Perspectives on Arab and Islamic Affairs (1906–1975)]. Riyadh: King Faisal Center for Research and Islamic Studies, 2001.

Huyette, Summer Scott. *Political Adaptation in Saudi Arabia: A Study of the Council of Ministers*. Boulder, Colo., and London: Westview, 1985.

Ibrahim, Youssef M. "Saudi King Issues Decrees to Revise Governing System." *New York Times*, March 2, 1992, 1.

"ICHR-GAP Lauds New Saudi Rights Group." *Arabia Monitor* 2, no. 5 (May 1993): 1, 6.

Ignatius, David. "Royal Payoffs: Big Saudi Oil Deal with Italy Collapses after Fee Plan Is Bared." *Wall Street Journal*, May 4, 1981, 1, 21.

———. "Some Saudi Princes Pressure Oil Firms for Secret Payments." *Wall Street Journal*, May 1, 1981, 23.

"Interview: Kissinger on Oil, Food, and Trade." *Business Week*, January 13, 1975, 66.

"Interview with Minister of Petroleum and Mineral Resources Shaykh Ahmad Zaki Al-Yamani." *Al-Mustaqbal* (Paris)258 (January 30, 1982): 49–52.

"Iran 'Waiting for UAE' to Agree to Talks on Islands." *Mideast Mirror*, November 25, 1993, 17.

"Islam Against Nationalism." *The Economist*, June 2, 1962, 903.

Islami, A. Reza S., and Rostam Mehraban Kavoussi. *The Political Economy of Saudi Arabia*. Seattle: University of Washington Press, 1984.

Al Jabariti, Anwar Abdul Majid. "Al Amir Abdallah Wal-Suq" [Prince Abdallah and the market]. *Al-Hayat* 13378 (October 24, 1999): 23.

Jarrah, Najm. "Small Step Forward." *Middle East International* 457 (August 28, 1993): 12–13.

al-Jawwad, Muhammad ʿAli. *Al-Tatawwur al-Tashriʿi fil-Mamlakah al-ʿArabiyyah al-Saʿudiyyah* [Legislative development in the Kingdom of Saudi Arabia]. Alexandria, Egypt: Munshaʾat al-Maʿarif, 1977.

Jehl, Douglas. "Sheik Shares His Misgivings Over U.S. Policies." *New York Times*, May 31, 1998, 5.

Jerichow, Anders. *Saudi Arabia: Outside Global Law and Order—A Discussion Paper*. Surrey, U.K.: Curzon, 1997.

———. *The Saudi File: People, Power, Politics*. New York: St. Martin's, 1998.

Johnson, Lyndon Baines. *The Vantage Point: Perspectives of the Presidency 1963–1969*. New York: Holt, Rinehart, and Winston, 1971.

al-Juhani, ʿId Masʿud. *Al Hudud wal-ʿIlaqat al-Saʿudiyyah al-Yamaniyyah* [Borders and Saudi-Yemeni relations]. N.p.: Dar al-Maʿarif al-Saʿudiyyah, 1994.

Karasik, Theodore. *Azerbaijan, Central Asia, and Future Persian Gulf Security*. N-3579-AF/A. Santa Monica, Calif.: RAND, 1992.

Katz, Mark N. "External Powers and the Yemeni Civil War." In *The Yemeni War of 1994: Causes and Consequences*, ed. Jamal S. al-Suwaidi, 81–93. London: Saqi Books for the Emirates Center for Strategic Studies and Research, 1995.

———. *Russia and Arabia: Soviet Foreign Policy Toward the Arabian Peninsula*. Baltimore: Johns Hopkins University Press, 1986.

Kean, Thomas H., and Lee H. Hamilton, et al. *The 9/11 Commission Report: Final Report of the National Commission on Terrorist Attacks upon the United States*. Authorized ed. New York: W. W. Norton, n.d. [2004].

Kéchichian, Joseph A. "Democratization in Gulf Monarchies: A New Challenge to the GCC." *Middle East Policy* 11, no. 4 (winter 2004): 37–57.

———. "Islamic Revivalism and Change in Saudi Arabia: Juhayman Al-Utaybi's 'Letters' to the Saudi People." *The Muslim World* 70, no. 1 (January 1990): 1–16.

———. *Oman and the World: The Emergence of an Independent Foreign Policy*. MR 680–RC. Santa Monica, Calif.: RAND, 1995.

———. *Political Dynamics and Security in the Arabian Peninsula through the 1990s*. MR-167–AF/A. Santa Monica. Calif.: RAND, 1993.

———. "Political Minefields in the Persian Gulf: The Succession Issue." *Energy Compass* 6, no. 46 (November 17, 1995): 14–17.

———. *Political Participation and Stability in the Sultanate of Oman*. Dubai: Gulf Research Center, 2005.

———. *Power and Succession in Arab Monarchies*. Boulder, Colo.: Lynne Rienner, 2008.

———. "The Role of the Ulama in the Politics of an Islamic State: The Case of Saudi Arabia." *International Journal of Middle East Studies* 18, no. 1 (February 1986): 53–71.

———. "Sa'ud, Faysal Ibn 'Abd Al-'Aziz Al." In John L. Esposito, ed., *The Oxford Encyclopedia of the Modern Islamic World*, 3–4. Vol. 4. New York: Oxford University Press, 1995

———. "Saudi Arabia's Will to Power," *Middle East Policy* 7, no. 2 (February 2000): 47–60.

———. "Saudi/U.S. Partnership: The Ties That Bind." *Arabies Trends* 14: November 1998): 22–24.

———. *Succession in Saudi Arabia*. New York: Palgrave, 2001.

———. "Testing the Saudi 'Will to Power': Challenges Confronting Prince Abdallah." *Middle East Policy* 10, no. 4 (winter 2003): 100–15.

———. "Trends in Saudi National Security." *Middle East Journal* 53, no. 2 (spring 1999): 232–53.

———. "The United States and the Arab Gulf Monarchies." *Les Notes de l'IFRI* (Paris) 8 (1999): 1–58.

Kéchichian, Joseph A., ed. *A Century in Thirty Years: Shaykh Zayed and the United Arab Emirates*. Washington, D.C.: The Middle East Policy Council, 2000.

———. *Iran, Iraq, and the Arab Gulf States*. New York: Palgrave, 2001.

Kéchichian, Joseph A., and R. Hrair Dekmejian. *The Just Prince: A Manual of Leadership*. London: Saqi Books, 2003.

Keddie, Nikki R. *An Islamic Response to Imperialism: Political and Religious Writings of Sayyid Jamal ad-Din "al-Afghani."* Berkeley and Los Angeles: University of California Press, 1983.

Kelidar, Abbas R. "The Arabian Peninsula in Arab and Power Politics." In *The Arabian Peninsula: Society and Politics*, 145–59. London: George Allen and Unwin, Ltd., 1972.

———. "The Problem of Succession in Saudi Arabia." *Asian Affairs* 9, no. 1 (February 1978): 23–30.

Kelley, J. B. *Arabia, the Gulf, and the West*. New York: Basic Books, 1980.

————. *The Eastern Arabian Frontiers*. London: Praeger, 1964.

Kerr, Malcolm. *The Arab Cold War: Gamal Abd al-Nasir and His Rivals, 1958–1970*. London and New York: Oxford University Press, 1973.

Khadduri, Majid. *Arab Contemporaries: The Role of Personalities in Politics*. Baltimore: Johns Hopkins University Press, 1973.

————. *Arab Personalities in Politics*. Washington, D.C.: The Middle East Institute, 1981.

————. *Republican Iraq: A Study in Iraqi Politics Since the Revolution of 1958*. London: Oxford University Press, 1969.

Khalid, Taysir. "The Situation in Saudi Arabia and the Horizons for Development: Agencies, Political Decisionmaking, and the Special Role." *Al-Safir* (Beirut), February 1, 1981, 15.

Khalifa, Ali Mohammed. *The United Arab Emirates: Unity in Fragmentation*. London: Croom Helm; Boulder, Colo.: Westview Press: 1979.

Khan, Inammullah. "The Mo'tamar Al-'Alam Al-Islami: A Brief Description of its Sixth Conference Held in Mogadishu." *Islamic Review* 53, no. 6 (1965): 27–29.

Khoury, Adel-Theodor. *Un Modèle d'Etat Islamique: L'Arabie Saoudite*. Tendances et Courants de l'Islam Arabe Contemporain 2. Munich: Kaiser, 1983.

"King of Oil Surges Ahead." *Petroleum Economist* 58, no. 12 (December 1991): 7.

Kingdom of Saudi Arabia. *Faisal Speaks*. Riyadh: Ministry of Information, n.d.

Kishk, Muhammad Jalal. *Al-Sa'udiyyun Wal-Hal Al-Islami* [The Saudis and the Islamic solution]. Jeddah: Saudi Publishing and Distribution House, 1982.

Kissinger, Henry. *White House Years*. Boston: Little, Brown, 1979.

————. *Years of Renewal*. New York: Simon and Schuster, 1999.

————. *Years of Upheaval*. Boston: Little, Brown, 1982.

Klayb, Sami. "Ziyarat Khasat ma' Ahmad Zaki Yamani" [Private visit with Ahmad Zaki Yamani]. Al Jazirah Television Network, episode 1, September 9, 2006; episode 2, September 18, 2006; episode 3, September 26, 2006. Text version available online at http://www.aljazeera.net/NR/exeres/41B14B96-8AA4-457C-BECD-2549146D8311.htm.

Knauerhase, Ramon. "Saudi Arabia: Our Conservative Muslim Ally." *Current History* 76, no. 453 (January 1980): 17–21, 35–37.

————. *The Saudi Arabian Economy*. New York: Praeger, 1975.

Koburger, Charles W. Jr. "The Kuwait Confrontation of 1961." *United States Naval Institute Proceedings* 100:1, January 1974, 42–49.

Korn, David A. *Stalemate: The War of Attrition and Great Power Diplomacy in the Middle East, 1967–1970*. Boulder, Colo.: Westview, 1992.

Kostiner, Joseph. *The Making of Saudi Arabia, 1916–1936: From Chieftaincy to Monarchical State*. New York: Oxford University Press, 1993.

————. *Middle East Monarchies: The Challenge of Modernity*. Boulder, Colo., and London: Lynne Rienner, 2000.

Koury, Enver M. *The Saudi Decision-Making Body: The House of Al-Saud*. Hyattsville, Md.: Institute of Middle Eastern and North African Affairs, 1978.

Kramer, Martin. *Islam Assembled: The Advent of the Muslim Congresses*. New York: Columbia University Press, 1986.

"Kuwait, Saudi Arabia Upgrade Defenses against Sabotage of Trans-Peninsula." *Platts Oilgram News* 66, no. 87 (May 5, 1988)L 2.

"Kuwait Signs Defense Pact with Moscow." *Mideast Mirror*, November 30, 1993, 22.

Lacey, Robert. *The Kingdom*. New York and London: Harcourt Brace Jovanovich, 1981.

Lackner, Helen. *A House Built on Sand: A Political Economy of Saudi Arabia*. London: Ithaca Press, 1978.

Lalevee, Thierry. "Teheran's New Allies in Africa." *World Press Review* (September 1993): 20.

Lambton, Ann K. S. "Law and the State: Islamic Political Thought." In *The Legacy of Islam*, ed. Joseph Schacht and C. E. Bosworth, 404–24. 2nd ed. London: Oxford University Press, 1974.

Leatherdale, Clive. *Britain and Saudi Arabia, 1925–1939: The Imperial Oasis*. London: Frank Cass, 1983.

Lees, Brian. "The Al Saud Family and the Future of Saudi Arabia." *Asian Affairs* 37, no. 1 (March 2006): 36–49.

———. *A Handbook of the Al Saud Family of Saudi Arabia*. London: Royal Genealogies, 1980.

Legum, Colin, ed. *Middle East Contemporary Survey 1, 1976–1977*. New York and London: Holmes and Meier, 1978.

Lewis, Bernard. "Politics and War." In *The Legacy of Islam*, ed. Joseph Schacht with C. E. Bosworth, 2nd ed., 156–209. Oxford: Clarendon, 1974.

Lindsey, Gene. *Saudi Arabia*. New York: Hippocrene, 1991.

Lippman, Thomas W. *Inside the Mirage: America's Fragile Partnership with Saudi Arabia*. Boulder, Colo.: Westview, 2004.

Long, David E. "King Faisal's World View." In *King Faisal and the Modernization of Saudi Arabia*, ed. Willard A. Belling, 173–83. London: Croom Helm; Boulder, Colo.: Westview, 1980.

———. *The Kingdom of Saudi Arabia*. Gainesville: University Press of Florida, 1997.

———. *Saudi Arabia*. The Washington Papers 4, no. 39. Beverly Hills and London: Sage Publications (for the Center for Strategic and International Studies,), 1976.

———. "Saudi Oil Policy." *The Wilson Quarterly* 3, no. 1 (winter 1979):83–91.

———. *The United States and Saudi Arabia: Ambivalent Allies*. Boulder, Colo., and London: Westview, 1985.

Maachou, Abdelkader. *L'OPAEP et le Pétrole Arabe*. Paris: Berger-Levrault, 1982.

MacDonald, Robert W. *The League of Arab States: A Study in the Dynamics of Regional Organization*. Princeton, N.J.: Princeton University Press, 1965.

Mackey, Sandra. *The Saudis: Inside the Desert Kingdom*. Boston: Houghton Mifflin, 1987.

———. *The Saudis: Inside the Desert Kingdom*. Updated ed. New York: W. W. Norton, 2002.

El Mallakh, Ragaei. *Saudi Arabia: Rush to Development; Profile of an Energy Economy and Investment*. Baltimore and London: Johns Hopkins University Press, 1982.

Al-Manjad, Salah al-Din. *Ahadith ʿan Faysal wal-Tadamun al-Islami* [Reports on Faysal and Islamic Solidarity]. Beirut: Dar al-Kitab al-Jadid, 1974.

———. *Falsafat Faysal fil-Tadamun al-Islami* [Faysal's Philosophy in Islamic Solidarity]. Riyadh: King Faisal Center for Research and Islamic Studies, 1989.

Marchand, Stéphane. *Arabie Saoudite: La Menace*. Paris: Fayard, 2003.

McLoughlin, Leslie. *Ibn Saud: Founder of a Kingdom*. London: Macmillan, 1993.

McMullen, Christopher J. *Resolution of the Yemen Crisis, 1963: A Case Study in Mediation*. Washington, D.C.: Institute for the Study of Diplomacy, Georgetown University, 1980.

"MEED Special Report on Construction: Fast-Moving Market Starts to Consolidate." *Middle East Economic Digest* 37, no. 30 (July 30, 1993): 20.

"MEED Special Report on Saudi Arabia: The Need for Export Industries." *Middle East Economic Digest* 36, no. 45 (November 13, 1992): 36.

Ménoret, Pascal. *L'Énigme Saoudienne: Les Saoudiens et le Monde, 1744–2003*. Paris: Éditions La Découverte, 2003.

Metz, Helen Chapin, ed. *Saudi Arabia: A Country Study*. Washington, D.C.: Federal Research Division, U.S. Library of Congress, 1993.

"Military College Graduates Include Palestinians." *Al-Madinah*, July 2, 1992, 3.

Miller, Aaron David. *Search for Security: Saudi Arabian Oil and American Foreign Policy, 1939–1949*. Chapel Hill: University of North Carolina Press, 1980.

"Mitterrand to Press Saudis on Oil Threats." *Financial Times*, October 15, 1993, 5.

Mishawi, Tawfik. "A New Direction." *The Middle East Magazine*, May 1979, 12–14.

Momoi, Makota. *The Energy Problems and Alliance Systems: Japan*. Adelphi Paper Number 115, London: The International Institute for Strategic Studies, 1975.

Moore, John Norton. *Crisis in the Gulf: Enforcing the Rule of Law*. New York: Oceana, 1992.

Morris, Harvey. "Saudi Arabia/Iran: Partnership." *Arabies Trends* 22 (July–August 1999): 14–15.

Mosely, Leonard. *Power Play: Oil in the Middle East*. Baltimore: Penguin, 1974.

Munif, Abdelrahman. *Cities of Salt*. New York: Vintage International, 1989.

———. *The Trench*. New York: Pantheon, 1991.

———. *Variations on Night and Day*. New York: Pantheon, 1993.

Al-Muqrin, Abd Al-Rahman, and Abdallah al-Umayrah. "Prince Sultan: Feasibility Studies for Four Huge Military Factories." *Al-Riyadh*, April 27, 1987, 1.

Murawiec, Laurent. *La Guerre d'Après*. Paris: Albin Michel, 2003.

Murphy, Caryle. "Saudi Arabia Bans Rights Group." *Washington Post*, May 14, 1993, 35.

Al-Musaybah, Saud. "Acting for Al-Fahd, Crown Prince Observes Opening Ceremony Today at King Khalid Military College." *Al-Riyadh*, December 18, 1982, 4. In "Overview On King Khalid Military College," *JPRS Near East-South Asia Report* 2730 (April 1, 1983): 22.

Al-Muttalib, Fikri Abd. "Clandestine Opposition Movements in Saudi Arabia." *Al-Yaqzah Al-Arabiyyah* (Cairo) (December 1987): 27–39. In "Russian Author Traces Opposition in Saudi Arabia," *JPRS –NEA Report* 88–011 (February 26, 1988): 15.

Naaoush, Sabah. "A Catastrophic Financial Situation." *Marchés Tropicaux Et Méditerranées*, May 29, 1992, 1382–84.

Al Na'im, Mishari 'Abdul Rahman. *Al Hudud al-Siyasiyyah al-Sa'udiyyah: Al-Bahth 'an al-Istiqrar* [Saudi Arabia's political borders: Search for stability]. Beirut: Dar al-Saqi, 1999.

Nakhleh, Emile A. *The United States and Saudi Arabia: A Policy Analysis*. Washington, D.C.: American Enterprise Institute for Public Policy Research, 1975.

Nasrawi, Salah. "Saudi Prince Urges Changes." Associated Press, June 6, 1999.

Naumkin, Vitali. *Emir Faisal in Russia, 1932: Dedicated to the 70th Anniversary of the Late King Faisal Visit to Russia*. Riyadh: King Faisal Center for Research and Islamic Studies, 2002.

Nawwab, Ismail I., Peter C. Speers, and Paul F. Hoye, eds. *Aramco and Its World: Arabia and the Middle East*. Dhahran, Saudi Arabia: Aramco, 1980.

"New ARAMCO Supreme Council Includes Five Private Businessmen." In *Country Report: Saudi Arabia 2–1989*, 15–16. London: The Economist Intelligence Unit, Ltd., 1989.

Nimr, Sulayman. "Saudi Arms: Diversified Sources and Modern Sites." *Al-Mustaqbal*, September 6, 1980, 18.

9/11 and Terrorist Travel: A Staff Report of the National Commission on Terrorist Attacks upon the United States. Franklin, Tenn.: Hillsboro, 2004.

Nixon, Richard. *RN: The Memoirs of Richard Nixon*. New York: Grosset and Dunlop, 1978.

"No Change in Oil Policy Says Prince Nayif." *Middle East Economic Survey* 30, no. 4 (November 3, 1986): A5.

Obaid, Nawaf E. *The Oil Kingdom at 100: Petroleum Policymaking in Saudi Arabia*. Washington, D.C.: Washington Institute for Near East Policy, 2000.

O'Ballance, Edgar. *The War in the Yemen*. London: Faber and Faber, 1971.

Ochsenwald, William. *The Hijaz Railroad*. Charlottesville: University Press of Virginia, 1980.

Okruhlik, Mary Gwenn. *Debating Profits and Political Power: Private Business and Government in Saudi Arabia*. doctoral dissertation, Austin: University of Texas, 1992.

Al-Osaimi, Mohammed. *The Politics of Persuasion: The Islamic Oratory of Faisal Ibn Abdul Aziz*. Riyadh: King Faisal Center for Research and Islamic Studies, 2000.

Pahlavi, Mohammad Reza [Shah]. *Mission for My Country*. New York: McGraw-Hill, 1961.

"The Party Isn't Over." *The Economist* 327, no. 7817 (June 26, 1993): 57.

Peterson, J. E. *Saudi Arabia and the Illusion of Security*. Adelphi Paper 348. London: Oxford University Press (for the International Institute for Strategic Studies), 2002.

"Petromin." *Quarterly Economic Review: Saudi Arabia Annual Supplement, 1978*. London: The Economic Intelligence Unit, 1978, 12.

Pickett, Joseph. "Young Saudis Worry about Oil Policy, Rapid Change." *The Oil Daily*, March 2, 1981, 4.

Philby, H. St. John. *Arabia*. London: C. Scribner's Sons, 1930.

———. *Arabia and the Wahhabis*, London: Frank Cass, 1977. First published in 1928.

———. *Arabian Jubilee*. London: AMS Press, 1988. First published in 1952.

———. *Arabian Oil Ventures*. Washington, D.C.: The Middle East Institute, 1964.

———. *The Heart of Arabia: A Record of Travel and Exploration*. London: Constable, 1922.

———. *Saudi Arabia*. London: Ernest Benn Ltd., 1955.

———, Royal Decree 380, dated 22 Shawwal 1377 (May 11, 1958), trans. *The Middle East Journal* 12, no. 3: 320–23.

Pierre, Andrew J. *The Global Politics of Arms Sales*. Princeton, N.J.: Princeton University Press, 1982.

Pipes, Daniel, and Patrick Clawson. "Ambitious Iran, Troubled Neighbors." *Foreign Affairs* 72, no. 1 (1992/1993): 124–41.

Plascov, Avi. *Security in the Persian Gulf: Modernization, Political Development, and Stability*. Totowa, N.J.: Allanheld, Osmun, 1982.

Podeh, Elie. "The Struggle over Arab Hegemony after the Suez Crisis." *Middle Eastern Studies* 29, no. 1 (January 1993): 91–110.

Posner, Gerald. *Secrets of the Kingdom: The Inside Story of the Saudi-U.S. Connection*. New York: Random House, 2005.

Powell, William. *Saudi Arabia and Its Royal Family*. Secaucus, N.J.: Lyle Stuart, 1982.

Presley, John R. *A Guide to the Saudi Arabian Economy*. London: Macmillan, 1984.

"Prince Nayif Backs Gulf Rapid Deployment Force." *Al-Yawm* (Ad-Damman), February 23, 1982, 1.

"Prince Turki Discusses Saudi Role in Sudanese Crisis." *Al-ʿAshiqqah* (Khartoum), May 31, 1988, 17–22.

Quandt, William B. *Saudi Arabia in the 1980s: Foreign Policy, Security, and Oil*. Washington, D.C.: Brookings Institution, 1981.

———. *Saudi Arabia's Oil Policy*. Washington, D.C.: Brookings Institution, 1982.

———. *Soviet Policy in the October 1973 War*. Santa Monica, Calif.: RAND, 1976.

———. "U.S. Energy Policy and the Arab-Israeli Conflict." In *Arab Oil: Impact on the Arab Countries and Global Implications*, ed. Naiem A. Sherbiny and Mark A. Tessler, 279–94. New York: Praeger, 1976.

Ramazani, R. K. *The Gulf Cooperation Council: Records and Analysis*. Charlottesville, Va.: University Press of Virginia, 1988.

———. *Iran's Foreign Policy, 1941–1973: A Study of Foreign Policy in Modernizing Nations*. Charlottesville: University Press of Virginia, 1975.

———. *Revolutionary Iran: Challenge and Response in the Middle East*. Baltimore: Johns Hopkins University Press, 1988.

———. *The United States and Iran: The Patterns of Influence*. New York: Praeger, 1982.

Al Rasheed, Madawi. *Politics in an Arabian Oasis: The Rashidi Tribal Dynasty*. London and New York: I. B. Tauris, 1991.

al-Rashid, Ibrahim, ed. *Documents on the History of Saudi Arabia*. Salisbury, N.C.: Documentary Publications, 1976.

al-Rashid, Mashal. "Al-Jazirah Explores Opinions of Officials at King Abdulaziz War College on College's Educational Message." *Al-Jazirah*, May 15, 1984, 11.

al-Rashid, Zamil Muhammad. *Su'udi Relations with Eastern Arabia and 'Uman (1800–1871)*. London: Luzac, 1981.

Rattner, Steven. "Khalid Is Dead; Fahd Succeeds in Saudi Arabia." *New York Times*, June 14, 1982, A1.

Rejai, Mostafa. *Comparative Political Ideologies*. New York: St. Martin's, 1984.

Rentz, George. "Wahhabism and Saudi Arabia." In *The Arabian Peninsula: Society and Politics*, ed. Derek Hopwood. London: George Allen and Unwin, 1972, 54–66.

Richard, Robert. "Le Premier Voyage en France du Futur Roi Fayçal (1926)." In *Version Originale: Le Trimestriel de Réflexion; La Péninsule Arabique*, ed. Christian Desjeunes, 103–5. 1999.

Richards, D. S. "Fatimid Dynasty." In *The Oxford Encyclopaedia of the Modern Islamic World*, 7–8. New York and Oxford: Oxford University Press, 1995.

Al-Rifa, Ahmad Sharif. "The King and Responsibility, Part Seven: Oil and Politics; As a Result of Fahd's Great Stand, the World Was Spared an Explosion That Would Have Led to Disaster." *Al-Madinah*, October 4, 1982, 9. In "King's Position on Oil Production, Pricing Reviewed," *JPRS Near East-North Africa* 2661 (November 17, 1982): 130.

Rihani, Ameen. *Around the Coasts of Arabia*. London: Caravan, 1983. First published in 1930.

———. *Ibn Sa'oud of Arabia: His People and His Land*. London: Kegan Paul, 2002. First published in 1928.

Robins, Philip. *A History of Jordan*. Cambridge: Cambridge University Press, 2004.

Robinson, Jeffrey. *Yamani: The Inside Story*. New York: Atlantic Monthly Press, 1988.

Rodendeck, Max. "A Long Walk: A Survey of Saudi Arabia: All in the Family." *The Economist* 378, no. 8459 (January 7, 2006): 5.

Royal Decree 380, dated 22 Shawwal 1377 (May 11, 1958), and translated by H. St. John B. Philby, see Philby, trans., *Middle East Journal* 12, no. 3 (summer 1958): 320–23.

"Royal Saudi Air Force: Safeguarding Peace and Stability." *Saudi Arabia* 8, no. 1 (spring 1991): 7.

Rugh, William. "Emergence of a New Middle Class in Saudi Arabia." *Middle East Journal* 27, no. 1, (winter 1973): 7–20.

Rusinov, Colonel R. "Saudi Arabia's Armed Forces" [in Russian]. *Zarubehshnoye voyennoye obzreniye* (January 1994): 9–11.

Sabini, John. *Armies in the Sand: The Struggle for Mecca and Medina.* London: Thames and Hudson, 1981.

el-Sadat, Anwar. *In Search of Identity: An Autobiography.* New York: Harper and Row, 1977.

Sadria, Modj-ta-ba. *Ainsi L'Arabie Est Devenue Saoudite: Les Fondements de l'Etat Saoudien.* Paris: L'Harmattab, 1989.

Safran, Nadav. *Saudi Arabia: The Ceaseless Quest for Security.* Boston: Harvard University Press, 1985.

Al-Saʿid, Nasir. *Tarikh Al Saʿud* [History of the Al Saʿud]. 2 vols. Beirut: Al-Ittihad Press, 1985.

"Al-Salafiyah Opposition Training Camp Found." *Al-Ahd* (Beirut), October 29, 1993, 16.

Salameh, Ghassan. "Political Power and the Saudi State." *MERIP Reports* 91 (October 1981): 8.

———. *Al-Siyasah al-Kharijiyhah al-Saʿudiyyah munzu ʿam 1945* [Saudi foreign policy since 1945]. Beirut: Maʿhad al-anma' al-ʿarabi, 1980.

Samore, Gary. "The Persian Gulf," In *Energy and Security*, ed. David A. Deese and Joseph S. Nye, 49–110. Cambridge: Ballinger, 1981.

———. *Royal Family Politics in Saudi Arabia (1953–1982).* doctoral dissertation, Cambridge, Mass.: Harvard University, 1983.

Al Saʿud, Khaled bin Sultan (with Patrick Seale). *Desert Warrior: A Personal View of the Gulf War by the Joint Forces Commander.* New York: HarperCollins Publishers, Inc., 1995.

[Al-Saʿud], Khalid al-Faisal. *Poems*, translated by Alison Lerrick, Riyadh: King Faisal Foundation, 1996.

Al Saʿud, Talal bin ʿAbdul Aziz. *Risalah ilal-Muwatin* [A Letter to the citizen]. [Cairo?]: N.p., [1962?].

"Saudi Arabia." *Oil and Gas Journal* 91, no. 33 (16 August 1993): 40–47.

"Saudi Arabia—Cumulative Crude Oil Production (1,000 b), Table 38." In *OPEC Annual Statistical Bulletin 2004.* Vienna: Organization of Petroleum Exporting Countries, 2005.

The Saudi Arabia Report, Issue Number 55, London: Middle East Economic Digest, First Quarter, 2005, 19–24.

"... Saudi ARAMCO Merges for a Second Time." *Country Report-Saudi Arabia, 3–1993.* London: The Economist Intelligence Unit, Ltd., 1989.

"Saudi King Fahd Shares Bush Peace 'Instinct.'" *Reuters Library Report,* January 6, 1991.

"Saudi Oil Grant to Help Turkish Military." *Middle East Economic Survey* 35, no. 1 (October 7, 1991): A3.

"Saudi Oil Minister on OPEC Policies." *JPRS Near East-South Asia Report* 2713 (February 24, 1983), 4.

"Saudis Cooperated with Reagan, Bush." *World Oil* 213, no. 8 (August 1992): 9.

"Saudis May Buy Subs to Protect Coasts." *Journal of Commerce,* April 18, 1994, 7B.

"Saudis Welcome U.S. Troops to Stop Saddam." *Reuters Library Report,* August 29, 1990.

Sawfih, Wahib 'Abdul Fattah, and 'Adnan 'Abdul Fattah Sawfih. *Al-Mamlakah al-'Arabiyyah al-Sa'udiyyah: Numuzaj li-dirasat al-Azmat al-Dawliyyah* [The Kingdom of Saudi Arabia and the Gulf crisis: A study in international response]. Beirut: Dar al-Saqi, 1993.

Al-Sayegh, Marwan M. *Ziyarat Al-Malik Faisal Li-Afriqiyah* [King Faysal's Visit to Africa], Beirut: N.p., 1973.

Schwartz, Stephen. *The Two Faces of Islam: The House of Saud from Tradition to Terror.* New York: Doubleday, 2002.

Sciolino, Elaine. "Iran's Durable Revolution." *Foreign Affairs* 61, no. 4 (spring 1983): 893–920.

Seale, Patrick. *Asad of Syria: The Struggle for the Middle East.* Berkeley and Los Angeles: University of California Press, January 1990.

"Seeds on Stony Ground." *The Economist* 327, no. 7815 (June 12, 1993): 53.

Seymour, Ian. *OPEC: Instrument of Change.* New York: St. Martin's, 1981.

Shakir, Abdulmunim. "Saudi Arabia." In *Constitutions of the Countries of the World,* ed. Albert P. Blaustein and Gisbert H. Flanz, 1–17. Dobbs Ferry, N.Y.: Oceana, 1976.

Sharabi, Hisham B. *Governments and Politics of the Middle East in the Twentieth Century.* Princeton, N.J.: D. Van Nostrand, 1962.

Shaw, John A. and David E. Long. *Saudi Arabian Modernization: The Impact of Change on Stability.* The Washington Papers 10, Number 89. New York: Praeger, 1982.

Shazly, Saad. *The Crossing of Suez: The October War.* London: Third World Centre for Research and Publications, 1980.

Sheean, Vincent. *Faisal: The King and His Kingdom.* Tavistock, U.K.: University Press of Arabia, 1975.

Siddiq, Mohammed H. *Why the Boom Went Bust: An Analysis of the Saudi Government.* Kearney, Neb.: Morris, 1995.

Simons, Geoff. *Saudi Arabia: The Shape of a Client Feudalism.* New York: St. Martin's, 1998.

Sindi, Abdullah M. "King Faisal and Pan-Islamism." In *King Faisal and the Modernisation of Saudi Arabia*, ed. Willard A. Beling, 184–201. London: Croom Helm; Boulder, Colo.: Westview, 1980.

Sindi, Abdulla Mohammed, and Ibrahim Fahad Alghofaily. *Summary of Saudi Arabian Third Five-Year Development Plan*. Riyadh: Tihama, 1982.

al-Sowayyegh, Abdulaziz H. "Saudi Oil Policy during King Faisal's Era." In *King Faisal and the Modernisation of Saudi Arabia*, ed. Willard A. Beling, 202–29. London: Croom Helm; Boulder, Colo.: Westview, 1980.

Standenmaier, William O. "Military Policy and Strategy in the Gulf War." *Parameters* 12, no. 2 (June 1982): 25–35.

Standenmaier, William O., and Shirin Tahir-Kheli. *The Saudi-Pakistani Military Relationship and Its Implications for U.S. Strategy in Southwest Asia*. Carlisle Barracks, Pa.: U.S. Army War College Strategic Studies Institute, 1981.

Stookey, Robert W. *Yemen: The Politics of the Yemen Arab Republic*. Boulder, Colo.: Westview, 1987.

Strasser, Steven, ed. *The 9/11 Investigations: Staff Reports of the 9/11 Commission*. New York: Public Affairs, 2004.

"Studies to Produce Military Hardware Conducted." *Al-Khalij*, May 17, 1992, 18.

"Sudur Al-Nizam Al-Jadid li-majlis Al-Wuzarat wa a'da' wa la-wa'ih majlis al-shura fil-Saudiyyah" [New regulations for the Council of Ministers and Membership and Bylaws of the Consultative Council in Saudi Arabia]. *Al-Hayat* 11147 (August 21, 1993): 6.

Sullivan, Robert R. "Saudi Arabia in International Politics." *Review of Politics* 32, no. 4 (October 1970): 436–60.

Sultan, General Prince Khaled bin. "The Gulf War and Its Aftermath: A Personal Perspective." *RUSI Journal* 138, no. 6 (December 1993): 1–5.

"Support for Oil Price Increases," *Quarterly Economic Review Saudi Arabia*. London: The Economist Intelligence Unit, Ltd., 2 (1978), 9.

Tadjbakhsh, Shahrbanou. "The Bloody Path of Change: The Case of Post-Soviet Tajikistan." *The Harriman Institute Forum* 6, (July 1993): 1–10.

al-Tahawih, 'Abdul Hakim. *Al Malik Faysal wal-'Ilaqat al-Kharijiyyah al-Sa'udiyyah* [King Faysal and Saudi foreign policy]. Elharam, Egypt: Ein for Human and Social Studies, 2002.

Tahtinen, Dale R. *National Security Challenges to Saudi Arabia*. Washington, D.C.: American Enterprise Institute for Public Policy Research, 1978.

"Talal Ibn Abdulaziz Reveals the Secrets of the Base in Dhahran." *Al-Nahar Al-Arabi Wa Al-Duwali*, April 7–13, 1980, 18–19.

Teitelbaum, Joshua. *Holier Than Thou: Saudi Arabia's Islamic Opposition*. Washington, D.C.: Washington Institute for Near East Policy, 2000.

"Telephone Interview with Saudi Ambassador to Sanna." '*Ukaz*, April 21, 1992, 5.

Tinnin, David. "Saudis Recognize Their Vulnerability." *Fortune*, March 10, 1980, 48–55.

Troeller, Gary. *The Birth of Saudi Arabia: Britain and the Rise of the House of Sa'ud*. London: Frank Cass, 1976.

Toynbee, Arnold J. "The Proclamation of Sultan Abdul-Aziz bin Sa'ud as King of the Hijaz and the Islamic Congress at Mecca (1926)." In *Islam and International Relations*, ed. J. Harris Proctor, 309–19. New York: Praeger, 1965.

Truman, Harry S. *Memoirs, Volume I: Year of Decisions; Volume II: Years of Trial and Hope*. Garden City, N.Y.: Doubleday, 1955 (vol. 1), 1956 (vol. 2).

Tucker, Robert W. "Further Reflections on Oil and Force." *Commentary*, March 1975, 45–56.

———. "Oil: The Issue of American Intervention." *Commentary*, January 1975, 21–30.

Turner, Louis, and James Bedore. "Saudi Arabia: The Power of the Purse-Strings." *International Affairs* 54, no. 3 (July 1978): 572–86.

Tusa, Francis. "LAV's in the Gulf: Saudi National Guard Hopes to Resume Modernization Plans." *Armed Forces Journal International* 131, no. 10 (May 1994): 39.

Twitchell, K. S. *Saudi Arabia*. Princeton, N.J.: Princeton University Press, 1953.

"U.K. Offers Submarine Lease." *Sentinel: The Gulf States* 1, no. 7 (April 1994): 1.

Al Uthaymin, 'Abdallah al-Salih. *Al-Shaykh Muhammad bin 'Abdul Wahhab*. Riyadh: Dar al-Ulum, n.d.

Al Uthaymin, Abdul Saleh. *Nashat Imarat al Rashid* [Accomplishments of the Al Rashid emirate]. Riyadh: N.p., 1981.

———. *Tarikh al-Mamlakah Al-'Arabiyyah al-Sa'udiyyah* [History of the Kingdom of Saudi Arabia]. Vol. 1. Riyadh: N.p., 1984, 1995.

Unger, Craig. *House of Bush, House of Saud: The Secret Relationship Between the World's Two Most Powerful Dynasties*. New York: Scribner's, 2004.

United Nations, General Assembly, Thirtieth Session, "Resolution Adopted by the General Assembly, 3379 (XXX), Elimination of all Forms of Racial Discrimination," November 10, 1975, at http://www.cinu.org.mx/biblioteca/documentos/palestina/ares3379.htm

U.S. Department of State (Office of the Historian). *Foreign Relations of the United States, 1943*. Vol. 4, *The Near East and Africa*. Washington, D.C.: Department of State (Office of the Historian), 1964.

———. *Foreign Relations of the United States, 1955–1957*. Vol. 13, *Near East Region; Jordan-Yemen*. Washington, D.C.: Department of State (Office of the Historian), 1988.

———. *Foreign Relations of the United States, 1955–1957*. Vol. 16, *Suez Crisis July 26–December 31, 1956*. Washington, D.C.: Department of State (Office of the Historian), 1990.

———. *Foreign Relations of the United States, 1958–1960*. Vol. 12, *Near East Region; Iran; Iraq; Arabian Peninsula*. Washington, D.C.: Department of State (Office of the Historian), 1992.

———. *Foreign Relations of the United States, 1958–1960*. Vol. 13, *Arab-Israeli Dispute;*

United Arab Republic; North Africa. Washington, D.C.: Department of State (Office of the Historian), 1992.

———. *Foreign Relations of the United States, 1964–1968.* Vol. 21, *Near East Region; Arabian Peninsula.* Washington, D.C.: Department of State (Office of the Historian), 2000.

Van Der Meulen, D. *The Wells of Ibn Sa'ud.* London and New York: Kegan Paul International, 2000.

Vassiliev, Alexei. *The History of Saudi Arabia.* London: Saqi Books, 1998.

Wahbah, Hafiz. *Arabian Days.* London: A. Barker, 1964.

———. *The Arabian Peninsula in the 20th Century.* London: Slim Press, 1961.

Walt, Joseph William. *Saudi Arabia and the Americans: 1928–1951.* Doctoral dissertation, Evanston, Ill.: Northwestern University, 1960.

Wells, Donald A. *Saudi Arabian Development Strategy.* Washington, D.C.: American Enterprise Institute for Public Policy Research, 1976.

Wenner, Manfred W. *Modern Yemen, 1918–1966.* Baltimore: Johns Hopkins University Press, 1967.

"When Saudi Arabia Says No to Storing Oil." *Al-Mustaqbal* (Paris) 248 (November 21, 1981): 53–55.

Wilkinson, John C. *Arabia's Frontiers: The Story of Britain's Boundary Drawing in the Desert.* London and New York: I. B. Tauris, 1991.

Wilson, Evan M. *Decision on Palestine: How the U.S. Came to Recognize Israel.* Stanford, Calif.: Hoover Institution Press, 1979.

Wilson, Peter W., and Douglas F. Graham. *Saudi Arabia: The Coming Storm.* Armonk, N.Y.: M. E. Sharpe, 1994.

Winder, Bailey. *Saudi Arabia in the Nineteenth Century.* New York: St. Martin's, 1965.

Wolffsohn, Michael. *German–Saudi Arabian Arms Deals 1936–1939 and 1981–1985; with an Essay on West Germany's Jews.* Frankfurt am Main: Verlag Peter Lang, 1985.

Wright, J. W., Jr. *Business and Economic Development in Saudi Arabia: Essays with Saudi Scholars.* London: Macmillan, 1996.

Wylie, James. "Iran: Quest for Security and Influence." *Jane's Intelligence Review* 5, no. 7 (July 1993): 311.

Yamani, Hani A. Z. *To Be a Saudi.* London: Janus, 1997.

Yamani, Mai. *Changed Identities: The Challenge of the New Generation in Saudi Arabia.* London: Royal Institute of International Affairs, 2000.

Al-Yassini, Ayman. *Religion and State in the Kingdom of Saudi Arabia.* Boulder, Colo., and London: Westview, 1985.

Yizraeli, Sarah. *The Remaking of Saudi Arabia: The Struggle Between King Sa'ud and Crown Prince Faysal, 1953–1962.* Tel Aviv: Moshe Dayan Center for Middle Eastern and African Studies, 1997.

Yodfat, Aryeh Y. *The Soviet Union and the Arabian Peninsula: Soviet Policy Towards the Persian Gulf and Arabia.* London: Croom Helm; New York: St. Martin's, 1983.

Young, T. Cuyler. "Pan-Islamism in the Modern World: Solidarity and Conflict among Muslim Countries." In *Islam and International Relations*, ed. J. Harris Proctor, 182–98. New York: Praeger, 1965.

Zanoyan, Vahan. *Saudi Arabia's Finances: Current Realities and Short-Term Prospects.* Washington, D.C.: Petroleum Finance Company, 1993.

Index

Index

Index

Kirk, Alexander C., 39

Kissinger, Henry, xv, 37, 139, 141, 142, 148–49, 152, 164, passim; and 1973 War, 157–63; and 1974 energy conference, 141; and détente policy, 87, 112, 150, 158, 165; and face to face with Faysal in Riyadh, 161–63; and Faysal, 150–54; and Saudi foreign policy style, 246n17; and shah of Iran, 154–56; and "Shuttle Diplomacy," 167–68; and threats to attack Saudi Arabia, 168; and view of the Middle East, 150–51; and views of Faysal, 162

Koran. *See* Qur'an

Kuwait, 49, 50, 193, passim; and 1899 treaty with Britain, 70; and borders with Saudi Arabia and Iraq, 49; and "Neutral Zone" with Saudi Arabia, 70; and relations with Saudi Arabia, 70

Kuwaiz, 'Abdallah Ibrahim El-, xv

Labaki, Salim, 106

Lawrence, HMS, 29

Lawrence of Arabia, 30

League of Arab States, 3, 69, 70, 71, 88, 105, 184; and 1967 Khartoum "No" Summit, 147, 177–78; and 1973 Algiers Summit, 5; and 1974 Rabat Summit, 5, 180

League of Nations, 47

Lebanon, 56, 65, passim

London (U.K.), 43, passim

Los Angeles (Calif.), 42

Luway, Khalid bin, 31

Madinah (Medina) (Saudi Arabia), 32, 57, 146

Majlis al-Shurah, 118

Makkah (Mecca) (Saudi Arabia), 13, 31, 32, 57, 72, 88, 146, 175, passim

Marseilles (France), 30

Mawlad, 192–93

Mecca. *See* Makkah

Medina. *See* Madinah

Mikado, The (Gilbert & Sullivan), 30

Mikoyan, Anastas, 188

Molotov, Vyacheslav, 36

Mossadegh, Mohammed, 127

Mosul (Iraq), 52

Motabbagani, Mazin Salah, xiv

Muhammad 'Ali (viceroy of Egypt), 13, 14

Muhammarah (Treaty of), 52

Murphy, Richard W., xv

Musnad, 'Abdallah al-, 118

Muslim Brethren, 16. *See also* Ikhwan

Muslim World League 3, 72, 191

Muwahiddun (Wahhabis), 7, 12

Naguib, Muhammad, 51, 63

Al Nahyan, Zayed bin Sultan, 188, 194, passim

Najd region (Saudi Arabia), 13, 14, 16, 17, 26, 27, 28, passim

Najran (Saudi Arabia), 53, 72, 81, 175

Nasir, 'Abdallah bin Muhammad, xv, 4

Nasir, Gamal 'Abdul, 37, 51, 60, 63,, 66, 69, 76, 84, 108, 133, 143, 147, 176, 190, passim; and end of era, 147–48; as "al-walad al-mudalal," 146

Nasiriyyah Palace, 77, 193

National Guard (Saudi Arabian), 17, 55, 106, 111, 114

National Front for the Liberation of Saudi Arabia, 114

NBC Television Network, 138

Neuralia, SS, 30

New Mexico, 42

Newsweek, 138

New York, 42, 43

Nikbah (Arab catastrophe), 177

Nixon, Richard M., 136, 149, 154, 165; and 1973 War, 158–60; and doctrine, 154; and "Twin Pillar" policy, 156; and visit to Faysal, 166–67

Numayri, Ja'afar al-, 180, 194

OAPEC. *See* Organization of Arab Petroleum Exporting Countries

October War (1973), 137–38; and aftermath of airlifts, 158–60

Odessa (Ukraine), 36

Oil: and challenging the embargo, 138–39, and skyrocketing prices, 139–143

Oil policy under Faysal, 119–44

Oil and security issues, external, 133–38

Oil and security issues, internal, 130–32

Oil as weapon: and 1967 war, 134–35; and Arab-Israeli conflict, 165–66; and consequences of embargo, 169–71; and early failures, 134–35; and effectiveness, 160–61; and linkage with Israel, 135–36; and meaning, 143–44; in 1973–74, 135–36

Oman, Sultanate of, 28, 60, 185, passim; and Buraymi Oasis, 60

OPEC. *See* Organization of Petroleum Exporting Countries

Operation Hardsurface, 86

Organization of Arab Petroleum Exporting Coun-

Index

Index

Joseph A. Kéchichian is the CEO of Kéchichian and Associates, a consulting partnership that provides analysis on the Arabian/Persian Gulf region. In 1985, he received a doctorate in foreign affairs from the University of Virginia, where he also taught (1986–88) and assumed the assistant deanship in international studies (1988–89). In the summer of 1989, Kéchichian was a Hoover fellow at Stanford University. Between 1990 and 1996, he was an associate political scientist at the RAND Corporation in Santa Monica and a lecturer at the University of California in Los Angeles.

From 1998 to 2001, he was a fellow at UCLA's Gustav E. von Grunebaum Center for Near Eastern Studies, where he held a Smith Richardson Foundation grant (1998–99) to write *Succession in Saudi Arabia* (2001). In 2003, he held a Davenport fellowship at Pepperdine University in Malibu and wrote *Power and Succession in Arab Monarchies* (also on a Smith Richardson Foundation grant) (2008).

Kéchichian published *Oman and the World: The Emergence of an Independent Foreign Policy* (1995) and *Political Participation and Stability in the Sultanate of Oman* (2005) and edited *A Century in Thirty Years: Shaykh Zayed and the United Arab Emirates* (2000), as well as *Iran, Iraq, and the Arab Gulf States* (2001). In 2003, he coauthored (with R. Hrair Dekmejian) *The Just Prince: A Manual of Leadership,* which includes a full translation of the *Sulwan al-Muta‘* by Muhammad Ibn Zafar al-Siqilli.